The Financial Times
Marketing Casebook

■ ■ ■

Sheila Wright

Senior Lecturer in Competitive Marketing Strategy
Leicester Business School, De Montfort University

PITMAN
PUBLISHING

London · Hong Kong · Johannesburg · Melbourne · Singapore · Washington DC

PITMAN PUBLISHING
128 Long Acre, London WC2E 9AN
Tel: +44 (0)171 447 2000
Fax: +44 (0)171 240 5771

A Division of Pearson Professional Limited

First published in Great Britain in 1997

© Pearson Professional Limited 1997

The right of Sheila Wright to be identified as
Author of this Work has been asserted by her in accordance
with the Copyright, Designs and Patents Act 1988.

ISBN 0 273 62058 4

British Library Cataloguing in Publication Data
A CIP catalogue record for this book can be obtained
from the British Library

3 5 7 9 10 8 6 4 2

Typeset by Pantek Arts, Maidstone, Kent
Printed and bound in Great Britain by Clays Ltd, St Ives plc

*The Publishers' policy is to use paper manufactured
from sustainable forests.*

Contents

■ ■ ■

Preface

■ ■ ■

This book is about the practice of marketing – doing it, sometimes getting it right, sometimes getting it wrong, fixing it and learning from the experience.

It is a collection of topical articles which illustrate, and hopefully animate, the theoretical concepts and frameworks you will be becoming familiar with during your marketing classes. There are good and bad examples of marketing, and questions which aim to make you think carefully about whether or not the theories can be useful to help explain a firm's actions. There is never one clear answer in marketing, and it is precisely this which makes it so challenging an area to work in. Indeed several of your colleagues may vigorously argue for a course of action or a point of view totally opposite to your own, and yet you may both be right. In your discussions, accept that there are alternatives and try to evaluate rather than dismiss the ideas of others.

The Financial Times Marketing Casebook has been designed to be used alongside Brassington and Pettitt's *Principles of Marketing*, so students with this as their core text will especially benefit. At the end of each chapter introduction there are key points which students need to be familiar with. These points are further illustrated in the coinciding chapters of *Principles of Marketing*.

The Financial Times Marketing Casebook is an invaluable resource for any student of marketing, reinforcing their lecturers' input and further testing their understanding of a wide range of marketing concepts. The selection of articles has been made carefully to reflect the amount of preparatory work I might expect a student to carry out as seminar or tutorial preparation, and your lecturer may well use this book as a basis for such activities. Apart from the questions usually expected at the end of a case study, I have included some more wide-ranging activities, such as presentations, debates, background research and discussion tasks. These in particular lend themselves to formal assessment and you might find it helpful to approach these with this in mind.

Articles taken from the *Financial Times* have been used throughout the book. They are typical of the authoritative and detailed reporting which appears every day in this and other broadsheet newspapers. As you are a student of marketing and the world of business in general, I would urge you not to ignore the business press, it is probably the cheapest, and most accessible source of up-to-date quality information you will ever have.

Sheila Wright
April 1997

About the Author

■ ■ ■

Sheila Wright is a Senior Lecturer in Competitive Marketing Strategy at Leicester Business School, De Montfort University.

She holds an MBA from the University of Warwick, the Professional Diploma in Management from the Open University and is a Member of both the Chartered Institute of Marketing and the US based Society of Competitor Intelligence Professionals. She is also a Registered Marketer. Currently she is Programme Director for Leicester Business School's MA Marketing Administration and MSc Strategic Marketing Programmes.

Her teaching experience includes final year undergraduate Business Studies students, postgraduates on MBA, MA and MSc programmes, as well as several professional programmes organised by the Business School for consortia of local organisations and delegations of managers from Russia, China and South Africa. She is also involved in consultancy assignments organised through De Montfort Expertise and a company she co-founded, Strategic Partnerships Ltd. She has worked on many international projects both industry and educationally based which have resulted in assignments in Turkey, Italy, Portugal, Belgium, France, South Africa and the USA.

With over twenty years of marketing and business development experience, principally in the food processing, agribusiness and technology transfer sectors, she advocates a very practical approach to marketing and is well equipped to bring the theory to life for the student. This particular expertise is demonstrated in this book where theories, concepts and frameworks are applied to examples taken from the *Financial Times*.

Acknowledgements

■ ■ ■

At the risk of making this sound like an Academy Award acceptance speech, my thanks are due to:

Pradeep Jethi at Pitman Publishing for agreeing to run with the idea of a marketing casebook based on articles from the *Financial Times*.

Frances Brassington and Stephen Pettitt for writing *Principles of Marketing* which provided the impetus and structure for my efforts.

The *Financial Times* for the kind use of the articles.

The Editorial team at Pitman Publishing for polishing the manuscript and Glenda Bourne for attending to the administrative issues.

Paul Child for his help in selecting articles and scissoring skills.

Family, friends and colleagues for putting up with the occasional temperamental outburst.

And, finally, Misty, my sweet natured, beautiful border collie who has performed sterling feet warming duties throughout the entire project and gave me the perfect excuse to go for a walk when it was most needed.

1

Marketing Dynamics

Marketing in many organisations today provides the overarching framework within which the firm does business. It shapes the product or service offering to meet customer and consumer needs, mostly within a traditional buyer–seller relationship. Money need not be the exchange medium. Indeed for organisations such as political parties, churches, schools and universities, it is the message, the knowledge or just an idea which is being presented. For charities, which now fully appreciate the role of marketing for fund-raising and other activities, it may just be an invitation for you to part with unwanted items which you accept.

Many critics of marketing think of it as 'just sales', and when you find that their exposure to marketing has been 'just sales', then it is easier to understand their viewpoint. However, sales and marketing is a vibrant activity, a highly creative task and an enormously exciting area to work in.

This is not to say that the other functions within an organisation are dull or unexciting, but, unless the firm is an investment bank where revenue comes from money management, it is useful to remember that when the accountants are worried about the bottom line, that is simply an expenditure issue. Marketing is the only department which can affect the top line in that it is marketing and selling which brings in the revenues. Without the top line, the rest of the organisation might just as well pack-up. All the latest management fads such as Business Process Re-engineering, BS 5750/ISO9000, Investors in People, Downsizing, Rightsizing, Upsizing are one off, unrepeatable gains. Only through sustained improved market performance can a firm continue to show increased profit and returns to shareholders.

A graduate of De Montfort University who came back to visit, proudly told of his firm's £140 million increase in the bottom line which had been achieved through a recently completed, radical, restructuring programme of disposals, redundancies, amalgamations of divisions and product categories. The Board was understandably delighted; bonuses were massive, the shareholders ecstatic. While obviously happy at his success, I asked him whether there had been any real improvement in market share or market performance. 'No,' he said, 'all attention had been on the restructuring.'

'So what are you going to do next year when they want another £140 million improvement in profit,' I asked? Predictably, there was no answer and I think he got the point.

Business orientation has gone through many phases. Mass-manufacturing made a lot of desirable goods available to the general public, but there were many geographical variations of availability and little choice. The focus here was on making profit through volume production and sales. A slight shift towards a product orientation meant that product features were stressed to customers in the expectation that they would be as thrilled with it as the technician who produced it. Although quality was constantly improving, profit still came through volume sales.

The introduction of travelling sales teams and performance targets, heralded the selling era, where aggressive tactics were supported by a lot of advertising and sales promotion. Still, the focus for profit was on high volume but this time through a speedy turnover of stock. Finally, the marketing era allowed a more personal touch where manufacturers and intermediaries tried to define what customers wanted and then provided it. Customer needs tended to drive production schedules and profit came through customer satisfaction and repeat business. There is now talk of a new era as we approach the next century and enter into the information age. Customers will have greater choice, but this will be informed choice, as product information becomes available to individuals through such vehicles as the Internet, on-line data-bases, satellite and cable TV. Firms who wish to maintain their success into the year 2000 and beyond, will have to respond to this thirst for knowledge and learn how to transfer technical information to its customers in an easily understandable manner.

In order to successfully complete the tasks in this chapter you will need to be familiar with:

- marketing/business orientation;
- satisfying customer needs;
- cause-related marketing;
- competition;
- marketing mix.

1A

Giving wisely

Getting a return on charitable investment is the aim of 'cause-related marketing', reports Diane Summers

A year ago Midland Bank, like many other big busi-nesses, realised it was seeing very little return on its charitable donations in the UK. It might seem rather hard-nosed to expect a return but, increasingly, companies are managing their charitable budgets with the same rigour as other parts of their business. Purely philanthropic giving is out, 'cause-related marketing' is in.

Midland was typically receiving 1,300–1,400 requests to its headquarters from charities each year and, out of that, making donations to about 250.

Many of the donations were for under £1,000, which, as Belinda Furneaux-Harris, Midland's head of sponsorship and donations observes, 'isn't even enough to buy a wheelchair'.

Efforts were fragmented, she says: 'We were trying to do too much with too few funds. It was a case of trying to cover the field, rather than looking at a few things and doing them well.'

The bank began to question the entire basis of its charitable giving, which amounts to about £1m, split between central donations, divisional budgets and support for a staff scheme. After a year's work, Midland has decided to sweep away the plethora of small donations and concentrate on working with just three 'charity partners' for greater impact.

It will be formally announced next week that Shelter, the national campaign for homeless people, will be the main beneficiary, receiving £180,000 a year for the next three years; Age Concern, which provides services for older people, will get £65,000 a year over the period; and the National Deaf Children's Society, a small charity founded by parents of deaf children, will receive £65,000 a year.

In return, Midland has been very clear that it wants specific projects to fund, clear measurement of results and positive public relations opportunities. For about the same expenditure, the bank is hoping to raise its profile as a corporate donor and gain recognition for its support. Charitable giving by companies has actually declined over recent years, and now, says Furneaux-Harris, 'people want a bang for their buck'.

Charities understand this harder-nosed approach and are themselves becoming more professional, tailoring projects with corporate donors in mind, she says. There are 180,000 charities, with one formed every 15 minutes, she points out. Often, several are competing to raise money from the same sources: 'They are only going to be able to compete by having a unique selling point. They've got to be more professional than the next, or they are going to have to merge,' she adds.

Cause-related marketing is the jargon being applied to this more commercial approach to giving. Already well-established in the US, it is gaining increasing attention in the UK. Business in the Community (BITC), the business-led charity which supports links with community activities, has set up a working group on the issue, led by Dominic Cadbury, chairman of Cadbury Schweppes.

Cadbury's itself is behind the highly successful 'Strollerthon', the annual sponsored walk through London which has raised more than £800,000 for the charity, Save the Children. The company benefits from the publicity and goodwill, as well as assembling names of participants on its database and using the event to give out samples of its products.

Other cause-related marketing examples include Tesco's Computers for Schools promotion, and a cross-branding scheme, masterminded by the International Red Cross, called HeldAd.

All the schemes fit BITC's definition of cause-related marketing as being when 'a company with an image, product or service to sell, builds a relationship or partnership with a "cause" or a number of "causes" for mutual benefit'.

The Midland's review of its charitable giving began when Furneaux-Harris joined the bank from Charles Barker, the public relations company where she had worked with Cadbury and had seen the success of the Strollerthon.

At Midland she found existing policy guidelines meant donations were going to broad and sometimes ill-defined categories, including education and training, the 'disadvantaged and deprived particularly among young people', the environment, and 'local or regional culture and tradition'. The danger of such lack of clarity, says Furneaux-Harris, is that 'you end up with a policy that isn't a policy and you give to almost everything'.

Following an evaluation of all the main areas of charitable activity, Midland settled on supporting: youth activities, particularly in relation to homelessness, drug abuse and unemployment; the elderly; and disability projects.

The appeal for Midland of supporting youth charities is clear, for young people account for half of all new accounts opened with the bank. The elderly sector was one where Midland felt it could make a mark – few other businesses want to identify with 'grey' issues, and the bank was keen to identify an area it could make its own. On the selection of disability, Furneaux-Harris points out that many customers are disabled, and the area of disability is likely to have a raised political profile in coming months, as the government's Disability Discrimination Act takes effect.

Finally, there was the question of making the selection of the charities themselves, and here the process had more in common with the appointment of an advertising agency than usual philanthropic procedures. A shortlist of charities in the three selected areas was invited to tender – each got a detailed document setting out what the bank was looking for and an individual briefing presentation. The charities had five weeks to work up their ideas for specific projects that would meet Midland's requirements, before pitching for the business.

From start to finish, the bank spent a year formulating its new policy and selecting the charities that would best fit its cause-relating marketing objectives. 'Take time and don't rush it,' is Furneaux-Harris's advice to other companies contemplating a similar exercise. 'Otherwise you'll end up with something that's very akin to what you've already got.'

Source: Financial Times, 1 January 1996

1.1 Outline how marketing as a concept has entered into the process of charity donations by large firms.

1.2 Throughout the remainder of your course, identify as many examples of cause-related marketing as you can and try to identify the benefits which are obtained by the giver and the recipient.

1B

Most people in west aware of the Internet

By Paul Taylor

Most westerners have heard of the Internet or the World Wide Web, even though many do not have the capability to use it, according to a survey of 18 countries conducted by the Belgium-based International Research Institutes (Iris).

The survey, which was based on interviews with 15,835 adult consumers in 18 countries in Europe, North America, Mexico and Australia, shows that only a very small proportion of consumers in each country are able to access the Internet from their homes and only a small percentage of adults, mainly upper-income males aged under 55, have had hands-on experience with the Internet.

Within Europe, 91 per cent of consumers in Sweden have heard of the Internet or the World Wide Web, the graphics-based part of the Internet which is based on 'pages' of information connected by 'hot-links'. Bottom of the league table come Spain and Cyprus, where consumer familiarity is 44 per cent and 39 per cent respectively.

Among the survey's other findings:

● Personal computer penetration is highest in Australia (41 per cent), but although many countries have achieved a fairly high level of PC ownership, many households still do not have a modem – a communications device which enables a computer to exchange information over a standard telephone line.

In the US and Canada about a fifth of all households have a PC with a modem. Mr Jim Fouss of Response Analysis in the US said: 'The Internet is quickly becoming the communications medium of higher-income consumers in the US, which holds significant implications for how products and services that appeal to higher-income households are marketed and sold in the US market.'

● Across the globe, a strong relationship exists between Internet awareness and income levels. In the US, Canada and the Netherlands the proportion of high-income adults who use the Internet at the office is twice that of the general population.

● Men are more likely to be accessing the Internet at home than women in most countries.

This gender gap is biggest in Finland, where the ratio is 8:1, but non-existent in France and Turkey.

Source: Financial Times, 27 August 1996

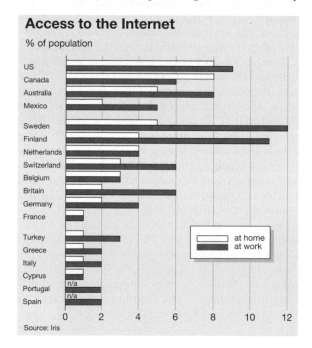

Access to the Internet

% of population

US
Canada
Australia
Mexico

Sweden
Finland
Netherlands
Switzerland
Belgium
Britain
Germany
France

Turkey
Greece
Italy
Cyprus
Portugal   n/a
Spain   n/a

0   2   4   6   8   10   12

□ at home
■ at work

Source: Iris

Battle of the Internet browsers

Peter Martin on the difficulties of choosing between Microsoft and Netscape software for the World Wide Web

Oh, our eyes have seen the glory of the coming of the Net,
We are ramping up our market share, objectives will
* be met.*
Soon our browser will be everywhere, you ain't seen
* nothin' yet,*
We embrace and we extend!

Out in cyberspace lurks this ditty, masquerading as Microsoft's new marching song. Real or parody, it is the anthem of the battle the company never thought it would have to fight: the war for Internet software.

In Netscape, his upstart rival, Mr Bill Gates, the Microsoft chairman, has at last come up against a competitor with comparable aggression and ambition. The two companies are leap-frogging each other in a battle to dominate the market for software for the Internet's World Wide Web. Scarcely a month goes by without a new version of one or the other program. But does it matter to ordinary computer users?

This week Microsoft introduced Internet Explorer 3.0, its new browser (the type of software with which users access the Web). Netscape, a much smaller company but the leader in this market, launches the latest version of its browser, Navigator, on Monday.

Each side claims its product is the fastest, most powerful, most compatible. Each is signing up mighty allies – in Microsoft's case, Internet service providers and the publishers of Web content; in Netscape's case the big companies which have adopted its software as standard.

The battle is relevant to ordinary computer users for three reasons. The first is that it is producing extraordinarily rapid improvements in software. Both companies have crammed into a few months the sort of product enhancements that typically take years. Users inundated with the two sides' competing claims will want to know whether it is worth upgrading – and if so, which program to choose.

The second reason is that this choice may be an important one. As Microsoft and Netscape drive out other competing browsers, users will find that their favourite web sites take sides in the battle, working better with one or other of the two rival programs.

The third reason is that the battle between Netscape and Microsoft is more than a side-show. It may well decide whether Microsoft is able to extend its remarkable dominance of personal computer software into the Internet era.

Until this week, Microsoft has been on the defensive, essentially trying to whittle down the huge lead Netscape has enjoyed in market share and Web credibility (it is estimated that four-fifths of all browsers in use are Netscape ones). Now, Microsoft is starting to attack.

The flood of new features in the rival products means that all but the most casual Web users will need to upgrade their browsers in the next few months. It would normally be a trivial decision. But this time the stakes are higher. By their choice of browser, users have an unusual opportunity to influence the shape of the software market for years to come. So here, to help you make the choice, is an unashamedly subjective assessment of the rival products, under five headings: functions, performance, compatibility, availability and sentiment.

● **Functions**. Until recently Netscape had a clear lead here. Now Microsoft has closed the gap: it even has a slight edge by offering 'whiteboarding', the ability for users thousands of miles apart to pore over and mark up a shared spreadsheet or document. Netscape's strong point is a more mature sub-program to handle e-mail and discussion groups. Verdict: pretty much a draw.

● **Performance**. As browsers have got bigger and more complex, performance has become a more important issue. Microsoft stole an early lead by producing a faster, more compact program. Now Netscape is claiming to have caught up and passed its rival. Verdict: subjectively, Microsoft still feels faster.

● **Compatibility**. Publicly, both sides are claiming to be compatible with everything in sight; privately, both are trying to match all their rival's features and then provide some unique features that the other cannot easily emulate ('embrace and extend'). Microsoft now runs third-party accessory programs, or 'plug-ins', designed to work with Netscape. Both run mini-programs written in the fashionable Java language that put animations on users' screens.

Verdict: for most users, there's not much to choose between the programs. But, with a much bigger market share, Netscape now sets the standard for compatibility.

● **Availability**. Both programs are downloadable over the Internet. Microsoft's is free; Netscape's is on free trial. Both programs are now so big that downloading is time-consuming and inconvenient, at least over a slow link. Both programs are handed out by Internet service providers; Microsoft's is also given away free with some magazines. Verdict: slight edge to Microsoft – at least as long as the program continues to be free.

● **Sentiment**. Netscape started as the clear sentimental favourite: its co-founder, Mr Marc Andreessen, wrote the first modern browser; it invented the idea of offering its software on free trial on the Internet; and, above all, it seemed to offer a way for the industry to scramble out from under Microsoft's thumb.

Then it became clear that Netscape had just as all-embracing a set of ambitions as Mr Gates. And Microsoft's programmers started on a heroic effort to catch up with Netscape. Suddenly, Microsoft looked like the underdog.

Verdict: for real Microsoft-haters, the answer is easy. For the rest of us, it is more evenly balanced. Still, the rapid improvements brought about by the competition show the benefits of having two companies in the field. Even those people who prefer the Microsoft program will benefit from keeping the competition with Netscape needle-sharp.

Source: Financial Times, 17 August 1996

1.3 In the war between Microsoft and Netscape, what type of orientation do you detect?

1.4 How well do you think this situation addresses customer concerns?

1.5 Assess Microsoft's motivations. Is it a company that is genuinely interested in meeting customer needs, or simply generating huge profits, or striving for market dominance?

1.6 In terms of marketing history and business orientation, does the Internet herald a new age for marketing?

1D

Postal staff accused of 'madness'

Royal Mail fears loss of market to couriers and electronic mail, by Andrew Bolger and Michael Cassell

Postal workers were yesterday accused of 'mid-summer madness' after their union gave notice that tomorrow's one-day strike will be followed by a second 24-hour stoppage next week.

Royal Mail said it had been notified by the CWU postal workers' union of a stoppage from noon next Thursday to noon the following day by 134,000 delivery and sorting workers.

In spite of another round of talks yesterday on a pay and conditions package, the union remains opposed to management's insistence that flexibility is improved through the introduction of teamworking.

Royal Mail said there was no reason for the union to 'rob the nation' of its mail service while talks were continuing. Strike action was pointless and would put business at risk.

The decision to stage a second stoppage, with the possibility of more, has heightened the fears of Post Office managers that the dispute could cause long-term damage to its business.

Volumes handled by Royal Mail have risen in recent years. The 70m items delivered daily represent an increase of almost 50 per cent from a decade ago. But its market share has been declining in the face of competition from electronic mail, overseas postal administrations and private sector courier companies.

After the last prolonged postal strike in 1988 the Post Office lost business to the rising number of facsimile machines installed by businesses. Installations have been increasing at a yearly rate of 30 per cent. The latest threat involves electronic data interchange, adopted by a rapidly rising number of companies.

Royal Mail says its share of the UK's £30bn a year communications sector has fallen in the past 15 years from 20 per cent to 16 per cent.

The impending disruption to a service whose customers demand speed and reliability comes just ahead of the introduction next month of the first increases in inland letter rates since 1993.

Commercial customers, who account for 90 per cent of the mail business, are stepping up contingency arrangements for alternative delivery after yesterday's news that this week's stoppage will be repeated.

Royal Mail has been talking to its biggest customers – 3 per cent of them are responsible for 75 per cent of Royal Mail income – to try to help minimise the effects of the stoppage. There is concern that the biggest companies, seeking the most effective and value-for-money method of communication, could be permanently lost because of repeated interruptions to Royal Mail.

Mr Richard Dykes, the new managing director of Royal Mail, said last night he did not want to exaggerate the impact of limited industrial action, but it would inevitably undermine customer confidence. More protracted action could pose a serious risk to the business.

Royal Mail is particularly anxious to protect the higher value special services which are already open to competition – such as special deliveries and registered post.

There is also concern that public confusion over the extent of the strike will lead customers to believe that Parcelforce services, which deliver about 400,000 parcels each day, will be disrupted. Parcelforce, which will not be affected, is the UK's biggest parcel company but competes with more than 4,000 private couriers in a market already suffering from overcapacity.

Courier companies, which cannot charge less than £1 for providing a letter service, are unlikely to benefit significantly from the Post Office's immediate problems. DHL International (UK) said its priority was to maintain its international business, but that it would try to help customers with domestic deliveries where possible.

Source: Financial Times, 20 June 1996

1.7 How damaging do you think the series of strikes will be on the Royal Mail in its effort to become more marketing orientated and satisfy business customer needs?

1.8 What would be needed to successfully introduce marketing as a business philosophy throughout the Royal Mail organisation? What do you think would be the biggest hurdle to overcome?

1.9 Because of regulations, courier companies are prevented from offering a letter service, yet the rest of Royal Mail's activities are open to competitors. What are your views on this?

Plan to unravel language of packaging

Consumer Council wants claims by manufacturers to be regulated, reports Diane Summers

When Reckitt & Colman advertised that its Down to Earth washing-up liquid 'looks after rivers', with independent experts conducting stringent tests for biodegradability, it hit trouble with the Advertising Standards Authority.

Rival manufacturer Unilever complained the implication was that competitors' products were less biodegradable and did more harm to the environment.

The ASA agreed, Reckitt & Colman was unable to demonstrate its product was less harmful, and the complaint was upheld.

But any manufacturer wanting to make a similar claim on its packaging, rather than in an advertisement, would not have to worry about the watch-dog snapping at its heels.

Voluntary advertising codes of practice, policed by the ASA, do not extend to product claims on packs; at a statutory level, there appear only ever to have been four successful prosecutions under the Trade Descriptions Act 1968 against companies making false claims on labelling. There is some dispute as to whether the Act even applies to such cases.

It is against this background that the National Consumer Council yesterday recommended the rules should be overhauled to deal with the explosion over the last decade in 'eco-friendly' claims and the plethora of symbols, such as rainbows and globes, now appearing on products such as aerosol cans and toilet rolls.

It argues that the distinction between advertising and packaging is essentially false and that 'in the real world of marketing, labels and claims carried on products or their packaging generally form part of integrated marketing campaigns, of which the product design, its name, appearance and the messages on it are but one part'.

It would appear from the NCC's report that it is not so much the downright dishonest claims which are causing confusion as the 'woolly and unverifiable'. For example, the NCC takes issue with the term 'biodegradable' as applied to many paper products and on washing powders. All UK detergents exceed European Union standards on biodegradability, while paper products do biodegrade naturally but, says the NCC, 'most landfill is designed to stop this happening'.

The NCC's preferred option for reform is a code of practice for businesses, backed by reform of legislation which would reduce the standard of proof required to prosecute offending companies. The government backed the idea of a code but was initially unenthusiastic about fresh legislation, although it promised to examine the suggestion.

The code of practice policed by the ASA for advertising gives some idea of what a packaging code could look like. That states, for example, that claims such as 'environmentally friendly' should not be used without qualification unless advertisers can provide convincing evidence that their product will cause no environmental damage. All will now depend, if a self-regulatory system is to operate, on whether industry, government and consumers can agree common rules and who will police them.

Source: Financial Times, 16 March 1996

1.10 **Which elements of the marketing mix does this article discuss and which are omitted?**

1.11 **Is this a good example of social marketing? Justify your response.**

1.12 **Would the claims made by Reckitt & Colman encourage you to buy these products? Why?**

2

The European Marketing Environment

Scanning the external environment, is a major element of the marketers' job, i.e. trying to anticipate changes in sociological trends; avoid nasty price rises in raw material costs; capitalise on technological development and pre-empt political interference. When carried out frequently, a STEP analysis (Sociological, Technological, Economic and Political) helps the firm to become more aware of its macro-environment, and to have at least as much information, if not more than its competitors.

The much stronger role played by the European Commission in the day-to-day activities of organisations in all member states, has brought macro-environmental scanning on to a much broader stage. It is now vital, that an electrical components manufacturer in Swindon is not only monitoring its competitors in Birmingham and Coventry, but also those in Milan, Dusseldorf and Lisbon.

The STEP framework is very helpful and remains the most common, but recent debate has centred on whether this should be extended providing a SWEPT framework, to include that most variable of external factors, the weather. Other suggestions have been to sub-divide sociological and demographic elements to produce DE-SWEPT, or whether legal should be segregated from political to produce DE-SWELPT, and so it goes on.

The European regulatory framework in particular, produces a great deal of tension between domestic laws, EC directives, national voluntary self-regulation, lobbyists, pressure groups and marketing decision makers in each and every member state. It sometimes makes you wonder how anybody could have ever thought it would be successful.

In order to successfully complete the tasks in this chapter you will need to be familiar with:

- STEP analysis;
- environmental scanning;
- single European market;
- European regulatory framework.

European Commission grapples with the content of chocolate

Alison Maitland on a contest between cocoa growers and confectioners

The European Commission faces a sticky problem over the next few weeks as it grapples with new chocolate manufacturing rules which developing countries fear could badly damage their cocoa exports.

Far from engendering universal pleasure, the composition of European Union chocolate places cocoa producers at loggerheads with EU confectioners and splits member states down the middle.

At issue is the use by seven member states, including Britain, of vegetable fat in chocolate products as an alternative to cocoa butter. The other eight countries, including France, Belgium and Germany, are not allowed to use any vegetable fat other than cocoa butter.

The Commission, which has been struggling to replace the outdated 1973 chocolate directive for the past three years, is due to discuss the problem next Wednesday. The chocolate manufacturing industry says it expects a new draft directive this month or next.

Manufacturers argue that using more malleable vegetable fats allows development of innovative products such as chocolate with bubbles or twists, offering consumers greater choice.

Pressure for reform began when member states called for a simplification of food directives at the Edinburgh summit in December 1992. But the problem soon became one of harmonising the Ecu17bn (£14.3bn) chocolate market under single market rules.

Britain, Denmark and Ireland are allowed to use up to 5 per cent vegetable fat in their chocolate under an exemption from the 1973 directive. But the legal position of Portugal, which joined the EU in 1986, and new members Austria, Sweden and Finland, all of which also use vegetable fat, remains uncertain. They are anxious for clarification.

Cocoa producers, fearful the Commission will bow to manufacturers' pressure to allow all member states to use vegetable fat, have mounted a strong campaign in the EU.

During a break at last week's meeting of the International Cocoa Organisation in London, Mr Kouame N'guessan, spokesman for cocoa-growing countries, warned such a move could lose them 200,000 tonnes of exports to the EU a year.

The cocoa organisation, which represents producers and consumers, last year estimated the potential additional loss of cocoa beans could be between 88,000 and 125,000 tonnes. The EU uses about 1.1m tonnes a year, mainly for chocolate – at least 50 per cent more than a decade ago.

'We don't understand why, with a surplus of cocoa, people are looking for alternatives,' said Mr N'guessan. 'Producer countries have organised themselves to provide abundant supplies.'

Mr Martin Bangemann, EU industry commissioner, is anxious to find a compromise. He has suggested allowing member states to continue producing chocolate the way they do now but insisting on clear labelling to indicate whether it contains vegetable fat.

Mr N'guessan conceded that keeping the *status quo* would be 'a little less bad' than permitting the whole EU to use vegetable fat. But he said producers wanted vegetable fat content 'harmonised at zero'.

The producers are backed by the British charity Oxfam, which says African countries would lose revenue if all member states used alternatives to cocoa butter such as sheafat, which is three times cheaper.

Caobisco, the European chocolate, biscuit and sugar confectionery association, whose members together represent the world's biggest single purchaser of cocoa beans, maintains producing countries would lose no more than 25,000 tonnes of exports a year.

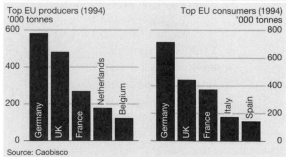

Chocolate & chocolate confectionery

Top EU producers (1994) '000 tonnes

Top EU consumers (1994) '000 tonnes

Source: Caobisco

Mr Baudouin Michiels, Caobisco president, says maintaining the EU *status quo* would be unacceptable. Confectioners wanting to export have to abide by the production rules in the target country 'and this makes the production process more complicated'.

If the existing split were enshrined in EU law, companies could take legal action against the Commission, he said. 'The single market is not just on paper, it has to be a reality.'

Even Mr Bangemann's apparently straightforward proposal on labelling could prove contentious. Cocoa purists want labelling to specify 'chocolate with vegetable fats' on the front of the bar or package. Manufacturers say the place for vegetable fat content is the ingredients list on the back.

The Commission has another headache. The International Cocoa Agreement, to which the EU is a signatory, says the Commission will not do anything that would reduce cocoa consumption. 'Legally it's complicated,' said a Commission official.

Officials fear stalemate when the issue is referred to member states – and they say the chocolate row could run and run.

Source: Financial Times, 30 March 1996

2.1 Why do you think the European Commission would want to get involved in determining how each member state manufactures chocolate?

2.2 British confectionery has been criticised for having a 'greasy' taste in comparison to continental chocolate. This is perhaps due to the partial substitution of vegetable fat for cocoa. Cocoa is very expensive and this makes continental chocolate more of a luxury in the UK. What would your reaction be if British manufacturers were told by the EU to stop using vegetable fats? Why?

2.3 What is your view on the labelling issue? If this was the only stumbling block, how could it be overcome?

2B

Campaigners fight against metrication

Traders face £5,000 fines if they breach regulations after M-Day, reports Neil Buckley

Campaigners to preserve imperial measures in the UK vowed yesterday to take their fight to the European Court – as laws come into force tomorrow making it a criminal offence to sell pre-packed goods in non-metric measures.

The man leading the anti-metrication campaign is Mr Vivian Linacre, an Edinburgh surveyor who has formed the British Weights and Measures Association to fight the changes. Mr Linacre, who called for a 'massive, national campaign of passive public resistance' against metrication, said he was launching an 'October revolution'.

He claimed to have legal advice that he had an 'open and shut case' for the European Court that compulsory metrication breached the Treaty of Rome, but warned the fight would be lengthy and costly.

Although Mr Linacre said he was unable to say how many members his association had, he claimed to have 'sackfuls of mail' in support.

The government, he said, had used statutory instruments to comply with a European Commission directive passed in 1989, with no debate or vote in parliament.

'That is the sum total of the democratic process that has led to the abolition of our whole system of weights and measures, and compulsory metrication backed by penal sanctions,' he added.

Tomorrow is Metrication Day, or M-Day, when British traders will be forced to sell pre-packed goods in grams, litres and centimetres, rather than pounds, pints and inches. There are exceptions, however – pints will be permitted for beer (but not shandy) in pubs, and for doorstep milk deliveries.

Anyone breaching the regulations will be subject to fines of up to £5,000, although government inspectors have promised lenience at first.

Food sold loose, including meat, poultry, fruit and vegetables, will not have to be sold in metric measures until the turn of the century.

The extent of support for Mr Linacre's campaign is uncertain and he may face a long and somewhat lonely struggle. However, the Federation of Small Businesses, with 75,000 members, has also launched a poster campaign condemning 'metric madness' and urging consumers to write to MPs.

The federation does not want to preserve imperial measures for ever, but would like more time for businesses to make the change because altering weights and labelling will cost its members thousands of pounds.

It said: 'We are complaining about the fact that people have not been educated about the changes. We are worried that there are fines hanging over the heads of people who fail to comply.'

The federation and other opponents say the government has deliberately failed to publicise the metrication move to avert a row with Eurosceptic MPs, leaving many businesses and consumers unaware of the changeover until recently. They accuse the Department of Trade and Industry of failing to distribute millions of leaflets printed to explain the metric measures.

The government says it has already postponed the move for nine months after the original target date – January 1 – to give businesses more time.

Moreover, metrication has plenty of support. The British Retail Consortium, which represents the majority of British retailers – 300,000 retail outlets – backs the move, while the National Consumer Council says it does not go far enough.

The Association of Convenience Stores said it did not believe metrication would have a significant impact on businesses, but was concerned it might cause confusion among customers.

Trading standards officers in some areas have warned consumers to be on guard for traders exploiting unfamiliarity with the measures to put prices up. They say some traders increased profits in 1971, when Britain adopted decimal currency, by generously 'rounding up' converted prices.

Source: Financial Times, 30 September 1995

2.4 Using the information in this article, your experience and that of your family and friends since M-Day, identify the STEP factors which affected this event. Include both positive and negative elements.

2.5 How marketing orientated do you think the Department of Trade & Industry has been in providing information for this event?

2.6 With the benefit of hindsight, what do you now think the DTI could and should have done to prepare the public for this change?

When banana skins abound

Misfortune and EU bureaucrats have put the skids under Geest, writes David Blackwell

Black sigatoka disease, tropical storm Debbie and the EU banana regime form an unlikely trinity of villains. Nevertheless, the three have combined to put the skids under Geest's share price over the past couple of years. From a high of 371p in January last year, shares in the fresh produce and prepared food group have tumbled to a low this week of 107p.

The slide began in January 1994 when the group warned that black sigatoka, a fungal disease, had attacked its banana plantations in Costa Rica. An exceptional charge of £8.9m to cover the costs of fighting the disease pushed the group £5.4m into the red for 1993.

News of Geest's troubles surprised the market as sigatoka is a routine hazard for banana growers in Latin America and normally is controlled by spraying. In this case, the group blamed weather patterns in the rainy season which led to a loss of control.

Then, in September last year, Debbie hit the Windward Islands, which usually provide more than half the group's total banana volume. The storm caused extensive damage and cut production by about 40 per cent. While the group exceeded forecasts with profits of £12.8m for 1994, they would have been £7m higher if Windward banana production had reached its usual level.

This week, the group issued its third profits warning of the past two years. It blamed the vagaries of the EU banana regime for an over-supply in Europe in the final quarter.

The banana regime regulations, which are now set until the year 2002, have changed Geest's field of operations from a regulated market in the UK to a regulated market in Europe. They are designed to favour bananas from former colonies, mostly countries in the African, Caribbean and Pacific (ACP) group. Import quotas are set for so-called dollar bananas from Latin America in order to satisfy demand.

Political complexities continue to surround the regime, however, with the US being particularly critical. As a result, the EU has already increased the dollar quota for 1995 from 2.1m to 2.2m tonnes. But further dollar banana licences have been issued to compensate ACP importers for the bananas lost to hurricane damage this year and last. The rolled-over licences must be used by the end of the calendar year.

It is these bananas which form the basis of Geest's complaint. Chief executive David Sugden, who believes the group has coped well with the changing market so far, said the situation was having 'a disastrous effect on the selling price'.

He is not alone. Earlier this month Chiquita, a US banana group, said its profits had been affected by 'inappropriate administration of the EU quota and licensing regime'.

In the UK, consumers have seen banana prices fall to the lowest level for almost 20 years this month as the supermarkets battle to outdo each other. Asda, which sells 8m bananas a week – more than any other single item – started to cut prices from 38p a lb on October 23. In the ensuing price war Asda, Tesco and Sainsbury all went down to 19p.

Sugden suggested that, realistically, bananas should retail at about 45p. While prices started to climb at the end of this week, they are likely to fluctuate for the rest of this month and December.

Because of this volatility Geest did not give a forecast. But exceptional charges announced so far this year mean that it is likely to end up in the red again.

City expectations have been reduced from about £14m to £9m, excluding exceptionals. In September, the group announced an exceptional charge of £5m, mostly for the disposal of its wholesale markets business.

This week, a further £7m of exceptionals was announced, some of which will be used to reduce the effect of continuing losses at Necta, the prepared pineapple business.

Sugden has been keen in the past couple of years to point out the growing importance of the group's food businesses outside bananas. Apart from Necta, the prepared foods businesses 'continue to perform well', the group said this week.

Speculation that the banana business was up for sale was fuelled when it was put into a separate division in June. In September Sir James Mitchell, prime minister of St Vincent, said he understood Geest had been negotiating with Noboa, an Ecuadorean company.

He wrote to the British government to express concern that a sale could harm the Windward Islands. But Geest denied there had been any negotiations although Sugden added: 'It would be foolish to say that we would never, ever sell.'

Analysts this week suggested that the market value of the whole group – just £87.6m on Thursday – was low enough to prove tempting to predators. Ironically, the political complexities of the banana market could be the only factor holding them at bay.

Source: Financial Times, 18 November 1995

2D

Flat batteries help drive record demand for lead

Supply shortfalls from eastern Europe and China have helped push up prices, writes Kenneth Gooding

Did your car battery fail recently? If it did, you are not alone in suffering this inconvenience. A long hot summer in 1995 in Europe and North America, coupled with two very cold winters in a row between 1994 and 1996, resulted in high levels of automotive battery failures.

It also caused record demand for lead because the main use for this metal today is for lead-acid batteries. In the US, 85 per cent of lead consumption is accounted for by battery makers. In the western world, 69 per cent of all refined lead produced goes into batteries.

Lead producers are struggling to keep up with the jump in demand. Global stocks have fallen to critical levels and London Metal Exchange prices have risen to their highest levels in nearly six years.

On top of that, the LME's lead market has been gripped by a ferocious technical squeeze and last week the board had to take emergency action to prevent 'an undesirable situation' developing. Traders were taken by surprise on Thursday when Mr David King, the LME's chief executive, halted trading just after midday to announce that the cost of carrying over a short position in lead for one day was to be limited to $27 (£17.60) a tonne.

This premium had been up to $40. Mr King said the lead market remained orderly but, because of the genuine tightness in lead supplies, 'some constraints were necessary to keep it orderly'.

Some traders complained that the LME's action had once again favoured those who had 'gone short' of metal, or sold lead they did not own on the expectation that the price would fall and they could buy it later and pocket the difference.

Mr King insisted that he had no sympathy for the 'shorts' but the LME had a legal duty to maintain an orderly market. It also owed a duty to the industries which used the market to hedge their risks. About 90 per cent of base metals industries use LME settlement prices and they expected those prices to reflect the fundamental supply-demand situation.

Those underlying fundamentals are certainly putting upward pressure on lead prices.

According to the International Lead & Zinc Study Group, an intergovernmental organisation, the present tightness in the lead market can be traced to big falls in output last year in China and Kazakhstan. Preliminary statistics from the ILZSG show that Chinese production fell 12.4 per cent or 58,000 tonnes compared with 1994, while the drop in Kazakhstan was 29 per cent or 47,000 tonnes.

This resulted in a big drop in exports from eastern Europe. The CRU International metals consultancy estimates net exports fell 36 per cent, from a record 253,000 tonnes in 1994 to 161,000 tonnes. This contributed to lead consumption in the western world exceeding supply by 172,000 tonnes last year compared with a 38,000 tonnes surplus in 1994.

Most analysts suggest the tightness will continue. Mr Neil Hawkes at CRU estimates the supply shortfall this year will be about 90,000 tonnes.

He points out that LME stocks are already below the critical level of five weeks' consumption and producers' stocks are usually low at this time of year.

Supply tightness has now been overlaid by a technical squeeze. This developed after merchants and investment funds moved some of their money into the lead market last month with the aim of driving the price of lead for delivery in three months on

Supply and demand of refined lead		
('000 tonnes)	1994	1995
Western world production	4,484	4,505
Western world consumption	4,761	4,881
Eastern European exports	253	161
US stockpile sales	62	43
Market balance	38	−172

Source: CRU International

Principal end-uses of lead

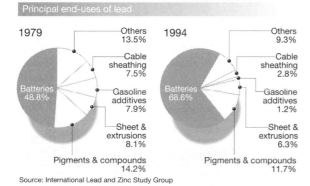

1979
Others 13.5%
Cable sheathing 7.5%
Gasoline additives 7.9%
Batteries 48.8%
Sheet & extrusions 8.1%
Pigments & compounds 14.2%

1994
Others 9.3%
Cable sheathing 2.8%
Gasoline additives 1.2%
Batteries 68.6%
Sheet & extrusions 6.3%
Pigments & compounds 11.7%

Source: International Lead and Zinc Study Group

the LME to $800 a tonne. In mid-December, the price had reached a five-year peak of $746 a tonne but fell when the US hedge funds started selling at the beginning of January.

The merchants and funds took a tight grip on stocks held in the LME-authorised warehouses in Helsingborg, Sweden, where about 80 per cent of total LME stocks were held.

They hoped that when the lead price reached $800 it would trigger a wave of buying by those commodity funds that use computer programmes and charts to track prices. This, in turn, could send lead up to $850 a tonne or higher. Last week, the three-month lead price was on the way, touching $828.50. But most of the pain was felt by those wanting lead for immediate delivery. The LME spot price reached $927.50 a tonne last Thursday, which meant buyers were having to pay a premium of $114 a tonne for immediate delivery. Prices have subsided a little since the LME intervened, but yesterday there was still a $25–$30 premium for immediate delivery.

While technical tightness seems to be easing, the underlying lead supply shortage remains. CRU's Mr Hawkes says: 'The key factor is the Chinese. Will they export more lead because of high prices? In the past they have flooded the market with refined metal at times like this.'

And what does this mean for battery prices? Mr Angus MacMillan, research manager at Billiton Metals, a Gencor subsidiary, suggests that high lead prices would have to persist for a prolonged period to cause a substantial battery price rise.

'Battery producers should have hedged their lead requirements because they could see the squeeze coming along time ago,' he says. 'Also, producers' battery stocks are high. Most important, there is over-capacity in battery production so the market is very competitive.'

Source: Financial Times, 26 March 1996

2.7 Using the information in these articles, produce an external environment analysis for both batteries and bananas. Within each analysis, rank each element according to its relative impact on the situation.

2.8 The weather was an important element in the series of events described, but where would you place 'the weather' in a traditional STEP analysis?

2.9 How many more industries, markets or activities can you identify which are significantly affected by the weather?

2.10 The purpose of environmental scanning is to try and pick up early signs of emerging trends and thus plan future activity appropriately. What steps could a manufacturer, a seller or an organiser take to anticipate and deal with favourable or unfavourable weather?

Nursing home operators look for healthier future

Government plans for long-term care could give the industry a much-needed boost in occupancy rates, writes Mark Suzman and Motoko Rich

Insurers are likely to be the most obvious beneficiaries of this week's government proposals to encourage people to make greater provision for long-term care. But the nursing home industry is also hoping for a significant boost.

The proposals will provide for 'partnerships' under which the government will disregard a proportion of money paid for care costs through insurance or an annuity when assessing an individual's eligibility for state assistance. Currently the state contributes to the cost of care only for people with assets of £16,000 or less.

If individuals are assured of coverage, this should reduce the disincentive to enter a home, and analysts expect it to provide a much-needed fillip for nursing home occupancy rates. Since 1992 these have fallen from 94.5 per cent to about 90 per cent – depressing company profits and forcing many small, privately-held homes to close or merge.

This is in part the result of simple overcapacity. The number of for-profit nursing home places has soared in recent years, from 52,000 in 1987 to 178,800 in 1994.

A bigger problem, however, has been the 1993 care in the community reforms, which devolved responsibility for funding long-term care from central government to local authorities. With those budgets capped by the government, the result has been that many authorities have faced shortfalls in paying for care, with detrimental effects for providers.

Some companies believe the problem is exacerbated by a failure to ringfence funds specified for long-term care. Mr Keith Bradshaw, managing director of Takare, the nursing homes group, said that there was 'genuine suspicion that community care funds are being used to pay teachers or to help maintain the town hall'.

According to Mr Andrew Richmond, analyst at Collins Stewart, the brokers, even if funds are spent on long-term care, these funds may be inefficiently allocated. 'They [the authorities] are possibly misdirecting funds into areas of care that are not cost effective as they should be,' he said.

Public companies active in long-term care

		No of homes	No of beds
1	Takare	51	6930
2	Westminster Health Care	70	4748
3	Cresta Care	48	2914
4	Ashbourne	22	1805
5	Court Cavendish Group	32	1517
6	Goldsborough Healthcare	30	1439
7	Quality Care Homes	28	1408
8	St Andrews Homes/Vaux Group	24	1241
9	Country House/Boddington Group	29	1194
10	ANS	18	1112
11	APTA Healthcare	23	844
12	Community Hospitals Group	13	704
13	Greenacre Group	13	680
14	CareUK	10	528
15	Tamaris	6	343
16	Compass Healthcare/Compass Group	2	128

Ranked by beds owned at July 1995   Source: The Fitzhugh Directory 1995

One such area is domiciliary – or home – care, which is difficult to provide more efficiently or cheaply than care in a nursing home. According to Laing & Buisson, the specialist health sector analyst, the number of people being cared for in their own house rose to 2.38m in 1995, from 1.69m in 1992.

Such care, said Mr Paul Saper, director at Laing & Buisson, has diverted funds and residents away from the nursing home groups, who have expanded in line with demographic, rather than community care funding, trends. 'New building has carried on, and instead of the expected increase of people coming from the demographic changes, they have effectively been transferred to domiciliary care,' he said.

Whatever the causes, the result has been increasing competition and lower margins, severely exacerbated by a sharp fall in the average length of stay in a home. According to Mr Tom Hamilton, chief executive of Ashbourne, the nursing home group, this has fallen from three years to 18 months. 'The combination of local authorities toughening up, and private individuals deferring the decision to go into a nursing home, has put downward pressure on the average length of stay,' he said.

It is these people who analysts believe will take advantage of the new proposals and enter the market in greater numbers, helping secure long-term growth. Although it will be several years before policy changes have a discernible effect, further rationalisation may help rebalance a market which is expected to show real growth of about 50 per cent in the next 25 years.

'Overheads are being reduced by companies buying each other,' said Mr Chai Patel, executive chairman of Court Cavendish, which bought Greenacre, another public rival, late last month. 'That will compensate for drops in occupancy.'

Source: Financial Times, 9 May 1996

2.11 Identify the forces within the external environment which have provided the increase in occupancy rates in the nursing home industry.

2.12 As a nursing home manager with responsibilities for long-term planning, how could you respond to these?

2.13 Suggest an appropriate, and tasteful promotional programme to create a better awareness of your facility in the local area.

2F

Doorstep milk decline takes toll on Park Food

By David Blackwell

The decline in doorstep milk deliveries was blamed for profits coming in below expectations at Park Food Group, which specialises in the sale of Christmas hampers.

The shares were marked down sharply, closing down 18p at 92p, in spite of the rise of almost 16 per cent in pre-tax profits from £11.8m to a record £13.7m. The City had been forecasting about £15m.

Mr Peter Johnson, the chairman and managing director, who owns 65 per cent of the company and is also chairman of Everton Football Club, said he appreciated that the results were below market expectations. He put the blame firmly on the wholesale hampers division. The group was now closing its dairy office in Windsor and consolidating the wholesale operation in Birkenhead.

Milkmen traditionally have made half the sales of the wholesale trade in Christmas hampers, which account for about 20 per cent of hamper turnover.

About 80 per cent of the hampers are sold through agents. The number of agents has retreated to 80,000 from almost 90,000 last year, the first fall in the company's history, although the company believed the 1994 level was exceptional.

Group sales were 25 per cent higher, rising from £137.3m to £171.1m. However, the latest figure included £8.7m of sales from the hamper business of Heritage Food Group (UK), acquired for £10.5m last year, and £12.7m from the first full year of Handling Solutions, whose operations include dispatching goods for coupons for other companies.

The Heritage hamper business contributed £1.07m to profits, while Handling Solutions made £2.34m. Profits were also enhanced by £1.7m of investment income, down from £2.02m previously.

The group also announced a delay in Project Q, its new potato processing business, following the receivership of the builders. The shell of the building is up, but production has been put back to late autumn.

However, the group is confident that the product will be well received. It is hoping for an annual turnover of £3.5m from the plant, and is negotiating a deal with an international catering company. But it will not be selling through retail outlets as it feels it could not meet demand.

Earnings per share rose from 5.04p to 5.84p. A final dividend of 1.88p is proposed taking the total to 2.88p (2.4p).

Source: Financial Times, 10 June 1995

2.14 Peter Johnson has asked you to advise him on how to increase the sales of doorstep milk and Christmas hampers in preparation for next year. He has asked you to look into the matter and prepare a presentation so that he can:
- identify those factors in the external environment which may have caused the decline;
- decide how to respond;
- take another look at the product offering and in view of this;
- decide on a new promotional plan.

2G

Electronics' driving forces

Car makers face social, political and economic pressures to change the systems in vehicles, writes Paul Taylor

New factors are reshaping the use of electronics in cars, as the industry prepares to respond to environmental regulations and to technological developments, such as traffic management systems.

The next few years are likely to bring both strict exhaust emission laws for petrol and diesel engines and advanced driver information services.

These two trends, according to Dataquest, the market research firm, mean that the world market for automotive electronics is likely to grow to $57bn (£36bn) by the end of the decade from $36bn last year.

Emerging electronic automotive applications will be influenced by a combination of factors as vehicle manufacturers, governments and local authorities act to curb vehicle congestion and limit the effects of air pollution in cities.

Mike Williams, a Dataquest industry analyst and author of the report, believes that another impetus for further growth will come from the newly emerging communications applications for road transport/traffic and vehicle systems. 'These new applications will generate a huge market exploding towards the year 2000,' he says.

Historically, powertrain electronics – systems which affect the motion of vehicles including engine management, suspension control and vehicle handling – and safety systems have increased the use of electronics in the automotive industry. They remain the biggest segment of the market accounting for a third of the total automotive electronics market last year.

Other market segments include safety and convenience electronics, in-car entertainment, driver information and car body control including multiplex door wiring and car security.

Electronics applications first appeared in cars in commercial volumes 30 years ago as voltage regulators and ignition controls. The energy crisis in the 1970s spawned electronic controls for fuel injection and carburettor engines. However, Dataquest estimates that growth in automotive electronics is reaching maturity for powertrain electronics, which now account for nearly half the world automotive electronics market.

US legislation in the 1980s prompted electronic engine control systems to curb exhaust pollution, and by the start of this decade electronics were found in many vehicle applications including engine management, air conditioning, dashboard, security systems, tracking devices, safety applications and for route planning and traffic information.

Electronics and vehicle electrics account for nearly 12 per cent of the total costs of a mid-range car, a figure which is expected to exceed 25 per cent 10 years hence.

'Virtual market forces, aside from legislation and regulation, are now emerging,' says Williams. For example, insurance companies are starting to require the use of electronic devices for car security.

By the end of the decade social, political and economic factors enforced by governments and the fleet transportation industry will drive the use of electronics in cars. The millions of dollars spent on research and development for the transportation industry will also be expected to yield dividends for the commercial sector.

The European Union and the European car manufacturers have committed more than $1bn to the Prometheus research programme, which aims to halve the 50,000 annual deaths on EU roads by the end of the decade through greater use of in-car electronic information systems and other technological developments. Similar programmes are under way in the US and Japan.

The next generation of 'smart' cars will be intelligent vehicles that can illuminate long distances in the dark using infra-red and ultraviolet headlights, cruise intelligently by automatically keeping pace with the vehicle in front, know exactly where they are by using satellite navigation systems, and summon emergency services to the scene of a breakdown or accident without driver action.

New systems beginning to appear in cars include electronic steering and suspension, keyless and remote-entry systems, devices that remember a driver's seating position, mirror position and radio settings, and navigation based on dead-reckoning technology and the global positioning satellite.

Dataquest says the growth of automotive electronics represents a tremendous opportunity for the semiconductor industry. For example, silicon sensors, pioneered by Motorola, represent a large potential market and could provide solutions to problems that can no longer be solved using older technologies.

At present, the automotive elec- tronics sector represents a rather fragmented semiconductor application market, but eventually all the component parts of automotive electronics systems will become integrated.

Tomorrow's car

Worldwide automotive electronic production revenues ($ million)

FUTURE 1

Segment	1993	1994	1998	2000
Entertainment	5,870	6,191	8,453	9,652
Body control	3,077	3,495	5,532	6,594
Driver information	5,464	5,893	7,584	9,068
Powertrain	10,607	11,929	16,425	18,541
Safety and convenience	7,193	8,521	11,486	13,257
Total	32,211	36,029	49,480	57,112

As a result, Williams predicts, automotive electronics will become one of the five largest global markets for semiconductors and passive electronics components. Overall, the average semiconductor content of a vehicle is currently around $100, but by the end of the decade this will have reached $200.

Worldwide automotive semiconductor consumption last year was $5.2bn but by 2000 this is expected to grow to at least $10.2bn. Williams points out that this growth forecast is for in-vehicle electronics systems only.

'The figure can be multiplied by about five for the infrastructure issues,' he says. 'Then we are looking at growth of around $25bn.'

Source: Financial Times, 25 May 1995

2.15 **Using the information in this article and your own experience, produce an analysis which identifies and ranks the sociological, technological, economic and political issues facing manufacturers as they approach the year 2000.**

3

Consumer Behaviour

A lot of money, time and effort is spent on trying to understand precisely what it is which motivates the individual consumer to make a purchase. Sociologists, behaviourists, scientists, philosophers and even astrologists, all try to predict our behaviour, yet few of us fit neatly into the various categories used to typify lifestyle and propensity to buy. These classifications are useful as a starting point, just so long as the marketer realises that 'times they are a'changing'.

Recent research has revealed that many more people, both male and female, are perfectly happy to be living alone and have no desire to permanently share their lives with anybody, other than perhaps a dog or cat. This has a marked effect on how marketers need to design their promotional messages to appeal to such groups of consumers. TV adverts showing the traditional two + two happy family and budget priced products, is quite likely to be a turn-off for this usually affluent group.

Product development teams are now willing to critically examine pack sizes, realising that not everything has to be in large quantities or packs of six. This is true not only in the familiar chilled meals section of the local supermarket, but also in packs of non-food items, such as toiletries, electrical and household maintenance products.

Many influences play a part in developing our individual personality. Some we are born with, but most we acquire through parental influence or through our association with different social groups. We all have different motivational needs, some being keen on a conspicuous display of wealth and material possession, while others prefer to play down their self-esteem. Anticipating, recognising and even forecasting when an individual or a group of similar types of people are likely to buy, and placing your product appropriately to appeal to their needs, wants and desires is the key to successfully understanding consumer behaviour.

In order to successfully complete the tasks in this chapter you will need to be familiar with:

- consumer decision making process;
- sociocultural influences;
- psychological influences;
- buying situations;
- motivation.

Men as magpies

Diane Summers looks at a study of male shopping habits
which offers retailers food for thought

The picture of the typical male shopper as a figure who fills his trolley with booze and biscuits but forgets the spuds and soap powder, may be outmoded. Indeed, there is evidence that some men not only enjoy supermarket shopping more than women, but take pride in their superior expertise in the aisles, members of the Market Research Society heard last week.

The competitive side of the male personality is 'highly apparent in the store experience', according to Nichola Riley and April Blanchard from market research company The Research Business.

Many of the men they talked to for their qualitative study of male shoppers 'considered themselves "better shoppers" than women in a number of ways'.

Their MRS paper, entitled 'The secret life of the male shopper', identified three forms this competitive shopping behaviour may take:

● 'Magpies' pride themselves on being more experimental, exciting shoppers than women, buying new and interesting products, and being more likely to try new items that catch their eye. They were more open to 'brand switching' than women, making them excellent targets for new product launches and brand variants.

However, the researchers warned there were dangers in making choices too complex.

For example, during store observations 'a number of men spent considerable time browsing the cook-in sauce category, picking up a wide range of brands and varieties, reading the labels, revisiting particular brands, only to revert to their standard purchase of a jar of Dolmio, as a result of cognitive overload from a complex fixture'.

● 'Bargain hunters' expressed their competitive edge over their partners by saving money. Riley and Blanchard found men were more likely than women to base purchase decisions on the lowest price and money-off promotions for certain types of goods.

● 'Go-fasters' got their reward by attempting to beat their personal best times for getting round the store and were particularly annoyed if a change in layout slowed them down. These men shopped in a 'grab and go' mode, relying on familiar brand names and packaging to help them get what they wanted quickly.

The research concentrated on the shopping habits of young, working, single men, and fathers of young children. There were group discussions, accompanied shopping trips, diaries and 'cupboard audits'. Four categories were explored in detail: cook-in sauces, household goods, savoury snacks and toiletries.

It was in this last category that men appeared least comfortable. With 'pack design and product presentation soaked in female values', toiletries fixtures could be seen 'to challenge masculine sexual identity'. For women the toiletries section was often the 'treat' element of their shop. But men described the toiletries section as an area where 'men do not belong'. Instead of the female 'indulgent browse,' men go into 'scanner mode,' found Riley and Blanchard. They skim along the aisle 'desperately searching for some male cues, such as black and silver, or chunky packaging, as with Gillette. Very little price comparison is conducted – the prime desire is to get out of this area as quickly as possible'.

For the same reasons, chemists shops were disliked, with men feeling they had entered a world for females only. In small chemists they felt they were under scrutiny from female assistants.

Overall, the supermarket environment was found to suit men well: organised layouts appealed to the functional elements of the male personality, while the anonymity offered allowed them to browse unchallenged.

Source: Financial Times, 28 March 1996

3.1 The consumer decision making process identifies many influencing factors on the five recognised stages of a purchase decision, i.e. problem recognition, information search, information evaluation, decision, post purchase evaluation. Apply this to the following types of purchaser identified and assess which stages of the process are taking place and which are being skipped:
- Magpie;
- Bargain hunter;
- Go-faster.

3.2 As a retail manager, what could you do to encourage each of these purchaser types to participate in each stage of the process?

3B

The X-files

Diane Summers reports on research into what 20-somethings the world over really think

The Generation X stereotypes spring readily to mind. Twenty-somethings, lost, aimless souls, trekking disillusioned in the urban wasteland; alternatively, they are style and status-conscious materialists, fixated by the Internet and able to relate only to yobbish, 'in-your-face' advertising.

As might be expected, the true picture contains elements of the stereotypes but is infinitely more complex. This is illustrated by an international qualitative study of young adults, based on 160 discussion groups in 35 countries, carried out by Research International, the WPP market research subsidiary.

Marketers may not be as in tune with this important age group as they believe. Besides talking to 20-35-year-olds (a slightly older age group than the usual focus of Generation X studies), researchers in each country questioned 'experts' from marketing, advertising, social science and journalism.

The experts' assumptions about enthusiasm for the Internet and virtual reality were not borne out by young adults themselves, says Research International, 'neither is the accepted view of them as acutely image-conscious and status-oriented consumers, at least in the developed western markets, where the research points to a move away from overt consumerism'.

If one universal observation can be made about this generation, it is that universal observations are unreliable. Individualism appears to be one basic defining characteristic, although the term is open to interpretation in different countries.

In emerging markets such as India, China, African countries and some south-east Asian and Latin American markets, individualism is about moving away from a traditional family-centred way of living, to a more 'modern' western lifestyle. In Japan, individual choices are made within the boundaries of collective values: young adults want choice but do not want to stand out or be rejected by others for being different. In the more mature markets of northern Europe, the US and parts of southern Europe, young adults appear ready to make choices irrespective of what their peers think.

Together with this individualism, the study finds the demise of a collective approach to, for example, environmental, social and political issues, and a retreat into 'micro orientation' – concern with immediate, personal issues such as financial security or finding a partner. The study found the prevailing attitude was that 'it was up to the state, rather than the individual' to resolve wider issues.

Four segments, by outlook, were identified within the age group:

- 'Enthusiastic materialists' were most prevalent in emerging markets such as India, Africa, China and south-east Asia, although some of their values were shared by the developing markets of Europe, such as Turkey and the Czech Republic, and some Latin American countries, including Colombia and Chile.

Those in this group were enthusiastically adopting western values, setting great store by 'outward show and the material trappings of status and success'.

Their goals can basically be defined as 'earn a lot, have a nice car, a nice house'. They are not prepared to spend years making progress like their parents. They are entrepreneurial and strongly optimistic.

● 'Complacent materialists' were identified only in Japan. Their 'cocooned, affluent upbringing seems to have sheltered them from economic reality so they feel secure and complacent'. They appear convinced they will prosper with little effort. As in some other mature markets, young adults subscribe to the 'new moderation': there is a backlash among many young Japanese men against their fathers' total dedication to their work. They are very micro-oriented and a 'passive sense of optimism' prevails.

● 'Swimmers against the tide' are struggling to maintain material ambitions but are suffering from the economic downturn. 'As a result, they frequently feel impotent and out of control . . . They feel their life has become a vicious circle, whereby they work hard to maintain the lifestyle they aspire to – but have no time to enjoy it'. Countries where this attitude was found included Brazil and parts of southern Europe, including Greece, Portugal and Spain.

● 'New realists' were found mainly in the mature markets of northern Europe, including the UK, France and Italy, and the US, Australasia and white South Africa. This group had come to terms with the 'new economic reality' – that they are never going to achieve the material affluence of their parents' generation, and have amended their goals accordingly. 'Their attitude is one of pragmatic resignation in a climate of underlying pessimism.'

One aim of the study was to identify 'levers' for communicating advertising messages to young adults. Humour, if relevant to the local culture, and approaches which reflect consumers' own values and lifestyles, were found to be highly engaging.

Advertising which humorously reflects the imperfections of modern life and which acknowledges 'current feelings of confusion, stress and cynicism which young people experience, or reflects their sense of living in a crazy world', generated strong identification. Tango in the UK, Nike in the US and Becker beer in Chile were all cited as particularly in tune with the age group.

Brands which offer themselves as the consumer's ally in a tough world, 'providing encouragement and empowerment to the individual', were successful. Nike was again cited as an example, with its 'Just do it' message.

Creating a sense of complicity by using codes or language understood only to this age group, or acknowledging the consumer's intelligence through subtle, intriguing or surprising advertising was appreciated. Levi's advertising was mentioned in many countries around the world, particularly the controversial commercial featuring a glamorous 'woman' in the back of a New York taxi who turns out, to the cabbie's horror, to be a transvestite.

There was international agreement on approaches that irritate – ads which insult the intelligence of young adults, use stereotyped images, knock the competition, look cheap or try too hard to be 'hip'.

Above all, the study warns against the risks, particularly in the more sophisticated, developed markets, of campaigns that are purely entertainment. An 'interactive, challenging relationship' with young adults need not preclude entertainment, it concludes.

Source: Financial Times, 18 January 1996

3.3 **Social class is still used as a means of identifying types of consumer, with occupation the main determinant for the UK. How relevant do you think the supposed link with income and social class is today, and why do you think the sociologists and marketers persist in using such a system?**

3.4 **What type of sociocultural factors would you expect to influence the 20-somethings discussed in the article?**

3.5 **You work for a manufacturer of laptop computers and your manager has recruited you with the specific purpose of trying to understand the 20-something market. Current purchasers are typically aged 34 and are motivated to buy because of business needs. You have been asked for your ideas on how to sell laptop computers to Generation X. Outline how you could make your product appealing to each of the three types identified in the article (ignore pricing issues at this stage).**

Growth in number of people living alone

By Diane Summers,
Marketing Correspondent

The number of people living alone is set to rise to 8m by the end of the century, from 6.8m last year, making single-person households the fastest-growing group of all household types, forecasts Mintel, the market intelligence group, in a study published today.

Mintel says the boom has implications for a number of sectors. Younger, single home-makers – who are increasingly likely to be owner-occupiers – will be interested in cheap ways of brightening their homes.

Convenience foods, home security devices and services linked to socialising will also have extra market potential.

Singles are also getting younger, more upmarket and more positive about living alone than they used to be, the report finds.

Single-person households made up 24 per cent of all households in 1985, and 28 per cent last year. By the year 2000 the figure will have grown to 30 per cent. The rising divorce rate and the tendency towards marrying later partly account for the trend among younger age groups, while steadily increasing life expectancy has contributed to the growth in numbers of older single-person households.

Nearly half of people who live alone are aged 65 or over but non-pensioner groups have shown the highest rate of growth in recent years.

The proportion of single-person households belonging to socio-economic group ABC1 (professional and non-manual) has increased to 45 per cent from 38 per cent in 1990. However, this is smaller than for the population as a whole, where ABC1 accounts for 49 per cent of households.

Ms Angela Hughes, Mintel's consumer research manager, said that out of a sample of nearly 800 adults living alone, half 'can be classified as "happy singles", who can see only positive, and no negative, aspects of living alone. Meanwhile, only one in 10 are "struggling singles", for whom negative factors such as loneliness or expense are not balanced by increased freedom or feelings of achievement'.

There was a drop in those saying they were lonely, from 36 per cent of those questioned in 1992, to 30 per cent last year, while those saying they gained a sense of achievement from living alone increased from 49 per cent to 53 per cent over the same period.

Singles have more leisure time than other groups – an additional eight hours a week for those under 55.

Source: Financial Times, 20 March 1996

More women holding own mortgages and cash cards

Social trends: Survey reflects growing financial independence of female population, writes Krishna Guha

The proportion of mortgages held solely by women in Britain more than doubled between 1983 and 1994, with women now accounting for more than 17 per cent of mortgages – a share close to that held by sole men.

The figure, published today by the Central Statistical Office, is part of the CSO Social Focus on Women. The report shows that in 1993 almost three-quarters of women had some form of 'plastic card' – credit, debit and retailer card.

The most common cards were those for drawing money from cash machines, held by six in 10 women. Slightly less than half held debit cards, such as Switch or Delta. A third held credit or charge cards – the most popular of which was Visa, held by one in four women. One in five had a retailer card, such as a Marks and Spencer charge card.

According to the report the rise in mortgages and plastic cards held by women reflects increasing financial independence as more women work, marry later and divorce more.

'It is not surprising,' said a spokeswoman for the Council of Mortgage Lenders. 'Women's changing employment patterns are likely to have implications for the mortgage market.

'Dual-income supported mortgages are also common, and lenders have to take into account risk associated with the loss of earnings should the female decide to have a family. Some are already recognising this by building in flexibility in the form of discounts and payment holidays.'

The CSO statistics show that nearly eight in 10 women in the UK had a bank account in 1993 and two-thirds had a building society account. Older women tend to invest in premium bonds, held by 28 per cent of all women, while younger women are more likely to invest in mortgage and non-mortgage endowment policies – each held by about a quarter of women.

More than one in four women hold shares, either directly or through personal equity plans, unit and investment trusts. Direct shareholdings were split almost evenly between non-privatisation shares (owned by 9 per cent of women) and privatisation shares (owned by 8 per cent).

Women's consumption preferences differ from those of men. Based on the comparison of single-person households, the CSO found that women were more likely than men to own telephones, freezers and microwave ovens, but less likely to own compact disc players, video recorders and motor vehicles.

Leisure patterns are changing. One in three women now does DIY work, such as household repairs. More play sport. While only slightly more than half of women have driving licences, compared with four-fifths of men, almost three-quarters of women in their 30s have licences, and one in two is the main driver of a car.

Women on average watch 28 hours of television a week, mainly soaps and drama series in the evening, although more listen to the radio in the mornings.

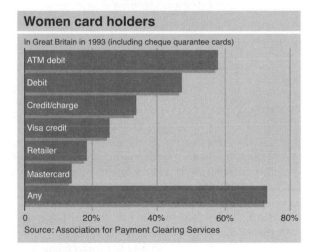

Women card holders

In Great Britain in 1993 (including cheque guarantee cards)

ATM debit
Debit
Credit/charge
Visa credit
Retailer
Mastercard
Any

0   20%   40%   60%   80%

Source: Association for Payment Clearing Services

MORTGAGES: by gender of borrower

	Percentages	
	1993	1994
Woman only	8.2	17.2
Man only	17.1	20.2
One woman, one man	73.4	61.3
Two women	0.4	0.6
Two men	0.6	0.4
Other	0.3	0.3
All mortgages (thousands)	6,846	10,410

Source: Council of Mortgage Lenders

More than half read national daily newspapers, the Sun dominating the under-35s market.

The statistics show women have distinctive concerns. Eighty-seven per cent describe themselves as very or quite concerned about the environment, and half save papers for recycling. More women belong to a religious group than any other type of social organisation.

The lifestyle changes reflect developments in the labour market. The proportion of women who are economically active rose from 44 per cent in 1971 to 53 per cent in 1994. In particular the proportion of women aged 25 to 35 in the labour market rose from 46 per cent to 71 per cent, as women are marrying and having children later, often cohabiting in the meanwhile.

Although women outnumber men in part-time employment, more women work full time than work part time. Earnings remain below equivalent male wages, and peak at the age of 35, compared with 45 for men, as a result of career breaks which cause earning power to fall.

Overall, however, social change is probably greater than total figures imply. As a result of life expectancy patterns there are relatively large numbers of elderly women. One in 10 women is now aged over 75, and women outnumber men in that age bracket by three to one. Such women are generally single, mostly widowed, have low income, and rely heavily on state benefits.

Source: Financial Times, 9 August 1995

3.6 How could the information in these articles affect the traditional marketing efforts of manufacturers and sellers of the following items:
- **household DIY products;**
- **sports/health club facilities;**
- **gardening equipment;**
- **security lighting;**
- **satellite/cable TV?**

3E

Sweet smell of skin-care

Lucia van der Post on a beauty products shop about to open

Jo Malone has been tending some extremely high-profile faces for several years in her sweet-smelling flat near London's Sloane Square.

From Queens and Princesses to fashion editors and the *beau monde* every day, an impressively elegant troupe heads up her narrow stairs.

Jo used to stay up late mixing her own creams and lotions and her customers soon became addicted to them. For some time they were sold only to private clients. But word began to spread, and demand increased, Jo began to broaden the range and sell it to a wider public.

Next week Jo opens her own shop selling the complete Jo Malone range.

Conventional make-up is not on offer – the beauty products are entirely related to skin-care. There is a cleansing milk made from apricot kernel and avocado

oil, a skin tonic with juniper, a moisturising lotion with apricot, avocado and almond oil as well as UV screens, eye gel with apricot and loe, night cream with orange and geranium. All smell wonderful.

The girls in the shop have been trained by Jo to give proper skin-care advice, not just to sell bottles of products.

But as well as the skin-care range, the shop, all cream and white like an old-fashioned French perfumer's studio, will sell sweet smells in a multitude of different packagings – bath oils, body lotions and colognes scented with basil and mandarin, nutmeg and ginger, muguet, Verbenas from Provence, grapefruit and Vertyver with spiced orange, and wild lavender with amber.

Then there are scented artichoke trees, bundles of scented wild lavender, pot-pourri smelling of orange and cinnamon, all beautifully packaged in simple solid glass bottles with chrome tops.

It should be a splendid source of Christmas presents – heart-shaped folding mirrors, scented candles and candle-holders, a sweet-smelling spray for the linen cupboard, as well as a small selection of old-fashioned linens.

Source: *Financial Times*, 15 October 1994

3.7 What type of buying situation do you think would be satisfied by a visit to Jo Malone's shop?

3.8 What type of customer would you expect to see in Jo's shop and what is likely to be their motivation to visit?

3.9 Given your answers to 3.7 and 3.8 above, what do you think Jo should do to appeal to such psychological influences?

3F

The armchair shopper

Louise Kehoe on the commercial appeal of 'virtual shopping malls'

A giant shopping centre will soon be built right on your doorstep. There will be hundreds of stores, banks, a supermarket, car dealerships, billboards – all within sight of your living-room armchair.

But don't rush to organise a protest. There will be no concrete poured in the construction of this mega-mall. It is a 'virtual' shopping centre, just a few seconds down the information superhighway.

Electronic shopping centres are proliferating as retailers spot the chance to create a direct, low-cost marketing channel to a fast-growing and predominantly affluent group of consumers – home-computer users.

More than a third of all US households now have a personal computer and 12 per cent – approximately 11m people – are equipped with a modem that allows them access via the telephone to the electronic data networks. Among US households with an annual income exceeding $50,000, the percentage of 'net travellers' – users of such networks – rises to 27 per cent.

This level of access has prompted a charge into electronic shopping, led by commercial networks such as Compuserve, America Online and Prodigy. They now have more than 5m subscribers who use their on-line discussion groups, live chat 'rooms' and news services, as well as electronic shopping.

Each has an 'electronic mall', with more than 100 stores selling products from a Brooks Brothers suit to honey-baked ham.

The Internet – a global web of computer networks with an estimated 25m–30m users – is also going commercial. Last month, Home Shopping Network, which operates the Home Shopping cable TV channel, acquired Internet Shopping Network (ISN), a fledgling Silicon Valley company that began selling computer products on the Internet five months ago.

'It is a bold step towards opening up a huge new market,' says Mr Randy Adams, founder of ISN. Home Shopping is planning 'a major push into the digital environment, a first step towards interactive television', he says.

With distribution and billing facilities already in place, Home Shopping Network is poised to create the first large-scale electronic shopping service on the Internet. Already there are dozens of smaller retailers on the Internet. Merchants from Palo Alto, in California's Silicon Valley, for example, have posted listings of their wares while the city's restaurants provide menus on-line.

For consumers, the main appeal of on-line shopping is convenience. Electronic stores are open 24 hours a day, seven days a week. The services draw 'too busy, two-income families', say the electronic merchants.

Most of the computer shopping services available today take the form of product lists with detailed descriptions of the merchandise and discount prices. For people who know what they want – a particular brand of clothing or a specific model of a household appliance – on-line shopping is a quick way to find a bargain. Without even a picture of the product, however, it is hard to imagine buying an outfit for a special occasion or a piece of furniture from an on-line service.

But multimedia computers are beginning to make electronic shopping much more interesting. Industry analysts predict that on-line sales of goods and services will mushroom into a multi-billion dollar industry over the next three years as the technology becomes more widely available.

A high-performance multimedia PC (now selling in the US for about $2,500) with a fast modem can handle graphics, audio and video clips, giving shoppers a much richer view of the products available. Multimedia also expands the range of goods and services that can be marketed effectively on-line.

For instance, the Global Network Navigator, a free Internet service provided by O'Reilly & Associates, a California publishing group, has established a 'travel resource centre'. Users can watch a video clip promoting the delights of a holiday resort, read travel articles, join a discussion group where people share travel experiences or check weather forecasts.

Even with a fast modem, however, on-line access to multimedia services through the telephone network can be tediously slow. A compromise approach that is gaining popularity involves publishing a multimedia catalogue on a CD-Rom disc which carries the images and sound. Updates on prices and availability, as well as ordering, are available on-line.

'The problem with the on-line world today is that the technology is long in the tooth,' says Mr Stephen Tomlin, vice-president in charge of interactive technology development at QVC, Home Shopping Network's rival in the cable TV shopping market.

'To be a good merchant you have to have a rich interaction with the customer – show the merchandise, demonstrate its features and have a real dialogue. We are limited by current modem speeds,' says Mr Tomlin.

Yet electronic shopping may be on the brink of a technology breakthrough that could give 'virtual' shopping malls a competitive edge on the real thing. The latest computer network technology for electronic commerce provides 'intelligent assistants' – computer programs that travel the data networks in search of information, or products, at the behest of their owners.

AT&T, the telecoms group, recently launched PersonaLink network service, the first commercial application of this technology. Using software developed by eShop, a California software venture, PersonaLink will create a 'market square' with electronic shopping assistants to help subscribers browse, select and make purchases.

These 'cyberpersonas' will get to know your interests and tastes, what sports you enjoy, your shoe size, your spending habits and more. Retailers will provide these 'electronic assistants' to help you to make your purchases.

You might also want to create your own electronic assistant, who will look through several electronic stores to find what you need at the best available price.

These assistants will emulate the role of the high-street tailor who knew your measurements, the corner grocer who used to deliver a regular weekly order to your home, or the saleswoman who helped you to select Christmas gifts.

Many retailers see these developments as an opportunity to experiment in the brave new world of 'virtual' shopping before it becomes a 21st century mass consumer service on 'interactive television'.

'It makes sense to get into the game, to understand what is going on,' says Mr Tomlin.

So when are they going to start building that virtual shopping centre?

'It's not around the corner, but there is no doubt that it is going to happen,' says Mr Adams. 'We are young enough to wait.'

Source: Financial Times, 22 October 1994

3.10 What type of consumer would be attracted to armchair shopping?

3.11 For what type of buying situations would armchair shopping seem to be most appropriate and why?

3.12 How comfortable would you be with buying a £350 gold and sapphire bracelet through QVC? What type of guarantees would you expect the supplier to offer?

India's new glossies

Mark Nicholson on the potential of an untapped elite

India, land of the bullock cart, has traditionally viewed conspicuous consumption with some suspicion. While former prime minister Indira Gandhi only wore wristwatches turned out by the state-run Hindustan Machine Tools company, her son Rajiv, when he was prime minister, inflamed the socialist establishment by sporting Gucci loafers.

Come the mid-1990s, however, after four years of economic reform, deregulation, open trade policies, foreign investment and, critically, the arrival of satellite television, a revolution appears to be under way.

Little exemplifies this better than the arrival on news stands over the past two months of two new glossy magazines: Verve, a Vogue-like high art magazine for 'the spirit of today's woman'; and India Today Plus, a similarly glossy product bearing on its cover a half-clad model, perched on a motorbike.

Inside are buyers' guides to home gyms, cellular phones and the new foreign cars about to arrive on Indian roads. Ads for luxury luggage and Piaget watches nestle between article on whether to ski next year in Gstaad or St Moritz.

Both magazines, their publishers declare, are aimed at an untapped market. 'It often seems that India's recent and rapid globalisation will throw up a new contemporary species of woman. And no one has recognised her,' writes Anuradha Mahindra, editor and publisher of Verve.

In the past, says Aroon Puri, publisher of India Today Plus, 'the more affluent sections of society were branded as being rather vulgar'. This, he said, has changed: 'That stigma seems to have vanished for many.' India's 'burgeoning middle class' is more international, aspirational, sophisticated and liberal, more adventurous and more leisure conscious.

By addressing the aspirational reading and consuming desires of this new audience, both magazines are seeking at the same time to corner an advertising platform which does not exist in India for premium consumer goods, luxury foreign brands, holidays, indeed the panoply of 'lifestyle' products. 'If you looked around,' says Mahindra, 'there wasn't any medium which fitted these brands.'

Other publishers agree. The staples of English-language Indian publishing – the common arena of this new consuming Indian elite – are either news, in magazines such as the 400,000-circulation India Today, father of India Today Plus, and the numerous English newspapers or specialist magazines.

'The advertisers we're looking at have not had the appropriate editorial environment,' says Sreekant Khandekar, editorial director of Spectrum, a specialist publisher which itself is about to launch a monthly 'leisure and lifestyles' men's magazine called Mantra.

Moreover, according to Indian advertising executives, the creation of a specifically Indian context for glossy, brand advertising is likely to prove vital, particularly to foreign brands establishing themselves. Rajeev Agarwal, managing director of Nexus Equity, a leading Bombay-based advertising agency, says incoming multinationals have found that their marketing succeeds best if tailored to Indian consumers.

The publishers of Verve, India Today Plus and Mantra, when it arrives, are testing the market cautiously. Mahindra launched Verve based on the success of Interiors magazine, a lavish coffee-table magazine published annually. Verve, to begin with, will appear twice a year. Its launch print run, which sold out, was just 15,000.

India Today Plus will at first be a quarterly and launched with a run of 100,000. Khandekar, more ambitiously, believes Mantra can launch later this year with a run of 500,000, though he also sees the magazine pitching at a wider, slightly less affluent, audience.

Research by I Natarajan, chief economist at the National Council of Applied Economic Research, an independent economic think tank, calculated there to be more than 500,000 Indian households with income exceeding Rs1m (£19,350) a year, a figure he believes likely to be understated given that India's rich tend to underdisclose their incomes.

Luxury good sales are also suggestive. Cellular phones have been available only since October, but even with handsets costing between $500 (£326) and $1,000 each, there are already 30,000 users in Bombay and 25,000 in Delhi. Mercedes-Benz launched its $60,000 E220 model last year and expects to sell 15,000 this year.

'Let's not forget,' adds Natarajan, 'we are still the world's largest buyers of gold – Indians bought 500 tonnes of it last year.'

Source: Financial Times, 28 March 1996

3.13 How successful do you think *Verve* and *India Today Plus* will be and why?

3.14 As a European manufacturer of TV's, VCR's, satellite dishes, hi-fi systems, cameras and camcorders, how valuable do you think this newly identified market could be to you and why?

4

Organisational Buying Behaviour

The previous chapter introduced you to the consumer and all the complexities which will eventually decide whether the individual will purchase a product or not.

Organisational buying behaviour is intended to be much more rational, more scientific, even calculated in its approach. Typically, a purchase requirement will be anticipated, a product specification drawn up, potential suppliers selected and a decision taken. Within each of these stages there will be sub-events, such as the vetting of potential suppliers in terms of quality standards, delivery and payment terms. Specific order routines will be initiated and there will always be some form of performance feedback and evaluation of the purchase cycle.

Another dimension to the organisational buying process, is the number of highly skilled professional staff involved at each stage. Engineers, designers, operators, information technologists, marketers and suppliers can all be involved in determining product specification; accountants will take part in supplier selection by way of credit checks and assessing the validity of any warranties offered; purchasing will put their skilled negotiators to the task to discuss prices and payment schedules and the quality departments will want to check everything! Quite a contrast to the 'I like it, so I'll have it' scenario discussed in Chapter 3.

In recent years, manufacturers have learned to develop closer links with their suppliers, recognising that they too can assist in the design of new products; bringing their expertise and funds, to develop joint research and development programmes. This has since become known as 'relationship marketing' and although not entirely centred on organisational buying processes, it has drawn attention to the benefits of collaborative, as opposed to adversarial, supplier handling.

In order to successfully complete the tasks in this chapter you will need to be familiar with:

- relationship marketing/relationship life cycle;
- commodity position matrix;
- organisational buying decision making models;
- single/multiple sourcing;
- buying criteria/buying centre;
- roles in the buying process/decision making unit.

Honda draws closer to components maker

Car industry excited by Unipart's joint ventures, writes John Griffiths

The long view came from a Unipart executive. 'History will probably consider there to be three landmark events for Unipart: the privatisation in 1987, an eventual flotation – and that will probably be over [group chief executive] John Neill's dead body – and this.'

The 'this' being referred to last week by the executive of Rover Group's former motor parts and accessories division, was the disclosure that the group whose headquarters is in Cowley, near Oxford, is launching, almost simultaneously, four joint ventures in motor components manufacturing which altogether entail an investment of more than £80m and will eventually employ between 400 and 500 people.

It is the ingredients making up three of the ventures, however, that have stirred interest well outside the circles of the immediate partners.

For, in a highly unusual step, Honda, the Japanese car maker, is itself taking a direct stake in the ventures, alongside three separate Japanese component suppliers who will also be Unipart's partners.

Honda first came into contact with Unipart via Honda's former partner, Rover. The components are destined primarily for Honda's assembly lines at Swindon in Wiltshire.

The ventures in the past few days have been hailed by Mr Ian Lang, the trade and industry secretary, as another boost for UK efforts to attract more foreign inward investment. Meanwhile Mr Kentaro Kato, the new managing director of Honda of the UK Manufacturing, is citing them as the clearest evidence to date that Honda is committed to establishing long-term relationships with its UK suppliers.

Honda and Unipart say the ventures are particularly important in two areas: there will be a significant transfer of technology, both in respect of the components produced and the manufacturing processes.

And even these ventures, which in themselves mark by far the biggest single expansion of Unipart's relationship with Honda, are expected to prove only the forerunners of bigger things to come.

Honda is already committed to a 50 per cent increase in its capacity of 100,000 cars a year at Swindon by the end of 1998. However, like Nissan at Sunderland, it is planning to introduce a third model to the Swindon lines alongside the Accord and Civic models.

While the company is reluctant to discuss the third model plan openly, hints coming from inside Honda are that it could be coming off the Swindon lines as early as the end of the decade. Honda is earmarking some £240m for the project.

Meanwhile, the number of markets to which Swindon-built Hondas are being consigned are proliferating beyond the UK and continental Europe. Swindon-built Civics and Accords are already on sale in several Middle Eastern countries and are destined for African and east European markets as well.

It is thus not inconceivable that by the early years of the century Swindon could be building 200,000 cars a year, providing organic growth for all Unipart's joint ventures. However Mr Kato and his colleagues make clear they have no wish to keep the ventures as captive suppliers to Honda and are encouraging them to seek business among other vehicle makers. Unipart has no false pride about the ventures, in spite of being the single largest shareholder in each.

'In order to get up and running fast we need the best know-how available in the manufacturing processes. Thus the Japanese partners have been asked to provide the managing directors for each venture,' says Mr Neill.

Unipart, which employs 4,000 staff in distribution, sales and manufacturing of parts and accessories, now believes it can double its manufacturing employment by the end of the century.

Source: Financial Times, 16 July 1996

4.1 Outline the benefits for both Honda and Unipart in these ventures.

4.2 How could Unipart further demonstrate its commitment to these ventures?

4.3 At which stage in the relationship life cycle are these ventures and how would you expect them to naturally develop?

Suppliers see drawbacks of openness

Many small companies have reservations about close partnerships
with big customers, writes Chris Tighe

As a senior instrument engineer with a big oil company, Mr Steve Pearson had the job of spreading the word about how partnership and openness between customers and their suppliers could drive down costs and increase efficiency.

As the founder and managing director of his own company, which sells its expertise in the management and computerisation of engineering documentation to big businesses, he can see the other side of the equation.

'I was on one side, pontificating this culture, but on the other side it's very difficult to buy into it. You feel you're exposing yourself,' says Mr Pearson, whose Teesside-based company, Pearson-Harper, employs 26 people and turns over more than £1m a year.

Self-interest, more than mutual interest, is, he believes, the motivation for some large companies which publicly champion the cause of partnership sourcing and long-term, open relationships with selected suppliers. 'They are looking for the best deal for themselves,' he says.

In spite of these reservations, Mr Pearson has entered into long-term relationships with several large oil and gas and pharmaceutical companies. These agreements are working well, and to mutual advantage. Even so, establishing a reliable method for identifying and distributing the achieved savings is not proving easy.

The concept of long-term supply agreements and partnership – intended to replace the adversarial culture of mistrust based on price-driven haggling – has gained ground in British industry in the last few years.

Inward investors such as Nissan, the Japanese carmaker, have been at the forefront of moves to raise quality and constantly drive down costs by forging long-term relationships with hand-picked suppliers, whose manufacturing processes and costs are minutely scrutinised.

At the sharp end though, attitudes are often sceptical.

'They are hoping to squeeze you so close to the bone they'll squeeze all your profit away,' says Mr David Whelan, UK manager of Bio-Chemical and Technical Services, a Newcastle-based anti-corrosion treatment specialist. 'How do you know when you're at the optimum cost? Who says how much profit you can make? At the end of the day it's the big company, you have no power.'

HNL Instruments and Control, based on Teesside, is involved in partnership supply agreements. They can mean good, steady business, says Miss Alex Hayward, the company's sales and marketing manager, but the downside is having to absorb price increases if materials or labour costs shoot up. Some customers, she says, seem genuinely to want to share benefits; for others it is an excuse to get prices down. 'You have to be wary.'

At the Northern Offshore Federation, whose 275 member companies include HNL, Pearson-Harper and Bio-Chemical and Technical Services, director Mr Alastair Rodgers is well aware of small companies' anxiety about partnership sourcing.

'The message has to be got across to these small companies that we are talking about cost reduction, not profit reduction,' says Mr Rodgers, whose organisation was set up to strengthen and promote the north's offshore industry.

Mr Rodgers is working on an ambitious plan to run workshops this month and next at which small groups of suppliers, drawn from the federation's membership, will sit around the table with a large fabricator to discuss the potential, and problems, of partnership sourcing. Each supplier will represent a different specialism to reduce their wariness of speaking in front of each other.

This, says Mr Rodgers, is a unique platform for small companies: 'The trust has to be built up. You need a genuine exchange of views.'

Frank discussion should, he believes, separate genuine problems from those which are only perceived.

But, he adds, the burden should not all be on the supplier. A contract is a two-way transaction. 'You have to get the customer to examine his performance too,' he says.

Source: Financial Times, 8 January 1996

Forging chains to bind the inward investors

By Chris Tighe

In supply-chain management, two little words separate the dinosaurs from the enlightened, says Mr David Bowles – 'price' and 'cost'.

Mr Bowles leads the Northern Development Company's drive to strengthen indigenous companies and ensure it retains its inward investors by supply-chain development.

NDC, the economic regeneration body for north-east England and Cumbria, says its supply-chain programme has generated nearly £100m in contracts for companies over the last year.

As larger companies become more aware of the need to be globally competitive, says Mr Bowles, they have inevitably come to focus on supply-chain management to cut costs.

NDC's business development managers – who try to develop the regional economy by ensuring that companies use local sources as much as possible – have helped unlock for local suppliers the buying power of some prestigious big companies operating in the region.

One of Mr Bowles's biggest successes is in sourcing components within the region for Samsung's new £450m electronics complex in Teesside.

But in spite of the potential spin-off of such a big customer on the doorstep, the reaction of many local companies is disappointing, says Mr Bowles.

'Two out of three suppliers don't want to know, or aren't capable,' he says. 'They want to expand their business but on their terms, and their terms are no longer good enough. The view of the manufacturers has changed out of all proportion.'

One small north-east supplier held up by NDC as a model of partnership sourcing is ARD Components, a pressings specialist based in Tyne and Wear. ARD, a second-tier supplier to Nissan's Sunderland car plant, last summer became the first north-east company to be appointed by Samsung to supply components to its Teesside complex.

Source: Financial Times, 8 January 1996

A relationship worth cultivating

Tim Dickson on the benefits of a link with Japanese companies

Sir Ivor Cohen, chairman of the Japan Electronics Business Association, makes the comparison with a pair of Sumo wrestlers.

'They circle each other for ages, throwing salt on the ground, patiently waiting for the right moment to pounce. Suddenly there's a surge of energy and the contest begins.'

Sir Ivor is describing the slow and sometimes frustrating build-up which typifies many partnerships between large Japanese companies and foreign suppliers. Such relationships, he believes, are not only worth cultivating but help explain why small and medium-sized British companies are now producing 30 per cent of the component needs of locally based Japanese electronics manufacturers, against just 15 per cent five years ago. JEBA, an industry-led organisation which emerged from the Department of Trade and Industry's Priority Japan campaign, is aiming to boost that UK share still further.

One company which has shown the way is Scunthorpe-based Roxburgh Electronics, whose transnational partnership with Mitsubishi Electric UK can be traced back to 1992. Hitherto a successful, but relatively unexceptional, distributor of electronic components, Roxburgh's Japanese alliance has been an impetus for new growth over the last three-and-a-half years. This has enabled the company to make two significant acquisitions, thereby forming the Deltron Electronics Group, and to ready itself for a stock market flotation in the near future. Sales are currently £27m–£30m.

Set up in 1969, Roxburgh initially specialised in the distribution of switches and printers, only later adding other more sophisticated products such as audible alarms and encoders. The first investment in the design and manufacture of Radio Frequency Interference filters and transformers was not made until the early 1980s.

The Mitsubishi relationship began almost by chance at the Euro-EMC (Electro-magnetic Compatibility) Show in London in October 1992 when a Mitsubishi UK representative visited the Roxburgh stand with a technical problem: how to produce a lightweight RFI filter unit which would fit the Japanese company's motor drives and comply with upcoming EMC legislation.

Mitsubishi supplied Roxburgh with 'footprints' and samples and specifications were sent to Japan for inspection by mid-1993. It was not until November 1994, however, that Mitsubishi issued a press release announcing that the British company was to be its worldwide partner for research, production and design in this particular technology.

Roxburgh's technical achievement has been to produce a unit which, unlike existing filters, was able to fit under the motor drive, immediately next to the source of mains and radio interference, while adding only a few centimetres to the depth of the drive.

On the strength of this, Roxburgh is now working with four Mitsubishi divisions and has so far received orders worth more than £1.5m from the group's operations in Japan, North America, Germany and the UK, as well as business from other international filter users. The company is expanding its capacity with a £2m factory extension at Scunthorpe to be opened today by Sir Peter Parker, UK chairman of Mitsubishi Electric. And it is discussing an agreement with the Japanese group to develop the next generation of filters.

Sir Peter believes that the process of internationalisation inside big Japanese companies is 'intense' – and that herein lie great opportunities for foreign partners. Someone such as Takashi Kitaoka (president of Mitsubishi Electric Corporation) is 'a new kind of man', he says, 'trying to change attitudes and encourage others to open up'.

He concedes that Europe has accounted for only 5 per cent of Mitsubishi revenues in the past – against 15 per cent from the US – but believes a market with 350m people (including eastern Europe) will be a significant lure in the future.

Source: Financial Times, 21 May 1996

4.4 **Why do you think that so many Japanese companies are keen on establishing long-term supplier relationships?**

4.5 **Outline the risks which a small company should be aware of when entering into a long-term partnership sourcing agreement with a large multi-national organisation. Do you think these risks are worth taking?**

4.6 **Where on the Commodity Position matrix would you place the supply of electronic components by Roxburgh Electronics to Mitsubishi Electric UK?**

4.7 **What type of cultural problems are at the root of the problems faced by the Northern Development Company?**

BSkyB sets digital decoder design

Call for suppliers shows determination to launch 200 channels late next year, writes Raymond Snoddy

British Sky Broadcasting has sent out confidential specifications for the production of up to 1m digital satellite television receivers in a strong signal that it will launch 200 UK channels next year.

BSkyB wants the decoders ready for the shops by September next year. The order would almost certainly be worth more than £250m at factory prices.

The issuing of specifications for such a large volume of the 'black box' decoders is the clearest evidence yet of how determined BSkyB is to launch digital satellite television in the UK in the final quarter of next year.

The company, controlled by Mr Rupert Murdoch's News Corporation, may expand the service to as many as 500 channels in the longer term.

Apart from a large number of different channels the service would feature near-video-on-demand, which devotes a large number of channels to a top movie so that there are many opportunities to view.

If pay-per-view deals can be agreed with the Premier League all the top matches could be available live to purchasers of an electronic season ticket.

BSkyB also sets out in the specifications the annual forecasts for how many decoders would be needed in each subsequent year as the market develops.

There are no plans to chose a number of 'exclusive' manufacturers – anyone who meets the specifications will be able to manufacture.

BSkyB is particularly interested to see what prices manufacturers can propose. The company wants the new digital boxes to retail for about £200.

The company is in talks with groups such as British Telecommunications and Barclays to see whether the initial retail cost of the boxes can be subsidised in return for their involvement in the development of interactive services such as home shopping and home banking.

The BSkyB specifications for digital satellite decoders are designed to be compatible with terrestrial digital services. Digital terrestrial uses digital technology and needs digital decoders but is broadcast from normal land-based transmitters and can be received without satellite dishes. Most of the UK could probably receive about 20 channels using digital terrestrial.

Yesterday the BBC, BT and Pace, the satellite equipment maker, said that they had started joint live field trials of digital terrestrial from two transmitters – Crystal Palace in London and Pontop Pike near Newcastle upon Tyne.

Lord Inglewood, the broadcasting minister, told a forum of the UK digital TV group that Britain would be at the forefront of the digital television revolution.

'If digital is going to work anywhere in Europe it will be here,' Lord Inglewood said.

Source: Financial Times, 5 July 1996

4.8 Using the organisational buying decision making model proposed by Robinson *et al.* (1967), apply the various stages to the situation in the article.

4.9 Which stage has this purchase decision reached?

4.10 How rigidly do you think BSkyB will carry out the remaining stages?

4.11 Do you think that BSkyB will go for single or multiple sourcing? Support your response by outlining the advantages and disadvantages of both methods.

The growing trend towards the east

West European companies are developing a new source for purchasing components, says Kevin Done

West European companies are increasingly looking to central and east Europe for new sources of supply for raw materials and components, as they seek to cut costs and improve their competitiveness against rivals from Asia and North America.

According to a survey by management consultants Booz-Allen & Hamilton, big companies in Germany, France, Italy and the UK are planning to triple their spending in east European countries during the coming years to 5 per cent of their total purchases by 1998.

West European companies will then be spending as much in east European countries as they do in North America or south-east Asia. There are still misgivings among many companies in west Europe about the quality of products and the reliability of delivery from suppliers in east Europe, but the trend is clear.

Jean-Baptiste Duzan, purchasing director of Renault, the French car and commercial vehicle maker, warns that 'in spite of their attractive cost base and the skills of their workforce, very few eastern European suppliers are able to adapt to the exceedingly tight requirements of our industry.

'However, there is no doubt that they have all the necessary ingredients to become important partners in the near future.'

The Booz-Allen survey of purchasing intentions covers 214 companies across all sectors of industry in the four leading economies of west Europe.

The proportion of purchases companies have made in their domestic markets has declined steadily from 69.3 per cent in 1988 to 64.2 per cent in 1993, and this is forecast to fall again to around 57.6 per cent by 1998.

The drop in home market purchasing in the late 1980s and the early 1990s mainly benefited suppliers in other European Union member states, a move accelerated by the creation of the single market and the abolition of tariff barriers.

In coming years it is countries in eastern Europe that are expected to gain most, however, with their share of west European companies' purchases rising to 5.1 per cent by 1998 from 0.8 per cent in 1988 and 1.6 per cent in 1993.

West European industrial equipment, automotive, chemicals and electrical and electronics companies are the most active buyers from eastern Europe,

according to the Booz-Allen study. 'Their main motivation appears to be access to cheap labour, allowing manufactured goods to be produced at competitive costs,' says the report.

The average savings in purchasing costs (including transportation) obtained by companies in these sectors range between 15 and 30 per cent compared with the price paid to traditional suppliers. More than one company in seven has managed to cut its costs by more than 30 per cent.

The only exception is the chemicals sector, which has developed a supply base in east Europe but has achieved cost savings of less than 10 per cent. Here the purchases have chiefly been made by German chemical companies of primary raw materials. They have been looking for cheaper commodities and also seeking to penetrate east European markets with their products.

German companies were often the first westerners to penetrate east European markets and to develop effective relationships with the most competitive suppliers.

Companies are more likely to engage east European suppliers when they are purchasing products with a high labour content, such as semi-finished products, electrical and electronic components and equipment, and mechanical equipment.

Hungary, Poland and the Czech Republic are the countries most favoured by west European companies, in particular those from Germany and France, although the choice of supplying country does vary according to the country of the buyer.

Hungary is the primary supplier of electrical and electronic components and equipment, says the report, whereas the Czech Republic and Poland have exploited their capability in mechanical equipment and finished products. The countries of former Yugoslavia have focused previously more on raw materials and packaging, although their role as suppliers has clearly been drastically diminished by the recent wars in Bosnia and Croatia and the sanctions against Serbia.

The degree of difficulty experienced by west European companies rises substantially as they move further east with greater distances involved and a greater degree of political instability, says the report.

'Countries in the Balkans and in the Commonwealth of Independent States are perceived more negatively by western buyers.'

While the level of purchases made in east Europe is set to rise sharply many problems remain. Quality is the main issue and is cited in 70 per cent of the cases, where supply relations have failed.

Despite the problems, Booz-Allen forecasts a boom in purchases from east Europe, particularly from those countries that are geographically close to west Europe and have done most to develop market economies and democratic political regimes.

Source: Financial Times, 19 January 1996

4.12 What do you think is the principal buying objective discussed in this article?

4.13 What are the dangers of sourcing components on this basis?

4.14 Why do you think that Western European companies have taken this route when the trend in the UK, Asia and USA has been the opposite?

4G

All the answers

James Buxton on a Scottish company that has established itself as a supplier to BT

The latest British Telecom answering machine is so sophisticated that it is almost a voice-mail system for a small office: it can play a variety of announcements, record 99 messages and forward them at preset times to other phone numbers.

But perhaps the most remarkable thing about the Response 2000 is that it is not, like many UK consumer products, imported from a big electronics manufacturer in East Asia: it was developed by a Scottish company called Phonebox which employs 15 people, and is assembled in Scotland.

Small UK companies frequently complain about the difficulties of penetrating organisations as large as BT and establishing themselves as suppliers: the story of the Response 2000 is an exception, although not without its share of pain.

Phonebox is the main subsidiary of Cairntech, a small telecommunications design company set up in 1982 at Dalgety Bay, Fife, by Timothy Laing, a former army helicopter pilot. After years of meagre results a breakthrough came in 1992 when it presented BT with a specification for a tapeless answering machine with many special features.

Laing recalls that the then group product manager at BT was stunned by the specification. 'He then told us it was almost exactly the same as one they were soon planning to put out to tender.'

Laing had earlier dealt with another part of BT's purchasing operation from which his company had won a small contract to supply an audio-conferencing product. The product did not sell well but Laing was given what he regards as a crucial introduction to the consumer products department.

The specification for an answering machine which the Scottish company presented to BT was the basis for what is now the Response 2000. The timing of the Scottish team's visit to BT was excellent, Laing says, because the telecommunications group was also seeking to obtain a simple combined telephone and digital answering machine.

Eventually Phonebox won both a contract to design the Response 2000 and another to design and later to supply the Response 120, another answering phone. The Response 120, which resembles a standard BT domestic telephone, has become one of BT's best-selling products: more than 600,000 have been sold since it was launched in late 1993, compared with original forecasts of 120,000 a year.

But initially Phonebox had serious problems persuading any Scottish manufacturer to consider assembling the Response 120 under contract. A nearby plant belonging to GEC Marconi initially said it could do it, then changed its mind, and Cairntech subsequently had trouble being listened to by several other big electronics plants in Silicon Glen.

The reason for their refusal was an understandable doubt about Phonebox's financial strength. Although it was expecting an initial order from BT worth about £10m, and the telecommunications company was satisfied with the results of its own due diligence, Cairntech had a record of heavy losses and annual sales of less than £300,000.

Eventually, however, Phonebox signed a contract to have the Response 120 assembled by the US company Hughes Microelectronics at its plant at Glenrothes in Fife. Hughes is also making the Response 2000, which took about two years to design. At one point Phonebox feared it might not win the order to supply the product.

The orders from BT were a dramatic event for Phonebox but were also a remarkable step for BT which has most of its consumer products made by bigger companies in East Asia.

John McGrath, BT's current group product manager for consumer products, agrees that 'you can buy answering machines at 10-a-penny from big electronics manufacturers in the Far East'. What makes the difference with Phonebox 'is the degree of innovation they give. They take existing and new technology and combine it to create a leading-edge product.'

He says that in the case of the Response 2000 the most innovative aspect is the user interface, a relatively large display on which the user programs the machine as if using a menu on a personal computer. 'This was their idea and it is extremely user-friendly,' he says. He also says the quality of voice recording is superior to that of many other digital machines.

McGrath says: 'The UK finds it difficult to compete with the Far East in making simple electronic products. But Phonebox is competitive because it does something different.' Manufacturers in East Asia, he says, are more interested in producing in large volumes than in 'pushing forward the frontiers of technology'.

For this reason, he says, BT is usually prepared to talk to small companies which come to it with ideas and products. 'We will see most people, otherwise we might be shutting something out. In some ways we prefer dealing with smaller companies because we get better attention from them. But they've got to add something, and most companies don't.'

The large orders from BT catapulted Cairntech from turning over about £20,000 a month to monthly sales of about £700,000. Unfortunately, the transformation was not reflected in its bottom line: it had costed the Response 120, which has some imported electronic components, when the pound was at $1.90.

The subsequent rise in the dollar against the pound distorted the economics of producing it, and Phonebox and its parent Cairntech still made losses in the year to September 1995. BT was not particularly sympathetic, Laing implies: 'We managed to squeeze a modest price increase out of them, but there never seemed to be a recognition that if they didn't help it could have been the end of us.' Laing believes his company will do better with the Response 2000, which BT has priced at £229.99, compared with the Response 120 which cost only £69.

Having established the production chain for the Response 2000, Phonebox is now starting to market its designs, on which it has intellectual property rights, in continental Europe. It is looking for partnerships with telecommunications utilities and consumer electronics companies to design derivatives of the two answering machines it has successfully developed for BT.

Source: Financial Times, 25 June 1996

4.15 Using the information in this article, identify the key roles in the buying process from BT's viewpoint.

4.16 The initial contact by Phonebox to BT's group product manager was an example of access at which stage of the buying process?

4.17 Which other elements of the buying process did Phonebox subsequently have to overcome in order to secure the Response 200 contract.

4.18 How much easier do you think it was for Phonebox to win the Response 120 contract? Why?

4.19 What should Phonebox do now?

5

Segmenting Markets

At the centre of any marketing strategy, is a clear identification of the target market segments which the firm is wishing to attract.

The segmentation of organisational markets tends to focus on such things as company size, location, size of order, usage rate of the product to be provided and/or the application to which the firm puts the product once it is delivered. For example, a supplier of cement would probably segment its share of the market on the basis of order size, as high volumes to a fairly small number of customers is likely to be normal in this sector. On the other hand, a manufacturer of moulded plastic components will have a large number of customers, all with their own particular design requirements who put the final product to a very diverse range of uses, such as children's toys, utility furniture and even military applications.

Segmentation in the consumer market tends to concentrate on geodemographic, psychographic and behavioural factors which help the marketer to profile its consumer groups and attempt to predict how they will respond to a particular set of marketing stimuli.

At the outset, a firm needs to analyse its market carefully to decide on the type of segmentation targeting strategy required. This will have an important impact on the amount of marketing expenditure needed to reach the segment and the expected returns which might be expected for that level of expenditure. Trying to achieve a compromise between a relatively economic undifferentiated targeting strategy and a much more tailored, but expensive, differentiated approach is not an easy task. Yet a full and accurate understanding of the segments in your market is absolutely essential to a firm's success. If economies have to be made, this is not the place to do it.

> **In order to successfully complete the tasks in this chapter you will need to be familiar with:**
>
> - segmentation criteria;
> - brand loyalty;
> - geodemographic segmentation;
> - psychographic segmentation;
> - segmentation targeting strategies;
> - marketing mix.

When executives go Dutch

Amon Cohen samples the different styles of two new small airlines' services to Amsterdam

World Airlines and easyJet are both new, small British airlines in dispute with KLM. Both have complained to the European Commission that the Dutch flag-carrier is abusing its dominant position in the London–Amsterdam air market, not least through predatory pricing. In addition, easyJet has issued a writ against KLM.

Although they are united on this front, the two carriers could hardly offer a more polarised style of service, as I discovered when I flew from London to Amsterdam recently with World and travelled back with easyJet.

One of the main differences between them is their choice of London airports. Both use Amsterdam's Schiphol, but World, a one-route airline, chooses to fly from London City airport, whereas easyJet flies from its home at Luton airport.

On the day that I sampled the service of World, Ian Gibson, UK chief executive of motor maker Nissan, was enjoying a rare treat: a trip in business class. Gibson was one of four other passengers in business class, savouring a free upgrade secured for him by Nissan's travel agency.

In spite of his rank and the fact that he flies up to 200 times a year, Gibson is subject to the same egalitarian travel policy as all Nissan employees in the UK: all flights are economy class except for long-haul travel, when business class is allowed if the return journey is within a week.

The flight to Amsterdam was the luxurious leg of my journey. World prides itself on pampering its passengers, even though its BAe 146-200 aircraft are in the air for only 50 minutes. Selling points include luxury leather seats with a generous 33in pitch, sumptuous food, vintage wines, and a wide array of free magazines.

A return flight with World can cost anywhere between £87 in economy (for a heavily restricted fare) and £290 in business. World also offers business-class passengers a free night in an Amsterdam hotel. A return with easyJet, a cheap but relentlessly cheerful low-cost operation, is priced at between £70 and £130.

This was Gibson's second flight with World, and he was impressed. 'I am flabbergasted by the service.

It is not what you expect on short-haul,' he said, having tucked into a breakfast of smoked haddock omelette, asparagus, potatoes sauteed with rosemary, grilled tomatoes, fresh orange juice, melon, rolls and croissants. The aircraft itself also won top marks: the 146 is quiet, comfortable and spotless.

Gibson, based in Sunderland, was on the flight because he had spent the previous night in London and had just attended an early morning meeting in the City of London. From there, he was hopping over to Amsterdam for another meeting and intended to fly home to Newcastle airport that same evening.

It was because of this itinerary, and not the cosseting, that he was aboard the World flight. 'The things that I need are convenience of location, schedule and flexibility in that order,' he said. London City was therefore the obvious choice following his appointment earlier that morning.

The airport, not the airline, was also why Amsterdam-based Ronald Ouwens was aboard. Ouwens is financial controller of loss adjusters Cunningham Europe, and had been attending a meeting in London at the Tower Hill head office of Hambros, its parent company.

He was impressed with the service and said he would never fly with an airline such as easyJet. 'Low-cost travel is not for business purposes,' he said. 'Once you have bought a ticket, you cannot change it.'

But on the easyJet flight, Jan Van der Velden, a compatriot of Ouwens, said he did not find the inflexibility a hindrance. 'The fares are so inexpensive that it is not a problem if you have to buy a new ticket for a different flight,' said Van der Velden, who owns a small technical wholesale company in Haarlem.

Being self-employed, he said, he was driven primarily by price. 'When I worked for the national steel company, I used to travel business class, but that is only OK as long as you are spending someone else's money.'

However, airport location was also important. Luton is conveniently placed for the many clients he has in the Midlands. Flying with easyJet costs him Fl 99 (£38) one way, whereas he says a return fare with a more established airline to Birmingham would set him back Fl 800-Fl 900.

Van der Helden was perfectly happy with easyJet's inflight service where you certainly don't get what you don't pay for. The interior of the 17-year-old Boeing 737-200 was marked and scuffed and the carpets were threadbare, while catering consisted of a trolley selling drinks and a few snacks. The trolley was pushed by extremely youthful cabin staff wearing orange polo shirts and black jeans. For 70 minutes, though, it was perfectly bearable.

'It is like a bus. You just hop on and hop off,' said Van der Helden. 'The crew wear jeans but they are not sloppy. They are at least as safety-conscious as other airlines.' Furthermore, the flight, which had about 50 passengers on board – of whom approximately 15 were business travellers, judged by a count of suits – took off and arrived on time, while the ticketless check-in only took about 30 seconds.

Another passenger on easyJet, Martin Leith, had several grievances from earlier flights. Among them were waiting a long time for the catering trolley, lengthy check-in queues and a hatred of Luton.

Leith admitted that this last gripe was mainly founded on prejudice but it was also partly based on his lack of confidence in the shuttle to the train station, which theoretically runs every 15 minutes and takes 10 minutes to journey through the town's unappetising streets.

Matters will be improved next year, when a new station will open much closer to the airport.

Even without that improvement, however, the Luton airport transfer seems perfectly acceptable because it is a very short journey from the aircraft to the arrivals lounge. It took me about 70 minutes from leaving the aircraft to reaching London St Pancras railway station, which I reckon is just as fast, if not quicker, than travelling to central London from Heathrow.

In any case, as Leith admits, easyJet's good points outweigh any bad ones. With easyJet, cheap fares are clearly all important factor, although airport location matters equally for business travellers on both airlines.

Source: Financial Times, 12 August 1996

5.1 Although apparently aiming their service at the same target market, identify all the differences in the two offerings.

5.2 In terms of successful segmentation criteria, how sustainable do you think the segmentation strategies of both these organisations are?

5.3 You have just been appointed as marketing assistant at World Airlines. What criteria would you use to help you segment the business traveller market?

5.4 From your answer in 5.3 above, identify the type of customer you would like to attract and suggest how you might market your service to that segment.

5.5 Once successful in increasing passenger numbers, how might you encourage passengers to stay loyal to World Airlines?

5B

Some like it hot

Alan Mitchell searches for the holy grail of direct marketing

Some FT readers will have recently received a missive from Lloyds Bank inviting them not to make a move 'until you check with us' about the company's buildings insurance. They probably never gave a thought to how closely targeted they were: they were not hot prospects, or even hot, hot prospects. They were hot, hot, hot prospects.

Targeting, the elimination of the hated 'junk' from 'junk mail', is the holy grail of direct marketing. The better it is done, the less the exercise costs, the fewer consumer noses are put out of joint and the higher the response rates are. Now marketers are combining data from a wider variety of sources – including the gold mines of information that usually lie unexploited in their own accounting and other records – to get closer to that holy grail. Lloyds Bank Insurance Direct's building insurance campaign is an example.

To isolate its best prospects Lloyds first compared the prices of its panel of insurers with the competition – postcode district by postcode district. If one of its panel was 30 per cent cheaper than the average competitor price in that postcode, the postcode was identified as 'hot'. The rest were dropped.

Next, Lloyds trawled its own customer records to identify which of these 'hot' postcodes had recorded higher than average conversion rates from inquiry to purchase and lower claims rates. That produced a refined 'hot, hot' list.

Then, to maximise the efficiency of leaflet doordrops, it used recent census data to identify those postcodes where property values were higher than average, and where there were particularly high concentrations of home ownership. The resulting 'hot, hot, hot' target areas look like a few tiny isolated dots in a postcoded map of the country. But they are a sizeable market.

Further, by using data from a lifestyle survey company, NDL, which generates detailed information, including brand preferences and house moving dates from millions of named individuals each year, Lloyds has been writing to 'hot, hot, hot' individuals who moved house 12 or 24 months ago. They are particularly ripe because their insurance is likely to be due for renewal. Philip Loney, Lloyds Bank Insurance Direct general manager, says: 'We want to progressively target our marketing expenditure where we get the maximum benefit. This is beautifully simple. We have identified the people who we can offer the best deal to, and now we are talking to them – and the results are markedly better.'

Technical developments such as this are doing more than generating better response rates. According to Chris Lovell, managing director of Lovell Vass Boddey, the marketing consultancy that helped Lloyds in this project, future media planning could be shaped by this type of 'micromarketing'.

Posters can be sited more accurately on key local roadside sites, for example. Bus-side ads can be placed on routes travelling through the postcodes in question. 'Too often,' says Lovell, 'advertising effectiveness is a matter of post-campaign evaluation rather than pre-campaign planning.'

Others are going further, trying to move their direct marketing beyond its traditional sales promotion by mail role to become relationship-building exercises.

Next month, for example, the car park at stately home Packington Hall, near Birmingham, will fill with Jaguars, Mercedes and other luxury cars. After refreshments, their owners will be chauffeur-driven to the door of the Motor Show, a privilege not even granted to big exhibitors. Before going home, they will be able to play at chauffeurs themselves – driving BMW's new Seven Series car.

Over the next few years BMW will keep in touch with these carefully selected prospective customers, sending them glossy magazines, stories about BMW, and the occasional chance of a freebie such as the Motor Show. By the time they come to replace their old car, BMW hopes it will have persuaded them to buy its new car.

The next step is to combine both approaches, using data from a variety of sources to target individuals for long-term, direct, relationship-building programmes – as Ford is now attempting. In July it sent out questionnaires to 1m named individuals – people who it knew from lifestyle surveys currently drive rival brands.

The Ford Driving Survey asked them details such as car age, replacement intentions, most important considerations in car purchase, marital status, occupation, number of children and income.

Existing customer records were then examined, using sophisticated modelling techniques to identify the key characteristics of who buys which Ford models, and why. This information was then matched to the 200,000 Driving Survey replies, so that the people most likely to choose each Ford model could be selected for the right sort of soft-sell mailing.

Says Anthony Marsella, strategic analysis manager at direct marketing specialist Wunderman Cato Johnson, which runs Ford's direct marketing operation: 'With car buying cycles you need to keep in touch with a potential customer over three years or more. When it gets to the point where they are going to buy, we will communicate a selling message to them.'

Marsella estimates that Ford, by fine-tuning its technique, has doubled its direct marketing efficiency over the past five years. But such technical developments are also having a more profound effect: they are beginning to change the way some marketers think about marketing.

Says Grant Harrison, loyalty controller at Tesco, which is currently testing a Club Card with enormous data-gathering potential: 'Marketing is moving very significantly away from trying to change or twist consumers' behaviour to understanding them and giving them what they want.'

The ultimate aim, says Mark Patron, managing director of CMT, one of the main lifestyle survey companies, is to use technology to mimic the days of the old corner shop. 'The owner would say, "Hello

Mrs Brown, how's Doris? I know she likes orange sherbets. Now we've got some lemon flavour. Give her this, and see if she likes it."'

Most marketers are still a long way away from that, but as they get closer Mrs Brown may find her-self investing as much care and attention in choosing which organisations deserve her trust and informa-tion – her 'relationship' – as she does in choosing which brands deserve her hard-earned cash.

Source: Financial Times, 15 September 1994

5.6 **You work for a supplier of gardening and horticultural products both the retail and organisation markets. Your manager has just given you this article. It is the first time he has heard of geodemographic segmentation or 'micro-marketing', as it is called here. He has asked you to prepare a presentation to be addressed to departmental members which will inform them of the benefits of geodemographic segmentation. He has also asked you to say whether there are any ideas in the article which the firm could use and has invited you to add any other ideas you might have on the subject.**

5C

Sales pitch that fills rooms

Tim Minogue visits a hotel that found success by creating its own cricket square

Encouraging parties of amateur cricketers to leave their wives and girlfriends at home for several days and stay in a hotel with a 24-hour bar sounds like a recipe for disaster. Hoteliers of a nervous dispo-sition might imagine fragile profits shattering along with the crockery in the course of boisterous boys' nights in.

In fact, concentrating on catering for amateur cricket tours proved to be the salvation of Linda Harrison and David Buck's hotel business.

The couple, who both worked in marketing and conference organisation, impulsively purchased a 15-year lease on the seven-bedroom Old Vicarage Hotel at Hinton, Hampshire, for £72,000 in 1992.

The business was in receivership, having lost £88,000 in the previous year. What made Buck and Harrison believe they could succeed where others had failed?

Harrison, who is 43, says: 'None of the partners worked here. The restaurant had a bad reputation. There was little control over costs and the marketing was unprofessional.'

Having cut costs and raised standards, Buck and Harrison played on the hotel's strengths: a quiet rural location, 10-acre garden, in the New Forest yet only a mile from the sea. Mailshots targeted poten-tial customers. Yet, at the end of their first season, they were struggling to break even.

Buck, 42, says: 'We realised that whatever we did, we were not going to make a living out of British holidaymakers.'

Foreign visitors loved the place, but usually only stayed a night or two.

'What we needed,' says Harrison, 'was to find a niche – something no one else in the Forest was doing – that would guarantee room occupancy during the week.'

In the summer of 1993 they took a lease on an overgrown neighbouring field with the idea of using it as a car park for wedding receptions. When he had cleared the chest-high nettles, however, Buck realised that he was standing in the middle of what could become, with imagination and hard labour, a delightful, rustic cricket oval. Could cricket be the niche they had been searching for?

A crude square was prepared and an advertisement placed in the *Cricketer* magazine, suggesting the hotel as a base for teams touring the area.

'We expected about six replies,' says Buck. 'We were astonished to receive more than 50 serious inquiries.' Within weeks, 25 cricket teams had booked to stay at the Old Vicarage in the 1994 season.

Buck invited an old friend, former Hampshire county cricketer John Rice, to inspect the wicket. 'His advice was to dig it up.' Hampshire's groundsmen at Southampton and Portsmouth gave some tips on basic groundsmanship. An advertisement in the local paper produced a nucleus of players for a revived Hinton Admiral CC – there had not been a team in the village since the 1970s – and offers of equipment. The local blacksmith made a roller. A scoreboard was painted on the back of a decrepit stable. The result is a ground which looks as though it has existed for 100 years, yet in fact is not a year old.

Buck, who reached the pinnacle of his own cricketing career in the 1970s with three or four appearances as a fast bowler for Hampshire Second XI, was impressed by the enthusiasm if not the talent of his recruits, who range in age from 24 to 74 and include the hotel's chef, a couple of City types, an engineer, a roadsweeper, a toymaker and a retired major. Intensive coaching sessions are slowly paying dividends: Hinton's record to date is played 17, won three, lost 13, drawn one, compared with a 100 per cent record of defeats at the end of July.

Buck provides prospective touring teams with a fixture contact list for more than 100 local sides in Hampshire and Dorset. The bar, crammed with cricketing memorabilia, stays open as late as the guests wish. Only on one occasion have victory celebrations got out of hand, when a 2am water fight ruined several mattresses.

Half of the teams which stayed at the Old Vicarage in 1994 have made firm bookings for 1995.

Harrison says: 'The cricket enables us to plan ahead. We know we will have that cash flow in a year's time.'

The couple believe that only two or three other hotels in Britain have their own cricket pitches. It is proving an attractive asset for corporate entertainment. Plessey, Lloyds Bank and Chase Manhattan Bank have all held staff cricket matches and barbecues at the Old Vicarage; another company plans to use the ground for an archery day.

Buck and Harrison expect to make a small profit this year on a turnover of about £130,000.

A bonus for Buck is that he gets to be captain of his own cricket team. He can afford to be more philosophical about losing than most skippers: 'I like to see our visitors go home happy. Anyway, when they've won, they spend more at the bar.'

Source: Financial Times, 3 September 1994

5.7 **Outline how the owners of the Old Vicarage Hotel, used the marketing mix elements in order to reach the niche segment of cricket tours. Identify which type of segmentation targeting strategy it is using.**

5.8 **This strategy would appear to only work in the summer months. Suggest other segments which could be targeted to fill the other seasons of the year.**

5.9 **From your answer to 5.8 above, select one idea and design an appropriate marketing mix.**

5.10 **If the Old Vicarage Hotel implemented your ideas in 5.9 above, what type of segmentation targeting strategy would they now be following?**

5D

Whisky's youthful look

By Christopher Price

The search is on for a lost generation of UK whisky drinkers. Over the next few months, United Distillers and Hiram Walker will re-launch their two best-selling brands to attract younger customers.

The move has been prompted by the rise of white spirits, such as vodka and tequila, and the growing market share of foreign beers and wine. But there is also a fear that whisky's reputation as a drink for older professional men – an image promoted by the producers themselves – is alienating a whole generation of younger customers.

'Most young people relate to whisky drinking in terms of their fathers,' says Pat Doble, core brands development director at Distillers, which manufactures the market leader, Bell's. 'Our challenge is to make them look at whisky in a different way and to see it as an energiser, not a winding down drink.'

Distillers plans to spend £30m over the next two years re-launching Bell's. The twin themes of the campaign will be to promote whisky as a mixer drink and to lower its customer age profile.

But in order not to alienate its core older customer base, Bell's is also to be marketed as a more mature Scotch, with a guarantee that the blend is made of whiskies which are at least eight years old.

Hiram Walker is to relaunch Teachers, the third biggest selling brand, to attract younger drinkers.

'There will be no pictures of wildlife, claymores or countryside. We have to recapture the aspirations of our customers,' says David Jarvis, managing director of Allied Lyons, owner of Hiram Walker.

Underpinning the campaigns is the decline in sales in the UK, the product's biggest market. UK off-trade sales dropped from 68m litres in 1983 to 60m last year, according to Stats MR, the market research group. In the same period, vodka sales jumped from 13.45m litres to 20.05m.

Distillers has been encouraged by its campaign to revamp Dewar's – the biggest-selling Scotch in the US – which halted its sales slide. The company also points to the remarkable rise of Venezuela, Thailand and Greece as leading whisky markets which now contribute 20 per cent of Distillers' profits.

'Whisky is seen as *the* young person's drink in these markets,' said Doble. 'If we can do it there, we can do it here.'

Source: Financial Times, 19 May 1994

Glenmorangie rises to £6.57m

Internet plays growing role in plan to attract younger drinkers, writes David Blackwell

Glenmorangie, which yesterday reported a 15 per cent rise in profits, said it was aiming to attract younger whisky drinkers.

Mr Peter Darbyshire, managing director, said yesterday that the group had been the first to offer a tour of the Tain distillery on the Internet. It was attracting between 4,000 and 5,000 hits a week. This summer it would also start to sell whisky through the Internet in the US, where the technology was ahead of Europe.

Pre-tax profits for the year to March 31 rose to £6.57m (£5.71m). Sales grew from £35.4m to £38.8m.

The group, which recently changed its name from Macdonald Martin Distilleries, lifted volume sales 21 per cent to 608,000 bottled cases of whisky. Malts were 20 per cent ahead at 215,000 cases, and blends grew 25 per cent to 350,000 cases.

Mr Darbyshire said the whisky industry had been complacent in the past about attracting younger customers. The group was looking at innovations such as the launch of three different 12-year-old Glenmorangie malts aimed partly at recruiting female drinkers.

Last year Glenmorangie sales were 55 per cent ahead in the US, against 35 per cent growth for whisky sales as a whole. In the UK Glenmorangie grew by 6 per cent – double the market growth.

Half the blended business was own-label, but the group was aiming at the premium end of the market.

The tax charge fell from £1.96m to £1.11m, or about 17 per cent, following the £12m investment in new production facilities at Broxburn, near Edinburgh airport, and the sale of the old Leith site. The tax rate is expected to return to 30 per cent this year.

Earnings rose 45 per cent from 27.49p to 39.97p for the A shares and from 13.745p to 19.985p for the B shares, which are held mainly by the controlling Macdonald family.

The final dividends of 9.25p and 4.625p respectively, lift both totals 13 per cent to 12p and 6p.

● Comment

Glenmorangie has undergone a period of significant change over the past couple of years, including sweeping changes in the top management. It looks like the right decision not to fight on price, but to go for quality. Prices of blends are likely to remain flat, with only small increases for malts in the US. But strong volume growth is flowing from the concentration on advertising, marketing and promotion. Forecast profits of £7.7m this year put the group on a prospective multiple of about 16 – lower than Highland, Burns Stewart and Macallan. It deserves better.

Source: Financial Times, 24 May 1996

5.11 **What is your view on the whisky distillers' aim to target younger drinkers?**

5.12 **Which segmentation variables would be helpful to you when trying to profile existing and potential customers?**

5.13 **How brand loyal do you think customers are in this sector and what impact might this have on persuading them to switch brands?**

5F

Dream consumer 'becoming endangered species'

Changing face of Britain:
Marriage is waning, divorce booming and 'empty nesters' may be a myth,
by Diane Summers, Marketing Correspondent

The marketer's dream consumer – the middle-aged, leisured 'empty nester' with a high disposable income – is becoming an endangered species, reports Mintel, the consumer market analysts, in a survey published today.

Middle-aged parents 'may spend many years sandwiched between the demands of elderly parents (who are living longer, and are less likely to be cared for by the state) and their own children', says the report on marketing to 45- to 64-year-olds.

The move to later parenthood means more of this age group have young children and, says the study, 'older off-spring, unable to find jobs in the current climate, are staying in the parental home for longer'.

A sample of 366 people aged 45 to 64 studied by Mintel showed that, in the age range 45 to 54, 16 per cent had children under 16 living at home, while 34 per cent had children over 16 still living with them. By age 55 to 64, 21 per cent still had older children at home.

When higher rates of divorce and step-parenthood are added to the picture, 'it becomes clear that the self-contained, comfortably off, empty-nester couple, if not becoming extinct altogether, is migrating to an older age group – the late fifties and older', says Mintel. The group is set to become increasingly important demographically: by 2005 there will be nearly 15m people aged 45 to 65 in the UK, making up 30 per cent of the adult population, compared with 28 per cent today. The largest increase will be among people aged 55 to 59, as postwar baby boomers join the age group.

The study highlights what it says 'may well be a new mood of disenchantment with the world of work' among the middle-aged. Out of 2,500 adults in the age group questioned in 1992, 41 per cent said they would carry on working even if they did not need the money. By 1994 this had dropped to 37 per cent.

Mintel says: 'It is certainly true that the widespread changes in working practices over the past decade, including greater reliance on new technology, and a more 'results-oriented' ethos in many companies, are more likely to have been unsettling for more established members of the workforce.'

The marketer's vision of the leisured middle-aged woman is particularly challenged by the survey

Stresses of the 'sandwich' generation

Mrs Irene Johnson is, in many ways, typical of the 'sandwich' generation – meeting the demands of an elderly parent at the same time as looking after her own child – described in the Mintel report published today, Diane Summers writes.

Mrs Johnson, 48, lives in Cannock, Staffordshire, with her husband of the same age who retired this year on medical grounds. She cares for her very frail 89-year old mother, and her 16-year-old daughter lives at home.

Her mother has lived with the family for the past two years because, says Mrs Johnson, 'the social services care that was on offer was not sufficient for her'.

Her daughter is anxiously awaiting tomorrow's GCSE results and hopes to become a nursery nurse. Mrs Johnson says it would be impossible for her to live away from home during her training.

'We couldn't afford it. Although we are better placed than many, my husband is now on a pension. I get £35.25 invalid care allowance a week, plus the family allowance for one child, which is £10.40, but that goes straight to my daughter.'

Mrs Johnson jokes that she 'wouldn't want to make it too comfortable' for her but accepts that the jobs market means it is likely that her daughter will remain at home 'for quite a few years'.

Like many of the women questioned by Mintel, Mrs Johnson's health has suffered because of the demands made on her. She is also increasingly typical of smokers of her generation: she smokes, while her husband does not, and she cannot envisage, with current pressures, giving up.

She has been ill, and 'ended up with mental and physical exhaustion' in hospital in February. 'It was simply the strain of caring for the family. Caring is an extremely stressful occupation,' she says.

---

findings. Many women in the 45 to 64 age group 'still seem to be leading the frenetic lifestyles associated with younger working mothers and may be neglecting their health because of it', says Mintel.

A survey of over 1,500 adults showed that men aged 45 to 54 enjoy 41 hours of leisure a week, while women got 34 hours. By aged 55–64, men had 59 hours leisure, compared with women's 46 hours. More women than men said they rushed their meals, were more likely not to take exercise, and were more likely to be smokers than men.

The percentage of over 45s who smoke has fallen in recent years, as it has done for all adults. However, reports Mintel, in 1975 almost half of 55–64 year old men smoked, compared with a third of women. In 1994, one in four women smoked, compared to one in five men.

When a sample of nearly 1,400 45–64 year olds were asked what their main problems were, 20 per cent of women chose health, compared with 17 per cent of men. Health education campaigns aimed at women in this age group should show how healthy eating and exercise can be incorporated into lifestyles 'which seem to be increasingly busy at an age when, a decade or two ago, women would have been starting to slow down'.

Family status and living arrangements, 1993–94

	45–54 %	55–64 %
Live alone	9	21
Live with spouse/partner	84	70
Children/step-children under 16 living at home	16	2
Children/step-children over 16 living at home	34	21
Have grandchildren	23	51

Source: BMRB/Mintel

Source: Financial Times, 23 August 1995

5.14 As a result of reading this article, assess how it might affect the following organisations:
- a nursing home for the elderly;
- a travel company;
- a health club;
- a cigarette manufacturer.

5.15 In view of your answer above, select one organisation and set out any marketing mix changes which the marketing manager might recommend.

6

Marketing Information and Research

Marketing Information Systems and Marketing Research has been subject to many changes in the past few years. Most of these changes have been driven by improvements in the technological capabilities of the agencies and their clients. The main issue for the industry therefore has shifted, from one of insufficient data, to one of too much. The main task in the forthcoming decade is going to be one of managing data into information, streamlining collection methods, prioritising research objectives and obtaining real results from the vast amount of money often spent on this activity.

Secondary information, which until fairly recently consisted mostly of paper based trade directories, government reports or sector reports, presented a broad perspective, but took a long time to compile, print and disseminate. The well-regarded Mintel and Keynote reports (sometimes costing in excess of £800 per copy) were often difficult to justify when there was little opportunity for the marketer to interrogate the raw data, or manipulate it easily to help answer a research question for the firm. Such information can now be downloaded from electronic sources, fed into a spreadsheet on a computer and be ready to use rather than simply read and filed.

Primary research, while still expensive to conduct, is still perhaps the most desired information, especially as it provides the opportunity for the firm to tailor the event to its own particular research requirements. The ubiquitous questionnaire is probably the most common form of primary research, to such an extent, that consumers, are getting 'questionnaire fatigue' as the forms get longer and the questions more invasive. Successful market research practitioners are having to devise more creative and less intrusive methods of gaining access to such information.

A robust Marketing Information System, which can link external data with internal sources, such as sales records, customer records and competitor information, will provide a strong basis for informed marketing decisions.

In order to successfully complete the tasks in this chapter you will need to be familiar with:

- secondary research techniques;
- primary research techniques;
- marketing information systems;
- sampling methods;
- sampling sizes;
- research evaluation.

It's a vision thing

By Meg Carter

Forecasting tomorrow's consumer trends today is an imprecise science – all too often qualitative research is out of date before the ink is dry.

Now a joint venture between Simons Palmer, the advertising agency, and The Insight Track, the research company, is aiming to help companies spot factors likely to affect business six, nine, or even 18 months ahead.

The new venture, called Headlight Vision, will use a group of 'visioneers'. These opinion-formers will be drawn from around the world and will include City analysts, fashion designers, magazine editors, psychologists and even philosophers.

Mike Perry, Simons Palmer group development director, says the visioneers will be people 'whose livelihoods depend on understanding and influencing what is going to happen next'.

Each client will be offered a tailored panel of 10 or 12 visioneers. The panel members will be paid a fee and told about the subjects under discussion two weeks in advance.

During the two weeks of preparation, visioneers will be expected to use their own contacts in order to forecast factors likely to affect businesses. According to Perry, 'smart companies are networking – this formalises that process'. Interviews with panel members will be individual, rather than in a group, and the visioneers can be revisited as often as required.

Nike is the first company to sign up for Headlight Vision. Clare Dobbie, UK head of communications, says youth brands in particular are likely to benefit from the approach: 'The real value lies in tailored, rather than generic, 'rear window' [retrospective] research. The application of practical, predictive research can have a real impact on marketing strategy.'

Perry believes the method would have allowed, for example, the vogue for all things Irish, or the snowboarding fad, to have been forecast earlier by marketing departments.

Source: Financial Times, 25 April 1996

6.1 **Identify the type and style of research which is being proposed by Headlight Vision.**

6.2 **For a company such as Nike, how representative of its market do you think the panel of 'visioneers' will be?**

6.3 **What other type of marketing research would you expect Nike to be carrying out to supplement any findings produced by Headlight Vision?**

Picked out by programs

Peter Marsh on marketing companies' use of computers to select target groups of consumers

From banks to blood collection agencies and from casinos to charities, different types of organisation are turning to highly specialised computer systems that enable them to market themselves better.

The computers sift vast volumes of data about groups of consumers, categorising them according to where they live, their incomes and likes or dislikes for types of food and other products, and so on.

Among the banks and financial services groups which use such systems, for instance to decide which types of customer should receive invitations to buy particular financial products, are American Express, the Spanish bank Banesto and the Swiss insurance group Winterthur.

Both CCN and CACI, two UK-based companies that are among the world leaders in the software needed to run these systems, say use of their services is growing as consumer markets become more fragmented and companies require more sophisticated tools to supplement traditional marketing methods.

Of the two companies, CCN, part of the Great Universal Stores retail group and with annual sales in marketing-related software and services of some £33m, is the more international. It says it holds in its computer files consumer information about 706m people in more than 15 countries. It receives about a quarter of its revenues in this part of its business from outside Britain.

CCN – which has total annual sales of some £100m and employs 2,600 people, mostly at its headquarters in Nottingham – is one of the world's biggest companies in services related to consumer data. It obtains a large chunk of its revenue from supplying confidential information about the finances of individuals to retailers, banks and loan agencies around the world, with the data being used to check credit requests.

CACI, which is US-owned, earns virtually all its £20m annual revenues from selling marketing-related software to British customers. This is because, says Greg Bradford, managing director of CACI's marketing systems arm, UK retailers and related groups are 'more research-oriented and interested in scientific techniques' than their counterparts in other countries.

A third, much smaller group has recently entered the area of selling software to help companies' marketing efforts. Marketing Sense, based in Edinburgh and with six employees, is selling compact discs containing details of 38m people in the UK – with the data limited to where they live and taken from the official government electoral roll.

The information on the discs can be used as a basic template to be added to companies' own internal and highly private sales information – for example, about the specific products and services bought by their customers and their average amount of annual spending.

In the past, Marks and Spencer, the UK retailer, has used marketing software of this sort, supplied by CCN, to work out which parts of Britain are the most suitable for opening new branches. Asda, another supermarket chain, has analysed with similar systems the particular mixes of special offers that it thinks will appeal to particular groups of consumers in selected stores, in a process that enables it to target promotional deals at specific locations.

One big user of such software is Circular Distributors, a privately-owned UK company that claims to be the leader in Britain in delivering advertising leaflets and free samples door to door.

The company, based in Maidenhead, Berkshire, delivers 1bn items of this sort a year, a fifth of the UK total. It claims to deliver, using an army of mainly part-time workers, to 19.5m out of the UK's 22m households. It works on behalf of a range of customers including big store chains such as Boots, Wickes and Ikea, as well as small enterprises which think leafleting will improve their custom among people living close by.

'We would not be able to operate as we do without software that enables us to target particular consumer groups according to where they live and the kind of life-styles they have,' says Charles Neilson, the company's planning director.

In Circular Distributors' case, it uses software supplied by CCN called Mosaic that splits UK residents into a number of consumer types, categorised by income levels, addresses (grouped into postcode areas) and tastes as indicated by use of certain products and services.

The data on these people have been built up by CCN using a range of sources including census details and marketing information supplied by other consumer companies with which it has business contacts.

A similar system called Acorn is supplied by CACI. It splits up the UK's population into a variety of socio-economic types, split into regions.

As a general rule, for instance, people in Merseyside spend 20 per cent more per head on toys and other products for children (such as prams) than people elsewhere in the UK. In Surrey, people are 20 per cent less likely to visit pubs regularly and only half as likely to go to wine bars as the average British citizen.

Using this type of data from CCN, and split up into much smaller areas, Circular Distributors can decide on which areas of Britain, comprising around 700 or so households, are most likely to be receptive to specific promotional offers or adverts that one of its own customers wants pushed through people's letterboxes on a targeted basis.

In this way, for example, literature related to special deals in a cut-price supermarket would find its way to poorer households in a run-down inner city area, while more wealthy families in the suburbs might receive leaflets asking them to take expensive holidays.

Another user of CCN's services is Mieke van Os, database manager at the Dutch arm of Air Miles International, a global group which organises promotional campaigns on behalf of participating consumer organisations by rewarding people who use specific products and services with prizes such as free air trips, theatre tickets or holidays.

'Our database has information about 2m households in the Netherlands, broken down to geographical areas, which contains general data about their way of life and how they spend their money so we can target products and services at them more effectively,' says van Os.

With the database built up by van Os, Air Miles in the Netherlands organises about 500,000 mailshots a year, trying to build up consumers' use of the products and services offered by companies associated with the Dutch part of Air Miles and which include Shell, the ABN Amro bank and Albert Heijn, a leading Netherlands food retailer.

Among the non-corporate users of geographically based marketing information supplied by specialised software groups is the Scottish National Blood Transfusion Service which wanted to increase its number of donors.

Using software and data supplied by CACI, it targeted for appeals groups of people living in Scotland judged to have the greatest 'propensity to give blood' – which boiled down to one fairly affluent group in professional or managerial jobs and with relatively high educational qualifications, and another less well-off corps of people who are public spirited in attitude, live close to the centres of towns and cities and who are fairly likely to live alone.

Unicef is one of a number of charities which have used such systems to work out which groups of people are most likely to give money. The charity has used specialised geodemographic targeting in Spain and Italy.

Such services have also been used by Sun International, the South Africa based operator of luxury hotels and casinos. The company is using a worldwide database of wealthy people both to decide which areas of the world are most suitable for new developments and to target potential customers.

Source: Financial Times, 24 May 1996

6.4 What type of marketing research is being discussed in this article and why has it become important to so many organisations?

6.5 This type of consumer data was first exploited by the retail sector but has since been recognised as valuable to other sectors, especially charities. How do you think that this information can help organisations to better segment and target customers?

6.6 There is a view, that the provision of this type of information on a vast scale has been enthusiastically embraced by organisations just 'because everybody else is doing it', and that they have little idea whether it has had any effect on their sales figures. Rather, it has simply provided sales and profits for the data base providers, the Post Office, the printing industry, mailing houses and waste disposal firms. What do you think?

6C

A point in question

Technological and social changes are altering the
face of market research, reports Diane Summers

The woman with the clipboard and a string of personal questions about your washing, eating or voting habits is an endangered species.

The market research industry, which has more than tripled in size in current prices in the UK and is now worth over £520m a year, is being swept by technological advances, profoundly affected by social changes, and potentially threatened by the competing demands of direct marketers.

First, the paper questionnaire-carrying clipboard is being rapidly replaced for many applications by the laptop computer. Computer-assisted personal interviewing (Capi) will probably be used in more than 60 per cent of face-to-face interviews by the end of this year, according to BMRB International, one of the UK's biggest market research agencies.

Computer-assisted telephone interviewing (Cati) is already firmly established as an alternative to the more laborious written questionnaires that telephone interviewers used to complete.

For both Capi and Cati, interviewers tap survey answers straight into a computer, cutting down on data processing time and improving accuracy. Surveys can be more complex and more closely targeted because the computer automatically selects the interviewer's 'routing' – which question should follow on from a particular answer.

Bill Blyth, technical director of Taylor Nelson AGB, the UK's largest market research group, says quality control is much better with computer-assisted interviewing because it is possible, for example, to check from the clock inside the computer what time the interview was conducted and even, using 'spy in the sky' satellite technology, to check where the interview took place and verify expense claims.

But he would like to see the new technology being employed more imaginatively than at present, when it is usually used simply to replace the paper and pencil. For example, he cites approvingly the way some market researchers in the US have been using the interviewer chiefly to 'sell' the idea of the survey to the respondent, rather than ask the questions. The respondent is then handed a laptop, plus headphones, and left to complete the questionnaire in privacy.

Increasingly, respondents are doing more of the work themselves. Taylor Nelson AGB has a panel of what will by next year be nearly 11,000 homes. These households, equipped with data terminals and barcode pens, scan all their supermarket purchases as they unpack them, providing a wealth of data on who buys what, where and when. Members of another panel of 'frequent flyers' are given electronic personal organisers on which to record their air travel experiences.

For the future, developments in linguistics and computers are likely to change further the face of market research, says Blyth. Speech recognition by computers will cut out the interviewer for some types of phone interviewing. Meanwhile, progress is already being made in getting computers to write reports after they have analysed the data.

After technological developments, the second most important factor altering the face of market research is social change. A forthcoming report from the market intelligence group Mintel, for example, details the effect of crime rates and the increasing number of women in the workforce.

Interviewers, it suggests, may be unwilling to venture into some high-crime inner-city areas, while householders may be afraid to answer the door to strangers, says Mintel. With women increasingly looking for regular employment, 'it is even becoming harder to find the standard type of person who used to be the backbone of fieldwork – the reasonably well-educated housewife looking for part-time work'.

Some of these social changes mean one potentially very damaging consequence for market research: slipping response rates as more people refuse to be, or cannot be, interviewed. Michael Warren, director general of the Market Research Society, the industry's professional body, says falling response levels are not just a UK phenomenon. He is concerned that the quality of research will begin to be affected, for the lower response rates are, the greater the departure from ideal cross-sections of opinion, and the less accurate findings are likely to be.

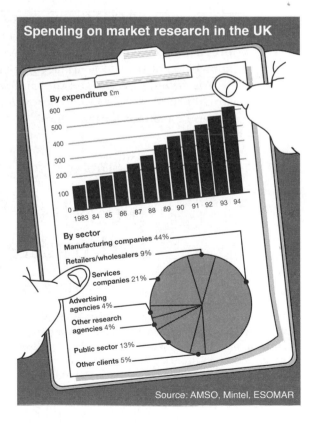

Spending on market research in the UK

By expenditure £m

By sector
Manufacturing companies 44%
Retailers/wholesalers 9%
Services companies 21%
Advertising agencies 4%
Other research agencies 4%
Public sector 13%
Other clients 5%

Source: AMSO, Mintel, ESOMAR

Another problem is 'data fatigue', as the public becomes tired of filling in questionnaires and more cynical about the real motives of 'market researchers'. 'Sugging' – selling under the guise of research – is a practice that the Market Research Society has had to fight for years. Recently Warren has come across a new phenomenon – 'frugging' – fundraising under the guise of research. This is a technique employed by some charities to stimulate donations as they struggle to overcome the public cynicism which is sometimes said to be affecting their own sector – donor fatigue.

Using research findings to sell products to respondents attacks the very core of the professional market researcher's code of ethics, which promises to safeguard the respondent's anonymity. Tensions are developing between the traditional market researchers and the newer discipline of database marketing. To a database marketer, the whole point of a finding out about an individual is to attach information to a name and address, to which offers, product information and money-off vouchers, for example, can later be mailed.

Warren is concerned there may be confusion in the public's mind about these very different activities and the Market Research Society plans later this year to investigate public perceptions of the confidentiality of the two forms of data collection.

Edwina Dunn, director of DunnHumby Associates, the company which is helping Tesco to collect and analyse the data from its Clubcard scheme, acknowledges the conflict but believes both disciplines have much to learn from each other.

Some purist market researchers are 'sticking their heads in the sand,' she says. 'Database marketing isn't going to go away.' Market research has much to teach the database marketers about devising open questions and interpreting data, she says.

While the woman with the clipboard may be threatened, she is not dead. According to Dunn, some market researchers are still using 'some pretty archaic approaches which are very labour intensive,' and they could benefit from the database marketer's computer wizardry.

Source: Financial Times, 29 June 1995

6.7 You have been invited for a final interview with Taylor Nelson and in preparation for the interview they have sent you this article. You are required to prepare a presentation based on the article, supplemented with your own knowledge of the problems facing the market research industry.

You haven't been asked for solutions, but the job is very attractive and you would like to make a good impression so you decide to include your ideas and recommendations for the future.

6D

No relish for cheese and pickle sandwich

By Richard Donkin

In a rare display of corporate humility yesterday one of the world's best-known companies admitted to making a big mistake when it unveiled a secret weapon to take on the UK's supermarket chains.

McDonald's, the hamburger chain that brought the world the Big Mac, thought it had another winner when it announced the new product to its expectant staff.

Enter the McPloughman's, a cheese, pickle and salad sandwich. Mr Paul Preston, president of McDonald's in the UK, told the conference that the McPloughman's was devised to compete with supermarkets in the cold sandwich market.

Instead of applauding this marketing innovation, however, staff were unimpressed. Mr Preston admitted: 'If we had done our homework we would have found that our customers didn't want the product and our staff were embarrassed even to have to say McPloughman's, let alone to have to sell it to our customers.'

In a masterly piece of understatement, he added that if the company had carried out market research 'we would have found that this was not a highly desirable product'.

When it did survey customer attitudes it found even more shocks were in store. Customers, he said, told McDonald's they were 'loud, brash, American, successful, complacent, uncaring, insensitive, disciplinarian, insincere, suspicious and arrogant'. He said: 'We thought we knew about service. Get the order into the customer's hands in 60 seconds – that was service. Not according to our customers. They wanted warmth, helpfulness, time to think, friendliness and advice. What they told us we were giving was horrifying.

'What we had failed to see was that our customers were now veterans in the quick-service market and their expectations had gone through the roof.'

The McPloughman's market test was restricted to central London and shortlived. Only now, more than three years after the sandwich debacle and the first customer survey, has the company felt confident enough to reveal the episode.

Mr Preston said the research, first carried out late in 1991, had been a turning point for McDonald's in the UK which had led to a radical change in its business approach.

Rather than relying on gut feeling that it knew what customers wanted, the company had developed a fact-based approach to planning.

Source: Financial Times, 28 October 1994

6.8 What type of marketing research could McDonald's have carried out before launching the McPlougman's in London?

6.9 In your work group, build a profile of the typical McDonald's customer.

6.10 Visit your local McDonald's restaurant to see if your profile seems accurate.

6.11 How do you think McDonald's is doing in its attempt to be more customer responsive? Justify your response.

6.12 Devise a market research programme which would help inform McDonald's of their customers' preferences. Try to be a little more imaginative than simply asking customers to fill in a questionnaire.

Rich lift spending power at cost of poor

Wealthy see recent improvement in quality of life as society polarises, writes Neil Buckley

The rich want expensive holidays and to own their home. They like new technology, think their quality of life has improved in the past five years – and they are getting richer.

The poor rate buying things for home and family as more important. They are suspicious of technology, believe 'things ain't what they used to be' – and are getting poorer.

A report today by Mintel, the market research group, portrays a Britain where the rich are increasing spending power at the expense of the poor, and a society polarising towards the two extremes.

Yet, Mintel finds, there is no strong demand from either side for redistributive taxes to even things out. Only 27 per cent of the poor say the rich do not pay enough tax and 22 per cent of the rich agree.

Rich and poor agreed that a 'safe neighbourhood' was the most important 'necessity for a good life'. The next priorities for the rich were cars, money in the bank and home ownership. For the poor, next most important were money in the bank, telephones and cars.

The rich, defined by Mintel as the top 20 per cent of earners (average gross household income of £42,818 in 1993), have increased their share of total household spending from 35 per cent in 1979, when the Conservatives came to power, to a forecast 49 per cent this year. The share of spending of the poor, defined by Mintel as the bottom 40 per cent of earners (average household income of £6,088), has halved in the same period from 24.5 per cent to 12.5 per cent.

Meanwhile, the proportion of adults in the middle-income category is declining. The number of rich has increased since 1979 from 9m to 11.1m, and the poor from 16.5m to 17.3m, but the middle-income category has shrunk from 30.7m to 30.1m.

Mintel says that makes targeting rich and poor groups of growing importance to consumer goods companies and retailers.

The changing proportions reflect the shift from manual to office-based jobs, an ageing population, growth in part-time and casual work, and the rise of an 'underclass' of poorly trained and educated adults with few prospects.

Based on interviews with 1,500 adults last December, Mintel finds wide differences in spending patterns. The poor devote a higher proportion of household spending to food, fuel, light and power. They also devote a much lower proportion of spending than the rich to leisure and sport, clothing and personal goods.

Asked to name spending priorities, the rich give greater priority to holidays, cars, home improvements or moving house. The poor are more likely to mention buying something for the home, new clothes or shoes, or something for all the family.

Essential items account for 54 per cent of spending by poor households, while non-essentials take up 58 per cent of spending by the rich.

But the report says that the rich have been more affected by recession and poor consumer confidence. Half the rich said they cancelled significant spending plans in 1994 because of financial uncertainty and 56 per cent said they had to cut spending to make ends meet.

'Targeting the rich is not the easy option,' said Ms Emma Besbrode, Mintel's project manager. 'In the current economic climate it requires a great deal of persuasion for them to spend money.'

The rich do, however, feel better generally. Thirty-five per cent said their quality of life had improved in the past five years, compared with 18 per cent of the poor. And while only two in 10 of the rich agree that 'things ain't what they used to be', four in 10 of the poor think this is true.

About 60 per cent of the rich say technology has improved their quality of life, but only 36 per cent of the poor.

'The poor are more conservative in outlook,' says Ms Besbrode. 'They have a strong streak of nostalgia for the good old days.'

Source: Financial Times, 12 July 1995

6.13 **This report was based on interviews with 1500 adults. Do you think this is an appropriate sample size? Why?**

6.14 **In order to assess the validity of the findings in this report, what additional information would you need to know on how the data was gathered?**

6.15 **Gather this data, or a similar Mintel report, in either your university or local library and report on whether the information you identified in 6.14 above is disclosed.**

6.16 **Based on your answer to 6.15 above, provide a view on the validity of this type of market research and its relevance to marketing decisions.**

7

Anatomy of a Product

A product or service offering is at the heart of the marketing exchange. If the offering does not meet, match or even exceed customer requirements, it will not sell. The basic offering from an organisation, is an attempt to either satisfy the customer's need or solve a particular problem. There are other levels of product though which the organisation may wish to use in its attempt to move the competition away from basic needs.

Competing at the core product level usually means the organisation is competing on price alone. Differentiation is far easier to achieve and more difficult for the competition to copy at the tangible level. It is here that the forces of branding, design and innovative packaging come into play. Competing at the augmented level usually involves add-on extras which do not form an intrinsic element of the product, but which make the offering more attractive to the purchaser. Warranties, credit facilities, after-sales service and training being common examples. Augmented product offerings are relatively easy for competitors to imitate and some would argue that it simply raises the final cost to the consumer. After all, 'free five-year guarantee' or 'free delivery' is rarely so, it has simply been built into the product's original pricing structure.

Products typically fall into classifications which help marketers decide on the most appropriate marketing mix tactics. From durable products, such as cars and capital equipment, through to shopping goods and raw materials. Purchasing behaviour in each of these categories differs according to many elements, e.g. the level of risk, decision making unit, product knowledge and volumes required, being just a few. Different product types demand different approaches and recognition of this is critical in ensuring that products are offered to customers appropriately.

In order to successfully complete the tasks in this chapter you will need to be familiar with:

- levels of products;
- product classification;
- purchasing decision;
- product mix;
- product line – length, depth and width;
- branding.

A brand enigma

Roderick Oram looks at Guinness's lager travails

Enigma is turning into an expensive riddle for Guinness. Who is going to drink the premium lager it launched just over a year ago?

The initial advertising campaign, arty and obscure even by Guinness standards, failed to carve out a clear brand identity and following for the lager. Thus, Guinness has just decided to can £8m of annual advertising and switch to some £5m a year of promotions.

The price of Enigma, which ranged as high as £4.89 for a four-pack shortly after the launch last April, is now often down to £3.99 in special offers.

'You need to build a reason for people to trial you in a very crowded and very competitive sector,' says Julian Spooner, marketing director of Guinness Brewing Great Britain.

So far Enigma has won a 1.6 per cent share of the take-home market for bottled and canned premium-priced lager, equal to some small established brands such as Tennent's Extra. 'It has strong appeal to a small group of people but it is too early to say whether it will grow substantially from here,' says Spooner.

Guinness's lager travails offer a number of lessons for all brewers as the British beer market becomes swamped with new products and brands. Some 470 new beers or variations and a raft of competing alcoholic soft drinks were launched last year, estimates Tom Wright, director of brands, research and development at Carlsberg-Tetley, which launches Calder's on Monday into the booming cream ale market.

Precious few are phenomenally successful. Caffrey's has been the most notable example in recent times, hitting its stride last year, its second year in the market since establishing the creamy Irish ale segment. It is already Bass's third largest brand by revenue. Closer competition to Enigma is Bass's Carling Premier lager launched at the same time as the Guinness product but off to a stronger start.

With Enigma, Guinness hoped to create a sector – widgeted lager. It believed consumers would like the creamy head created by the nitrogen device in the bottom of the can which had been a big hit with ales. Guinness is not alone in the struggle. Whitbread has made slow progress so far with its widgeted Newquay Steam lager. But competitors are particularly harsh critics of Enigma, starting with the name.

'It sounds as though Guinness couldn't find a better name than the code they'd used for the project,' says one. 'It is all concept – the widget – and no heritage,' says another. Similarly, the packaging is dull and the advertising pure attitude and no product.

Enigma, available only in the take-home trade, has two further disadvantages: history and distribution. Guinness is very closely identified with its dominant stout while its lager credentials through Harp are weak. Without owning pubs as Bass and other brewers do, it cannot easily build a new brand in the on-trade to reinforce off-trade sales.

Carling Premier, in contrast, is building on Carling Black Label's dominance of the standard lager market and benefits from Bass's pub distribution. Even so, Bass admits Premier was slow to catch on in the take-home market.

'With on- and off-trade you can build consumer experience more quickly but it doesn't mean you have to have both,' says Spooner. To encourage more drinkers, the brewer is giving the packaging a 'warmer' look but is keeping the name. It is also satisfied with the taste which it believes has broad appeal from its smoothness.

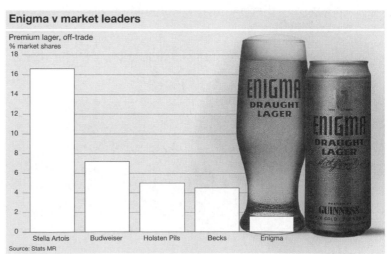

Enigma v market leaders

Premium lager, off-trade
% market shares

Source: Stats MR

(Stella Artois, Budweiser, Holsten Pils, Becks, Enigma)

But it is this very lack of distinction which is Enigma's greatest problem, rivals say. Thus, despite the switch in promotion strategy, some in brewing and retailing speculate that Guinness might let the lager fade away. But, says Spooner, 'we have absolutely no plans to withdraw the brand from the market. It is profitable for us'.

Source: Financial Times, 20 June 1996

7.1 How valuable do you think the Guinness brand name is to the future of Enigma? Provide supporting arguments which will justify your response.

7.2 Given that the company accepts 'there has to be a good reason for people to trial the product in a very crowded and very competitive sector', why do you think that Guinness launched Enigma and who do you think it was targeted at?

7.3 Identify the advantages and disadvantages of Guinness not making Enigma available to the on-trade.

7B

Brands at bay

Diane Summers examines new research which warns companies to be wary of making own-label goods

Those who predict the death of the brand are sometimes overgloomy. Yet the startling decline in respect among consumers in the principal European economies for the big brand names over the last five years is inescapable.

For example, in 1991, 81 per cent of Spaniards, who are among the greatest brand enthusiasts, agreed with the statement: 'It's best to buy famous brands because you can rely on their quality.' By last year this figure stood at 68 per cent, having sunk in 1993 as low as 50 per cent.

Such figures, which have just been updated for 1995, are gathered across Europe each year by the UK-based Henley forecasting centre, in conjunction with market research company Research International. They form one strand of the continued monitoring of changes in consumer behaviour and trends in Germany, the UK, France, Spain, Italy and the Netherlands.

Hand in hand with this declining respect for brands is the increasing regard in which retailers' own-label goods are held in both Europe and, to a growing extent, North America. In Europe, own-label sales have grown over five years by an average of 7.5 per cent a year at current prices, compared with 3.4 per cent for overall retail sales growth, according to market analysts Euromonitor.

Meanwhile, in North America, Euromonitor finds that in the packaged food sector, for example, private-label's share rose from less than 20 per cent of the market in 1990 to nearly 25 per cent four years later.

The social and economic reasons for these profound changes are numerous. James Murphy, Henley associate director, sees a continued lack of consumer confidence, pressure on prices and the 'shifting respect for emblems of authority,' as contributory factors. Consumers begin to question why they are paying more for the benefit of a brand logo when private-label versions may be just as good.

But those big brand manufacturers currently weighing up the pros and cons of own-label production, there is unequivocal advice from John Quelch, professor of marketing at Harvard Business School, and David Harding, a director of strategy at consultants Bain & Company. Writing recently in the Harvard Business Review, they state: 'Our recommendation to companies that do not yet make products for the private-label market is simple. Don't start.'

Like the development of an addiction, things may begin in a small way, they argue. Own-label production that starts as a method of using occasional excess production capacity can end up cannibalising the main body of a company's branded goods. 'Private-label production can become a narcotic,' say Quelch and Harding.

This road to ruin is paved with the apparent attractions of marginal production costs, with own-label production often looking like 100 per cent profit, says Henley. Managers can be seduced by this simple calculation – what is more difficult to measure is the potential corruption of the long-term value of the company's brands, Henley says.

Quelch and Harding argue that any company making own-label should answer three questions to get at the real economics of production: what is the true contribution from private-label products; what fixed costs are attributable to private-label production; and how much will the private-label goods cannibalise the company's brands.

They demonstrate the point with the example of Consumer Corporation (not its real name). The contribution from a popular food product was $0.40 per pound for the national brand and $0.23 per pound for the private label. So the company had to sell almost two pounds of the private label product to equal the contribution generated by the sale of one pound of the national brand. Once cannibalisation had been taken into account, Consumer decided that the risk outweighed the marginal reward and opted instead to invest more in the branded product.

Additional manufacturing and distribution costs, such as changing labels and packaging for each own-label customer and holding stock for each account, should also be added into the calculation, as should the costs of maintaining separate sales relationships with retailers and 'unproductive use of management time in reducing conflicts' between the two sides of the operation, they argue.

For those companies which have already chosen the own-label route, Quelch and Harding recommend, as a first step in keeping operations under control, that an audit is carried out. 'Amazingly, top-level executives at many companies do not know how much private-label business their organisations do,' they say. Second, true profitability, on both a full-cost and marginal-cost basis, and the impact of private label in the individual sectors in which the company's brands operate, should be calculated.

Finally, excess capacity should be closed, they say. 'The option of shutting down unused capacity is almost never considered in the private-label debate. Yet in five categories, Consumer found that the profitability of manufacturing rationalisation (including exit costs) was superior to filling excess capacity with low-return private-label business,' they state.

In spite of declining respect shown by consumers, Henley sees the brand as far from dead. The trick now seems to be for manufacturers to imitate the imitators – it is now time for the brand producers to establish relationships with consumers that are as strong as those built by retailers such as J. Sainsbury in the UK and the Netherlands' Albert Heijn.

Rational product-focused marketing campaigns, continuous innovation, and serious dialogue with consumers are some of the measures that can revitalise brands, says Henley.

Source: Financial Times, 17 March 1996

7.4 Identify the reasons why a manufacturer would wish to get involved in own-label manufacturing.

7.5 What problems do you think an involvement in own-label or badged products would give a manufacturer of branded goods?

7.6 As so many manufacturers now have contracts for the supply of own-label products, why is it that some consumers are still sufficiently motivated to pay a higher price for branded products?

Siemens tries out 'no-frills' controls

By Peter Marsh in London

Siemens is test marketing in Britain a new range of machine tool controls destined for China on the grounds that the UK's 'value for money' approach to factory automation is closer to east Asia than that of any other big European country.

'Britain is half way to Asia [in its attitude to using machine tools],' said Mr Norbert Armbrüster, Siemens' marketing director for machine tool controls.

What some might take as a back-handed compliment to the UK concerns a new set of cheap, 'no frills' controls which Siemens has developed largely to meet the fast-growing market in east Asia, excluding Japan. Siemens is Europe's biggest electronics and electrical goods company.

In the world's DM5bn-a-year machine tool controls industry, Siemens is the second biggest company, accounting for about a fifth of sales. Fanuc of Japan is the leader, with 40 per cent of the market. In Europe and the US, Fanuc sells its controls through a joint venture with General Electric of the US.

Siemens' marketing efforts concern a new set of machine tool controls which sell for about DM16,000 ($10,500), less than half the price of more sophisticated controls in which the German company has traditionally specialised.

It is stepping up its attempts to sell the products to UK-based machine tool companies, many of which are accenting low-cost machines aimed at small jobbing shops, as a prelude to launching a still cheaper version of the controls system in China next year.

Mr Armbrüster said he was specifically targeting the UK's 600 Group and Bridgeport and Cincinnati Milacron of the US, both of which have large UK factories, for sales of the new systems.

In the past, the German company has been accused of 'over-engineering' its machine tool products, especially in relation to Fanuc's cheaper controls.

Siemens believes the east Asian region, outside Japan, will account for sales in 2000 of 42,000 controls, worth DM640m. Last year, in contrast, Siemens reckons the region bought 23,000 units, valued at DM400m.

The forecast 83 per cent growth in sales in the region, in unit terms, would be far higher than the comparable 16 per cent growth Siemens foresees for the whole world.

The projections hinge on the rapid industrialisation of the region, much of which is based around hundreds of thousands of small jobbing shops meeting the demand for locally made components from groups such as multinational car companies.

Source: Financial Times, 19 July 1996

7.7 What level of product has Siemens traditionally operated at and why is the new range dramatically different?

7.8 In terms of product classification, which category would Siemens' products fall into?

7.9 What implication would you expect this to have on the purchasing decision and purchasing process?

A sticky problem

Sellotape is trying to break free from the trap of being a near generic name, explains Diane Summers

Sellotape has a sticky problem. The brand is so well known in the UK, Ireland and New Zealand, where it is the dominant adhesive tape brand, that it appears in the dictionary as both a noun and a verb. Like Biro, Thermos, Hoover, Walkman and Jeep, the name runs the danger of coming to stand for any brand in its product group.

The near-universal consumer recognition of the Sellotape name in its main markets would be envied by many brand owners. But the downside of being a near generic is that a shopper setting out to buy Sellotape might pick up a rival product or a cheap unbranded roll on a market stall, and still consider the mission accomplished.

As David Haigh, a director of Interbrand, the brand consultancy, points out: 'If your name becomes so closely associated in the consumer's mind with the category, it removes your ability to achieve a price premium. Your brand has stopped being a brand and becomes a category reference point.'

And because Sellotape is so closely identified in consumers' minds with just one item – clear adhesive tape – the familiarity of the name runs the risk of inhibiting the development of other products in the range.

Sellotape, the company, makes a range of industrial, DIY and stationery products, and is even to be found on sea-bed pipelines, in outer-space on telecoms hardware, as well as holding up babies' nappies.

To fix these sticky problems, the company, which is a privately owned French concern with a £90m turnover, is spending £2m on a new corporate identity, as well as repositioning and repackaging its retail and office products.

Neil Ashley, who heads the consumer business at Sellotape and is based in the UK, is leading the project. The UK accounts for 45 per cent of the group's business but the new look will be adopted in all the company's markets worldwide.

About a year ago, Ashley selected Identica, the identity and innovation consultancy headed by Michael Peters, which has as one of its specialities, boosting 'tired trademarks'.

Peters was founder of the Michael Peters Group, the design company which floated in 1983. The group subsequently expanded outside its areas of expertise and was a victim of the recession. It went into receivership in 1990, with Peters moving on to form Michael Peters Limited, and then Identica in 1992.

One of the first steps has been to change the name of the consumer side of Sellotape from Sellotape Limited to The Sellotape Company – a subtle but not unimportant difference, argue Ashley and Peters. The new name conveys that the group makes more than simply clear sticky tape and opens up the possibility of the company endorsing products that are not necessarily called Sellotape and which the company may not itself make.

The distancing of the company's identity from the brands is reinforced by the use of different logos: The Sellotape Company has a new corporate symbol of an athlete running with a baton to symbolise its new-found agility. The symbol will be used within the company and in trade communications, while the familiar blue and yellow Sellotape lozenge will continue to be used on retail packaging.

For the first time, the range of office stationery supplies will, as Sellotape Office, have a separate identity, and more exciting presentation in office supplies catalogues will help the products stand out from the usual dull array of passport-style pictures.

The creation of sub-brands targeted at different sectors is one of the most important features of the revamp and becomes increasingly possible as the identity of the company is distanced from its products. Packaging of the main retail stationery lines has been redesigned to emphasise the different functions of the lines.

From early next year, double-sided and invisible sticky tape, for example, will be distinguished clearly from each other and original Sellotape by different colour packs and bold labelling. The old packaging not only made Sellotape easy to confuse with its competitors, but also failed to highlight the extent of the range.

Ashley and Peters say that, unusually for a manufacturer, they consulted widely with retailers about the changes, allowing them to short-cut some of the usual research and consumer testing. Sellotape has been a victim of own-brand competition to a limited extent only: Ashley maintains that it is in retailers' interests to take their share of the generous premium that the brand commands, rather than compete with their own, cheaper versions.

Tesco switched to own label but back again to Sellotape, while W.H. Smith excluded the brand from its office supplies catalogue but will re-include it next year 'because of the logic of the marketplace', he says.

Changes have already been implemented in the DIY market, where Sellotape had not been taken seriously because of its over-identification as a stationery company, says Ashley.

Identica redesigned packing for its tape, repair and insulation products, giving packs an architectural 'blueprint' background and a separate identity to the stationery goods. The company's fastest-selling new product last year was a grey cloth DIY tape called Elephant Tape, which is only lightly branded with the Sellotape name.

A departure for the future is a new range of children's products, which is likely to be in the shops from the second quarter next year. Targeting five-to-nine-year-olds, Sellotape is hoping to create a new category of 'collectable' characters, within the pocket money price range, which exploit the snail-like shape of sticky tape dispensers and will be sub-branded 'Stick It!'.

The object of the segmentation, say Ashley and Peters, is to increase the opportunities for purchase by making the sub-brands available at a number of different points in a store, along with, for example, children's items, stationery, gift wrapping, craft goods and in separate DIY shops. The aim is to encourage impulse buying and the 'collecting' of different products to fulfil different needs.

The strategy, hopes Ashley, will lead to an increase in frequency of purchase: 'Currently, a heavy purchaser buys one roll a year. A very heavy user buys one a year, and nicks a roll from the office.'

Source: Financial Times, 23 November 1995

7.10 **In terms of product classification, which category do you think Sellotape would fall into?**

7.11 **What implication would you expect this to have on the purchasing decision and purchasing process?**

7.12 **Visit your local stationery store and make an assessment of products available to solve the 'it needs sticking' problem. Draw up a product mix chart for products carrying a single brand name – Sellotape if possible (Office World is a good location). Supplement this with an analysis of product line length, depth and width.**

7.13 **You are a guest at the annual dinner of the Institute of Mechanical Engineers. During an intense discussion, another guest derides Marketing as not being a proper job and states loudly: 'The best thing which can happen to a product is for it to become generic so what's the point in marketing?' Resisting your immediate desire to explain it to him there and then, you decide to leave. On your way home, you start to wonder whether he may be right. You decide to ask your sales team to consider this in more depth and will put it on the agenda for the next meeting.**

In preparation for this, draw up your arguments for and against a product becoming a generic name and outline the difficulties that can occur when this happens.

Marrying brands

Today's merger of Lloyds Bank and TSB Group raises questions of identity, says Alison Smith

Personal customers of high street banks are notoriously inert. Even they, however, might generally be expected to notice and respond to the creation of the bank with the most extensive branch network in the UK.

The aim of those masterminding the merger of Lloyds Bank and TSB Group, which becomes effective today, is that customers should realise only gradually that a new entity has been created. The announcement of the deal in October made it clear that the TSB brand would continue to exist alongside the brands that Lloyds already offers its retail banking customers.

To an extent this is mere pragmatism: short of getting the individual consent of millions of customers, the two organisations cannot formally merge their customer bases until a private bill has been passed by parliament.

The commitment to keep the TSB bank brand alive in Scotland, where Lloyds has hardly any presence, is absolute. Although the commitment to the brand's survival in England is slightly vague, the present intention seems to be that Lloyds and TSB branches will co-exist in different regions, depending on their relative strength.

The move marks the expansion of Lloyds as a multi-brand financial services organisation.

In the past, the general pattern when one financial services company buys another has been for the brand of the one acquired to disappear. Most recently, this is happening in the acquisition by General Accident, a composite insurer, of Provident Mutual, a life office. It is due to happen with Abbey National's takeover of National & Provincial Building Society next year.

But this phenomenon is most common where both organisations are in exactly the same field. As the largest financial services organisations become more ambitious to offer a full range of products and cover the whole market, this is changing.

The inclusion of the TSB brand will take to four the total number of brands available to Lloyds Bank personal customers.

Apart from being offered products which bear the Lloyds name, customers can also be sold life assurance, investment and pensions policies from Black Horse Financial Services and mortgages and retail savings accounts from Cheltenham & Gloucester.

Lloyds bought C&G, formerly a building society, in August for £1.8bn with the specific aim of maintaining its separate identity in order to capitalise on its mortgage expertise.

It already sells its home loans in Lloyds' network as well as its own-brand branches, and is expected to take on the administration of existing Lloyds mortgages early next year. It will design and run TSB mortgages, and is likely to market them under its own brand.

But for Lloyds to maintain the TSB brand is a different proposition. Instead of keeping a name with a strong reputation in a specific and not generally overlapping area of business, the organisation would be maintaining two brands offering similar services to different parts of the market.

Tom Blackett, deputy chairman of Interbrand, a branding consultancy, does not believe this approach is tenable – even in Scotland.

'I can't see how the TSB bank brand will survive,' he says. 'There is no rationale these days for maintaining a small, regional brand, even if it is quite strong.

'The whole trend is towards big, national brands.'

An additional approach open to the new group, however many bank brands it maintains, is retaining the brand name for use on certain products, which would then be available from all branches.

In areas where Lloyds was seen to have the stronger products – for example, perhaps in the basic current account – its brand would be sold throughout the network. Equally, where TSB appears to have the stronger name – such as services aimed at young people – that name would survive.

If Lloyds TSB adopts this strategy, it would highlight the anomalous and autonomous position of C&G within the group: it has not only retained its own branches, but currently does not sell any other brand of products from its network.

Blackett is clear on the advantages of keeping existing brands in some form. 'While the identity of the total network needs just one name, it makes very good sense to use the old one on products because in financial services it takes a long time to build a brand,' he says.

The length of time needed to establish a name seems to be a particular feature of life assurance, where the customer is buying a promise – of protection for dependants or a good investment return – that can take several years to be kept.

This may be one reason why a new note is being struck in some quarters, as financial service companies consider the rationalisation of the life assurance sector.

There are signs from one or two potential purchasers that they might be prepared to recognise the value of additional brands in any acquisition. If, for example, Prudential, which is the UK's largest life assurance group and sells mainly through a direct sales force, bought a life company selling through independent financial advisers, it might consider holding on to that brand if it had associations with high levels of service or particular expertise in designing products for the independent adviser market.

One instance where this approach of keeping the brand has worked is the purchase by Abbey National of Scottish Mutual in 1992.

'With Scottish Mutual we were going for a different market, the independent adviser market,' says John Fry, deputy chairman of Abbey National.

There was clearly an advantage for Abbey in staying with the brand known by independent financial advisers, rather than trying to persuade them that they should deal with an organisation primarily known for its mortgages and savings accounts.

The financial sector is still a long way from the clusters of brands owned by groups such as Kingfisher (Woolworth, Superdrug, Comet and B&Q) and Burtons (whose chains include Top Shop, Principles and Dorothy Perkins).

But as the largest financial services organisations expand further into each others' markets, then they are likely to grow closer to high street retailers in this regard.

Source: Financial Times, 28 December 1995

7.14 When looking for life assurance, mortgage services or a bank account, would you seek a brand name in much the same way as you would when buying a chocolate bar or a pair of jeans? Why?

7.15 How appropriate do you think it is for banks to extend their product line in much the same way as Kellogg, Lego and Kodak do?

7.16 Lloyds Bank obviously sees benefits in being able to offer their customers several products with differing brand names. How do you think the customer will perceive this?

7.17 Do you think that the Lloyds Bank move into related products is a genuine response to customer needs or, more cynically, just a way for them to horizontally integrate and make more money? Justify your response.

8

Product Management

Effective product management is fundamental to any organisation's success. Recognising when a product has had its day and really should be deleted from the portfolio, and gearing the firm up to produce new products, is an essential part of the marketing management function.

Critics of the product life cycle concept, doubt the notion that all products are born, grow, reach maturity and then die. Many examples can be found of products which have reached maturity and have stayed in the market for years. Very little change has been seen to generic shopping products, such as toilet paper, soap, baked beans, or to industrial goods, such as cement, bricks, lawn seed, television aerials, yet it would be foolish to treat these products as approaching decline, when clearly they are still in great demand.

The launch of new products and the decision on where, and to which type of consumer to position that product, is also fundamental to a successful launch. Product line extension and range filling, is often an organisation's response to the consumer's demand for different pack sizes, enhanced formulations, refill facilities, etc, yet this also carries with it the risk of small, if any, increase in sales.

This applies as much to services as it does to physical products. Insurance companies have been quick to satisfy the increased demand for critical illness policies, recognising the effect this may have on the sale of straight life insurance policies. Similarly, banks and building societies, have had to introduce customer service functions which simply serve to keep the company competitive and retain customers, yet it is difficult to see how this can increase profits by any substantial amount.

Perceptual mapping is very helpful in identifying gaps in the market, and this in turn, helps to decide the product positioning issue.

> **In order to successfully complete the tasks in this chapter you will need to be familiar with:**
>
> - product life cycle;
> - consumer adoption process;
> - product positioning;
> - perceptual mapping;
> - product line management.

How to keep the customer happy

Peter Marsh explains three companies' different approaches to mass customisation

Offer your customers what they want – within limits. For many businesses, the challenge is to embrace enough product variation to satisfy the marketplace while retaining the benefits of the standardised production line.

But getting the balance right is far from easy. The blend of skills required to succeed with 'mass customisation', to use the management jargon, may take decades to build up. Hence, the strategy is more likely to be adopted by companies which plan on a long timescale.

Three companies in widely different sectors which have made significant headway in putting these concepts into practice are Stuttgart-based Trumpf, Europe's biggest machine tool maker, J.C. Bamford Excavators of the UK, the construction equipment maker, and L.B. Plastics, a manufacturer of plastic components for windows and furniture with plants in the UK, the US and Germany.

The three companies are privately-owned, plough a large part of revenues into research and development and have distant horizons. Their respective chief executives (who in each case own the company) have been in charge for an average of 25 years, well above the norm for most parts of industry.

Berthold Leibinger, president and 75 per cent majority shareholder in Trumpf, would probably take around £100m should he ever decide to sell up. Sir Anthony Bamford, JCB chairman, has a £10m home in Gloucestershire and flies around Europe in the company helicopter. Leon Litchfield, who has run L.B. Plastics for 40 years, likes to relax on his £12m sporting estate in Scotland.

In the case of Trumpf, its main products are sophisticated cutting and punching machines which use lasers rather than conventional tools.

The company started moving towards a greater degree of product standardisation six years ago, after realising that it was spending too much time on 'customising' machines to meet particular needs, and in the process making the systems too costly and complex. Following a design and production rethink in the early 1990s, the company now raises about 60 per cent of its revenues from a family of six machines, roughly half the number of the late 1980s.

Each system within the same family is built to the same basic design to simplify manufacturing and reduce costs while permitting optional variations to be added at a relatively late stage in the production process.

According to Leibinger, who joined Trumpf as an apprentice in 1950 and bought out the previous owner in the 1970s, the reduction in costs would not have been possible without a 'master plan' for the design of each new product which brings together engineering, production and marketing specialists.

The rethink, he says, has involved much effort persuading Trumpf's engineers that it is equally rewarding intellectually to work on 'standards' as on the 'specials' that involved tackling one-off problems.

At JCB, one of Britain's biggest privately-owned manufacturers, the effort at 'mass customisation' is best seen in its 'special products' group, one of its fastest growing divisions. Based in Cheadle, Staffordshire, the division was originally an archetypal 'backroom' operation. It was started in 1986, says Sir Anthony, largely as a service to customers who wanted something slightly different from JCB's standard construction machines.

But it has since evolved into 'company within a company', turning out a stream of products developed specifically in response to customer requests and termed 'standard-specials'.

The division had sales last year of £62m, or roughly 9 per cent of JCB's total revenues. Most of the growth of the 'special products' business has been in the past four years, in which output has increased from 1,200 machines in 1992 to an expected 4,000 this year.

Jim Edwards, who has run the division since its inception, says his staff must listen to customers about new product possibilities – but must restrain their inventiveness. 'We have a drawerful of ideas but try to direct them as much as we can to the existing five [product] families.'

L.B. Plastics, based in Nether Heage, Derbyshire, has annual sales of about £60m, three-quarters of which come from 'standard' products – including systems of PVC components for double-glazing and furniture kits. The company has 60 per cent of its 850 employees in the UK, with other plants in Germany and the US.

Much of the company's sales growth has stemmed from a decision more than 25 years ago by Leon Litchfield to steer away from the jobbing-shop mentality favoured by many small plastics businesses.

Started in 1956 by Leon Litchfield's father, its first products included plastic-covered clothes lines, curtain rails and plastic toys. It launched its first system of plastic components for knock-down furniture in 1968, and 11 years later introduced the 'Sheerframe' system of plastic window parts which can be tailored into products for specific retailers and customers with fairly small changes on the production line.

Litchfield is currently looking at plastics-based replacements for steel, which would be strong and rigid, yet cheap and corrosion-resistant. 'I'm still looking for new products,' he says. 'It's inconceivable that all the new ideas are exhausted.'

Source: Financial Times, 21 August 1996

8B

Chains on 'mass customisation'

Peter Marsh reports on a technique set to become an important strategic tool for industrial companies

David Cotterill likes frightening his customers. He is not a mobster but chief executive of Manchester-based Renold, one of the world's leading makers of engineering chain sold to a range of industries including automotive, shipbuilding and food-processing.

Part of the company's marketing strategy is to instil a sense of worry into businesses about the consequences of them buying cheap components from other chain suppliers that are more likely to break.

'You can buy chain from all kinds of places,' says Cotterill. 'But you're not going to put your cheap chain on [machinery in] Space Mountain in Disneyland, nor in a bottling plant that you're concerned about. You know if it breaks you're in deep shit.'

Renold's marketing efforts, backed up by production disciplines based on cutting lead times and being more responsive to customers, seem to have paid off.

This week the company unveiled pre-tax profits for 1995 up 61 per cent from the previous year, with the figures rising from £11.6m to £18.8m, on sales 21 per cent higher at £179.3m.

Renold is among the world's five biggest makers of engineering chain. The two top players in the sector are Tsubaki Moto of Japan and Rexnord, part of the BTR industrial group. Of Renold's total sales, about 60 per cent is from chain and the rest from other engineering components such as gears and rotors.

Chain is among the best examples in engineering of a simple product that is put to a huge range of uses – virtually anything which contains moving parts which need to be linked – and consequently has to be made in a large number of types.

It lends itself to ideas of 'mass customisation', in which manufacturing and marketing skills come together. The process is aimed at making products efficiently from a small number of basic components.

The batch runs must be small and the order turnround quick, to suit the sharply different and ever-changing needs of a large volume of customers.

'Mass customisation' – in the view of management gurus led by Richard Schonberger, the Seattle-based manufacturing consultant – will in the late 1990s be one of the most important strategic tools for industrial companies as markets continue to split and customers become more demanding.

In Renold's case, it makes chain sold in thousands of variations, at prices varying from a few pounds to up to £25,000 for the chain used in big marine diesels and sold to companies such as Hitachi and Hyundai.

Other big purchasers include the Linde and Nacco lift-truck makers, and large car businesses such as Ford, General Motors and Nissan.

About half of Renold's products are made in the UK – where its biggest factory is at Bredbury, south Manchester – with the company's other main plants in Germany and France.

A key to the company's improved financial performance in recent years, after a gloomy period in the late 1980s, has been better links between the marketing and production sides of the company.

'We've moved away from banging out products at high volume to asking customers what they want and operating plant flexibly,' says Tony Ward, Renold's operating director for chain products.

A case in point is the Bredbury factory, which makes a fifth of Renold's chain output and is its second biggest after the Einbeck plant in Germany.

While Einbeck contains a large amount of automated machinery for turning out chain of the same basic type in relatively high volumes, the accent at Bredbury is more on making large, heavy chain to customer specification. Often, the plant makes chain in one-offs, using what amounts to a jobbing-shop mentality.

The work boils down to assembling a fairly small number of welded and machined metal components into a large range of chain types.

Cotterill, who joined the company in 1992, indicates that when he arrived he was not over-impressed by the Bredbury plant. This opened in 1990 and is the group's showpiece for 'cell production' techniques in which responsibility for manufacturing is devolved to workers in small teams. Between 1990 and 1993, the company invested about £8m on new machines for the Bredbury plant.

'The factory had wonderful new equipment that was not joined together,' he says.

Since then, in line with the increased accent on customer responsiveness, spending on capital equipment has been cut back, and the company has concentrated on adapting the equipment to make output more flexible. According to Cotterill, customer orders for standard products, which do not need new design work, can be met in five days, compared with more than a month in 1991.

And this focus on listening to customers, he hints, can be profitable. A company that wants a special chain delivery urgently – say for a ship's engine that has just broken – and finds it can be met in days rather than weeks, is not going to worry too much about the price.

Source: Financial Times, 12 June 1996

8.1 Describe what you understand the term 'mass customisation' to mean, and state its main purpose.

8.2 Identify the type of organisation which would be able to engage in mass customisation and try to think of some specific examples in addition to those given in the articles.

8.3 Outline, from both the manufacturer's and customer's point of view, the advantages and disadvantages of mass customisation.

8C

Corel confident of a perfect repackaging

By Bernard Simon

Senior executives of Corel, the Canadian software maker, were at WordPerfect's offices in Orem, Utah, last Friday for a burst of corporate cheerleading to welcome the word-processing software group into the Corel fold.

Corel, which brought WordPerfect in January from Novell, the networking software specialist, is eager to show WordPerfect's 600 employees, as well as sceptical outsiders, that the deal has the makings of an exciting and rewarding partnership.

Over the next few weeks, each WordPerfect employee will be linked to head office in Ottawa by Corel's new video communication system, which includes a small camera mounted on every PC monitor.

Nor is Corel wasting any time applying its vaunted marketing skills. A renamed and repackaged Corel WordPerfect is to be launched within the next few weeks. 'It's going to be supported by megabucks of advertising,'' promises Mr Michael Cowpland, Corel's founder and chief executive. More ambitious co-operative ventures are in store later in the year.

Corel's efforts underscore the high stakes riding on its new acquisition, both for WordPerfect and itself. The Canadian company needs WordPerfect to help broaden its base. Its flagship product, the popular CorelDraw graphics software, made up 74 per cent of sales, totalling US$196.4m, in the fiscal year to November 30.

Corel has left few stones unturned in perfecting and marketing CorelDraw in the six years since it was launched. 'The only things left for them were acquisitions or new products,' says Mr Tom Astle, analyst at Midland Walwyn in Toronto.

For WordPerfect, the arrival of a new parent offers hope of rejuvenation. WordPerfect remains one of the most popular word-processing programs, but has steadily lost ground in recent years, notably to Microsoft Word. Its business version, PerfectOffice, has market share of only about 5 per cent, versus more than 90 per cent for Microsoft Office.

Novell bought WordPerfect two years ago for $1.4bn, but received only $116m – excluding the value of licensing agreements – from Corel. This made it Corel's biggest shareholder, with a 16 per cent fully-diluted stake. Mr Cowpland says Novell 'really wasn't promoting [WordPerfect] strongly in the past 18 months'. Its Windows 95 version, WordPerfect 7, is due for launch in April, six months behind the comparable Microsoft product.

Corel appears to be better placed than Novell to revive WordPerfect. 'There's a much better culture fit with the folks at Corel than there ever was at Novell,' says one WordPerfect employee. While Novell's customers mainly comprise staid information technology specialists and engineers, Corel is driven by the pizazz of the retail market.

Mr Cowpland, a fast-talking Englishman with a collegiate management style, first came to prominence in the 1970s as co-founder of Mitel, the telephone equipment maker. His lifestyle is epitomised by a convertible Porsche with the registration COREL.

Advertising outlay made up 28 per cent of Corel's 1995 sales. While revenues rose 19.5 per cent, advertising spend shot up 72.8 per cent to $55.1m.

Mr Cowpland says this year's advertising budget will top $100m. The company spends heavily on sports sponsorship.

Concern about Corel's prospects has grown recently. Disappointing shipments of a new CorelDraw version designed for Windows 95 pushed the company to a $1m loss in the final quarter of fiscal 1995, compared with earnings of $11.2m a year earlier. The WordPerfect purchase has failed to revive Corel's share price, which has slipped to C$14.25 on the Toronto stock exchange, from last year's peak of C$26.62.

WordPerfect and PerfectOffice sales were US$400m in Novell's latest fiscal year, ended October 31. But first-quarter revenues this year were only about $50m. 'If they get $150m from WordPerfect this year, they'll be lucky,' says one analyst, who has told clients to steer clear of Corel.

Stronger results are likely over the next few months. But analysts caution against reading too much into the performance. Earnings are likely to be buoyed as the new versions of WordPerfect and PerfectOffice are pushed into the distribution pipeline.

Concerns about WordPerfect include the high proportion of users who still use the old Dos operating system and are not expected to upgrade to Windows or Windows 95 soon. They also worry that Microsoft might try to outflank Corel by bringing out a graphics product to take on CorelDraw.

Mr Cowpland dismisses these fears. He predicts that, with proper marketing, software users will better appreciate WordPerfect's superior features – for example, the one-tenth point increments in its font sizes, versus Microsoft's one-half point increments.

The new Corel WordPerfect will be more than a word processing programme. Starting with WordPerfect 7, extras are likely to be added to the traditional word processing package, such as a Netscape Internet browser, and various multimedia and graphics products. PerfectOffice may include Novell's electronic publishing and workgroup-sharing software.

As for the danger of Microsoft entering the graphics market, Mr Cowpland says that 'they'd have to buy a product that we've already demolished in the market place'. In any case, he expects any foray by Microsoft on to Corel's turf to be delayed at least six months by US antitrust scrutiny.

Even sceptical outsiders temper their concerns with respect for Corel's marketing flair and youthful energy. 'There is great leverage [in the WordPerfect deal],' Mr Astle says. 'They could make us all look silly.'

Source: *Financial Times*, 6 March 1996

8.4 Produce an up-to-date report on the situation between Corel WordPerfect and Microsoft Word.

8.5 In light of your findings above, use the product life cycle concept to illustrate Corel WordPerfect's current position.

8.6 Bearing in mind your response to 8.5, suggest ways in which you should now target, position and support Corel WordPerfect.

Royals consider radical changes to monarchy

By David Wighton, Political Correspondent

The Royal Family yesterday confirmed that it was considering radical proposals to modernise the monarchy but constitutional experts attacked suggestions that its public funding might be scrapped.

Plans being discussed include an end to the 300-year-old ban on the monarch marrying a Roman Catholic, reducing the number of family members involved in public duties and allowing women equal rights to succeed to the throne.

Senior family members and their advisers are believed to be looking at the future of public funding of the monarchy after the present arrangements expire in 2000.

But there is no suggestion they are considering changes to the monarch's powers to appoint prime ministers and dissolve parliament.

The discussions are taking place against a background of increasing political pressure for further reform and declining public support following two high-profile royal divorces.

While Buckingham Palace would not comment on particular proposals, it confirmed that 'strategic issues' were discussed at regular meetings between senior family members and royal advisers. It said no decisions were 'imminent'.

Downing Street said no officials had been involved either from the prime minister's office or the Cabinet Office. Buckingham Palace pointed out that significant reforms had been introduced since 1992, when the Queen agreed to pay income tax and the number of family members receiving public funds from the Civil List was reduced.

Buckingham Palace would not comment on suggestions that it was considering the scrapping of all public subsidy in exchange for the return of former crown lands now run for the exchequer by Crown Estates.

It seems unlikely that this would be acceptable to parliament given that last year the Crown Estates generated income of £94.6m, compared with total state funding for the royal family of £55m. Civil list funding amounted to just £8.9m.

The suggestion was attacked by Mr David Starkey, a constitutional historian at the London School of Economics, who said it would amount to 'the biggest privatisation of them all'.

He said: 'The obvious disadvantage is that the public functions of the Royal Family would not be recognised. With the Civil List, they are paid public money for doing public duties.' He added that returning the crown lands would make the Royal Family more like any other noble family, living off its estates. Lord St John of Fawsley, a constitutional expert and former Tory cabinet minister, said allowing Catholic marriages would not require severing the link with the Church of England.

The Queen is thought to be keen that the monarch remains head of the Church of England, although Prince Charles has suggested the link is outdated.

Source: Financial Times, 20 August 1996

A future for the monarchy

For the royal family the 1990s have so far proved a dismal decade. The breakdown of the marriages of the monarch's two eldest sons, played out in vivid detail by an unforgiving, and often hostile, press has been corrosive of the popular esteem on which the monarchy depends. Public confessions of adulterous relationships have turned private lives into public property. The Queen is now obliged to seek the protection of the law to shield her family from prying camera lenses.

No one doubts that she is still held in immense personal affection by her subjects. The same opinion polls which show that the institution has been tarnished point to undiminished respect for the monarch herself. Prince Charles, as heir to the throne, has been more subject to criticism but there has not been any measurable upsurge in republicanism. A large majority would still prefer a fallible king or queen to an elected president.

The passing of the age of deference, however, has inevitably raised broader questions about the proper shape and role of the British monarchy. There is recognition also that its historic grandeur often seems at odds with the nation's diminished role on the international stage. The news therefore that the Queen and her advisers are engaged in a strategic review to equip the monarchy for the 21st century is welcome. So too are the directions in which the review seems to be heading.

Public interest

By limiting the privileges of royalty to the monarch's immediate family, the Queen would buttress an earlier decision to restrict access to the Civil List, the taxpayers' contribution to the institution. A tighter net would also allow the personal indiscretions of 'minor royals' to be dismissed as of no public interest. The system works in the Netherlands, shielding Queen Beatrix from the colourful personal lives of relatives.

Scrapping the Civil List entirely would be more problematic. If the nation wants a monarchy it should be prepared to pay for it. And if ending Civil List payments meant returning to the Queen and her successors some of the much larger income from the Crown Estates which now flows to the exchequer, the exercise would be cosmetic.

Need of reform

There is an unanswerable case, however, for an end to the medieval practice which confers precedence on male over female heirs to the throne. The nation no longer needs a king to lead it on the battlefield. Few of her subjects would understand if in preparing the monarchy for the next century, the Queen defended a principle which so needlessly discriminates against women. There would be implications obviously for the House of Lords, but that institution anyway is in need of reform.

The 1701 Act of Settlement which bars the heir to the throne from marrying a Roman Catholic is a similar hangover from history. It derives from an age when protestantism and Englishness were deemed indivisible. Three hundred years on, it is offensive to Catholics and irrelevant in a plural, and increasingly secular society.

Since the Catholic hierarchy has relaxed its rules, there would be no theoretical bar on the child of such a mixed marriage becoming, as monarch, the head of the Church of England. In practice, revocation of the Act would provoke a public debate about eventual disestablishment of the Church. There are arguments on both sides, but there should be nothing for the monarchy to fear from such a debate.

There is no suggestion that all or any of these reforms are imminent. The cogs still turn slowly in Buckingham Palace. Significant reform would probably also need to await the outcome of the general election. The national mood too will be important. But the Queen has grasped the point taken some time ago by her fellow monarchs in Northern Europe. Traditional institutions survive and prosper when they adapt to a changing world.

Source: Financial Times, 20 August 1996

8.7 Accepting that 'The Royal Family' (TRF) is a powerful brand name consider the following issues:

- In PLC terms, where do you think TRF is currently situated? Justify your view with supporting arguments.
- What shape is TRF's PLC?
- TRF has responded to external pressures and is trying to re-position its brand. Identify the old and the new position and discuss the impact this has on TRF's marketing mix options.
- Identify how TRF has attempted to extend the product line length and depth.
- Identify how TRF managed its portfolio in terms of filling the product range, deleting old products, launching new products and cutting costs.
- Using a marketing approach, what would you advise TRF to do next in order to repair its battered image?

8F

Skoda's sales drive is no joke

Diane Summers on the Czech company's use of the Volkswagen connection to reposition its Favorit brand

Why does a Skoda have a heated rear windscreen? So you can keep your hands warm while you're pushing it. The Skoda has all the charm of the typical eastern European product in the British mind – a dubious car of comical design, renowned only for its joke status.

The complete repositioning of the brand, which Skoda is currently bravely attempting, must amount to one of the most daunting marketing challenges of recent years.

The impetus for Skoda to attempt the seemingly impossible comes as a result of Volkswagen taking control of the Czech company three years ago and, in the UK, the establishment last year of Skoda Automobile UK, a new wholly-owned subsidiary to import the cars.

The old Estelle model – the traditional Skoda of the joke – was superseded by the Favorit in 1989, and, over the past three years, Volkswagen has been further improving the specification and quality control of the Favorit range (priced between £5,600 and £7,700). Skoda proudly quotes a recent BBC television programme which gave the Favorit a test drive and found it 'completely free of rattles and squeaks'.

Skoda has never had more than 1 per cent of the UK car market – now the objective under the new Volkswagen management is to increase that share to 2 per cent by the end of the decade.

Robin Woolcock, managing director of Skoda Automobile UK, had no illusions about the magnitude of the job: 'It was clear to me very early on that this was a major marketing task. It wasn't about distribution strategy or retailing capacity – it was about changing the perception of a company that had come to epitomise eastern Europe.'

In the UK, the brand is a victim partly of its own success: the jokes exist because Skoda has a considerable presence in the market. Elsewhere in western Europe, the jokes would be meaningless and have therefore not taken root, says Woolcock.

A tight marketing budget meant that objectives had to be clearly defined and focused. With no marketing department, Woolcock's first stop was a market research consultancy called Quadrangle, which carried out qualitative studies among three groups: current Skoda owners; 'susceptibles' who might be persuaded to buy a Skoda; and 'rejecters' who would be unlikely to purchase.

Simon Lidington, a Quadrangle partner, discovered there was nothing odd about Skoda owners. 'They were just normal people who were characterised by being honest, straightforward and disliking hype. They had a very clear-sighted view of the kind of purchases they wanted to make, wanting to pay no more than they needed.'

Skoda owners loved their Skodas and had even come to love the jokes, says Lidington. The only problem was that there weren't enough owners, which is why the next group, the 'susceptibles', became so important.

Susceptibles were 'attitudinally similar to Skoda owners', found Lidington. 'They had been put off by the jokes and by their lack of awareness of the Favorit. If conditions were right, and they felt other people weren't going to laugh at them, they'd jump at the chance of owning a Skoda.'

Working alongside Lidington was the advertising agency GGK, whose job it became to develop a strategy for awakening the interest of the susceptibles. Steve Green, a GGK director, discovered it was not enough merely to point out the merits of the Favorit to potential purchasers.

'There was such a huge dissonance between what people – even susceptibles – have in their head about what Skoda is and means, and what we were presenting to them,' he says.

The most important lever has turned out to be the fact that Volkswagen – with its strong reputation for quality – now controls the company, says Green.

'The Volkswagen connection lit lights, hit the spot. People immediately latched on to it. It allowed susceptibles a route into the brand,' he says.

Press, poster and television advertising – currently showing – has all led on the VW link. After an outlay of £6m on press and poster advertisements last year, and £4.5m for the current TV campaign, Woolcock believes the benefits are beginning to materialise: after the first week of TV adverts, dealers are reporting a 50 per cent rise in sales, he says.

The final ingredient in the campaign has been public relations. PR company Shandwick has the task of monitoring press coverage and listening out for the jokes. Journalists, comedians, disc jockeys and other careless Skoda joke artists are likely in future to find themselves threatened with a test drive.

Says Shandwick: 'We don't intend to overreact but if anyone does make an ill-informed comment about Skoda, we will be offering them an opportunity to reconsider their views. We're also trying to educate the public that we're not a soft touch any more – we're not going to lie back and take comments that affect the brand value.'

Source: Financial Times, 12 May 1994

8.8 **In terms of the diffusion of innovation, what type of customer do you think would typically be interested in the Skoda Favorit?**

8.9 **Now under the control of Volkswagen, how would you position the Skoda brand name?**

8.10 **At the date of this article, Volkswagen planned to double Skoda's share of the UK car market from 1 per cent to 2 per cent by the year 2000. Find out how they are progressing towards this objective and assess whether Volkswagen will be able to achieve its goal.**

8G

Channel battle with only one winner

The cut-throat competition between Eurotunnel and the ferries means more bargains for travellers, writes Charles Batchelor

Mike Allmond set off from London yesterday evening with his wife and nine-year-old son for their regular trip through the Channel tunnel to their cottage near Boulogne in France. Mr Allmond uses the tunnel most weekends and is one of 100,000 Eurotunnel customers to make at least six annual crossings.

As a Eurotunnel shareholder, Mr Allmond gets a 50 per cent reduction on the ticket price and is a dedicated user of the service after years of suffering what he describes as the overcrowding and inconvenience of the ferries.

He needs no convincing of the tunnel's attractions, but other travellers clearly do: from today, Eurotunnel, the tunnel operator, is seeking to lure extra customers with new discount fares.

Earlier claims that it would not descend to a price war have been dropped. The company is now slugging it out with the ferries in the bargain basement in an attempt to pay off its £8bn ($12bn) debt.

Holiday motorists from the UK planning their fortnight in the sun this summer will have an unprecedented choice of cut-price travel deals and duty-free offers. Travellers will also have the pick of up to 60 ferry sailings a day and more than 100 'shuttle' train departures through the tunnel.

Travel agents have welcomed the boost that the price cuts will give to the French holiday market, despite the fact that lower fares will mean lower commission earnings. 'If this were a normal year, I would be unhappy but France is struggling because of the strength of the franc. This will give France a kick-start,' says Mr Cris Rees, commercial manager for Thomas Cook.

The bargain tunnel price that caught the headline writers' eyes was the £49 per car offer available to day-trippers who are prepared to board the shuttle train at 6am and return by midnight. For those who want to leave home in daylight, the day-return price rises to £59.

At least a quarter of travellers who use the shuttle do so to buy duty-free or cheap drinks and cigarettes, frequently travelling from points as far away as Exeter, Manchester and Liverpool. 'We have expanded the market for duty-free trips,' says Mr Dominic Fry, Eurotunnel's communications director.

But the main target of Eurotunnel's present discount offer is not the 'booze cruise' voyager but the family holidaymaker. Such travellers are now being offered an economy fare of £109 if they are prepared to set off between 10pm and 6am, rising to £129 for travel after 6am, compared with the previous price of £266.

'The real meat is the two-week traveller,' says Mr Fry. 'People do go across on the shuttle for dinner in Paris but three-quarters of our customers are going on holiday.'

For the traveller who is prepared to book 14 days in advance, there is an Apex fare for £99, regardless of the time of day.

P&O and Stena, the tunnel's two main ferry rivals on the Dover–Calais route, have dismissed its latest price reductions. They claim that while some ferry brochure prices may be higher their special offers and in some instances their regular fares still undercut Eurotunnel.

'They've come down to the fares we were offering anyway and on the key fares we are still cheaper,' says Mr Brian Reece of Stena, which is offering a day-trip rate of £15 per car plus £1 per passenger until the end of June, when rates rise to £19 per car and £4 per passenger. For the two-week holidaymaker, Stena still offers the best rate of £98.

Meanwhile, P&O has a £16 fare for a car with driver for day trips. Its standard return fares start at £149 but are now approaching their high-season rates of £225.

Ticket prices help to persuade travellers to choose either tunnel or ferry but duty- and tax-free sales provide another important incentive. Eurotunnel, which is not allowed to sell duty-free goods on its trains but can do so at its terminals, slashed prices by one-third last September.

It has expanded the duty-free sales areas at its terminals and introduced a range of VAT-free items as well. A litre of Gilbey's Gin sells for £4.65 compared with the average high street price of £14.15.

Once on the shuttle train, the traveller experiences a very spartan service, waiting in or beside his car in a brightly lit aluminium box, although Eurotunnel is considering installing interactive terminals to allow travellers to place duty-free orders.

But the ferries too are continually improving the quality of service. Stena is spending £8m on upgrading the Stena Emperor, which is to be moved from the Baltic to the Channel next month.

But financing these improvements is difficult while the ferry companies remain locked in competition with each other. As a result, P&O, which claims 33 per cent of the Channel market, applied to the government last month for permission to reopen talks about merging its cross-Channel operations, but denied it had a specific partner in mind.

Stena, which would be an obvious ally, says it has no need of a partner following the end of its long-standing agreement with SNAT, the French state-owned ferry company.

But the ferry companies will not be able to continue indefinitely with the present number of daily sailings. P&O's first-quarter earnings were badly affected by competition from the tunnel, and both companies depend on duty-free sales rather than ticket revenues for any profits they do make.

Eurotunnel has stopped publishing market-share figures because they caused disputes with ferries over accuracy but it does still claim 'undisputed' leadership of the market. The ferries say the tunnel peaked at 45 per cent of traffic at the end of last year and has since fallen back to 35–40 per cent.

Both the ferries and the tunnel have plenty of spare capacity, provided their pricing policies can persuade more travellers to use them at quiet times. Because it has to share capacity in the tunnel with freight services and the Eurostar long-distance expresses, Eurotunnel is restricted to four departures of its car and passenger shuttle trains an hour but says that is sufficient.

For the ferries the opportunities to make further price reductions while maintaining profitability have probably been exhausted. But the tunnel, which cost a lot to build but is relatively cheap to run, could reap benefits from attracting more travellers with additional fare cuts. There is a good chance that the discounts on offer for the summer will be continued into the autumn.

Source: Financial Times, 1 June 1996

8.11 How would you categorise the cross-channel travel market in PLC terminology?

8.12 As a late entrant to the market, how can Eurostar position its brand against its established competitors?

8.13 As the cross-channel travel market has massive over-capacity what future can you see for both categories of operators, tunnel or ferry, other than a continual price war?

8.14 As a ferry operator wishing to move the battle away from price, and bearing in mind the PLC position, how can you position your service against Eurostar? A perceptual map may be helpful here.

9

New Product Development

Organisations need a constant flow of new products in order to stay competitive and to continually grow sales and profit revenues, yet the path is littered with casualties.

Too many new products are introduced on the basis that the firm has to utilise excess capacity, or because 'the MD wants a new product'. This apparent disregard for attention to customer needs, is probably the reason for a commonly quoted figure, that 90 per cent of new products fail to reach their potential, i.e. recover development, launch and promotion costs and make a profit.

NPD success depends to a great extent on industry sector. It is far easier to launch a new product which utilises similar manufacturing technology, components, existing distribution channels and customer service skills than it is to develop something totally innovative. Consider the introduction of mountain bikes against the legendary Sinclair C5 vehicle. The mountain bike is indeed a new product, designed to do different things, accept rougher treatment, yet utilising many of the same components of the traditional cycle and sold through similar outlets. The Sinclair C5 was a totally new travelling concept which had peculiar manufacturing requirements, high customer information services and a less than obvious place in the distribution network. Should it be sold in a cycle shop, a car dealership or a motor-cycle outlet?

While never proposing to be a panacea, utilisation of the eight-step new product development process helps to avoid such difficulties.

In order to successfully complete the tasks in this chapter you will need to be familiar with:

- external environment/STEP analysis;
- consumer behaviour;
- product life cycle;
- eight-step new product development process;
- new product classification;
- new product failure;
- R&D management.

Kangaroo and ostrich good enough to eat

By Peter John

Skippy, the television marsupial, must be turning in his grave. Kangaroo meat could be on British school dinner menus shortly.

Freedown, an importer of exotic foods, says the phone has not stopped ringing since the government announced a link between BSE and its human equivalent last week.

Mr John Bengué, one of the company's two partners, says that education authorities in Dorset and central London had expressed an interest in finding a substitute to beef.

'It's been mayhem. We have been inundated with calls and, from a turnover of around £50,000 last year, we are now projecting annualised sales of some £300,000.

'Discussions with local councils are at very early stages but education officials are definitely interested.'

Freedown was established two years ago by Mr Daniel Russell, to market the venison produced by his brother's farm in Blandford, Dorset.

Soon afterwards, Mr Russell expanded into kangaroo, which he imported from Australia. Then, with Mr Bengué, he moved into ostrich, emu, wild boar, bison and crocodile from Zimbabwe.

The partners, who claim to be the UK's biggest importers of exotic meats, have been selling mainly to wholesalers. The remaining 50 per cent goes directly to retailers, restaurants and mail order customers.

They have already had an approach from a division of Whitchurch, the meat processing group, which is looking at supplying ostrich burgers – an established delicacy in South Africa – to offset some of the damage to its sales of traditional burgers.

A move into the school dinners market is a little further off. Even so, Mr Terry Thomas, the contracts officer for Dorset County Council, said: 'We have to look very closely at price and acceptability, but we don't rule out anything.'

Mr Thomas is responsible for providing around 15,000 meals a day. He says pupils are 'voting with their feet' and demand for beef products has tumbled.

But whether West Country fifth formers are ready for crocodile casserole remains to be seen.

Source: Financial Times, 29 March 1996

9.1 You work for Freedown and yesterday you were called to Mr Bengué's office where you learned of this article. As a newly appointed marketing assistant, you have been invited to a brainstorming session, which is trying to think of ways of encouraging customers to try your new products. In your work group you need to:

- Put yourself in the place of a customer and try to think what your reaction might be to being offered exotic meats.

- Consider whether any concerns you might have are based on fact, knowledge, emotion or fear. Also identify ways in which the marketing effort can help to change attitudes towards the consumption of exotic meats.

- Identify the current PLC and NPD stage for Kangaroo meat and discuss the impact this will have on marketing mix options.

Air bags blow new life into packing group

By Peter Marsh

An environmentally friendly technique to protect fragile goods from damage using plastic air-filled pillows is breathing new life into a small Midlands packaging company.

The pillows – a cross between flattened balloons and blown-up plastic sausages – are the invention of Coventry-based Amasec.

They are made at the rate of 1,000 an hour using special machines devised by the company and being sold or rented across Europe by Storopack, a German packaging group.

Each miniature air bag is about the size of a postcard. They are used to fill the voids in packaging cartons which are conventionally filled with polystyrene chips – materials falling out of favour on ecological grounds. A new European Union directive on reducing packaging waste has put further pressure on companies to move away from polystyrene.

Mr Barry Lobbett, one of Amasec's two directors, said the potential market for the machines was 'limitless'.

The 20-or-so users across Europe include Sony and Toshiba, the large Japanese electronics companies, SmithKline Beecham, the drugs and consumer products maker and glass group Edinburgh Crystal. Others include New Wave Logistics, a Japanese distribution company owned by the NYK shipping line, and Makita, a big Japanese machine tool company.

Britain each year gets through a mountain of polystyrene chips estimated at 15m cu ft – enough to fill St Paul's Cathedral – and worth about £7m. Not only are these chips notoriously messy, they are hard to recycle.

In contrast, the air-filled pillows, each costing about 0.5p, can be pricked like a balloon after use to produce, as waste, flat plastic sheets which are easy to reprocess.

The pillows – subject to worldwide patents taken out by Amasec – work out roughly half as expensive as the comparable amount of polystyrene, according to the company.

Amasec, whose main business is contract packaging for a range of customers, and has annual sales of about £300,000, devised the machines after receiving inquiries from companies anxious to get rid of polystyrene chips on environmental grounds.

They were designed by Mr Wilf Watkins, a former engineer at tractor maker Massey Ferguson and the father of Mr Dave Watkins, another Amasec director.

'I gave my father the idea and three days later he came up with the drawings,' said Mr Dave Watkins.

The pillows – which emerge from the machines joined to each other like a string of sausages – are made from polyethylene sheets filled with compressed air and with the joints between each 'sausage' sealed using thin strips of heated metal.

Ecologically minded companies in Germany, Switzerland and Denmark are expected to show special interest.

Source: Financial Times, 28 February 1996

9.2 **In terms of 'newness to company' and 'newness to the market', how 'new' do you think this product is?**

9.3 **What were the external pressures which encouraged Amasec to develop their air-filled pillows?**

9.4 **Do you think that Amasec should continue to manufacture the air-pillow as part of their contract packaging activities? Justify your response.**

An element of cash sought for kettle project

Radical plans are afoot for the common kitchen appliance

A small company is appealing to the venture capital industry for help in developing a flat heating element for kettles – to sit under the kettle rather than be immersed in the water.

Deeman, based in Winsford, Cheshire, plans a plant that would make flat heating elements using techniques borrowed from powder metallurgy and high-tech steel-making.

Flat elements are being studied by many European kitchen equipment makers including Philips of the Netherlands, Moulinex of France and Pifco of the UK as a way of increasing kettle sales throughout the world.

World sales of electric kettles have grown rapidly in recent years to a retail value of about £450m a year, with most of the growth coming from continental Europe. Of the 15m to 20m electric kettles sold each year, about a third find homes in the UK.

The new elements would be stuck to the underside of kettles, replacing the conventional, immersed elements which collect scale, look unsightly and make the kettle hard to clean. There have been health scares about the effects of the metal in the elements on the water being boiled.

Deeman's elements are made by spraying a nickel-chrome powder on a substrate and arranging for heat to be conducted across the kettle base through an electrical insulator.

It is thought that they could be made for just more than £1 each in full-scale, automated production, little more than the cost of an immersed element made from wire packed into thin steel tubes.

Flat elements are seen by big kettle makers, which also include France's Tefal, as vital to furthering the evolution of the kettle from a device mainly used for tea-making in Anglo Saxon countries to a general purpose kitchen tool.

According to industry estimates, sales of kettles could quadruple in the next five years if they could be made more appealing to consumers by omitting the immersed element. Apart from heating water, they could be used for preparing a variety of liquid foods such as soup.

The Deeman elements use about 10 per cent less energy than conventional elements. If fitted to all the kettles in the UK's 22m homes, they would save an estimated £35m a year in energy bills.

Deeman expects that heating elements could be used not only in kettles but have a range of other applications, from electric cookers to de-icing aircraft wings.

Mr John Crathorne, the chief executive of Stoves, a cooker maker based on Merseyside, said: 'I have studied Deeman's ideas and they are extremely interesting, though in my opinion they need some years more work.'

Deeman's techniques are not, however, the only ones being studied in the kitchen appliance industry.

It is believed that Philips and Pifco are fairly far advanced with alternative concepts for developing flat heating elements on the undersides of kettles, using thick-film printing techniques of a kind used in semiconductor and ceramics manufacturing.

Meanwhile, a number of Chinese kettle manufacturers are thought to be waiting in the wings. They have been scouting in recent years for opportunities to make products in Asia and sell them in large volumes in Europe.

Mr Inglo Bleckmann, the chief executive of Bleckmann, a leading European heating systems maker in Salzburg, Austria, interested in working with Deeman on its technology, said: 'There are about 15 Chinese companies keen to get access to European technology and building up sales in Europe. The way for European manufacturers to hit back may be to turn to the high-tech kettles with flat elements.'

Philips – which makes 3m kettles a year from a plant at Hastings, East Sussex – is already selling kettles using a novel form of 'under-floor' heating element using technology supplied by Bleckmann.

Mr Francis Smith, the chairman of Deeman, is one of Britain's most noted industrial metallurgists.

A former head of research at British Steel's strip mills division, he recently retired as chairman of Mixalloy, a north Wales-based company which is a world leader in powder-metal techniques used to make industrial diamonds, and a part of the De Beers diamond and metals empire.

Deeman is talking to three venture capital companies about raising £1m for a plant, probably to be based in Cheshire, to turn out heating elements using its technology. It is also studying the Bleckmann approach of a joint venture.

Deeman's ideas are based on concepts patented worldwide by Mr Jeffery Boardman, an industrial engineer who is the company's technical director. It envisages sales of elements of £14m a year by 2000, by which time it reckons it could show a £5m pre-tax profit.

Source: Financial Times, 11 March 1996

9.5 In terms of 'newness to company' and 'newness to the market', how 'new' do you think this product is?

9.6 Would you regard Deeman as a company involved in continuous innovation, dynamically continuous innovation or discontinuous innovation? Justify your response.

9.7 What impact do you think the flat element will have on the kettle market?

Innovation roulette

How do you launch a new product while ensuring the old model keeps earning? Richard Gourlay reports

It is an uncomfortable dilemma for a company. If you do not innovate, old products will be overtaken by new technology. If, on the other hand, you introduce a new range it can cannibalise the old product. Even more likely, sales of an existing model can dry up overnight once word gets out that a new product is imminent.

Yet companies must innovate. If you are Microsoft introducing Windows 95, this is less of a problem. Its marketing muscle and industry dominance are such that it could endure a fall in sales of Windows 3.1. When BMW announces a new 7-Series, it has at least got sales of the 5-Series and 3-Series to tide it over should old 7-Series sales slow down.

This is not the case if you are a small one-product company, as SDX Business Systems was in 1991. When the management team, led by Frank Bretherton, bought the Welwyn Garden City-based company from Northern Telecom of the US it realised its digital telephone exchange had a limited life. But because the company had only one product Bretherton knew he would have to 'bet the company' when introducing the new exchange, called Index.

SDX's range of digital business exchanges was developed by STC, the UK telecoms equipment group, soon after the market for telephone equip-

ment was liberalised in 1982. But it had received little investment particularly after STC was taken over by Northern Telecom in 1991. Sales were £9m, the company was beginning to lose money and Northern Telecom decided to sell the company.

'We were a division of a division in Northern Telecom and the product needed development. It was a nine-year-old product and showing its age,' says Bretherton.

The product's potential and weaknesses were equally clear to Jeremy Cooke, who joined the buy-out team as marketing director. 'We were optimistic about what the product had achieved and what was in the pipeline,' says Cooke. 'But we knew we had to re-engineer the switch if the business was to have a life expectancy of more than four to five years.'

The company faced two problems. The first was how to squeeze a bit more life out of the old product through upgrades and additional functionality without diverting limited resources from the development of Index.

The second issue was how to develop the new system and market it without stopping the sale of the existing SDX system in its tracks.

It is a problem that will be particularly familiar to small technology-based companies. Modern management theory, backed by a body of research, suggests successful companies have a high rate of product innovation. This reflects the decreasing window of opportunity for new products before they are overtaken by new technology.

For small technology-based companies, product innovation is riskier than for larger competitors because they are potentially cannibalising a larger part of their product range.

'This is a common marketing issue for fast-moving consumer goods and durable goods,' says Hubert Gatignon, associate dean at Insead in Paris. 'In making the transition, it is best to attempt to differentiate and segment the market but if the product is late in its life cycle this might not be possible. In that case it is best just to try to penetrate the market as quickly as possible and that needs resources.'

SDX decided there was more to lose from an abrupt fall in sales of the existing product should it announce Index long before its launch than there was to gain from potential new sales later on.

It began to formulate a plan that called for complete secrecy.

Before anything else, Bretherton and his team needed to find backers. Formal venture capitalists had refused to back the MBO after consultants had described the existing SDX products as outmoded and expensive. Or they were demanding too large a slice of the equity.

Eventually the team found Maurice Pinto, a founder of Sea Containers, the Bermuda-based leisure and ferries group, who agreed to finance the £4.2m purchase in return for half the equity. Northern Telecom accepted deferred payment.

By November 1992 SDX had designed Index. It began a development programme that would take $2\frac{1}{2}$ years and involve 24 of the company's then 67 employees.

To finance the development budget the company needed to maintain the growth of its existing SDX range. The management team decided to bolt on additional functions to the SDX range by buying in software developed for it outside the company. Functions such as automatic call distribution, computer telephone integration and caller identification were added.

'We had to add value during a $2\frac{1}{2}$ year drought when we had no engineering resource because it was all focused on the development of Index,' says Cooke. 'We were extending the life of a dying product.'

It did the trick. While revenue growth from the SDX product was slowing, the added functions helped SDX's sales rise to £18.7m by October 1994.

As that year ended, the team began to realise just how risky the launch could be. 'We suddenly realised our sales of the old exchange system would dry up overnight because we were offering enhanced features at lower cost,' says Cooke.

'We were a one-product business in one market [the UK],' says Bretherton. 'It was tremendous technology but the question was: would it work.'

In order to test the new product while keeping it secret from its dealers, SDX paid £500,000 to buy a small installation and servicing company and put test models in sites such as the Port of London Authority.

It then developed a launch plan. This included telling the owners of the 35 approved resellers confidentially that the product would be launched at the UK's main telecommunications trade show in November 1995 and that no documentation, pricing details or name for the product would be available until the last moment.

Bretherton then took the dealers and the market by surprise by announcing the launch in mid-September.

SDX faced two remaining problems. What would happen if there was a bug in the Index product which led to its withdrawal? Unilever might have been able to survive the withdrawal of Persil Power after its disastrous launch when the new product was found to damage clothes. But for SDX, a product recall would have been terminal. 'We would have been deciding who should switch off the lights,' says Cooke.

SDX therefore decided to finance the build-up of stock of the old system at the same time as it was building up stocks of Index.

Its other problem was how to educate the resellers and the distributors in a very short time about a highly complex product. Cooke commissioned a multimedia publishing house to produce a 350MB CD-Rom encyclopedia of Index to act as an aide memoire and marketing tool for the promotion pack.

When Index was launched in September last year, it took resellers and competition by surprise. 'Usually dealers get wind of these things,' says Patrick Sparkes, managing director of Combined Communications, an independent reseller. 'The launch was one of the best-kept secrets dealers have seen in the telecommunications industry.'

Bretherton says the Index launch has gone smoothly and is being well received. The company has sold 300 systems. Sales for the company are heading for £31m this year, up from £24m at the end of last October, he says.

Now SDX is facing another dilemma – whether it should raise more capital to take the product to a wider market or link up with an industrial partner with greater marketing muscle.

Source: Financial Times, 23 January 1996

9.8 This article illustrates very clearly how difficult it can be to test market a product, especially in a highly competitive market. Having been successful once, SDX have now sought your advice on the following issues:

- Having placed deliberately misleading signals into the market regarding their product launch plans, how can SDX go about convincing customers that they are able to put **their** needs before their own in future?

- How do you think SDX's competitors will react to any future press release put out by SDX?

- While obviously very pleased with themselves at having 'pulled it off', how damaging do you think this article could be to SDX's future. What do you think they should do now?

Testing times

Drugs companies are being forced to become more efficient at drug trials, says Daniel Green

Drug testing can make or break a pharmaceuticals company. UK company Boots, for example, sold its drugs business in 1994 after the failure in the final stages of testing for its heart drug Manoplax.

US biotechnology company Synergen collapsed in the same year when its septic shock drug failed at a similar stage. Other biotech companies have succumbed to similar fates.

At the same time, the people good at running clinical trials can make fortunes for their employers. Every drug that reaches the top 100 best-sellers can count on eventual revenues of $1m (£600,000) a day. Since the lifespan of a drug is limited to 20 years of patent protection, each day cut from testing creates an extra day of patent protected sales. An extra week means a lot of extra revenue.

According to the industry-sponsored UK Centre for Medicines Research, it takes $11\frac{1}{2}$ years for a typical drug to pass through basic research, clinical testing and regulatory approval. The time needed for basic research may now be getting shorter, thanks to a better understanding of the structure and functions of drug molecules.

At the same time, regulators are working more quickly, partly under pressure from patient lobby groups and partly as a result of computer analysis of drugs trial results.

The net effect, according to Boston Consulting Group, the management consultancy, has been to increase the proportion of pre-product launch time taken up by clinical trials from 46 per cent in the 1970s to 55 per cent in the early 1990s.

Stuart Walker, director of the Centre for Medicines Research, says that drugs companies have woken up to the problem. 'The aim for the main companies is to cut the time a drug spends in clinical trials from almost seven years to five,' he says.

Yet clinical trials managers face increasing pressures to lengthen, not shorten, trials.

- Regulators demand ever more rigorous tests with more people and greater statistical reliability. According to Peter Farrow, senior director of European clinical development for US drugs company Pfizer, 'the average amount of data included in the submission to regulators is up four-fold over the past decade'.
- Pharmaceutical marketing departments want extra information about a drug's performance. If economic data show that a new drug can cut costs elsewhere in healthcare – perhaps in allowing a hospitalised patient to go home sooner – they can charge a higher price. They also want quality of life data. For an arthritis drug to be put in a hospital's list of first choice drugs, it is not enough that a patient has less pain and more mobility. The drug's effect must be

measured on scales that cover everything from psychological well-being to whether the patient can carry shopping home.

● Senior management wants to move into untapped markets with drugs for conditions that are poorly treated. But many of these 'new' diseases act slowly. Jörg Reinhardt, senior vice-president of international development at Swiss drugs company Ciba, says it can take two-and-a-half years to conduct a single large-scale trial on a disease such as Alzheimer's.

Fortunately for the industry, there is plenty of room for improvement, says one senior pharmaceutical industry watcher. 'They [drugs companies] have been inefficient in the past because they have been too successful. They have been able to make money without trying to become more efficient.'

At the core of the effort to improve is information technology. Reinhardt says a typical large drugs company spends £20m–£50m on information technology in capital costs alone.

The aim is to allow data to be collected electronically at the hospital. The data can then be transferred to a central location and analysed rapidly. The period between the end of a trial and the completion of statistical analysis can be cut from months to weeks. Reinhardt says the total time consumed by trials could eventually be cut by 20 per cent or 30 per cent.

In addition, fewer different trials are being conducted. National regulators are increasingly willing to accept results from trials held in foreign countries. Companies have found it cheaper to conduct all trials to the same standards, even if this means using higher standards than might be necessary in some markets.

The increasing importance of clinical trials has triggered the emergence of a new industry, contract research organisations (CROs), which specialise in running trials.

CRO sales are rising at 15 per cent a year, according to Boston Consulting Group. This year's revenues in the US alone will be $1.8bn. CROs are no cheaper than in-house drug development, says Farrow. But they are faster because the drug company does not need to recruit staff to run the trials.

To move beyond the changes that are already under way, both in-house drug developers and CROs are beginning to pick apart the components of clinical trials. Some changes are simply adopted from other industries. Walker says benchmarking – in which several companies' methods are compared to try to identify best practice – has caught on in the drugs industry as never before.

Elsewhere, the very basics of trial design are being questioned. Geoffrey Tucker, from the Department of Medicine and Pharmacology at Sheffield University in the UK, last year questioned the standard practice of recording the responses of patients to one size of dose. A range of doses, to try to take account of differences in the metabolism between individuals, might be more difficult medically and statistically, but it could be more economical.

That still leaves the question of whether to bother researching drugs in disease such as Alzheimer's, where testing can take much longer than with, say, antibiotics.

Increasingly, companies are taking the more difficult option, largely because areas that are easy to test are already crowded. Companies that do so ensure their portfolio of drugs in development is balanced by research where testing is quick, such as in cancer or vaccines.

The feeling in the pharmaceuticals industry is that the work on improving the efficiency of drug testing has only just begun. Information technology will continue to spread. Contracting out to CROs will gain further in popularity. The push into new diseases will redouble the emphasis on benchmarking. The reward for success is $1m a day.

Source: *Financial Times*, 11 January 1996

9.9   On the basis of the information provided in this article, conduct a full STEP analysis and rank each element identified in order of its impact on the industry.

9.10   Discuss how the views expressed in this article could change the shape and nature of the more traditional eight-step approach to new product development.

9.11   You are responsible for R&D in a large pharmaceutical company. You have been asked to draw up a presentation, identifying the advantages and disadvantages of using CRO's. Conclude your presentation with a recommendation on whether or not to use CRO's.

10

Pricing: Context and Concepts

Price is a multi-faceted weapon for the marketer and conveys much more than the simple amount of currency you will have to exchange in order to purchase an item.

In the premium branded product sectors, such as Rolex, Cartier and Porsche, it helps to position a product as high price is often associated with high quality. In other sectors, notably FMCG, travel and insurance, low price, or at least good value for money, is frequently the key determinant in the motivation to purchase.

A number of influences determine the scope within which an organisation can set its price, and these can be external or internal pressures. The classical demand curves put forward by economists suggest that as price decreases, demand increases. This, however, does not take into account the market situation. Price may have dropped because the market is saturated, therefore an increase in demand is unlikely to occur, although there may be potential to attract a more price sensitive segment of the market, but at decreasing gross margins. On the other hand, maintaining a high price not only suggests exclusivity, but it somewhat arrogantly sends out signals to the competition that you will fight to retain that position and puts your product at the top of the table for comparative purposes.

The key task for the marketer, is to shift the competition away from price-based tactics. Whatever you do with price, it is very easy for competitors to match and beat your offer, almost to the point of selling below cost – an unsustainable proposition. Reducing price is often a 'knee-jerk' reaction to declining sales or increased stock levels, yet it rarely produces long-lasting results.

In order to successfully complete the tasks in this chapter you will need to be familiar with:

- demand curves;
- price elasticity of demand;
- price sensitivity;
- customer's price assessment;
- market structure;
- external and internal influences on pricing decisions.

Philip Morris opens fight over US breakfast bowls

By Richard Tomkins

Philip Morris, the US tobacco and food group, yesterday set the scene for a price war in the US breakfast cereal industry by slashing the list prices of its cereal products by an average of 20 per cent.

The move came almost three years to the day after Philip Morris made a similar move in the US cigarette market, slashing the price of Marlboro and its other premium cigarette brands by nearly 20 per cent to win back market share from lower cost rivals.

The price war that followed so-called Marlboro Friday temporarily devastated tobacco industry share prices and profits, but Philip Morris eventually came out on top by gaining market share for its premium brands.

Philip Morris is one of the biggest breakfast cereal makers in the US.

Through its Kraft Foods subsidiary, it owns Post Cereal, which sells 22 cereals in the US under the Post and Nabisco brands – among them, Post's Grape Nuts and Nabisco's Shredded Wheat.

Breakfast cereals represent the biggest category in US supermarkets after fizzy drinks. Food industry analysts have long said that the sector could be ripe for a price war because the big brands face fierce competition from cheaper private-label products which have been gaining market share.

Until recently, the big cereal makers had adopted a policy of charging high prices for their products, but lowering effective prices to consumers with money-off coupons and special offers such as one free pack for every pack bought.

In 1994, the other big US breakfast cereal makers, Kellogg and General Mills, announced that they were cutting this promotional spending.

General Mills also trimmed prices, but Kellogg kept its prices the same: so in effect, consumers ended up paying more for Kellogg products at the check-out because there were not as many special offers.

Post Cereal said yesterday that it was also cutting back on promotional offers such as money-off coupons, but it would allow any Post or Nabisco coupon to be used for any Post or Nabisco cereal.

The price cuts will reduce the suggested retail price of most Post products to $2.99 for the popular sized pack. Previous prices ranged from $3.88 to $4.13.

Kraft Foods acknowledged that the price cuts would have a short-term impact on profits, but said it was making the sacrifice in the expectation of increasing volumes and, in the long run, generating better returns.

Kellogg said yesterday that it would continue its pricing strategy, making its decisions on a product-by-product basis. General Foods could not be contacted for comment.

Source: Financial Times, 16 April 1996

Kellogg joins price war in US breakfast cereal market

By Richard Tomkins

The price war in the US breakfast cereal market escalated yesterday as Kellogg, the biggest cereal company, slashed the prices of some of its top-selling products by up to 28 per cent.

The company tried to put a positive spin on the cuts, announcing them with a fanfare in New York.

But they were seen as a defensive move following steep price cuts in April by Philip Morris's Post subsidiary, one of Kellogg's biggest rivals.

Kellogg acknowledged the price reductions would result in a slump in earnings per share from 77 cents to 45 cents in the second quarter to June, and said it expected earnings per share for the full year to be no higher than last year's.

US cereal companies' share prices fell as Wall Street responded to the threat of tumbling profits. Kellogg was off $2\frac{7}{8}$ at $72 in early trading, General Mills fell $1\frac{5}{8}$ to $55\frac{3}{4}$, and Ralcorp, a large maker of private label breakfast cereals, dropped $\frac{7}{8}$ to $23\frac{5}{8}$.

Separately, Ralcorp announced it expected profits to fall this year because of the 'negative pricing trends'. It said it was cutting 100 jobs as part of a plan to trim costs by $25m–$30m a year.

Kellogg said prices to retailers would fall by an average of 19 per cent on brands comprising about two-thirds of its US business. It said the price of Kellogg's Frosted Flakes, its best-selling product in the US, would fall 18 per cent.

The company said it would also cut the distribution of money-off coupons. Only 2 per cent of the coupons printed were redeemed, it said.

Mr Arnold Langbo, Kellogg's chairman and chief executive, said the price cuts had been made possible by cost savings achieved through a global streamlining initiated last year. This included a 15 per cent cut in the US workforce.

However, Mr Langbo acknowledged that the company had also seen a fall in its market share since the decision by Philip Morris in April to cut the prices of its Post and Nabisco branded cereals by an average of 20 per cent. Philip Morris also reduced the distribution of coupons.

US cereal companies have traditionally maintained high list prices for their products, but lowered effective prices at the check-out with coupons and special offers. Their change in strategy has been forced by increasing competition from lower-priced products and private label brands.

Source: Financial Times, 11 June 1996

Crunch time for US cereal makers

Consumers are tired of overpriced cornflakes, writes Richard Tomkins

If you want to make an American shopper apoplectic, just mention the cost of cornflakes. The usual response is a tirade against the prices charged by the big breakfast cereal manufacturers.

Yet munchers of Cocoa Krispies, Grape Nuts and Spoon Size Shredded Wheat are finding themselves with less to complain about following the outbreak of a price war in the US cereal market. In the last few weeks, each of the three biggest cereal companies – Kellogg, General Mills and Philip Morris's Post subsidiary – have slashed prices in an attempt to win back fading consumer enthusiasm for their products.

The price-cutting bears the hallmarks of a similar episode the US tobacco industry that started with Marlboro Friday – the day in 1993 when Philip Morris cut the prices of its premium cigarette brands to regain market share.

Analysts say the big cereal manufacturers, like the big tobacco companies three years ago, are guilty of sheer greed. Over a period of many years, they have pushed up prices in the belief that consumers will go on buying their products on the strength of their brands.

The result of this policy is that branded cereals have become extraordinarily expensive in US stores. In a London branch of the J. Sainsbury supermarket chain last week, a 500g box of Kellogg's Corn Flakes was selling for £1.06, or $1.63 at current exchange rates. In New York, a 510g box of the same product was selling for $3.39 in a branch of the D'Agostino supermarket chain – at more than double the UK price per gram.

Significantly, not everyone pays such high prices. In an attempt to stimulate demand, cereal companies typically distribute billions of money-off coupons a year, enabling the thrifty to buy their favourite cereal at a discount.

The strategy, however, has failed. Infuriated by the high prices and constant coupon-clipping, US consumers have started turning away from cereals, either skipping breakfast or switching to alternatives such as muffins or bagels. In the year to April 22, US cereal sales fell 3.7 per cent to $7.85bn, according to Information Resources, a Chicago-based market research group.

Meanwhile, those consumers who still need their daily fix of flakes are saving money by buying

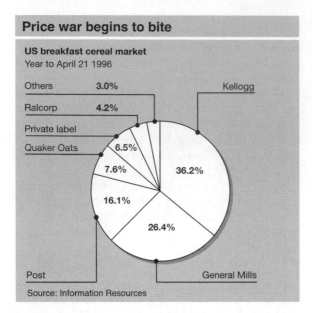

Price war begins to bite

US breakfast cereal market
Year to April 21 1996

Others — 3.0%
Ralcorp — 4.2%
Private label
Quaker Oats — 6.5%
7.6%
16.1%
26.4%
36.2%
Kellogg
General Mills
Post

Source: Information Resources

of Post and Nabisco products; earlier this month, Kellogg followed by cutting prices by an average of 19 per cent across two-thirds of its US cereal sales; and last week General Mills, not to be outdone, announced it was cutting prices by another 11 per cent on brands accounting for 42 per cent of sales.

The manufacturers' apparent objective is to fight off the challenge from private-label products and restore growth to the cereal sector as a whole. 'We believe the long-term benefits of these actions far outweigh their costs,' said Mr Stephen Sanger, chairman and chief executive of General Mills.

Yet the price war is hurting the participants. Kellogg said its earnings would dive from 77 cents to 45 cents a share in the second quarter to June, and that its earnings for the full year would be no higher than last year's. General Mills said the cuts would cut earnings by $30m–$35m, or about 20 cents a share, in its fiscal year ending May 1997.

Another victim is Ralcorp, a manufacturer of private-label cereals, which stands to lose some of the market share it has won. Last week it announced plans to cut jobs and production at one of its plants, and said it would take an undisclosed charge in the quarter to June.

No-one knows where the price war will end, but the size of the price premium still being charged by the big manufacturers suggests there could be more cuts to come. One Wall Street analyst, Mr Mark Altherr at Salomon Brothers, thinks one or more companies may even disappear before the war is over.

'There are basically too many cereal producers out there, and it may be that the end game in all of this is to get rid of somebody.'

Source: Financial Times, 27 June 1996

private-label products instead of branded goods. Defying the shrinking market, private-label sales rose 9.1 per cent to $514m in the year to April 21, says Information Resources – hardly surprising when a box of private-label cornflakes can cost half the price of the Kellogg product.

Two years ago, General Mills became the first big cereal company to respond to weakening demand when it announced it was reducing couponing and cutting the cost of its biggest-selling products by an average of 11 per cent.

Now, faced with declining sales, all the big cereal makers are cutting prices. In April, Post announced it was reducing list prices by 20 per cent across its range

10D

General Mills profit ahead 28% for year

By Richard Tomkins

A big rise in breakfast cereal sales helped General Mills, the US food company, report a 28 per cent increase in underlying net profits to $476m for its year to May 26. Earnings per share rose 28 per cent to $3, the company said yesterday.

The figures were in line with predictions by General Mills last week, when it announced that it was introducing a second round of price cuts in its breakfast cereals, following a first round two years ago.

General Mills also reiterated last week's warning that the latest price cuts would hit profits in the current year, reducing net income by $30m–$35m, or about 20 cents a share. Between 50 and 75 per cent of the impact would come in the first quarter, it said.

Last year's fourth quarter was the strongest of the year, General Mills said, with net losses of $13.3m the previous year turning into net profits of $77.5m.

Excluding restructuring charges in the previous year, earnings per share rose from 10 cents to 49 cents.

The profits growth was driven by a 13 per cent increase in sales to $1.38bn, with unit volume up more than 11 per cent.

For the full year, General Mills said its Big G cereals business led the company's performance. Sales and unit volume both rose by nearly 10 per cent, and its share of the market by volume rose 1.3 percentage points following the price cuts of the year before.

Source: Financial Times, 27 June 1996

Using the information presented in these four articles:

10.1 Identify and discuss the demand curve for breakfast cereals.

10.2 Identify and discuss the price elasticity curve for breakfast cereals.

10.3 Identify and discuss those factors which you think may influence price sensitivity in the breakfast cereals market.

10.4 How do you think the customer views the pricing tactics of the branded cereals manufacturers?

10.5 How may this influence their purchasing behaviour?

10E

BT seeks to make the most of its lower prices

Andrew Adonis reports on the tactics of telecoms companies as competition becomes keener

It is not just British Telecommunications hype. The telephone really is becoming steadily cheaper to use, particularly for business callers who clock up long-distance and international minutes. And prices are set to fall further as regulation and competition continue to bite.

This week's price cuts from BT mean that UK long-distance calls are barely a third of the cost a decade ago, allowing for inflation. From the end of this month a three-minute weekday morning call from London to Hereford will cost 30p. In January this year it was 50p.

Not all prices have come down. Line rental charges have risen 10 per cent in real terms in the past decade,

and will continue rising. Oftel, the telecoms regulator, supports BT's efforts to reduce its deficit on maintaining basic line connections. But it has forced the company to bring its call charges down sharply, reflecting the falling cost of delivering calls as new technology slashes overheads.

Oftel's price cap obliges BT to reduce its total charges by 7.5 per cent a year, once an increase for inflation has been allowed for. In round figures that equals price cuts worth £500m, with £100m recouped from a 2 per cent real-terms increase in line rental charges. BT is free to target the cuts as it chooses.

Mr Michael Hepher, BT's managing director, says three factors determine its price-cutting strategy.

Ideally, cuts will stimulate usage. They ought to give BT 'the most favourable stance against the competition' and they should 'do something to sparkle the imagination'.

The abolition of the morning peak rate earlier this year met the last two criteria. This week's abolition of the higher long-distance rate, at a cost of £244m over a full year, was firmly directed at the first and second – particularly at competition in the business market.

Mercury, BT's main competitor, has a quarter of the large business market and about two-thirds of the City of London's outgoing traffic. But it is increasingly hampered by BT's falling prices on one hand and by new entrants pursuing its bigger customers on the other.

The price gap between BT and Mercury is steadily narrowing in the business market. For many big businesses the saving is down to 6 per cent or less for UK traffic.

Mr Terry Rhodes, Mercury's competition director, said his company had to break out of the 'BT-but-cheaper' syndrome. He believes the message still has strong appeal to small and medium-sized businesses – those with annual telecoms bills of less than £150,000. But Mercury's efforts are shifting to building 'brand loyalty' through added-value business services such as network management and improved data telecoms links.

A host of new operators has moved into the City, the UK's telecoms honeypot, and targeting Mercury first and foremost.

The most successful to date appears to be Worldcom, a US group which set up in London in 1991. Worldcom re-sells international lines to big business at a discount. It boasts 250 business customers and claims to have cornered nearly 3 per cent of the UK's outgoing international telecoms traffic. Mr David Hardwick, managing director, said: 'Our marketing is based on 10 per cent to 15 per cent off Mercury's best business price.'

Worldcom is also about to enter the small and medium-size business market, and plans to offer a long-distance UK service in addition to its international service, interconnecting to existing long-distance networks.

MFS, another US group, is already active in the UK long-distance business. Launched in March this year, MFS offers free line rental to customers with usage bills of £600 or more per line per year. Its fibre network covers most of the City and Docklands and is being built out to Southwark and Westminster. The company is considering a plan to extend the network to the Thames Valley, putting MFS within reach of 35 per cent of the UK's big telecoms users.

Long-distance telecoms capacity is abundant, giving plenty of scope for re-sellers to expand. In addition to BT and Mercury, Energis, a subsidiary of the National Grid which has erected a long-distance network on electricity pylons, is opening for business. The regional electricity companies covering Yorkshire and Manchester are building their own networks, and targeting business users.

Source: Financial Times, 2 September 1994

BT cuts prices to counter cable threat

By Alan Cane

British Telecommunications, the UK's largest telecoms operator, yesterday moved decisively to counter inroads on its profitability by cable television companies offering lower prices.

Only a fortnight after BT's annual results showed that cable operators – which are allowed to offer telephony in addition to television programmes – were hurting revenues and profits, the operator announced a package of price cuts designed to level the playing field.

It also announced the start of the much anticipated per-second pricing to replace the obsolete and complex per-unit system. Virtually all BT customers will be charged for calls by the second rather than by the unit from June 28, the company said yesterday.

Yesterday's package of price cuts was aimed chiefly at residential customers – the principal attraction is a weekend rate for local calls of 1p-a-minute including VAT.

BT said the effect of the cuts would be to reduce call charges by a total of £310m, equivalent to a 5 per cent decrease in the average phone bill.

Mr Don Cruickshank, director general of Oftel, the industry watchdog, welcomed both the shift to per-second pricing and the price reductions which will mean that BT will have exceeded its obligations under its price control agreement by more than £200m for 1994–95.

BT has been forced to cut its prices by more than £1bn since December 1993 because of controls which prevent it raising the price of a basket of services by more than the retail price index minus 7.5 per cent. Some £204m of the cut will come from a 9 per cent reduction in the cost of local calls with a further £98m spread among cheaper longer-distance UK calls and international call prices coming down £8m. A further £10m of the cuts will come from rounding call charges down to the nearest penny. The move to per-second pricing and the price reductions is partly a public relations exercise designed to persuade consumers that the telephone is neither a luxury nor as expensive as it is popularly perceived.

The Consumers' Association said yesterday that its computer analysis suggested cable companies were cheaper than BT even after the latest round of price cuts. According to the association, the average quarterly bill for the cable company Nynex is £54 compared with £72 for BT.

BT said that the Consumers' Association was comparing the best prices available from cable operators with BT's basic, or standard, prices. Mr Michael Hepher, BT group managing director, said in most cases its new prices would mean call charges would be close to, and in some cases cheaper than, cable operators' charges.

Per-second charging is simpler to understand than the per-unit system widely used by BT's competitors. BT has been unable to offer it before now because of the limitations of its remaining electro-mechanical exchanges.

● NatWest Group is outsourcing its UK telecommunications operations to BT in a deal worth £350m over five years.

Sixty-four NatWest staff will join BT on equivalent terms and conditions of service and BT will assume control of NatWest's internal network. It will provide an agreed level of service and manage relationships with NatWest's other telecoms suppliers, Mercury, Colt and Racal.

Outsourcing telecoms operations is becoming increasingly popular with large companies wishing to concentrate on their core business.

Source: Financial Times, 1 June 1995

BT claims cheap calls will devastate industry

By Alan Cane

British Telecommunications said yesterday that price controls proposed by the telecoms watchdog for the period after 1997 would result in lower call prices at the cost of a devastated industry.

In talking about a 'cash starved industry littered with business failures' BT made it clear that there remains a huge conceptual gulf between itself and Mr Don Cruickshank, the director-general of Oftel, the industry regulator.

It seems increasingly likely that BT will reject Mr Cruickshank's decision on how its prices should be controlled, leading Mr Cruickshank to refer the question to the Monopolies and Mergers Commission for adjudication.

To safeguard customers and promote competition, most of BT's prices are controlled by a formula (RPI-X) which is currently equal to the rate of inflation minus $7\frac{1}{2}$ per cent. Oftel's proposed price regime after 1997 is the rate of inflation minus between 5 per cent and 9 per cent.

BT said: 'There is no industry solution in the retail range of X, 5–9, that will not seriously damage newer entrants, service levels and choice to all customers.'

The reason is that BT's competitors compete chiefly on price with the dominant operator. If BT's prices are controlled unduly harshly, the profitability of the competitors is jeopardised.

Mr Peter McCarthy-Ward, leader of the BT price regulation team, said that Oftel's proposals did not reflect the growth of competition in the UK. In calculating a value for X it had wrongly estimated BT's cost of capital, the likely efficiencies the operator would be able to make and the growth of the UK market.

BT reiterated that it sees no reason to link the price control review with a general anticompetitive power Mr Cruickshank is threatening to write into BT's licence.

BT has consistently complained that such a power would leave it no final mode of appeal; Mr Cruickshank's answer is that present legislation does not allow him to offer such a process.

Mr Alan Whitfield, BT's solicitor, said he was sure a compromise could be agreed: 'There could be a temporary amendment to BT's licence which would fall away when the necessary legislation was passed.'

He said there was no reason why a referral to the MMC would prevent a deal with Cable & Wireless, if the current merger talks are successful. He agreed, however, that tough price controls could depress BT's share price and subsequently affect the price at which the deal could be struck.

Source: Financial Times, 30 April 1996

10.6 Using the external influences on a pricing decision (customers & consumers, legal & regulatory, channels of distribution, competitors, demand and price elasticity) as a framework, produce an analysis of BT's pricing policy.

10.7 Do you think BT's fears are real or are they just trying to generate publicity?

10.8 In a free market economy, why is it necessary to have price watchdogs such as Ofwat, Oftel, Ofgas, etc?

10.9 What market conditions do you think would have to be present in order for there to be no need for price watchdogs?

10H

Compaq launches cut-price challenge to competitors

By Christopher Parkes

Compaq, the world's leading personal computer maker, today presents a fresh challenge to its competitors with the world launch of a number of high-powered machines for business users at US prices 10–15 per cent lower than its previous range.

It will be the latest shot in a vicious computer price war which has undermined manufacturers' profits and knocked the US stock market. Compaq will today also start deliveries of the new range outside the US. Prices will depend on local market conditions but reductions are expected to be similar to those in North America.

'We are anticipating a reaction from competitors,' said Mr Lewis Schrock, Compaq's business product manager. 'But the cost and price savings have been designed into these machines from the ground up. It will be harder for them to come back at us this time,' he claimed.

New manufacturing processes had helped cut production costs at Compaq's factories in Houston, Scotland and Singapore by 17 per cent.

Retail prices for the most basic model, which includes a Pentium 100MHz microprocessor, start at $1,100 (£705) in the US. One leading US mail order supplier was last week still offering a 75MHz Compaq Deskpro business computer for $1,499.

The top of the new range, equipped with Intel's Pentium Pro 200MHz chips, are expected to sell for $4,800.

The introduction, just before the group is expected to release flat results for the three months to the end of June, completes a revamp of Compaq's marketing and model range.

It comes a week after Dell, Compaq's closest competitor and the leading direct marketer of PCs in the

US, reduced prices on its business computers for the third time this year.

Although aggressive pricing has long been a characteristic of the PC market, the pace and range of cuts has been stepped up by manufacturers anxious to boost slowing sales to business customers.

Compaq, which yesterday also announced reductions of up to 23 per cent on its existing business machines, revived its falling revenues in the quarter to the end of March by slashing 20 per cent off most prices.

However, such tactics have hit margins and earnings across the industry, and a nervous Wall Street was rattled further when Hewlett-Packard recently reported slowing sales.

In the past few weeks Compaq has introduced enhanced models for the consumer, laptop and network server markets which will be managed as distinct market segments. The new Deskpro range completes the process.

Source: Financial Times, 22 July 1996

10.11 **Identify advantages and disadvantages of mounting a market challenge in this way.**

10.12 **What effect (if any) do you think this will have on existing Compaq customers and their loyalty to the brand name?**

10.13 **Do you think Compaq's move will significantly improve their market share? Justify your response.**

10.14 **What type of pattern can you see emerging in Compaq's behaviour?**

10I

When there is room for negotiation

Hotels may do a price deal, says Scheherazade Daneshkhu

If you thought bartering was something you only did in a souk for a souvenir, think again. It seems that business travellers are bargaining their way into cheaper hotel rooms, too.

A clutch of surveys shows that you need never pay an advertised room rate. According to Pannell Kerr Forster, a consultancy, the average discount on published room rates at four and five-star hotels in Europe last year was 33.4 per cent on advertised prices.

Discounting works for the hotels as well. Last year they had to offer favourable rates and pursue volume business such as groups and tours, the consultants said. According to the survey, average room occupancy rose 6.7 per cent last year compared with the previous year to 67.3 per cent.

The survey converts room rates into D-Marks and found that the average achieved room rate across Europe, as opposed to the official rate, declined 1.5 per cent to DM206 (£92). But getting a discount depends on where and when you are travelling: Pannell Kerr found that discounting was less widespread at the top end of the market in Paris and London, the two most expensive European cities. The best discounts were at off-peak periods.

After Paris and London, Moscow and Geneva were the priciest cities. In Paris, the average achieved room rate was FFr1,182 (£151) a night. In London, the average price paid was £106, while in Manchester, the cheapest of the 26 cities surveyed, the average rate paid was £51 a night. After Manchester, the cheapest rooms were to be found in Birmingham, Helsinki and Lisbon.

The largest discounters were in Athens, Brussels and Helsinki, which all discounted by an average of between 46 per cent and 50 per cent on the published room rate. Although London emerged as the second most expensive European city for quality hotels, it also offered some of the biggest discounts, depending on the hotel.

Hotels at business destinations tend to employ fewer staff per guest than at the very top end of the market – a consequence of further cuts in staff last year due to the recession. In cities where business travellers predominate, such as Birmingham, Frankfurt, Helsinki and Stockholm, the number of staff per guest room was much lower than the European average staff to room ratio of 0.73. The highest levels of service were at the luxury end of the quality London market, where guests are pampered with a ratio of 1.84 staff members to guests.

The 55 London hotels surveyed, which included the Savoy group, Copthorne Tara, Holiday Inn Mayfair, the Marble Arch Marriott, the Gloucester and the Selfridge, were divided into three categories based on price. The upper tier comprised hotels that secured an average rate of more than £155 a night last year, while prices paid on the third and lowest tier averaged less than £105 a night.

The survey found that the lowest tier offered average discounts of up to 48.5 per cent on its official rates, a discount level second only to hotels in Athens, which gave average reductions of up to 50 per cent. On the other hand, discounting at the top end was very low with an average of only 7.3 per cent.

'The indicators are that in the corporate meeting, groups and incentive market that London has regained its popularity as a destination, although there is still sensitivity to rate as London competes with other international destinations,' said Mr Chris Cowdray, general manager of the Churchill Inter-Continental hotel.

There will always be rooms for those with more to spend. London's luxury hotels still seem to have been able to increase prices this year, says Arthur Andersen, the accountant and business adviser.

Its survey of 18 five-star hotels showed that average occupancy was up to 65.3 per cent in the first quarter of the year compared with 62.8 per cent in the same period last year. Average daily room rates also increased to £146 from £138. The survey found that smaller hotels were charging higher average room rates than larger competitors.

Surprisingly, another survey last week found that London hotels are among the cheapest in the world. Hogg Robinson, the business travel agent, found in its survey of prices in the first third of the year that at an average paid room rate of £83.43, London emerged cheaper than Zurich, Geneva, Frankfurt, Basle, Brussels, Düsseldorf, Copenhagen, Amsterdam, Stockholm and a number of other European cities. Unlike the other two surveys, however, it did not confine its research to the top end of the market.

But the trend to cheaper hotel rooms may have had its day. The rise in occupancy last year means that Pannell Kerr Forster is predicting that room rates this year will rise on an average across Europe.

Source: Financial Times, 26 June 1995

10.15 If it is common knowledge that nobody ever pays the proper rate for a hotel room, why do you think that hotels still advertise such highly inflated rates?

10.16 What effect might continual discounting have on a customer's perception of value, quality and style?

10.17 What external influences might affect a hotel operator's decision on whether or not to offer a discount?

10J

Low prices make cost of travelling light

Travel agents still have more than 1m overseas package holidays available for the summer season, writes Scheherazade Daneshkhu

Travel agents have more than 1m overseas package holidays unsold for the summer season, which extends to October, but expect not to have to resort to 'silly' prices to shift them.

'The market is better than people are suggesting,' said Mr Andrew Jones, marketing manager at Going Places, which is the second biggest tour operator.

'What's been new this year is the extended availability of low prices. There are quite substantial bargains available for mid-September,' he said.

The market this year has also been different from other years in the amount of 'tactical' discounting available.

This kind of discounting involves a special offer being made for a limited period – sometimes only one day – in order to encourage people to go to travel agents.

The number of late availability holidays has also been greater this year, according to Thomas Cook.

The western Mediterranean is almost sold out but there are still many holidays in Greece, Turkey and Cyprus to be sold.

'When Best Travel, which specialised in holidays to Greece, collapsed last year a lot of tour operators rushed in to increase their share of the market, but the volume just hasn't been there,' said one travel agent.

Thomson, the biggest tour operator, this week revised its estimate of a 5 per cent growth in the sale of summer holidays to no change from last year.

It said that higher than expected discounting was proving necessary to achieve late sales but added that the price at which it had been selling holidays this month had been higher than in July.

It has stopped advertising its late availability holidays because of a rise in demand.

Going Places, which is owned by Airtours, the second biggest tour operator, is advertising one week September holidays to many parts of Greece and Turkey from £179. Lunn Poly, the biggest travel agent, has halved the price of air fares to Dublin to £49.50 per person for September to October departures.

It is also offering £100 off brochured First Choice and Sunworld holidays but stopped guaranteeing free child places on Sunworld holidays last night.

The heaviest discounting is on holidays immediately prior to departure but travel agents do not advertise these deals.

There has been a growing trend towards late booking, which travel agents are keen to discourage.

Lunn Poly is promising a 10 per cent discount as well as free child places to those who pre-register for a summer 1996 holiday, the brochures for which are due out on September 1.

Meanwhile the English Tourist Board said yesterday that Britain was enjoying its best ever summer tourist season.

'The continuing fine weather has encouraged many more people to visit resorts in Britain, including people who have not taken a holiday in this country since they were children,' said Mr Stephen Mills, the board's assistant director of development.

Source: Financial Times, 18 August 1995

10.18 Identify the organisational objectives, marketing objectives and cost elements which might influence a travel agent's pricing decision.

10.19 Draw up an analysis of the benefits and drawbacks of very late bookings for both the customer and the travel agent.

10.20 Identify two different travelling scenarios – one where you would be happy to accept the consequences of a very late booking and one where you would not. Examine your purchasing behaviour and objectives in each of these situations.

11

Pricing Strategies

Within many markets, there are continual difficulties experienced when establishing prices. Financial pressures of profit, margins and cash flow, conflict with marketing objectives of share, position and volume. If your firm is the market leader, then there are the additional considerations of whether you should lead the market in price changes or allow a competitor to make the first move. Pricing truces are common, even to the point of manufacturers being put under pressure to refuse to supply retailers who won't 'come into line' with pricing policies.

Pricing policies help to convey an impression of quality and a policy of continual low prices tends to damage a firm's reputation and image. It is unusual for someone to buy anything at full price from MFI. If you wait just a few days, it is virtually guaranteed that there would be another 'fifty per cent off everything' announcement. The MFI cycle of continuing 'sales', while obviously effective at the outset, is now very difficult to break.

High prices can be sustained with products which are new to the market, and which attract the type of consumer who is willing to pay the premium to have something just that little bit different. High prices are also essential to allow the firm to recoup development, testing and launch costs. This is known as a skimming pricing policy, where profits are 'creamed' in the early stages of a product's life. Skimming is often followed (in varying time scales, depending on the product) with penetration pricing. Here the key objective is an increase in market share and mass exposure. Penetration, or market share pricing is most common in sectors where demand is either reaching, or has reached maturity. The product life cycle is a useful tool to remember when looking at pricing policies, as there are major links between the stage of a product in the life cycle and the strategies which are appropriate for that stage.

In order to successfully complete the tasks in this chapter you will need to be familiar with:

- conflicting price objectives;
- market dominance;
- pricing methods;
- pricing strategies;
- pricing adjustments.

Esso serves its competitors a 'good sweating'

The oil company's low price policy may help it claw back market share from the supermarkets, writes Robert Corzine and Neil Buckley

Esso, the UK subsidiary of Exxon, one of the world's largest oil companies, acted true to its heritage on Wednesday when it switched to a low price policy to bolster its eroding position in the retail petrol market.

The company is a direct descendant of Standard Oil of the US, whose legendary founder, John D. Rockefeller, had a simple solution to falling market share: Give competitors a 'good sweating'.

Analysts were yesterday assessing the likely impact of Esso's decision to match prices at its 2,100 service stations, the country's largest retail network, with the lowest available.

On Wednesday Esso executives said they had 'no intention to undermine the market'. Nor did they want to start a price war.

The cheap petrol policy was a strategic response to a fundamental shift in the retail market, they claimed. Market research showed motorists are now prepared to drive further to buy cheaper petrol. Price, they said, is now the motorists main concern.

But some analysts yesterday saw Esso's move in a different light. 'Esso's target is the supermarkets,' said Mr Matthew Hall, an energy analyst at brokers SBC Warburg in London. 'But their victims are likely to be the independent retailers' who will find it hardest to withstand the falling margins which a price war will bring.

In the past few years supermarket chains have captured 22–25 per cent of the petrol market by offering fuel that is about 2p a litre cheaper than the big oil companies. They have done so by selling through 700 high-volume petrol stations, many located next to big out-of-town superstores that attract large numbers of shoppers and their cars.

Such sites have proved highly successful. As Sir Ian MacLaurin, chairman of Tesco, the biggest supermarket chain, points out: 'Where we have a superstore and petrol station next to it, we have a pretty captive marketplace.'

There have been charges and countercharges between the oil companies and supermarkets about predatory pricing and selling petrol below cost, but the complexity of the industry is such that there no definitive evidence has emerged.

Grocery retailers have a number of advantages over independent petrol retailers and oil companies. They can take advantage of a structural surplus of petrol in the UK and western Europe by buying in bulk, often from the refineries of the same oil companies with which they compete.

They can sell at low margins since the additional overheads involved in running a petrol station on an existing superstore site are small.

They also enjoy very high volumes. Mr Hall notes that the average supermarket site sells about 8m litres a year, compared with 3m–3.5m litres a year for the busiest oil company station and a national average of 2m litres a year.

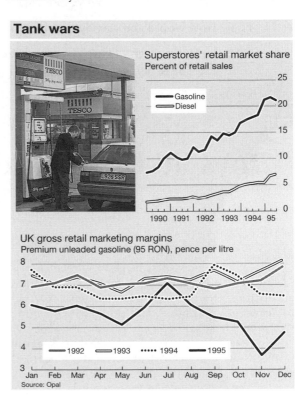

Tank wars

Superstores' retail market share
Percent of retail sales

UK gross retail marketing margins
Premium unleaded gasoline (95 RON), pence per litre

Source: Opal

Mr Ian Upson, Esso's managing director, says it is unwise 'to overplay the role of the supermarkets' in prompting Esso's move. But analysts say Esso, which is one of the lowest cost suppliers, must be worried about the longer-term intentions of the supermarkets.

The rate of new superstore building may slow due to tougher planning restrictions, but all the big four grocers – Sainsbury, Tesco, Safeway and Asda – are keen to open petrol stations on older superstore sites which do not already have them.

Sainsbury, with about 170 petrol filling stations and more than 4 per cent of the petrol market, announced plans last year to open 60 more. Tesco, with more than 230 superstore petrol sites and more than 7 per cent of the petrol market, has gone a step further by opening stand-alone petrol stations. These are independent of its superstores but have small convenience stores attached.

Tesco believes the format has the potential to be expanded nationally – putting further pressure on independent operators and oil companies.

But will Esso succeed in clawing back market share? One industry observer doubts the big grocery chains can be stopped. In France, he points out, they have captured half the retail petrol market.

Oil companies are challenging the grocers at their own game by opening convenience stores. Retail sales through forecourt shops in 1994 totalled £2bn, and are estimated to be growing three times faster than overall retail sales.

But industry observers say Esso's move is likely to depress already thin petrol retailing margins to the point where the smaller chains will consider whether the UK market, already among Europe's cheapest, is worth the effort.

Source: Financial Times, 19 January 1996

11.1 **Draw up a comparison of forecourt prices for the different types and brands of petrol in your area. Include Esso in your sample and produce a table of your results.**

11.2 **How truthful do you think Esso's statement is that they did not want to start a price war? Justify your response.**

11.3 **How would you classify their actions – financially, marketing or survival driven?**

11.4 **Looking at the retail petrol market long-term, who do you think will win? Provide arguments to support your decision.**

11B

Toys 'R' Us accused of acting unfairly towards US rivals

By Richard Tomkins

Toys 'R' Us, the world's biggest toy retailer, yesterday faced accusations by US competition authorities that it had used its market clout to force prices higher and stop toys reaching rival stores.

The Federal Trade Commission filed an administrative complaint against the company alleging it extracted agreements from toy manufacturers to stop selling certain toys to warehouse clubs, a form of discount store, because they were selling the items too cheaply.

But two of the five commissioners dissented from the decision to press charges, and Toys 'R' Us vigorously denied them.

Mr Michael Goldstein, chief executive of Toys 'R' Us, said he was 'astounded' at the FTC's complaint, which will be referred to an administrative court in the hope of obtaining an order against the company.

Toys 'R' Us, which last year had worldwide revenue of $9.4bn (£6.2bn), is the dominant toy retailer in the US, with 20 per cent of the market.

But in recent years it has faced a growing challenge to its reputation for low prices.

The competition has come from two main sources: discount store chains such as Wal-Mart Stores and Kmart, and warehouse clubs like Price/Costco, which reserve access to members who pay a fee.

The FTC said yesterday that membership clubs used to sell popular toy lines at substantially lower prices than Toys 'R' Us.

But as early as 1989, the FTC said, Toys 'R' Us started using its market power to extract agreements and understandings from manufacturers, under which:

● Manufacturers would not allow the warehouse clubs to buy the same toys that Toys 'R' Us carried.

● If such toys were supplied to warehouse clubs, they would have to be packaged as higher-priced 'specials' – typically, combinations of two or more items – that could not easily be price-compared with the Toys 'R' Us item.

● Manufacturers agreed to tell Toys 'R' Us which items they planned to supply to the warehouse clubs so that Toys 'R' Us could decide whether the sales posed a competitive threat.

'As a result,' said Mr William Baer, director of the FTC's bureau of competition, 'by 1994, most of the major US toy manufacturers stopped selling popular individual toys carried by Toys 'R' Us to the warehouse clubs.'

In a statement anticipating the FTC's complaint, Toys 'R' Us said on Tuesday it spent millions of dollars promoting toys throughout the year.

'The warehouse clubs then come during the six weeks before Christmas, without making any such investment, and select the few hottest selling items, selling them at or below cost to create customer traffic,' it said.

'Given that behaviour, and Toys 'R' Us's contribution to the industry, we have told manufacturers that we reserve our unquestionable right to refuse to carry the same items as warehouse clubs,' Toys 'R' Us added.

Source: Financial Times, 23 May 1996

11.5 How do you view the actions of Toys 'R' Us?

11.6 As the manager of a Warehouse Club which has been refused supplies because of this action, what would you do?

11.7 As a manufacturer of toys, you are likely to be the biggest loser in this argument, what can you do?

One in four pharmacies 'at risk'

By Christopher Brown-Humes

Up to a quarter of the UK's pharmacies and 3,000 jobs will be at risk if price-fixing on non-prescription drugs is abolished, pharmacists warned yesterday. The Community Pharmacy Action Group, citing independent research by accountants Deloitte & Touche, said more than 3,000 UK pharmacies could be affected.

The group was responding to an investigation into Resale Price Maintenance by the Office of Fair Trading and a high-profile campaign by supermarket group Asda to have RPM scrapped. RPM, a £1.2bn-a-year market, is Britain's last legal price-fixing arrangement, allowing manufacturers to set the shop prices of a range of health aids, cold cures and vitamin products.

The CPAG says that scrapping RPM would increase the burden on the National Health Service, push up travel costs, and hit vulnerable groups such as the elderly and people without cars.

'If a tenth of those who treat themselves with medicines bought from a pharmacy were to see the doctor instead, the annual cost to the NHS would be more than £4.7bn,' said Mr Tim Astill, a director of the

National Pharmaceutical Association. The CPAG also warns that pharmacies that survived would stock a narrower range of medicines. It claims that a typical pharmacy stocks some 700 lines – 10 times the number found in an average supermarket. Non-prescription drugs account for about 15 per cent of a typical pharmacy's turnover and about 22 per cent of gross profit.

Supermarkets have steadily lifted their share of non-prescription drug sales to 15 per cent – but pharmacies still have 70 per cent of the market.

One of the biggest problems for RPM supporters is the public perception that branded goods such as Lemsip and Anadin would be much cheaper if RPM was abolished. The CPAG accepts that savings of £180m could be achieved – Asda puts the figure at £300m – but says this is just £3 per person and is outweighed by the benefits of retaining it.

When the OFT last looked into RPM, in 1970, it said the system was in the public's interest. It is expected to report its latest findings in September. If it feels there is a case to answer, it will refer the matter to the Restrictive Practices Court, which has the power to scrap the system.

Source: Financial Times, 16 July 1996

11.8 Many products, including pharmaceutical items, are governed by resale price maintenance. If the Restrictive Practices Court decided to scrap the system, what do you think would be the outcome? Debate this from three view points:

- the consumer;
- the retailer; and
- the manufacturer.

11D

Potential cost of selling it cheap every day

Is Kingfisher's unexciting performance down to its strategy of permanently low prices, asks Neil Buckley

Is everyday low pricing the right retailing strategy for the 1990s?

Yesterday's relatively lacklustre UK results from Kingfisher – the Comet, B&Q, Superdrug and Woolworth group – raises a question of growing interest to City analysts and competitors in the retailing industry.

Kingfisher unveiled a jump in 1993 pre-tax profits from £205m, before exceptional items, to £309.3m – apparently a strong performance. But much of the gain came from last year's £1bn acquisition of French electrical retailer Darty, without which earnings growth since 1990 would have been unexciting.

The blame in some quarters is being put on the strategy promoted by Sir Geoffrey Mulcahy, Kingfisher chairman, of cutting prices, which has resulted in lower margins but disappointing volume growth. Sir Geoffrey, however, is adamant that the approach is sound, but that it needs time.

'The combination of a shift away from promotions and sales to everyday low pricing, stronger merchandise ranges and significantly improved customer service generally resulted in promising increases in like-for-like sales,' he insists.

Everyday low pricing dates back to the start of modern retailing last century, to Woolworth's 'Five and dime' stores in the US or Marks and Spencer's penny bazaars in the UK. There have always been 'discount' retailers concentrating not on high margins, but on selling large volumes of goods as cheaply as possible.

What refocused attention on the potential of that approach in the late 1980s – especially in the US – was the huge success of discount chains such as Wal-Mart and Kmart, and other new formats such as warehouse clubs, or 'category killers' like Toys R Us, whose central philosophy is EDLP.

The theory is that in chains which tightly control costs, lower prices should increase volumes and market share, generating increased profits and buying power which can be used to cut prices further – the so-called 'virtuous circle'.

Other retailers experimented with a consistently low-price stance. The shift to EDLP was given further impetus in the US when the consumer goods giant Procter & Gamble decided in 1991 to adopt an EDLP approach in supplying retailers, ending 'trade allowances' – periodic discounts to retailers to allow them to promote brands at lower prices.

By mid-1992, one US survey found six out of 10 packaged-goods manufacturers and almost half of all retailers had implemented or tested EDLP.

Now EDLP, value pricing, or 'investing in margin', are becoming buzzwords among UK retailers – partly in reaction to the recent influx of US and continental European discount formats.

Kingfisher has been the most vocal proponent, although Sir Geoffrey's EDLP campaign kicked off in earnest only a year ago, with the introduction of permanently reduced 'key lines' in his chains. Some retail experts support his claim that it is too early to judge the results.

They argue customers are slow to pick up the low-price message on high-ticket products purchased only infrequently – such as those in Kingfisher's B&Q DIY chain or Comet electrical chain.

Critics counter that the results of EDLP should have been seen more quickly in lower-ticket chains such as Woolworth. They also point to the apparent success of EDLP elsewhere.

One example is Marks and Spencer, which has not referred to it as such, but which some analysts argue has effectively adopted an EDLP approach. Its 'Outstanding Value' campaign, launched in autumn 1992, froze the price of 75 per cent of its products, and reduced the price of the remainder.

The campaign brought a significant increase in volumes, attested to by M&S suppliers, and a 21 per cent increase in profits in the latest half-year to £308m.

Moving to permanently low pricing has been central to the recovery of the Asda and Gateway grocery chains, after both ran into difficulties in the early 1990s. Asda was reported last week to be strengthening its commitment to EDLP with a call to its suppliers to move away from periodic discounts towards consistently lower prices.

Yet, strangely, a limited move to EDLP does not seem to have worked at the UK's biggest grocer J Sainsbury, which indefinitely cut the price of 300 own-label products accounting for 10 per cent of sales last October. The result, revealed in January, was a 0.4 per cent drop in gross margin and a 1 per cent underlying fall in sales.

Analysts suggest that Sainsbury's move, like Kingfisher's, suffered from poor marketing.

Yet both ran higher-profile campaigns than Marks and Spencer.

'I am still convinced EDLP will play a major role in UK retailing in the 1990s,' says Richard Hyman, director of retail research group Verdict. 'Kingfisher has taken an important step in introducing it into its corporate strategy.'

Whether or not such predictions come true, it is already clear that simply cutting prices may not bring customers streaming through the doors. Getting the range of products and customer service right, and effectively communicating the message to consumers, are an integral part of the process.

Source: Financial Times, 24 March 1994

11.9 **Draw up an analysis of those firms mentioned in the article which are involved in EDLP. Using just the views of your work group, place them on a price–quality matrix.**

11.10 **Which type of pricing strategy is EDLP consistent with?**

11.11 **Outline the advantages and disadvantages of following such a strategy.**

The price is right

UK car sales are rising on the back of manufacturers' discounts, says John Griffiths

The UK has become a lonely, glittering prize for Europe's recession-battered motor industry. Carmakers in continental Europe, surveying the wastelands of their domestic markets, where sales fell last year by up to a quarter, are casting covetous eyes at the one big market in Europe enjoying what now looks like strong and sustainable growth.

New car registrations in the UK increased by 11.6 per cent last year – far more than the industry dared to predict 12 months ago. Even pessimists in the industry now expect sales to climb throughout the year.

But the explanation for the British revival is not a straightforward tale of rising demand and suppliers rushing to catch up. Much of the sales growth has been the result of consumers being wooed as never before by carmakers seeking either to stem losses or hang on to profitability and to keep production lines going. With few signs of market recovery on the Continent, consumers can expect the wooing to go on.

The response of the consumer has caused some mayhem and not a little heartache among the big carmaking rivals. Where traditionally many motorists would stick with one manufacturer for a lifetime, they are now switching between makers according to which is offering the best deal.

'Today's customer has become mobile, choosy – and totally disloyal,' says Mr Alan Pulham, director of the National Franchised Dealers' Association.

The break up of customer loyalties is apparent in the Society of Motor Manufacturers and Traders' figures. Sales in relatively new market niches, particularly leisure four-wheel-drive vehicles such as Rover's Discovery and 'people carriers' like Renault's Espace, are still small but enjoying rapid growth.

Most spectacularly, those manufacturers which have established reputations for diesel models are enjoying a field day: diesel car sales last year almost doubled to 340,000 and they now account for one in five of new cars sold.

Mr Tom Purves, managing director of BMW (GB) says that the German executive carmaker had expected to sell 1,200 of its new diesel 3 and 5 series cars after their launch in the UK in the summer. 'We're past 1,800 and simply can't get enough.'

In such niche markets sales have risen unaided but in the mainstream the battle is being fought increasingly on price, with the biggest gains and losses in terms of sales last year correlating closely to the size of the discounts being offered.

Ford, once the market leader, is now struggling to maintain its pre-eminence, trailing behind both Vauxhall and Rover in December's sales figures. Last Spring, it cut the price of its new Mondeo saloon by an average of 6 per cent only a fortnight after launch. Subsequently sales revived.

At the same time, sales figures for last year have dispelled any suggestion that, as Japanese makers Nissan, Toyota and Honda strengthened their manufacturing capacity in the UK, they would push aside all other competitors.

The Japanese manufacturers are enjoying healthy growth – but having to invest as heavily in marketing as everyone else. Sales of Japanese models in the UK rose by more than 15 per cent last year.

In common with other manufacturers, the Japanese companies are having to fight much more strongly than they expected against some of the Continental manufacturers who were expected to be among their early victims.

A rash of well-received and competitively priced new models, combined with improved quality, successful marketing and generous offers on after-sales service, has led to companies such as Fiat, Peugeot and Citroen enjoying some of the best sales figures for any manufacturer last year.

Sales of Fiats, for instance, which had been falling in the UK since the late 1980s, increased by 38 per cent last year. The company was helped in particular by the introduction of the tiny, Polish-built Cinqueconto, which set the pace for a new generation of urban runabouts and which virtually no other European maker can yet rival.

The ferocity of the fighting for supremacy which waged throughout last year – and which can only intensify in the absence of any significant Continental market upturn – has led some in the industry to question whether the recovery is as strong as it appears.

In carefully-timed broadsides just before and during the London motor show in October, Mr Pulham, whose NFDA members sell four-fifths of all new cars, accused manufacturers of desperately trying to preserve market positions by 'forcing' the market.

He said dealers were being pressurised into registering cars for which there were no final buyers in order to qualify for manufacturers' sales bonuses. By intensifying the downward pressure on prices, he argued, the practice was having an adverse effect on dealers, and because of the knock-on effects in the second-hand market, ultimately on the motorists as well. According to Mr Pulham, August alone saw at least 40,000 such cases.

Such attacks on the tactics of carmakers may be prompted partly by dealers' self-interest. More than 2,000 dealerships have gone bust or changed hands in the past two years of recession, as sales margins have been squeezed. Meanwhile, the leading manufacturers are dismissive of the impact of their attempts to increase sales, saying 'pre-registering' has been part of the UK car market scene for years.

In addition, industry analysts such as Garel Rhys, professor of motor industry economics at Cardiff Business School, estimate that the net effect of pre-registration is probably only a slight over-statement of the new car market's size. Year-on-year comparisons hold good and yesterday's statistics are a fair reflection of the trend, he believes.

But another grievance of many dealers may prove of more significance: that the interests of individual consumers are being threatened by the practices of carmakers which sell direct to large fleet operators, bypassing the dealer networks.

The NFDA says that such deals, which can involve discounts of 35 per cent or more, now account for more than 300,000 car sales a year – nearly 20 per cent of the total. As recently as the late 1980s, such deals were rare.

The figures highlight the enduring popularity of the company car, many of which are now supplied from fleets, in spite of the progressive erosion in the past decade of their tax advantages. The latest changes to the company car tax regime, which come into effect on April 6, are expected to be broadly neutral.

The NFDA maintains that the discounts offered to fleet buyers have to be paid for somehow – and that small company buyers and private motorists are subsidising them. New car list prices could be cut by 5 per cent if such deals were outlawed, says the NFDA. But the association is not optimistic that its call for such practices to be outlawed will be heeded.

Such disputes over practices, however, cannot disguise a new found ebullience among both those who sell as well as make cars. This year, says Mr Ernie Thompson, the former Ford director recently appointed chief executive of the Society of Motor Manufacturers and Traders, sales should rise further by nearly 100,000, to 1.86m.

'To put that into perspective, it is still 20 per cent down on the 1989 peak,' he says. But for many dealers, the fact that the British recession is history will be enough.

Source: *Financial Times*, 9 January 1994

11.12 Why is there no such thing as a fixed price? Illustrate your answer using the car industry as an example.

11.13 Assess the impact that Daewoo has had on its entry into the UK market.

11.14 Through their actions, car dealers effectively control pricing in the market. What is your view on this?

11F

Reflections on price stickiness

A more competitive environment could alter the way companies set prices. By Robert Chote

Britain's industrial policy has undergone a subtle shift of late. Ian Lang, the trade and industry secretary, has quietly jettisoned the strategic interventionism favoured by his predecessor and said that he seeks above all else to promote domestic competition.

We have heard this all before. Whether the government should tenderly nurture national champions or let rival producers slug it out in home markets is a long-running debate. Indeed, the two alternatives seem periodically to swing in and out of fashion.

The first question to ask is which alternative is more likely to breed companies that are best placed to compete in an unforgiving global marketplace? On this, Lang's instincts are well placed. As management guru Michael Porter argued in *The Competitive Advantage of Nations*, world-beating companies often get up to scratch only by operating in an atmosphere of fierce domestic rivalry. But this is much easier to achieve in industries where economies of scale are relatively unimportant than, say, the supply of gas to residential customers or the production of jumbo jets.

A decision to promote domestic competition may also have macro-economic consequences, perhaps affecting inflation by altering the way in which firms set prices. An article in tomorrow's *Bank of England Quarterly Bulletin* sheds light on the way companies set prices in Britain.

The article describes the results of a survey of more than 700 companies carried out by the bank last autumn. Almost 40 per cent of the companies questioned said they set prices at the highest level they thought the market would bear. A further 25 per cent said prices were set in relation to their competitors'. In contrast, some 37 per cent said they set prices by adding a fixed or variable mark-up to their costs of production.

The survey asked the same question in a different way by asking firms to rank in order of importance a series of theories which sets out to explain why prices in the real world appear to be sticky. This suggested a greater role for cost-based pricing than the other question had, especially among small firms for which the expense of monitoring market conditions is relatively burdensome. The most popular theory was one suggesting that firms *do* change prices in response to fluctuations in market conditions, but only to a limited degree because their costs do not rise much as they increase output.

Next most popular after the cost-based theories was one based on companies' desire to avoid price wars. Under this hypothesis, businesses are reluctant to change their prices even in response to changing costs, fearing their competitors will follow suit and – in the case of a price cut – trigger a downward spiral.

One would expect policies that promoted competition to encourage market-based pricing at the expense of cost-based pricing. Competition should also reduce the size of the mark-up that companies

The ups and downs of companies' prices

% of firms citing given factor as most important reason to change price

Factor	Rise	Fall
Material costs	64	28
Rival price	16	36
Change in demand	15	22
Prices never change	4	12
Move in interest rates	3	1
Change in market share	2	11
Change in productivity	1	3

Source: Bank of England

(% of companies)

Number of price changes during the year: Over 12, 5 to 12, 3 or 4, 2, 1, 0

can sustain. This is difficult to assess, but some clues emerge from a recent study of mark-ups in the manufacturing sectors of industrial countries carried out by the Organisation for Economic Co-operation and Development. This suggests that the highest mark-ups have been whittled away in most countries in recent years, perhaps because greater openness to trade has made competition tougher.

Interestingly, the pattern of mark-ups from industry to industry has changed little since the 1970s. High mark-ups remain most prevalent in industries such as tobacco products, industrial chemicals, drugs, medicines and computers, and radio, television and communications equipment. Mark-ups are relatively low for textiles, food, printing, electric machinery and motor vehicles.

Mark-ups are higher in those industries comprising relatively few competitors than in those with many. They are also higher in industries in which companies produce differentiated products rather than homogeneous ones. But this does not mean that high mark-ups are necessarily a bad thing. They may provide a reward for expensive innovation.

A fall in mark-ups as a result of increased competition would have a direct, albeit temporary, effect on inflation. Greater competition might also reduce the danger that inflationary shocks become embedded in an upward spiral of wage and price increases – studies show that trade unions are much less successful in boosting pay when employers are under pressure from rivals. Greater competition might also affect inflation if it altered the relative stickiness of prices upwards or downwards.

Conventional wisdom has it that companies are much less willing to cut prices than to increase them. The Bank of England did not test this explicitly in its survey, but it did confirm that such decisions would be taken according to different criteria. Almost 65 per cent of companies said that rising raw material prices were the factor most likely to prompt a price increase, but only 28 per cent said that a fall in the cost of materials would lead to cuts. Changes in rivals' prices or the state of demand were more likely to trigger cuts than rises.

Downward price stickiness becomes more of a problem when inflation is low, because the relative price changes needed to signal scarcity or oversupply are more likely to demand that the prices of out-of-favour goods fall in cash terms. When inflation is higher, the price of out-of-favour goods can continue rising, only less quickly.

The psychological barrier against price cutting has clearly been weakened by the recession and by the continued mood of bargain consciousness among consumers during the recovery. But the fact that three times as many companies told the bank they never cut prices as said they never raise them, suggests it has by no means been eliminated entirely. This remains an obstacle to moving from what has been an era of historically low inflation to one of effective price stability.

A concerted effort to intensify product market competition would presumably help to weaken resistance to price cuts, and thereby help that transition. But the bank's survey suggests it would also encourage companies to review their prices more frequently and to change them more frequently, too. A more competitive market might therefore be one in which companies are quick to raise prices at any chance they get.

Source: Financial Times, 13 May 1996

11.15 **It is generally thought, that more competition produces a better deal for the consumer. With your knowledge of pricing objectives, strategies and tactics, discuss this article in your work group. Outline the benefits and drawbacks of increased competition with particular reference to pricing policies.**

12

Marketing Channels

Getting a product or service to the target market in an efficient and effective manner is the result of good channel design.

Many questions have to be answered such as 'can we distribute this ourselves, and even if we can, should we?' Intermediaries are often viewed simply as middlemen taking an unwelcome cut in the profit margin. However, for reasons of market coverage, value added at the distribution point and services offered to the manufacturer/supplier, intermediaries are more often than not, a vital link in successful channel management.

For many products, intermediaries are vital. For example, if you wished to buy a diamond ring you wouldn't telephone Consolidated Gold Fields in South Africa with your specification for size of stone and weight of gold! You would normally make the purchase at the retailer level, realising that the raw materials have been sold through an agent to a designer, who then sells the finished product on to the retailer for sale to the consumer.

Buying direct from a manufacturer, is more common in organisational markets where the purchase of raw materials is a daily occurrence. But even then, intermediaries may be involved, providing some form of sub-assembly service or grading process.

Distribution channels make it easier for the customer to obtain the product they wish to buy, and different levels of control are possible within the channel design. Building partnerships, facilitating co-operation and ensuring common objectives, helps to avoid the problem of channel conflict.

> **In order to successfully complete the tasks in this chapter you will need to be familiar with:**
>
> - behavioural aspects of channels;
> - power-dependency;
> - vertical marketing systems;
> - channel strategy and design;
> - intermediary types;
> - distribution intensity.

Suppliers re-learn lesson that customer is king

By Peter Marsh

An industrial suburb of Liverpool is an unexotic place for a works outing. But Diamond – a Norwich-based maker of electronic controls – has been sending minibus-loads of its staff to Prescot for a series of day trips.

The 40 managers who have made the 700km return journeys have been out hunting ideas from Stoves, the cooker company.

Stoves is a big customer of Diamond and one of Britain's most noted exponents of just-in-time production practices, which boost efficiency through making products only when necessary. But just-in-time methods rely on assembly companies having close links with their suppliers.

'We've learned a hell of a lot from Stoves,' said Mr Phil Hodge, sales director of Diamond, part of the Cortworth engineering group. 'We realised we could fit in with their way of doing things only if we took on board some of their techniques.'

With tips from Stoves picked up over the past year, Diamond has re-organised its factory along the lines of the Prescot company. Parts are channelled between production operations only when required, cutting warehouse space required and preventing unfinished parts clogging Diamond's plant.

The interchange between Stoves and Diamond is just one example of the closer links developing between suppliers and customers in many areas of UK manufacturing. In the past five years many big companies have cut back on suppliers, investing time and effort persuading those remaining to make and deliver products exactly to their wishes. In return for what can be painful changes, suppliers get a commitment that orders will continue.

Stoves has 80 suppliers, half the number it had in 1988. About 40 deliver every one or two days, with 20 sending parts direct to the production line as opposed to the company's warehouse.

Mr John Crathorne, Stoves's chief executive, said: 'It's taken four years of talking to get to the stage where we can rely on our suppliers to give us what we want. Our quality control people spend as much time in [suppliers'] factories as in our own.'

Mr David Plant, engineering sales manager of Nottingham-based Sturmy Archer, which supplies Stoves with metal caps for gas cookers, said: 'In the old days we'd be looking over our back all the time to check that Stoves wasn't about to buy the parts from someone else. Now there's more security.'

The new partnerships are not without problems. 'In a just-in-time system, your quality has to be perfect, and the change to taking over full responsibility for this can be frightening,' said Mr Ken Moore, deputy managing director of Thermax, a glass processor owned by St Gobain of France.

Every day Thermax sends to Stoves – from its plant in Bishop Auckland, County Durham – 5,000 pieces of glass for oven doors. 'We sometimes have fights with Stoves [over production procedures] but the disagreements are out in the open,' said Mr Moore.

For Mr Roy Bevan, managing director of B.U. Industrial Components of Telford, the just-in-time deliveries demanded by Stoves are 'absolute hell'. Every day his driver spends five hours delivering about 12,000 plastic knobs and moulded parts to seven different points on the factory floor. Two years ago, before Stoves changed its routine, the driver used to travel to Widnes once or twice a week, and, because he delivered to the warehouse, the trip was only two hours.

'They [Stoves] have laid a lot of their problems on their suppliers,' said Mr Bevan. 'The changes mean they keep a lot of their stocks on the M6.'

Similar changes have been implemented in other parts of UK industry. Motherwell-based Honeywell Controls, a US-owned company making heating control equipment such as thermostats, has installed computer links with 20 suppliers so information about parts requirements can be fed back and forth daily.

According to Mr Alf Stiegler, the managing director of R.A. Labone of Ilkeston, Derbyshire, which every week makes 100,000 small parts for Honeywell, the arrangement means that his company can react instantaneously to changes in demand.

For Bostrom, a maker of vehicle seats in Northampton, one of its key suppliers is Birmingham-based Genner Steels. Rather than buy 4,000 different unfinished steel parts from a range of companies,

Bostrom purchases all of them from Genner, which delivers every day. Instead of pricing all the items it supplies to Bostrom separately, Genner has devised a system which bases price largely on weight and makes invoicing easier.

'Because of our long-term relationship we can anticipate two thirds of the new orders we get from Bostrom every day,' said Mr Chris Mansell, Genner's sales director. 'If all our customers were as efficient as Bostrom, we'd be a lot more profitable.'

Perkins Engines, a US-owned maker of diesel engines based in Peterborough, has in the past five years cut its suppliers from 500 to 200, persuading many of them to adapt their production routines.

One such supplier is Alumasc Precision Components of Kettering, which makes aluminium camshaft covers. The company used to cast its products and then leave Perkins to finish the parts by sending them to machining businesses. But following demands from Perkins, Alumasc has added its own machining operations to save its customer this job and reduce costs.

'In the past few years we've had to spend about £500,000 a year buying new machine tools and taking on extra skills to project-manage a complete assembly,' said Mr Keith Waldern, Alumasc's chairman. 'It's part of the effort to fit in with what Perkins wants.'

Telford-based NDM Manufacturing, which makes air conditioning equipment for cars and is owned 75 per cent by Nippondenso of Japan and 25 per cent by Italy's Magneti Marelli, has 40 main suppliers – one of which is LVS Rubber Mouldings of Burntwood, near Birmingham. Each week LVS makes for NDM about 10,000 small rubber grommets, costing about 10p each.

Under the arrangement with NDM, which set up in the UK three years ago, the Japanese-controlled company insists on knowing how the cost of everything LVS makes for it breaks down between 15 areas including packaging, delivery, raw materials and processing.

Mr Lee Adams, quality manager at LVS, said the relationship with NDM had been 'helpful' in pushing his company towards examining ways of making products more cheaply. 'The relationship has made us think more carefully about what we do,' he said.

Another person happy to be working with a Japanese customer is Mr Geoff Miles, UK managing director of Alfred Engelmann, a German-owned maker of car mirrors. For several months a production engineer from Toyota, one of Engelmann's big customers, has been semi-resident in its plant in Corby teaching Engelmann employees new assembly routines and how to link up better with its own suppliers. Toyota also last year paid for three Engelmann managers to go to Japan for more tuition.

'Partly with this guidance, we have reduced our stock levels over the past few years by a factor of four and increased the productivity of some parts of our factory by 25 per cent – all with negligible investment,' said Mr Miles.

Source: Financial Times, 11 October 1995

12.1 **What type of power relationship did Stove used to have with its suppliers and what type of conflict did that result in?**

12.2 **What type of channel atmosphere do you think exists for the firms mentioned in this article?**

12.3 **As a supplier, identify the issues which you would wish to debate with your management team before committing the company to a future with either one or a few manufacturers.**

It's a big boys' game

Richard Gourlay on how integrated supply chains may help UK companies

Hidden away in Tottenham, barely eight miles from Trafalgar Square, is a factory that presses car mats from bales of raw rubber. It is a heavy industrial process that looks decidedly out of place amid the machine shops and general merchants of north-east London.

Some 75 miles up the road in Glemsford, Suffolk is the second arm of Cannon Rubber, a family-owned group now run by the son of its founder, which has sales of £35m. The Avent factory makes the baby bottle that has arguably become the first high-tech accessory every up-market baby simply cannot be seen without.

In a commercial world increasingly seeking focused businesses, the two companies lack any obvious industrial logic together. The combination is the result of the kind of historical accident that helps form many privately owned companies.

Yet Cannon Rubber's experience producing rubber car mats for the motor industry on a just-in-time basis is about to pay dividends in its baby product business.

At the moment Avent delivers weekly parcels of its 40 product lines to Mothercare's warehouse in Wellingborough where a contracted distributor repackages the goods for each of the 268 stores. But this autumn, Mothercare, which Avent supplies with a wide range of baby products, is to move to a stockless warehouse.

Cannon itself will then have to carry the stock for Mothercare. Guided by each store's stock control systems, Avent will each week make up parcels of products and barcode them for each shop.

Edward Atkin, Cannon Rubber's managing director, sees Mothercare's move as an example of the relentless pressure on smaller suppliers by big customers. 'The concentration of buying power is being used ruthlessly,' says Atkin. 'But it is the only game in town – you are playing with the big boys or you are out of business.'

Mothercare accepts that the new system means suppliers such as Avent are supplying smaller quantities more frequently and are also carrying stock that previously it had to hold. But Mothercare also says that by establishing a more closely integrated supply chain, it has reduced the number of suppliers from about 300 to 130. Those that survive as suppliers will get more business from the store.

The growing demands made by larger customers pose considerable challenges for smaller suppliers. Avent will have to address Mothercare's extra demands by installing sophisticated stock management and sorting systems or add expensive labour.

If the increased pressure from suppliers is clouding the horizon, Atkin believes there is a silver lining. The new level of integration of the supply chain leads to greater inter-dependency and could mean companies dealing with customers such as Mothercare will have to have a local UK manufacturing base. That should help to keep at bay the far eastern competition that has such a labour cost advantage.

'The momentum is swinging back in favour of UK suppliers because supply infrastructure is becoming increasingly important,' says Atkin. Rather than being a disadvantage, shorter supply chains could ensure a resurgence of UK manufacturing industry as more distant and cheaper suppliers are no longer capable of meeting the higher standards customers want.

Storehouse, the parent of Mothercare and BHS, hints that this might be more than wishful thinking. In the past two years BHS has seen 'a bit of a move back to UK sourcing because of the need for closer relations with the supplier'.

Talk of more harmonious relations – loosely what some businesses call partnership sourcing – is all very well, but Atkin recognises its limitations. It may provide a cushion of comfort, but companies have to work hard to achieve it.

He recognises that only by producing innovative products can the smaller supplier stay in the market. Cannon Rubber has invested heavily in computer numerically controlled machining equipment to make the moulds for its rubber mats and some baby products. Low-tech products, such as ice scrapers for cars and baby bottle heaters, are made with the aid of robots.

This has helped to keep foreign competition at bay. And in little more than 10 years Avent's product line has become market leader with some of the highest retail prices. In spite of the growth potential internationally, Atkin recognises that in the medium term the company must be run by a management that has the same hunger he and his father needed to build the company.

'Dynastic succession is not compatible with the pressures of commercial life now,' he says. Last month the family sold 20 per cent of the company to 3i for £5m. The sale reduced Cannon Rubber's gearing from more than 100 per cent. It also began a process that should lead to the Atkin family floating the company in the next few years.

Supporters of businesses staying in family hands may mourn this move, but Atkin suggests that conditions today require a kind of professional management that family companies may not be able to muster. To pretend otherwise would be sentimentalism.

Source: Financial Times, 20 June 1995

12.4 What type of VMS is in operation between Cannon Rubber and its customers?

12.5 Identify the advantages and disadvantages of this arrangement for Cannon Rubber.

12.6 Identify the advantages and disadvantages for the customers of Cannon Rubber.

12.7 What organisational influences are operating here between Cannon Rubber and Storehouse?

12C

Musical discord

Alice Rawsthorn on the struggle between record clubs and retailers

Eleven CDs For The Price Of One – there is nothing more likely to infuriate a US music retailer than advertisements like this, which are regularly placed in newspapers and magazines by the record clubs which sell music by mail order.

The feud has simmered for years, but it flared up publicly last month when a number of retailers called for legal action to curb the clubs' activities, claiming they were using unfair tactics to poach customers from record stores.

So far relations between the UK's record clubs and retailers have been calmer, despite occasional grumbles from the stores. However, developments in the US music industry are often replicated in the UK a few years later, and some of the underlying trends that triggered the current conflict in the US are now surfacing on this side of the Atlantic.

Record clubs are a long established phenomenon in the US, where for decades they were virtually the only way that people in remote rural areas could buy music. The clubs, most of which are owned by US record companies, gain the licence to recordings by paying fees to record companies and artists, and then manufacture their own cassettes and compact discs.

The clubs maintain that, rather than taking sales away from retailers, they sell records to people who would not otherwise buy them. They are only allowed to sell records three to six months after release, so do not appeal to pop fans looking for new albums, or to devotees of jazz or classical music interested in esoteric recordings.

'I don't see us as being in competition against retailers, our sales are incremental,' says Richard Wolter, chairman of Columbia House, the biggest US record club which is owned by Sony and Warner. 'There are some people who'll never buy music by mail, they can't deal with the delay.'

As a result clubs tend to attract people with middle-of-the-road taste, mostly consumers above the age of 30 who are likely to buy music by Elton John or Vivaldi, and find record shops too young and trendy.

However, the clubs reached a wider market in the early 1990s, when consumers were replacing their old vinyl collections with compact discs. The Record Industry Association of America calculates that the clubs' market share rose from 8.9 per cent in 1990 to 15.1 per cent in 1994, giving them sales of $1.9bn (£1.25bn).

This expansion provoked complaints from retailers, claiming that the clubs' licensing agreements gave them an unfair advantage, by enabling them to sell music at deeply discounted prices. Clubs typically pay licensing fees of $3 for each CD, half the wholesale price. An average CD album from Columbia House costs $5, against $4 from its arch-rival, BMG Music (a Bertelsmann subsidiary), and $12 at retail. Record labels not owning big clubs also complained, saying the licensing fees were too low.

However, criticism of the clubs has recently grown more vociferous, as the US market has slowed down, reflecting a dearth of exciting releases and fierce competition in the saturated retail sector. Clubs, like other areas of the music industry, have had to fight harder for sales, particularly as 'CD replacement' sales are now falling.

'We've got to become more competitive,' says Wolter. 'We've got to make our advertising better, to make sure that we're stocking what consumers want and delivering it to them faster.'

Columbia House and BMG have both improved customer service, with initiatives such as increased facility for telephone ordering, launching World Wide Web sites where customers can place orders and faster deliveries.

More controversial are their efforts to sharpen up their advertising by adopting more contemporary graphics and focusing on younger artists, such as Alanis Morissette, rather than Elton John.

Yet a number of record labels which do not own big clubs – including Geffen, Virgin and MCA – stopped supplying clubs last year, claiming they were cannibalising more profitable retail sales. And last month several retailers announced that they were considering taking legal action against the clubs, or referring them to the Federal Trade Commission.

While the US clubs try to ride out the storm, their UK counterparts, such as Britannia, part of Poly-Gram, and BMG, are hoping to avoid a similar conflict. They operate on a similar basis to US clubs, but buy CDs from record companies, rather than manufacturing their own, and are slightly less aggressive on pricing. The latest Britannia promotion offers five CDs, rather than 11, for the price of one.

Another distinction is that the UK music market has been so buoyant that, although the clubs' share held steady at 6 per cent of the £1bn market in 1995, the mood of the industry has been relatively cordial.

The UK clubs are trying to maintain the status quo, particularly as 'CD replacement' sales have now stabilised. Britannia sponsors the music industry's annual Brit awards, not only to raise public awareness of its name but to foster good relations with record labels and retailers.

'So far we haven't had the same problems as in the States,' says John Nelligan, chairman. 'As for the future, who knows?'

Source: Financial Times, 25 April 1996

12.8 **Do you think that the complaint lodged by US retailers against record clubs was justified? Why?**

12.9 **What type of intermediary is used in the UK for the sale of vinyl, cassettes and CD's?**

12.10 **What benefits would you normally expect the record labels and production companies to receive from this?**

12.11 **What benefits can you identify from this type of distribution method from a customer's point of view? Illustrate your response with examples from your own experience.**

National Savings' virtual shops

Diane Summers on an innovative strategy that uses newspapers as a distribution outlet

A strangely empty-looking advertisement is appearing in national newspapers this week. Apart from a swivel chair and a few apparently meaningless lines and symbols, all it contains are the words: 'Virtual shop. Reserved for National Savings. Opening here on [followed by a date early in October].'

The 'teaser' advertisement will run again next week, in the identical position in the same papers, with little further illumination. The following week, the 'virtual shops' will start trading: the empty spaces will become shop windows in which National Savings displays its wares, and readers will be able to buy products off the page. For at least a year, the virtual shops will be open for business at the same sites, on the same days of the week, in the same papers.

There will also be advertising for the advertising or, to extend the shop idea, support for the channel of distribution. Like other big retailers, National Savings will advertise its shops on TV, strengthening the brand, giving information about location and highlighting new products and special offers.

As it swallows the bulk of National Savings' £11m advertising budget over the coming year, managers will be hoping that the concept generates enough excitement, awareness of shop sites and, most importantly, direct sales. This will be necessary to justify what at first may seem simply an update of the often effective but hardly revolutionary concept of direct response press advertising that requires the reader to clip a coupon or phone a sales number.

The virtual shop is the brainchild of advertising agency Howell Henry Chaldecott Lury and its media strategy subsidiary Michaelides & Bednash. The agency is famous for injecting new life, sometimes by controversial means, into staid or obscure brands. Two of its best-known campaigns were for the Automobile Association (the fourth emergency service) and Tango, the fizzy drink (exploding grannies and practical jokes).

National Savings certainly needs new life. By the late 1980s its products, which include fixed-term savings certificates and investment accounts, were losing out to competition from the banks and building societies. A negative public sector borrowing requirement led to the running down of advertising and a focus on gross-of-tax products aimed at the poor, the young and the old.

When the government needed an injection of National Savings funding in 1992 to meet a sharp rise in the PSBR, research showed that the most lucrative prospects – better-off individuals in the 40–60 age group – viewed National Savings as 'secure but old-fashioned, trustworthy but uncompetitive'. Also, the link with the Post Office, as the retail outlet, was particularly unappealing to this more sophisticated target group.

Unbranded product tests produced enthusiasm among consumers for what was on offer but, says Anne Nash, National Savings' head of marketing, 'our image was getting in the way of what we knew were very good products'.

The first stab at changing this image came towards the end of 1992 with a series of press and TV advertisements using work by cartoonist Gary Larson. These helped shift the customer profile towards the target group, increase average value of receipts and build awareness, says Nash. Most important, funding targets, which required annual sales of around £10bn, have been met.

But simply updating an image does not necessarily amount to a long-term strategy. When National Savings was obliged under government rules to put its advertising work out to tender last year, it instructed competing agencies – incumbents McCann-Erickson, HHCL, Publicis, and Delaney Fletcher Bozell to concentrate on strategy.

Unusually, Nash and her colleagues made a full presentation to the agencies on the terms of the brief. The venue was the Natural History Museum, underlining National Savings' then 'financial jungle' advertising theme. Chris Satterthwaite, HHCL partner, describes it as 'the best briefing we have ever received in terms of clarity and intensity of message'.

He says that many clients appear initially to want change but, reading between the lines, it becomes clear they lack conviction. From the first page of National Savings' briefing document it was clear they were 'after a strategic leap'.

The agencies were also told not to consider distribution of the products and to work on the assumption that the links with the Post Office would continue more or less in their present form for at least five years.

HHCL decided to ignore this instruction. The Post Office was fine for traditional National Savings consumers, says Satterthwaite, 'but the younger, high net worth target audience does not have time to go to the Post Office'. Technological changes mean brand communication and distribution are converging, he says: 'As the world gets more digital, the TV will be a distribution point through which you can transact a purchase. A younger target audience understands that.'

And so to virtual shops. Simon Calvert, media strategist with Michaelides & Bednash, says there are three important features to the plan which justify the coining of the term. First, unlike ordinary direct response press advertising, there will be a permanence of location in the selected publications, so customers can find the 'shop' when they need it.

Second, there will be the kind of analysis used by retailers to match products to consumers: different 'branches' of the shop will offer different goods in different ways. And, third, the shops will be promoted, using advertising for the advertising. TV commercials will, says Calvert, 'let people know the shops are there permanently, explain the concept and, when there are products to promote, tell people to look in the shop windows'.

As the government's finances worsen, – August's PSBR exceeded even the gloomiest forecasts – pressures on National Savings to perform will increase. Nash and her colleagues will be waiting to see whether virtual shops produce window shopping or hard sales.

Source: Financial Times, 21 September 1995

12.12 What type of selection criteria do you think National Savings had in mind when it made its distribution selection? Try to separate your responses into strategic and operational elements.

12.13 How compatible do you think the new ideas are with the traditional image of National Savings?

12.14 Recommend ways in which the strengths of the traditional image can be married with the new.

13

Retailers and Wholesalers

After junk mail, the supermarket is probably the image which comes to mind when most of us think of marketing. For some, the level of exposure is never enough, yet for others it is entirely distasteful. There is no doubt, that the terrain of retailing has dramatically changed in the past 40 years. Small specialist shops have been replaced with department stores. The grocer, butcher and baker have been united into a super-market or hypermarket which can only be reached by transport, and all this in the name of progress.

Whatever our personal views, it is clear that out-of-town shopping centres, which provide one-stop shopping for nearly all our needs, will not go away, even if their march across the country has been briefly slowed.

Distribution channels are, of course, essential in getting products to the customer. Once goods pass into the hands of channel members, they are normally expected to perform some service on those goods to justify their cut of the profits. Wholesalers will break up large consignments and assemble a range of goods for delivery to a small shop, while retailers perform many additional services in order to help us make the right purchase. This can range from providing complex advice and information, through to simply providing a pleasing environment in which to shop.

Some organisations such as Marks & Spencer, Dixons, and Comet, chose to run a corporate chain of outlets, orchestrating a well-defined chain of events, striving for unity rather than diversity. Others will operate on a contractual system, where an outlet becomes approved to supply certain products or carry out particular activities such as dry cleaning, but has the freedom to introduce other products, such as 24-hour film developing, into its range to meet customer demands.

The independent store, of course, is free to stock exactly what they think will be attractive to their customers. However, with freedom comes responsibility. Faulty products, poor service, late or incorrect deliveries are just a few of the problems which the independent retailer has to solve alone, without the benefit of a large corporate machine to either help or blame.

In order to successfully complete the tasks in this chapter you will need to be familiar with:

- types of retail store;
- non-store retailing;
- level of service;
- breadth and depth of range;
- store image and atmosphere;
- discount operators;
- wholesaler/retailer relationships;
- forms of ownership;
- channel competition.

Avon calling for more troops to halt decline

The message behind an inspirational presentation was
that an image makeover is required, writes Richard Wolffe

As the disco lights swirled overhead and the stage filled with smoke, it was clear this was no ordinary staff presentation.

About 500 women had gathered to hear Mrs Sandy Mountford, the new chief executive of Avon Cosmetics, the door-to-door beauty company. Most were tapping their feet to the dance music well before Mrs Mountford, the first woman to lead Avon's UK operation, emerged from the smoke.

'Avon is in my heart and sales are in my heart,' she told her audience. 'I believe it's in my very soul.'

With autocue speeches and two huge video screens, Avon's annual conference in Birmingham's Metropole hotel – which ended yesterday – often seemed more like a TV game show than a strategy meeting.

The official purpose of the party was to launch Avon's range of Christmas products and learn of the year's stringent sales targets. But the show was really designed as an inspirational message for the troops – Avon's area managers. They would in turn inspire the 150,000 representatives back home.

It seemed to work. The audience leapt to its feet as the best sales managers were called on stage to receive a wad of £50 notes.

But there were some tough personal messages too. 'We have to upgrade our image,' admitted Mrs Mountford. 'Avon Cosmetics is not your mother's make-up company. We have great products and, in fact, I have a really hard time understanding why people in this company will wear and use competitors' products.'

The message was a sign of long-term difficulties which the UK company shares with other Avon operations in its 'mature markets' – mainly North America and western Europe.

The number of sales made has steadily declined in the UK from 37m in 1989 to 31.3m last year. Avon hopes to reverse that trend this year by lifting the number of sales by 1m and raising turnover from £153.2m in 1995 to £163.5m this year.

Avon admits it quickly needs to find more sales representatives – the commissioned saleswomen who knock on doors – and ultimately more customers. According to its own market research, about 12m women would buy Avon products if they were contacted by a representative. The company – based around its manufacturing plant in Northampton – reckons it has some 7m potential customers who are 'stranded' without a saleswoman nearby.

But Avon's central problem is its age. The US parent company is 110 years old, and its UK subsidiary – its sixth largest – was launched in 1959.

Although it has worldwide sales of $5bn (£3.2bn) the company still has an old-fashioned image which it is keen to shake off. It is now expanding into emerging markets, where the Avon image is more modern, through its 2m representatives in 125 countries.

However, it denies that its army of saleswomen is out of tune with the times and says it has the best-selling fragrance brand in the UK.

Mrs Mountford, who began her career as an Avon rep in Canada, rejected the trend in other industries towards telephone sales.

'In the 1980s the big shopping malls and department stores came to be very successful and at the time people said direct selling was going the way of the dinosaur,' she said after her conference speech.

'But it has changed again. There are more working women than ever before, trying to balance their lives. Time is their most valuable commodity and home-shopping is the thing of the future.'

The pace of the Avon sales drive is almost frenetic. Every three weeks, a new brochure is distributed with new products and a new marketing message.

But the driving force is still the company's ability to motivate its reps to knock on doors. 'Destiny is not a matter of chance, it is a matter of choice,' Mrs Mountford told the conference. 'Determining the future of this company is not a spectator sport.'

Source: Financial Times, 23 August 1996

13.1 Within your work group, discuss your impression of Avon and report on any contact you, your friends or family have had with its representatives.

13.2 Avon operate just one form of retailing. How well do you think this will serve Avon in the future?

13.3 Identify alternatives which Avon could use. Outline any cultural and operational changes the organisation would have to make in order to make a successful entry.

13B

Cargo Clubs fail to deliver the goods

Geoff Dyer looks at the ambitious strategy which has led to problems for Nurdin & Peacock

When Mr David Poole resigned in October as chief executive of Nurdin & Peacock, the cash and carry operator, the company was quick to stress that his departure would not affect the ambitious strategy he had put in place.

Four months later, observers are questioning whether the group, still without a chief executive, can really maintain that course. Moreover, N&P is now being talked about as a possible takeover candidate.

Worries about N&P were aggravated by the £16.2m exceptional charge to 1994 profits it announced nearly two weeks ago. The charge was more than £4m higher than indicated at the time of the interim results and exposed just how many problems Mr Poole's initiatives were creating.

Profits for the year are now expected to be between £15m and £18m, against £32.1m last year. The shares have fallen from a high of 234p last year to 141p yesterday.

No one denies that the management needed to introduce changes. Cash and carry stores sell food items in bulk and at large discounts to independent retailers, such as corner shop grocers. But these customers have been whiplashed by the expansion of Sunday trading and price competition between large supermarket chains and discount stores. N&P's like-for-like sales fell by 7 per cent in 1993 and 1 per cent in 1994.

Mr Poole said in 1993 that traditional cash and carry business had 'no future'.

N&P's strategy was to broaden its customer base. Its stores were converted into Trade and Business Warehouses, supplying stationery as well as food products. The group expanded in northern England with the £21.9m acquisition in May of M6, a cash and carry chain with 10 outlets.

Most ambitious of all, last year it opened three Cargo Club warehouse outlets, US-style shopping clubs. According to Mr Bill Currie, analyst at Barclay de Zoete Wedd: 'Any one of these initiatives would have been a huge strain on management. Trying all three at once was just too much.'

The diversification into new products exposed the group's lack of experience in non-food merchandise and the strain on working capital turned £2.7m of interest income in 1993 into an interest charge of £1.5m in 1994.

However, Cargo Club has caused the biggest problem. In the US, where it was introduced in the 1970s, the concept has been a great success. It offers large discounts to fee-paying members on items such as food, clothes and electrical goods at huge out-of-town warehouses. By 1993 they had 21m members in the US and accounted for an annual $35bn (£22.4bn) in sales.

N&P opened its first store in Croydon, south London, in March with a fanfare of publicity and a prediction that the company would have 30 warehouses by the end of the century. But the three opened so far incurred operating losses of between £3 and £4m in 1994 and ran up marketing costs of £3m. In the words of one analyst, 'they have been an unmitigated disaster'.

Critics say that N&P's approach of trying to attract retail customers, spending heavily on marketing and stocking a wide range of products ignores the US experience that warehouses survive on minimal costs and by selling a small range of items in bulk.

Mr Paul Morris, analyst at Goldman Sachs, observed that: 'The warehouses in the US that have fallen have been the ones that went for retail customers.'

According to Mr Nigel Hall, finance director at N&P: 'There is not a cash and carry industry of any size in the US so we have to differentiate. People in this country like to see a wide range of options.'

The sale of Cargo Club is now widely rumoured. The most likely buyer would be Costco Europe, which is 60 per cent owned by PriceCostco, the largest US warehouse operator, and which opened the first UK warehouse in Thurrock, Essex in 1993. Other large US operators such as Wal-Mart could see it as an opportunity to get a foothold in the UK market.

Mr Hall said that 'it is not the case yet' that N&P would need to sell the Cargo Clubs, which currently have 115,000 members, because of the losses they were incurring. He added that N&P had been 'in conversations with various parties' about providing finance for expanding them.

The falling share price means that N&P now has a market capitalisation of £179.5m, against net assets of £145.5m at the half year end on July 1, encouraging talk of a possible takeover.

All previous speculation was academic because 28.9 per cent of the shares are controlled by the Peacock family.

However, some brokers now believe that Mr Michael Peacock, who was chairman until 1991 and is now honorary president, would be prepared to sell if the right offer came along. Mr Peacock dismisses this as rumour: 'I hope N&P will go on as an independent company.'

The obvious candidate would be SHV, the Dutch private company which owns Makro, the wholesale store chain, and which has a 14 per cent stake in N&P. SHV has never declared aggressive intentions, but market observers believe that if it did want to make a move, now would be the time.

SHV said the N&P stake was 'a financial investment' and that 'we have our hands full with Makro at the moment'.

A bid from Booker, the food group, is thought unlikely because that would give it more than 50 per cent of the UK cash and carry market, raising competition concerns.

Source: Financial Times, 31 January 1995

13.4 **Establish whether Nurdin & Peacock managed to stay an independent company and draw up a schematic of the company's current interests in the retail sector.**

13.5 **Outline the external and internal pressures which resulted in Nurdin & Peacock's expansion. Identify the type of growth strategy they are following.**

13.6 **What level of service, type of merchandise, store image and atmosphere would you expect to find in a Cargo Club? How does this differ from a department store?**

Sowing the seeds of co-operation

Fruit and vegetable growers are being challenged to replace imports, writes Alison Maitland

Uniformly sized tomatoes, innovative baby vegetables and long-life strawberries are likely to be on the menu this week as UK fruit and vegetable growers are encouraged to sharpen up their marketing skills.

Growers visiting Britain's main horticultural show in Birmingham will be treated to the food industry's first 'reverse exhibition'. Among the stands promoting seeds, fertiliser and specialist equipment, they will find a handful of large retailers and caterers who are there not to sell their wares but to make contact with potential suppliers.

The National Farmers' Union, which is organising the exhibition, says: 'The aim is to put buyers in direct contact with individual growers to enable growers to offer alternatives to imports or grow innovative products by tailoring their production to the specific needs of buyers.'

The idea came from Margaret Charrington, chairman of the Horticultural Development Council, who is battling to close Britain's £3bn trade gap in horticultural products. While executive director of the Invest in Britain campaign from 1982 to 1992, she organised several 'reverse exhibitions' for the textiles, car and toy industries.

'We used to invite buyers to take a stand and bring a selection of material they were buying from abroad,' she says. 'I'd bring UK suppliers along and say: couldn't you deliver at this price, on this date and to this specification?'

Fruit and vegetable growers are often considered to have sharper selling skills than other farmers because they have not been cushioned by European Union subsidies. But Charrington believes there is room for improvement, especially as the independent-minded British do not enjoy the strength in numbers achieved by the powerful horticultural co-operatives in continental Europe.

Her concern is underlined by the fact that about half the £40m worth of fresh fruit and vegetables bought each year by Gardner Merchant, the UK's largest contract caterer, comes from abroad. Jayne Nightingale, fresh produce purchasing executive, is attending the exhibition to find out whether British growers can compete on quality and price.

'We look for consistency,' she says. 'In the Dutch market, tomatoes are highly graded. If you're ordering something, you know what you're going to get. In the English market, they're less graded. If you order a box of tomatoes, the size and ripeness of the fruit could vary.'

Gardner Merchant buys most of its fresh produce through about 20 wholesalers and distributors. But Nightingale says that dealing direct with a grower or a group of growers in Britain could have advantages. 'It could be cheaper and it would give us more control over what is on offer,' she says.

By inviting big food retailers to the exhibition, the NFU acknowledges the supermarkets' domination of UK fruit and vegetable sales. But the multiples are anxious to dispel their image among farmers as dictatorial on price and product requirements.

'We've got to get away from this old-fashioned idea of them and us,' says David Sawday, corporate affairs manager for Tesco. 'We want growers to see the customers in our stores as their customers as well. We've got to work together to get the product absolutely right, both in terms of quality and presentation.'

As part of the effort to reduce Britain's overall trade gap of nearly £6bn in food and drink, the supermarkets have made much of their recent switch from foreign to UK produce. Bob Hilborn, chief food technologist for Sainsbury, says its UK suppliers have worked hard to extend their growing seasons. English new potatoes, once available only between May and August, are now sold right up to Christmas.

He acknowledges that co-operation between growers can be important, but points out that a single producer in Warwickshire provides Sainsbury with up to 80 per cent of its specialty *feuilles de chêne* lettuces.

Charrington nevertheless believes supermarkets could do more, for example by promoting regional produce such as greens from Lincolnshire, or by buying fewer long-distance vegetables from low-cost producers.

Source: Financial Times, 19 January 1995

Supermarkets 'make farmers into serfs'

By Alison Maitland

Farmers are no more than 'up-market serfs' working to order for the supermarkets, a leading consumer and food lobbyist said yesterday.

Mr Tim Lang, professor of food policy at London's Thames Valley University, made a savage attack on the power of the multiples at a meeting of the Women's Farming Union.

'The power brokers in the modern food economy are the distributors,' he said. 'It isn't a market economy any more, it's a hypermarket economy.'

He rejected the view that the supermarkets represented consumers' interests. 'Every consumer organisation testifies to the lack of consumer power.'

Mr Lang told the farming union, which aims to bring producers and consumers closer together: 'The rise of the hypermarket symbolises what is wrong with the current policy. Far from being hands-off, government has actually allowed this concentration to occur.'

He pointed to the rise in the number of superstores bigger than 25,000 sq ft from 239 in 1980 to about 925 last year. He said the trend would continue for five to 10 years because of planning permission already granted, in spite of recent government moves to curb out-of-town superstores.

Mr Lang argued that competition policy should examine market share in local areas. 'One supermarket can have a 50–60 per cent share in some areas of London.'

Mr Lang, who is involved in projects on school meals and low income for the government's nutrition taskforce, said there were 'huge price advantages' in buying fresh fruit and vegetables from street markets rather than supermarkets.

He said 82 per cent of the British diet consisted of prepared or processed food, and supermarket fresh produce was dearer than processed food because of the high costs of transporting it long distances.

He said: 'You have got to put pressure on the government and the supermarkets to start getting food straight to people rather than going round the globe.'

Mr Lang also blamed the multiples for a rise in car journeys, with consequent damage to the environment. He cited a survey by the Henley Centre showing that the percentage of people using a car to do their main grocery shopping had risen from 62 per cent in 1985 to 73 per cent in 1993.

His remarks appeared to strike a chord among many of the women in the audience.

But a male questioner who said he did the weekly shopping for his family argued that Mr Lang's ideas on shopping locally and cooking every meal would add hours to household chores. 'You're not taking account of the cultural change that's taking place,' he said. 'It's the way we live now. How do we change that?'

Source: Financial Times, 16 November 1995

13.7 Why does it seem to be so difficult for UK growers to supply produce to the specifications laid down by the premium retailer groups?

13.8 What assistance could the Government and retailers give to the UK farmer to help them achieve such standards and thus promote British produce? Compare this with assistance provided for growers in other European countries.

13.9 'British growers should forget trying to compete for the premium retailer's orders and accept that their produce naturally fits in the discount sector where price is more important than consistency.' Discuss.

Magazine avalanche engulfs shops

Newsagents are unhappy with their wholesale agreements, reports Motoko Rich

Mrs Jackie Grafton at Jonathan's newsagents in East Dulwich, south London, is wondering what to do with magazines such as Boards, Women & Golf, and Traction.

Although she never ordered them, they and other obscure titles keep appearing in deliveries from her wholesaler.

She said: 'Every day I get loads of stuff I do not want, and it is just sitting on my shelf.'

Mrs Grafton is not alone. Mrs Olive Heanue at Lucky News in Ilford, east London, said: 'I have bundles of magazines that I could never sell. I could practically open another shop with them.'

Other newsagents have also been complaining about the wholesaler practice of routinely delivering unsolicited magazines to retailers.

Under terms set by W.H. Smith, John Menzies, Surridge Dawson and Johnson's, the UK's four leading magazine wholesalers, retailers have to accept what are known in the industry as 'box-outs' – new or promoted magazines – with their regular orders.

The Association of Newspaper and Magazine Wholesalers is working with the Periodical Publishers Association to develop a code of practice for magazine sales, which it hopes to present to retailers soon.

Retailers are often required to pay for the magazines as many as three weeks before they can sell them or are able to return unsold stock. That can impose cashflow problems on some smaller newsagents.

Many retailers say that the wholesalers are guilty of poor record-keeping, unpaid credits and bad judgment on the types of magazines they deliver in the box-outs.

Mr John Rowe, director of wholesaler operations at the National Federation of Retail Newsagents, said: 'The weight of anecdotal evidence is so compelling as to demand investigation into the wholesalers' service competence.'

Mr Ian Locks, chief executive of the PPA, said the magazine code of practice was being prepared partly in response to a newspaper code which was drawn up after the Monopolies and Mergers Commission found that some wholesaler practices were operating against the public interest.

The newspaper code, which comes into effect in October, guarantees retailers greater rights of access to newspapers if they meet certain conditions. Publishers are concerned that a change in practices could endanger magazine supply.

It is not clear whether the magazine code will address the newsagents' complaints. Some wholesalers are already trying to increase communications with their retailers. W.H. Smith, which supplies 43 per cent of the wholesale market, is meeting independent retailers in 22 regions to gather opinions in an initiative called the Independent Retailer Forum.

Both W.H. Smith and John Menzies, the second-largest wholesaler, with a market share of 27 per cent, say they operate systems to accommodate retailers' needs. New magazines are not randomly allocated but are supplied to retailers based on sales of titles in related categories. If a new women's fashion magazine were launched, for example, a computer would determine the number of copies to distribute to a newsagent based on the retailer's regular sales of magazines such as Elle or Vogue.

Mr Alex van Straubenzee of W.H. Smith said wholesalers were caught between the competing interests of publishers and retailers, but admits that 'since 1988 we have been exclusively focused on publishers, so we have adopted an amended strategy to take more notice of retailers'.

But Mr Shoaib Punjani, owner of Punjani's newsagent in Holland Park, west London said: 'The wholesalers do not listen to what we want. They look at computer projections and assume that the newsagent is ignorant. It is sheer stupidity if they think that they have to hold our hands and tell us what we want.'

The newsagents are afraid to play David to the wholesaler's Goliath. Mrs Mina Patel, owner of S & M Newsagents in Streatham, London, said: 'I have tried to get some newsagents together. But some are afraid that the wholesalers will stop sending them newspapers.'

Source: Financial Times, 26 September 1994

13.10 Identify the flaws in the wholesalers' approach to the launch of new magazine titles through independent newsagents.

13.11 The power in this relationship appears to lie very firmly with the wholesaler. Recommend ways in which wholesalers could improve their service to newsagents and encourage this to become a more equitable partnership.

Ford sets up factory for used-car venture

By John Griffiths

Ford is setting up a 'used-car factory' to prepare and sell to its dealers up to 85,000 nearly new vehicles a year.

The venture, called Ford Direct, is believed to be the first used-car retailing scheme in which the manufacturer is taking direct responsibility for preparing vehicles for sale and providing warranties for them.

It also represents a response to research carried out by Ford during the past 18 months which, the company admits, shows motorists to be 'deeply cynical' about the integrity of the motor trade – frequently with good reason.

The high level of complaints from consumers about used cars has led the Office of Fair Trading to start an investigation into the trade and its dealers.

The Ford Direct venture, which starts next month and in which the company is investing about £10m, initially is being confined to cars less than one-year-old. All will be returned vehicles from short-term rental companies which Ford has supplied, or from Ford's own company fleets.

This means initial maximum yearly sales through the scheme of about 45,000 vehicles. Yet if it is well received and proves commercially viable, it may be widened to embrace other sources of similarly aged cars and total about 85,000 cars a year.

Even at the 45,000-a-year level, the scheme would account for about 10 per cent of total annual sales of 'nearly new' cars under a year old.

Most of Ford's rivals run their own dealer-based 'manufacturer-approved' used-car retailing schemes, such as Vauxhall's Network Q operation, and may dismiss Ford's initiative as little different from their own schemes.

CONSUMER PERCEPTIONS v DEALER PERCEPTIONS

What affects your choice of car dealer?			Why do your customers come to you?
Dealer Reputation	6%	23%	Dealer Reputation
Type of car	29%	31%	Quality/Price/Value
Product choice	7%	13%	Product choice
Convenience	13%	4%	Convenience
Recommendation	9%	2%	Recommendation
Advertising	18%	4%	Advertising
Treatment in showroom	10%	4%	Treatment in showroom
I was passing by	8%	19%	Manufacturer-backed

Source: Ford Direct

Yet Ford maintains that its scheme eliminates the three most serious sources of concern aired by consumers about other operations: that dealer-based 'independent' pre-sale checks and tests are neither properly independent nor rigorous; that warranties offered are not comprehensive enough; and that too often dealers try not to honour them.

The fundamental difference, however, is the manner in which cars are to be processed for sale.

In the opening weeks of the scheme Ford has contracted three independent outlets to prepare the cars for inspection by its own personnel and RAC inspectors.

Mr Ian McAllister, Ford of Britain chairman, said the company was identifying a final site for the single 'used-car factory', which will process cars on flow-line principles similar to a normal assembly line.

The final stage will remain an RAC inspection after which the car is identified with what Ford insists is a non-forgeable Ford Direct hologram.

The cars' specifications will be entered on Ford's computer network as they are being processed, and the company's 1,000 dealers will bid for them via their Viewdata terminals.

Ford says that as part of the scheme, which includes the company's 12-month warranty, buyers will be able to exchange any car with which they become dissatisfied up to 30 days after purchase.

Dealers say tactic is not a runner

By Motoko Rich

Independent second-hand car dealers and their customers in London were yesterday sceptical about Ford's venture.

Mr Roger Firth, owner of Southwark Park Service Station in south London, said: 'I do not think the trade is going to lose sleep over it.'

Mr Terry Stockdale, manager of John's Autos in east London, said: 'I reckon the manufacturer's dealers will mark up their prices by at least £200–300 more than us.'

Mr Terrence Puleston (above), co-owner of T & T Autos, also in east London, said: 'I think Ford will come unstuck the way business is going. The trade is so bad that it comes in silly spasms, one week you might sell three cars and then another three weeks you might not sell any.'

One of Ford's biggest selling points for the scheme is its 12-month warranty. But most independent dealers already offer private warranty schemes. Mr Richard Davis, who

bought a used Ford Fiesta from John's Autos yesterday, said: 'I have bought about 10 cars from used-car dealers and I have been happy.'

A woman who had brought a male friend to help her look for a car at Westcombe Carriage agreed with the Ford finding that dealers prefer to talk to men.

She said: 'Used-car dealers think they can pull one over on the women.

'But I don't mind because it is the car I am going to drive not the person selling it.'

Source: Financial Times, 28 January 1994

13.12   As the potential purchaser of a Ford used car, what advantages and disadvantages would you see in Ford Direct?

13.13   Apart from the statements about customer service, what other advantages do you think Ford have identified for themselves in this venture?

13.14   As a thriving second-hand car dealership how much of a threat do you think this is to your business and how could you react?

13G

Branded bargains

Neil Buckley on plans for factory outlet centres throughout the UK

As the fuss dies down over the arrival in the UK of warehouse clubs, the US bulk-selling discount format, retailers are waking up to a new threat from the US: factory outlet centres.

After warehouse clubs, these discount centres or malls have been the fastest-growing form of selling in the US over the last decade, with sales reaching $10bn (£6.7bn) last year.

Now, both UK and US developers are planning to build on the success of the first two factory outlet centres in Britain – Hornsea Freeport and Clarks Village. Hornsea Freeport, which opened three years ago in Humberside, attracted 1.4m visitors last year and Clarks Village at Street in Somerset had 1m visitors between opening in August 1993 and the end of the year.

Developers have at least 15 further projects in the pipeline for the UK and then plan to move into continental Europe. These projects will put pressure on traditional retailers, particularly on small independent stores, and expose the clothing sector to the kind of price competition that has developed in the UK grocery industry in the last three years.

Discount factory shops, often situated on factory premises, where manufacturers sell off overmakes, slight seconds, or retailers' returns, are already well-established in the UK. Corporate Intelligence, the retail consultancy, estimates there are at least 1,400.

What developers started doing in the US in the early 1980s, and now want to do throughout the UK, is to group such outlets together in purpose-built malls. Shoppers can then choose from a wide range of branded goods from manufacturers such as Calvin Klein, Nike, Aquascutum or Laura Ashley, at prices up to 50 per cent below conventional retail outlets.

There are almost 300 factory outlet malls in the US, with about another 150 planned. Average size is around 150,000 sq ft, but some are more than 1.5m sq ft – as big as the largest UK out-of-town shopping centres. Forecasters expect total turnover to double to $20bn by the end of the decade.

The centres offer advantages to both manufacturers and consumers. Shoppers have the chance to buy branded goods they otherwise might not be able to afford. They can also turn a shopping trip into a day out, as factory outlet centres are designed as 'destination' shopping venues, offering facilities such as playgrounds and restaurants.

Manufacturers enjoy the ability to sell surplus stock at a profit, and in a controlled way that does not damage the brand. Traditionally, surplus stock has been sold into the discount wholesale and retail trade, which can include market stalls, where manufacturers do not control their brand image.

'Initially profit was not the driving factor, it was turning distressed stock into cash,' says Paul Knight, retail and factory outlet development manager at shoe manufacturer C & J Clark, which operates Clarks Village.

'But in the US people have realised these malls are not just means of disposing of stock, they are successful profit centres in their own right,' says Knight.

US manufacturers have turned factory shops into a powerful marketing tool. Some companies use them to test-market products before launching them in high street stores.

The outlets can also be used to sell current lines – for example, avant-garde designs that have not caught on in the mainstream retail market.

But opinions are divided on how successful the format is likely to be in the UK. Robert Clark, director of Corporate Intelligence, says there could be scope for up to 50 outlet centres, with annual sales of £1bn.

'We reckon they will prove very popular indeed. There is a thirst for that kind of retailing, and a realisation that these places not only offer good value but a good day out.'

Others are more cautious. Richard Ashworth, partner specialising in out-of-town retailing at Hillier Parker, the commercial property agents, says there may be scope for fewer than 30. 'The UK is not big enough for them to proliferate,' he says.

Factory shopping centres in the UK

Hornsea Freeport: Operated successfully by Peter Black Holdings for three years.

C & J Clark: Opened centre at Street, Somerset, last year. Opening another in Cumbria and seeking site for a third.

Prime Richardson Tarmac. Consortium of US and UK developers and UK construction company. Plans three centres in Wiltshire, Birmingham and Derbyshire.

BAA, McArthur/Glen: Joint venture between privatised UK airports operator and US outlet centre operator. Plans six centres. Seeking sites in continental Europe.

Value Retail. Consortium of SD Malkin properties and Chelsea Group of the US, and Argent Group and London Metropolitan of the UK. First centre at Bicester, Oxfordshire, due to open this year. Plans up to 10 on motorway corridors.

Guinea Holdings: Complex at Hartlepool due to open in August. Also plans a centre at Kinross, near Perth.

Tobacco Dock: Former jewellery retailer Gerald Ratner is advising a consortium developing a 75-shop centre in London's Docklands.

Factory Outlet Shopping Centres: Pilot centre opened in York last year. Plans 10 to 12 around UK.

US operators have built most factory outlet malls an hour or more's drive from the nearest large city. In the smaller, more densely-populated countries of Europe, few such sites exist.

Another potential problem is opposition from retailers unhappy at seeing their prices undercut by manufacturers selling directly to the public. So far, there has been little opposition from US retailers to the centres, partly because they have been sited well away from cities. McArthur/Glen, one of the biggest US factory outlet operators, says it is sensitive to high street retailers, and does not, for example, use specific brand names in advertisements for its centres.

But European retailers may defend their markets more aggressively. Costco, the US warehouse club operator, had to go to the High Court last year to fend off a joint legal challenge from the UK's three biggest supermarket chains Sainsbury, Safeway and Tesco, aimed at overturning planning permission for its first warehouse club in Britain.

Both the size of the market, and opposition from retailers, may depend on who factory outlet centres appeal to. In the US, where brand-buying is well established and designer labels sought after, factory centres have a broad appeal. In the UK, where retailers such as Marks and Spencer offer quality own-label alternatives more cheaply, it is less clear who the centres' target audience will be.

Knight says research at the Clarks Village suggested it appealed to 'brand-conscious, aspirational people. Those who didn't aspire to brands were the ones who went away disappointed,' he says. 'They were looking for "cheap", but we are not "cheap".'

But while factory outlet centres do not sell 'cheap' goods, and their share of the UK market could be limited, they are still expected to have a significant impact on UK retailing. Only 10 per cent of clothing in the UK is sold through discount outlets, compared with almost 50 per cent in the US, and factory centres are likely to narrow the gap.

By establishing new lower price 'floors' for branded goods they will further increase price competition among retailers, and help turn the 1990s into what retailers are already calling the 'value' decade.

Source: Financial Times, 6 January 1994

13.15 Produce a profile on the type of consumer who would

(i) be expected to buy from factory shops carrying branded goods; and
(ii) one for those who look but do not buy.

13.16 Given that factory shops appear to offer clear advantages over buying the same product through a retailer in the high street, what additional service are you expecting from the retailer to compensate for the higher price?

13.17 If factory shops were banned, what other forms of non-store retailing could the manufacturers engage in which would not be quite such a challenge to the high street store?

13.18 'Factory shops don't cut out the middleman, they just introduce a further layer of competition in the distribution channel.' Discuss.

14

Physical Distribution and Logistics

A cursory glance at the sheer number of delivery vehicles on national and international road networks, will demonstrate the reliance that firms have on physical distribution and logistics management. It is very expensive to have empty vehicles on the road and takes a great deal of management skill, effort and planning to ensure that this doesn't happen too often.

Decisions concerning the handling of materials supply, materials management and physical distribution is the domain of logistics. If efficient logistics management is practised, the close links with the customer provides an unrivalled opportunity to improve customer satisfaction. Physical distribution management is concerned chiefly with the actual movement of finished goods through channels such as warehouses, wholesalers and retailers, to the end user. You would find tasks such as order processing, packing, stock levels and channel selection within the physical distribution function.

The introduction of EPOS systems has enabled raw materials or semi-finished goods suppliers to play a greater role in satisfying the needs of manufacturers and retailers. This in turn, has led more recently, to a closer relationship with suppliers, often called partnership sourcing. It is difficult to see how such schemes could ever have been implemented had it not been for the wide-spread acceptance of computer-based data gathering, communication and interpretation. It is probably fair to say, that the development of computer technology from the main frame environment through to desk top and now hand-held applications, has been the largest single influence on logistics management and physical distribution activities in the past 50 years.

In order to successfully complete the tasks in this chapter you will need to be familiar with:

- physical distribution management;
- logistics management;
- customer service within distribution channels;
- efficient consumer response (ECR);
- pre-transactional, transactional and post-transactional variables;
- inventory management.

Logistics industry may deliver consolidation

Gossip had not focused on Salvesen, says Geoff Dyer, but closer examination explains Hays' choice

The logistics industry, which was one of the fastest-growing sectors of the 1980s, has been ripe for consolidation for the past two years.

Intense margin pressure and increasing competition have led to falling profits and plummeting share prices for many of the companies specialising in logistics – industry jargon for third-party distribution, warehousing and packaging.

So yesterday's announcement that Hays was planning to make an offer for its distribution rival Christian Salvesen should have come as no surprise.

In fact, City gossip had not focused on Salvesen until very recently – most analysts had predicted that bidders were more likely to look at TDG, which has performed sluggishly in recent years, or Tibbett & Britten, which has issued two profits warnings in the last year.

But on closer examination it is easy to see why Hays, which signalled earlier this year that it was on the acquisition trail, should have Salvesen in its sights.

The two stumbling blocks to any takeovers in the sector do not appear to apply in this case, analysts said. Third-party distribution contracts often have a change of ownership clause, in case customers end up with one distributor for the bulk of their business after a takeover.

However Mr Ronnie Frost, Hays' chairman, pointed out yesterday that the two groups only had two clients in common – Marks and Spencer and Tesco – and both of these were for different products. 'I wouldn't anticipate us losing any business by putting the two groups together,' he claimed.

As most logistics contracts operate from self-contained warehouses, there can be few opportunities to cut costs from taking over a rival's business. However, in this case there should be a fair amount of benefit from acquisition, such as closure of Salvesen's logistics headquarters and a reduction in the sales staff. Analysts expect savings of at least £20m.

Moreover, Hays starts from a position of strength. While its competitors have complained that customers were taking a scythe to margins when they renewed contracts, Hays has improved its profits from distribution by 26 per cent over the last two years.

The group has been skilful at persuading new customers to outsource their distribution and has made successful acquisitions in France and Germany, a feat that has eluded several rivals, such as NFC.

'This would turn them into the strongest operator in Europe and give them the clout to win more new business,' said Mr Robert Morton, analyst at Charterhouse Tilney.

The downside for Hays is that Salvesen has a large exposure to the UK grocery retail market, which has been the site of the most cut-throat margin pressure and which Hays has mainly steered clear of.

However, boosted by its acquisition of Swift Distribution in 1993, Salvesen has expanded its industrial customer base and reduced its dependence on the UK grocers.

The consensus among analysts was that a takeover would benefit the sector.

Some analysts also predicted that if the acquisition went ahead, it could spark a wave of takeovers in the industry. Alternatively, other groups could enter the race for Salvesen.

Possible bidders include Wincanton, Unigate's distribution arm, Mayne Nickless and TNT, the Australian transport groups, and Rider of the US. 'There are enough people out there who want to buy a UK logistics business,' said one analyst.

The benefits for Hays do not stop with Salvesen's distribution activities. Hays has been keen to expand its commercial division, whose businesses include Britdoc, an overnight mail service, and Rentacrate, a container hire operation

Mr Frost said that Aggreko, Salvesen's specialist plant hire company, would allow Hays to increase its industrial clients and reduce the dependence on office support activities.

Aggreko, which is providing temperature control equipment at the Atlanta Olympic Games, was the cause of a profits warning from Salvesen two years ago. However, it increased profits by 20 per cent last year and analysts believe it has the most growth potential of the group's businesses, as it has very few international competitors.

Source: Financial Times, 26 July 1996

14.1 **Establish whether the planned acquisition of Salvesen by Hays went ahead and report on the current situation with the two companies.**

14.2 **Bearing in mind your findings from 14.1 above, what customer benefits can you see from a combined company?**

14.3 **As a manufacturer of products which require physical distribution, identify the advantages and disadvantages of taking out a contract with a firm such as Salvesen.**

14B

Tighter links in the chain

Vanessa Houlder on further upheaval for retailers and suppliers

The relationship between UK retailers and their suppliers may be facing further upheaval. Somerfield, the UK supermarket chain, has begun to cede some responsibility for re-ordering stock to its suppliers, in what it believes is the first large-scale trial of a 'co-managed' inventory system in the UK.

The move is part the retail industry's drive to improve the efficiency of the supply chain, which has allowed them to cut down their stock holdings and improve the availability of stock to customers. Miles Clark, supply chain controller at Somerfield, describes it as 'a significant step towards the management of the supply chain as a seamless end-to-end process'.

Like many other improvements in supply chain management, the introduction of co-managed inventory – which was pioneered by Wal-Mart in the US – stems from advances in technology. Its success depends on providing suppliers with up-to-date sales information from the stores, which has been made possible by linking the computers of retailers and suppliers through a system known as electronic data interchange.

The exchange of this type of information has generally been done on an arm's-length basis. Now, however, Somerfield is asking its suppliers to use the daily updates about sales, together with shared knowledge about planned promotions, to replenish stocks without waiting to be asked. During the six-month trial, Somerfield will merely stipulate a basic level of availability.

By closely monitoring sales to customers, suppliers will have a more accurate and timely idea of what is required than if they waited for the retailer to place an order. That will allow them to respond more quickly, so shortening lead times, reducing stock levels and improving the availability of goods.

Somerfield believes the system will be mutually advantageous. 'The major point is that it is not the retailer imposing this. It is definitely a matter of working together,' says Karen Myers, Somerfield's supply chain director.

But suppliers, which have seen their negotiating position weakened by the increasing dominance of the large national retailers over the past 15 years, are aware of potential risks. Reduced lead times and more frequent deliveries add costs to the manufacturer, whereas the cost savings tend mostly to accrue to the retailer.

The suppliers taking part in Somerfield's project, which include Bass, Cadbury, Kraft Jacobs Suchard, Nestlé, RHM Foods and Chivers Hartley, are all volunteers.

Smaller suppliers may be more concerned about the introduction of co-managed inventory as they are usually less technically advanced and may have greater problems in a faster response and more frequent deliveries. But Somerfield is adamant suppliers will not be excluded if they are unable to adopt this technology.

The blurring of roles between supplier and retailer may have some disadvantages. Although suppliers may have more sophisticated models of future demand for their product, they will not benefit from Somerfield's knowledge about the sales of its entire product range.

Currently, suppliers informally give retailers intelligence about promotions by its rivals which it would be loathe to lose. 'Maybe there needs to be the right to be told about a competitive activity and a duty to inform,' says Clark.

If Somerfield's trial is successful, other retailers may follow suit. According to John Thorpe, managing director of GE Information Services which supplied the software, sharing responsibility for ordering with suppliers could become the norm in much of the industry.

The belief in the future of co-managed inventory is also shared by some suppliers. According to John Breeze, commercial director with responsibility for logistics at RHM Foods: 'People are beginning to realise that the information revolution is actually here.'

Source: Financial Times, 21 June 1995

14C

Europe's new interest in ECR

Alan Mitchell on how manufacturers and retailers could cut $33bn out of the grocery supply chain

The flights to Geneva that night were full to overflowing. If you did not check in early, you got bumped off to the next aeroplane. A conference on Efficient Consumer Response was the offending item. Its organisers had set themselves a target of 300 delegates. At 1,200 they closed their book. They turned another 300 away.

ECR has swept the US grocery industry over the past three years, but until now it has received a chilly reception in Europe. In the UK it has been widely dismissed simply as a US attempt to catch up with the UK's highly efficient supply chain. 'It sounds like a gimmick to me,' says the marketing director responsible for one of the UK's top 10 grocery brands.

So why the sudden stampede of interest? First, because in an unprecedented display of unity the big names of European grocery manufacturing and retailing have joined forces to promote ECR via the recently formed ECR Europe Executive Board, whose 18 blue chip sponsors include Nestlé, Mars, Coca-Cola, Albert Heijn and Promodès. Second, after a year of pilot studies, the board claims ECR could take 5.7 per cent worth of cost, or $33bn (£21bn), out of the European grocery supply chain.

Even more important, ECR offers a practical way to break the logjam of traditionally adversarial manufacturer/retailer relationships, which are beginning to make both sides vulnerable to new competitors.

At ECR's heart lies a realisation that the beggar-my-neighbour strategies often adopted by both sides simply shunt problems – and costs – up and down the supply chain. They do nothing to make the system as a whole more efficient.

Many of ECR's basic techniques are already well known, if not widely practised. They include automated store ordering (where point-of-sale scanning data is used to trigger new orders automatically), cross docking (where goods are moved from suppliers' lorries to retailers' lorries with no time being spent in a warehouse) and reliable operations (delivery of 100 per cent correct orders, in full, on time).

According to John Millen, vice president of sales for Procter and Gamble in the UK and Scandinavia, ECR implies 'a seamless flow of information and products involving manufactures and retailers working together in joint planning and demand forecasting. Both sides might take on functions traditionally handled by the other if they can do it better and at a total lower cost. It will drive changes in business process, organisation structure and information systems'.

In the European context, ECR means more than improved logistics, insist its new enthusiasts. It is, says the board, all about 'working together to fulfil consumer wishes better, faster and at less cost'. And that means focusing not only on replenishment, but also on the efficient operation of product introductions, promotions and assortments.

In a board-sponsored Europe-wide study, Coopers & Lybrand conducted a value chain analysis, which measures current performance in these 'four pillars of ECR' against best-known practice. That is where the $33bn savings figure comes from. The study is also the source of a set of 'maturity profiles' which companies can use to judge their relative performance in key ECR practices.

The resulting ECR 'scorecard' has another, more strategic, purpose: the creation of common measures and language for manufacturers and retailers to use in joint projects.

The big challenge is that ECR requires a change of culture, says Antony Burgmans, a member of the Unilever main board. 'It is a different way of doing business.' Yet today's industry leaders won their spurs in an adversarial environment. Now 'we have to change the latent sense of hostility to co-operation, to trust, to partnership'.

Well worn clichés? Yes, says Graham Booth, supply chain director at Tesco, and co-chair of the value chain analysis project. 'But now we are moving beyond clichés to doing it. I was very sceptical before I joined the ECR board,' he says. Now, however, 'I am very enthusiastic. We thought our business was pretty strong in supply chain terms,' he explains. 'For example, our in-store stock holding is down from 4.4 weeks to less than a week. We were looking for the next quantum leap and the VCA health check caused us to refocus.'

Tesco's ECR project, he says, 'changed some of the strategies we were going for, and in the end, the structure of the business'. That includes his job. He is now in charge of strategic supply chain development which, he says, 'definitely includes partnership development'. As if to emphasise the UK's greater emphasis on category management and marketing and the US obsession with logistics, his new cross-functional team is biased towards the first two.

Now, under the auspices of the Institute of Grocery Distribution, a UK ECR board is being established. To be launched in May, it already includes representatives from all the major grocery multiples.

Andy Robson, the IGD's head of supply chain projects, admits 'we have a fair mountain to climb' to overcome UK prejudices. Yet both manufacturers and retailers are realising the industry is crying out for change, says Millen.

Marketers' current behaviour is creating 'distrust and confusion' among consumers, he warns. A proliferation of line extensions offers them a staggering array of non-essential varieties but little real choice, continuous on-off promotions compound confusion and encourage consumers to shop around, while logistics failures mean that consumers often cannot buy what they were looking for. 'We have complicated our business out of sight and we're doing many things that do not add value,' he says.

Meanwhile, new players such as discounters are threatening to undermine the industry's traditional economic foundations.

ECR will take off, Italian Co-op president Vincenzo Tassinara told the conference, because if manufacturers and retailers continue their attempts to improve their own systems and profits in isolation, 'consumers will vote with their feet'.

Source: Financial Times, 8 February 1996

14D

Suppliers put in the picture

Alan Mitchell on Somerfield's trial in Efficient Consumer Response

Plans for supermarket promotions are usually kept secret until the last possible moment. It is against any marketer's instincts to tell competitors in advance about special offers.

But tipping off the competition up to two weeks ahead is just what Somerfield, Britain's fifth-largest supermarket chain, has been asking suppliers to do. The unusual request is part of an experiment in Efficient Consumer Response.

ECR began in the US and is a relation of just-in-time and partnership sourcing. Its central doctrine is that many practices that make good business sense to individuals in the supply chain often add cost or complexity when viewed from the perspective of the chain as a whole.

One ingredient of ECR can be 'co-managed inventory'. Instead of sending out orders to suppliers as stocks get low, retailers hand over the task of generating orders to the manufacturers. Both parties jointly agree forecasting techniques and the supplier takes over responsibility for replenishment using up-to-date sales information from the retailer.

The reasoning behind a manufacturer alerting competitors to a promotion in the Somerfield experiment is as follows: if Brand A has a special offer, there is little point in Brand B supplying stock that is not going to be sold.

A condition of the exchange of information is that advance warning of promotions is used for logistical purposes only. Nevertheless, Karen Myers, Somerfield's supply chain director, admits that 'it was one of our biggest hurdles'.

How widely such *glasnost* could be applied across the industry remains open to question. As one wary brand marketer says: 'It's all very well in an experiment with Somerfield, but what is going to roll it out across the whole of Tesco?'

The Somerfield experiment, which has just been completed, involves 12 manufacturers supplying 1,000 different product lines. First results since the trial went live at the store's Ross-on-Wye regional distribution centre last November are good enough for the retailer to plan extending the scheme to other depots, suppliers and products.

Stock levels were reduced by up to 24 per cent, and the percentage of the time shelves were empty decreased by up to 2.5 percentage points. An increase in sales of about 0.3–0.6 per cent was generated. That may not sound much, but Myers said turnover could be boosted by between £7.5m and £15m if the figure were translated across the whole organisation.

The immediate efficiency gains for manufacturers seem to have been minimal, although there have been benefits in building relations with retailers. According to Mike Trevor, head of logistics at Reckitt and Colman, and one of the participants, financial savings will only accrue for manufacturers once a critical mass is reached and control of replenishment allows production schedules to be fine-tuned.

One supplier pulled out of the trial, while others, including Reckitt and Chivers Hartley, hope to accelerate wider adoption by joining together to sell the concept to other retailers.

Somerfield's is one of the first trials in a UK-wide programme of ECR pilot projects. A 20-strong strategy group – including big names such as Tesco, J. Sainsbury, Safeway, Asda, Procter & Gamble, Lever, Nestlé and Mars – is initiating the experiments.

Meanwhile, according to Tom Vyner, deputy chairman of J. Sainsbury, the UK supply chain is already one of the most efficient in the world and the greatest headway could be made on marketing.

Vyner pinpoints three areas where marketing methods are 'significant drains on both manufacturer and retailer resources'. These are: new product launches, which have a failure rate of 80 per cent within two years; promotions, where benefits are often more than outweighed by reduced margins and extra packaging and distribution costs; and having the wrong products on the shelves at the wrong times.

Source: Financial Times, 20 June 1996

14.4 Assuming that ECR is successful, how do you think this would affect the traditional manufacturer–supplier–retailer chain?

14.5 What benefits do you think ECR could deliver in terms of pre-transactional, transactional and post-transactional variables?

Retailers aim to refill their shelves just in time

As stores seek to avoid large holdings of stocks, suppliers are having to adjust their methods, writes Motoko Rich and Graham Bowley

Ms Ann Iverson, the chief executive of Laura Ashley, the clothing and homewares retailer, is passionate about what she calls 'stock cleansing'.

'Managing your stock [of unsold goods] and getting rid of it before its sell-by date is very important,' she says. 'If you put more on your plate than you are capable of digesting, you end up paying the price.'

Ms Iverson is typical of many retailers. To avoid weighing down their balance sheets and store shelves with costly unwanted stock, they have made big efforts to improve the efficiency of their supply and distribution chains by installing just-in-time delivery methods. 'Obviously the ultimate objective would be to have the stock arrive at your back door when you actually want to put it on sale,' she says.

While this ideal may still be some way off, efforts in that direction have nevertheless yielded results.

Both manufacturers and retailers overestimated consumer demand in the second half of last year. But while resulting large build-up of stocks of has since forced manufacturers to rein back output sharply, retailers have experienced a relatively mild stock build-up which they have managed to shed quickly.

The latest official figures show that retail stocks rose by a seasonally adjusted £221m in the third quarter of last year, following a £285m rise in the second quarter, while the ratio of retail stocks to sales reached levels not seen since 1979. By comparison, manufacturing stocks grew by £769m in the third quarter, more than double the £354m increase in the previous three months. Wholesalers' stocks rose by £237m, following an increase of £40m.

More up-to-date data are not available yet, but the indirect evidence which has emerged in the months since then – a sharp slowdown in manufacturing output combined with a pick-up in retail sales – is consistent with retailers cutting back on new supplies and beginning to reduce their existing stocks. The latest Confederation of British Industry distributive trades survey, however, suggests that retailers' stock holdings are still adequate to meet demand.

In the drive towards greater efficiency, retailers have focused largely on improving systems which monitor their sales and stocks. Many high street chains have installed sophisticated computer programmes, known as Electronic Point of Sale – or Epos – systems, which track precisely how much they sell on a daily basis, helping them to improve stock ordering efficiency.

'Investment in technology has helped to control inventory and drive stock levels down and improve stock turn,' said Mr James May, the director-general of the British Retail Consortium.

Boots, the retail and healthcare group, is about to install a newer model of its Epos system. Mr Rod Scribbens, the group's director of logistics, says that the system, which allows stock levels to be adjusted on a store-to-store basis, has reduced the number of weeks the group holds stock before selling it by 15 per cent to 20 per cent. 'For most of our inventory we would not have stock for more than a week,' he said.

Such stock control in the retail sector has intensified the burden on suppliers, which are either forced to keep the stock or develop more efficient production methods themselves to reduce the amount of stocks sitting on their books.

'The whole thrust of Epos and just-in-time delivery is to keep down stocks in the retail sector and put the onus back on the suppliers,' says one retail analyst. 'It is more likely that the suppliers would suffer if there were a problem in relieving stock because the retailers by and large tend to hold the trump cards.'

According to one textile industry executive: 'Most retailers are trying to take one or two weeks out of their pipelines so we just have to make the goods a little later than we used to. Most retailers hold back in telling us what they want until later in the season.'

In many cases, retailers have been able to take full advantage of the rise in suppliers' stocks. 'The fact that wholesalers have been stocking up has been to our benefit in that we can use them for spot buying and keep prices under control,' says Mr Eric Holes, the finance director of QS Holdings, the discount retailer.

But the strong bargaining position of retailers is due in large part to the better high street trading conditions over Christmas and the new year. In spite of improve-ments in their stock management they remain exposed to any reversal in consumer sentiment.

Retailers may hold the trump cards for the time being but the consumer may yet have the final say.

Source: Financial Times, 12 February 1996

14.6 **The article reminds us that many retailers have installed sophisticated EPOS systems although this is not a common feature away from the high street. Identify alternative methods of inventory management and support each of your alternatives with an example.**

14.7 **What issues would have to be considered before deciding on an inventory management policy?**

14.8 **What impact could a 'stock out' situation have on an organisation? Include both positive and negative issues.**

14F

Taking the plunge

Partnership sourcing can be bliss but it can easily end in tears, explains Richard Gourlay

You own a components factory and a company such as Ford invites you to become a 'partner' in the integration of its supply chain. Should you reach for the champagne or find the emergency exit?

A businessman returning from a long stay on Mars and viewing the way suppliers relate to customers, and vice versa, would be forgiven for not knowing the answer.

From one part of industry he would hear the vocab-ulary of conflict: José Ignacio López de Arriortúa, head of purchasing at Volkswagen, demanding that its sup-pliers deliver substantial price cuts year after year; suppliers complaining that they could not 'make price rises stick' or, if they were lucky, crowing they 'had managed to pass on raw material increases'.

From another corner of industry, however, come the mellifluous phrases of partnership sourcing – an extension of supply chain integration or sup-plier development. Here such tempting notions as 'teamwork is better than combat' blend with the claim that suppliers and customers working in har-mony, trust and openness can release benefits for both partners.

According to Partnership Sourcing, a joint venture between the Confederation of British Industry and the Department of Trade and Industry, small and medium-sized enterprises are not confused.

'We have moved on from a small number of com-panies using partnering, not with all their suppliers but the strategically important ones,' says Neill Irwin, director of Partnership Sourcing on secondment from ICL. 'Now in the SME area partnership is spreading like wildfire.'

Much of what partnership sourcing preaches makes sense and did so long before the term entered the management lexicon. What, for instance, could be more logical for a customer than to involve suppli-ers in the redesign of a product from an early stage?

But as the idea spreads, more suppliers are recog-nising that formal partnerships can give them a competitive edge, Partnership Sourcing says. Take TR Fastenings, a UK-based maker of nuts and bolts for customers such as IBM, Compaq and Hewlett-Packard. For most manufacturers it supplies, the fastenings are less than 1 per cent of the product cost. But up to 80 per cent of that cost is incurred getting those parts to the production line, says Malcolm Diamond, managing director of TR Fastenings.

'We are doing more and more logistics management of items that are inexpensive in terms of unit price but expensive in terms of time,' says Diamond.

By relying on the partnership developed with its customers, TR Fastenings can provide a distinctive service even though it is selling a relatively low-tech product similar to those supplied by competitors. Instead of both the supplier and customer checking for quality, storing stock and constantly repeating the ordering process, TR Fastenings does everything.

The customer benefits by spending more time on those areas where it adds value; TR Fastenings gains additional business. It uses its trucks to supply other low-value items to some of its customers. And because it feels it has more long-term business, Diamond says he can plan further ahead; TR Fastenings is now investing in new plant worth £1m, a commitment which would have been more difficult if the company had been chasing a series of one-off orders.

For Terry Emery and Tony D'Alton, partners in Pinewood Structures, makers of timber frames, partnership made the difference between survival and failure. Soon after starting to develop a partnership with Laing Homes, the house-builders, Pinewood was forced to within a whisker of receivership by a £370,000 bad debt.

Laing decided it valued its partnership and was happy with Pinewood's performance on quality and price. So it increased its orders. 'Had Laing not responded as it did, I think Pinewood would not have survived,' says Emery. With the help of London International Mercantile Bank, which supplied a line for letters of credit, Pinewood is about to emerge successfully from a three-year company voluntary arrangement. What is more, Peter Taylor, Laing Homes' commercial director, says the partnership actually 'flourished' amid 'greater communication'.

Not all partnerships are so fruitful for the smaller suppliers. They seem to work best for those companies that seek partnership rather than have it thrust upon them.

Saying 'no' to the invitation could threaten sales to what may already be an important customer. And frequently partnership is no more than an extension of a (usually large) customer's cost-cutting programme.

Steve Young, vice-president of consultants AT Kearney, says some 'partnerships' simply do not exist. Research with the Manchester School of Management last year found no evidence that firms claiming partnership relationships behaved significantly differently from those that don't. 'True partnerships are a rarity,' he says.

What happens to an electronic components supplier, for example, sandwiched between a large customer demanding annual price cuts and a large raw material supplier, such as British Steel, which is raising the cost of a crucial input? The supplier's sense of partnership with its customer evaporates as quickly as its profit margins.

What is more, Young says, the quest for 'true partnership' can prevent companies adopting practices that fall short of this goal but which nevertheless would lead to better supply chain integration: electronic data interchange, automatic stock replenishment and the co-ordination of design functions, to name a few. 'There are many shades of grey between outright adversarial purchasing and partnership,' he says.

Partnership sourcing is now a revered management concept. But the old power imbalances between small supplier and large customer remain fundamentally unaltered, despite the cosy rhetoric.

It may be that small suppliers courted by a customer will have to tie the knot. But they should remember that the difference between a cuddle with a partner and a bear hug is a matter of degree.

Source: Financial Times, 14 February 1995

14.9 **Identify the various physical distribution tasks which firms like TR Fastenings and Pinewood Structures are undertaking for their customers.**

14.10 **Identify the benefits and pitfalls of partnership sourcing for both large and small firms.**

14.11 **What customer service and transactional variables are being satisfied through partnership sourcing?**

15

Communication and the Promotional Mix

Manipulating the many and varied elements of the promotional mix, is the principal way in which an organisation communicates with its existing and potential customers. All of the elements: Advertising, Sales Promotion, Personal Selling, Direct Marketing and Public Relations, have a well-defined role and quite specific levels of effectiveness in a given situation.

Getting this mix right is important, as is an accurate selection of the communication channel through which the firm can send the messages. With so many items of information bombarding us every day, overcoming the 'noise' within the communication channel is by far the most difficult, as it is an element over which there is little control. 'Noise', might be physical noise with just too many people talking at once, or it may be noise which is produced unintentionally. A promotional message which buries the information on where to buy the product in a barrage of 'low prices', 'get one free', 'new formulation', is unlikely to be purchased, however good the product is. Similarly, encoding your message to suit the target market is just as important. There would be little future in trying to sell relaxing family holidays in Scotland by showing footage of energetic parties from last year's Edinburgh Festival.

Promotion, and especially advertising, can be very expensive, thus the need for careful planning and target selection is essential. Many organisations really do not know how effective their promotional efforts are in terms of increased sales, higher brand awareness or improved market share. They think they know, but rarely is it possible to be certain. This makes it relatively easy for promotional budgets to be cut. Therefore, it is the marketer's responsibility to obtain feedback and evaluate the effects of a promotional effort, otherwise it might just as well be money down the drain.

In order to successfully complete the tasks in this chapter you will need to be familiar with:

- judgemental/data based budget setting;
- response hierarchy models;
- push/pull strategies;
- source credibility;
- VisCAP model of presenter characteristics;
- personal-impersonal communication methods;
- alternative media.

No accounting for advertising

Companies should tell shareholders more about the big amounts spent on campaigns, argues Kevin Parry

Advertising is one of the most effective means of communicating product value to consumers: indeed, some £2.4bn was spent advertising the top 100 brands in the UK in 1994.

Moreover, when co-ordinated properly in the marketing mix, advertising also plays a crucial role in directly enhancing shareholder value.

It might be expected, then, that directors would be keen to focus in annual reports on the amount spent on advertising, and to link that expenditure with current or expected improvements in corporate performance. Yet annual reports to shareholders are surprisingly coy about advertising expenditure and about the effectiveness of campaigns.

A KPMG review of the report and accounts of FT-SE 100 companies – whose brand advertising expenditure accounts for more than one-third of the UK total spent on the top 100 brands – shows that expenditure is rarely revealed, let alone justified, by the directors.

Judging the quality of information in annual reports is necessarily a subjective exercise; KPMG's review has used three broad definitions:

● Low or no coverage: advertising and marketing may or may not be referred to; but specific campaigns are not mentioned and there is no attempt to quantify levels of expenditure or its effects. For example, banks and insurance companies are high spenders on advertising, but provide little coverage in their annual reports.

● Moderate coverage: specific campaigns or launches are referred to, perhaps including pictures of the advertising, but there is little detail about the campaign, the underlying strategy for communicating with customers or quantification of results. For example, Cadbury Schweppes mentions that marketing expenditure is a priority to ensure the continuing strength and earning potential of its brands. It also reveals the overall

level of marketing expenditure at £467m, being a 10 per cent year-on-year increase and representing 11.6 per cent of sales in the current year compared with 11.4 per cent in the previous year. However, there is little detail about the nature of any of the campaigns and little quantification of the effects.

● High coverage: specific campaigns are discussed in detail, including the nature of the campaign and the underlying reasoning, and an attempt is made to quantify the effect of the campaign in, for example, monetary terms or the number of new customers reached or the expected impact on market share. Normally, pictures of the products and campaigns are given to highlight the impact of brands.

Guinness's discussion of its relaunch of Bell's falls in this category, with details of a £15m marketing support campaign, with information about tactics, launch packs, retail promotions and the effect on sales including the number of 'new' whisky drinkers. It also outlined the next step in the campaign – to focus on young trend-setting adults and to 'seed' Bell's at selected locations.

In the retail sector, Argyll's discussion of Safeway's strategy is also high-quality. Several pages are devoted to the company's approach to understanding its customers, and rolling this out into marketing

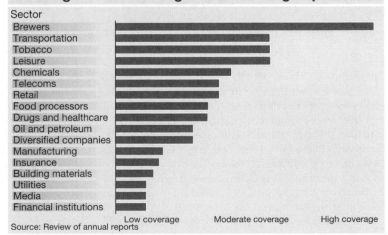

Coverage of advertising and marketing expenditure

Sector

Brewers
Transportation
Tobacco
Leisure
Chemicals
Telecoms
Retail
Food processors
Drugs and healthcare
Oil and petroleum
Diversified companies
Manufacturing
Insurance
Building materials
Utilities
Media
Financial institutions

Low coverage   Moderate coverage   High coverage

Source: Review of annual reports

and advertising initiatives. This provides an effective picture of the thinking behind the company's actions and engenders confidence in the strategies.

Ideally, greater quantification would have been provided for the number of new customers expected and the anticipated impact on market share and future earnings and profitability.

Companies which tend to give the best information are, not surprisingly, those which place great emphasis on the importance of brands and the development of brand loyalty among consumers. But some branded sectors, notably banking and financial institutions, give little coverage of their extensive advertising campaigns in their annual reports.

The need for advertising and marketing expenditure to be explained more fully in annual reports was recognised in 1993 by the Accounting Standards Board.

The Institute of Practitioners in Advertising, the advertisers' trade association, has for some years emphasised the need to measure the effectiveness of advertising. While quantification of effectiveness is not straightforward, it is not impossible and companies should rise to the communication challenge; advertising should be advertised.

The author is head of advertising and promotions services at KPMG.

Source: Financial Times, 11 January 1996. ©KPMG

15.1 **Obtain the Annual Reports from three different companies operating in either the brewing, tobacco or chemical sector, and three more from companies in either the telecoms, food processing or manufacturing sector.**

i **Draw up a comparison of the amount of information provided in the Reports on their marketing spend. Using the article as a basis for assessing the firm's willingness to disclose information, prepare your findings in a manner suitable for presentation to other members of your class.**

ii **Your presentation should also include your views, where possible, on which method of budget setting the firms might be using and a discussion on why firms might be reluctant to publicly disclose such expenditure items.**

15B

Peugeot: a media blitz

Car ads now focus on a brand's personality and attempt to tap into the feelings of drivers, say Diane Summers and Haig Simonian

Tonight, at about 10.15, one of UK television's largest roadblocks is being erected by Peugeot, the French-owned car manufacturer.

Whichever commercial channel a viewer turns to, it will be difficult to evade launch advertising for the company's latest model, the Peugeot 406. All of ITN's News at Ten commercial break will be devoted to the ad – the first time, it is claimed, this has happened – while airtime has also been booked on satellite and cable channels at around the same time.

The media costs of the advertising campaign will total £12.5m for the initial burst; on top of this will be

the expense of making the film (around £1m) and the additional public relations hype.

Spending on such a scale is not new for the sector: eight out of the 20 highest-spending advertisers in the UK last year were car makers. But the 406 launch is an illustration of the lengths to which advertisers are prepared to go, particularly when promoting models intended for the company fleet market.

Starting at about £12,500, the car is competing with models such as the Ford Mondeo, General Motors' Vauxhall Vectra and the Renault Laguna. All are aimed primarily at the same user – the middle-level company car driver.

The business car market in the UK accounts for about 65 per cent of all sales. While fleet managers will be primarily concerned with discounts and resale values, 'user-choosers' – those who have some say about what they drive – may be more swayed by a brand's 'personality', emotional appeal and, above all, what the car says about their status at work.

The 405, the new car's predecessor, gained a reasonable foothold in the fleet market, while its smaller sister, the 306, has also done well in the UK. Nevertheless, Peugeot's share of the UK car market fell to 7.4 per cent last year, from 7.7 per cent in 1994, mainly because buyers were awaiting the arrival of the 406.

The importance of making an impact quickly, establishing the right image and raising awareness, is emphasised by Tod Evans, commercial director of Peugeot's UK arm, hence the TV roadblock.

In spite of previous adventurous advertising, including the controversial burning cane fields ad in 1988, the Peugeot marque has a safe, dependable, but still rather boring image which the company is seeking to counteract. The latest campaign's theme could be summarised as: Peugeot knows you (the male company car driver) may look like an average chap doing an average job but, in reality, you are a seething mass of emotions with a strong heroic streak. Drive the 406, give rein to your inner life, and show you are someone a little out of the ordinary.

The film starts by stating the average person has 12,367 thoughts a day and then enters the mind of a 406 driver as he motors along. To the lyrics 'Search for the hero inside yourself' scenes of war, birth, a charging elephant, a drowning person, a ravishing woman, and a child threatened by a jack-knifing lorry, flash by in succession.

The car brochure reinforces the theme, using 'quotes' from 406 drivers, for example: 'They used to call me steady Eddie. Probably because I never appeared to do anything out of the ordinary. . . So the 406 was a little bit of a surprise for them. Now they're going to have to reconsider a few other things as well.'

The tagline 'the lion goes from strength to strength' has now been replaced by 'the drive of your life'.

In Germany and France, a separate campaign is being used which will emphasise safety, while in Italy and Portugal different versions are being used of the UK film. Evans describes the UK ad as a 'very mature film any of us can relate to' and an 'emotional experience'. Mark Wnek, executive creative director of Peugeot's agency, Euro RSCG Wnek Gosper, claims one hard-bitten senior company executive had tears in his eyes as he watched.

Hype or not, one thing is certain: there is very little about the car or its specifications in the ad. Evans says potential buyers will get details through press ads and information packs containing a video, as well as printed material.

Wnek, who is scathing about most car advertising, explains the more oblique approach by arguing that many manufacturers are frequently too direct and disrespectful to their audiences, in effect saying: 'You're a boring salesman in a Polyester suit and you'll like this car.' Viewers now have 'such a sophisticated anti-advertising radar, you have to sneak underneath to give yourself a chance', he says.

Chris Satterthwaite, a partner with agency Howell Henry Chaldecott Lury, argues that because cars are now so similar advertising is bound to move away from emphasis on technical features and play to 'softer' attributes. 'There is a lack of sustainable unique selling propositions in all products sectors – everybody copies everything so quickly. What you can sustain is a personality, and the software around the hardware,' he says.

His agency has taken a different approach again for Mazda, the Japanese car maker, with the reputation for innovative products which nevertheless has failed to make the sales impact it had hoped for in Europe. 'Interactive' ads have required TV viewers to tape ads and replay them for product information, 'puncturing the style of car advertising which, classicly, overplays the car's functions or overhypes the emotional thrill you get driving. Mazda is saying to people, make up your own mind', he says.

Even Ford, the Procter & Gamble of car advertising, which has traditionally gone for a straightforward demonstration of the product, is now tapping into the emotional feelings of car drivers.

Says James Page, business director on the Ford account at agency Ogilvy & Mather: 'Manufacturers are now looking to communicate more than simple product benefit. They are looking to emotional values, the way people feel and think about a particular brand.' The last Ford Mondeo commercial, for example, told the story of a man prepared to leave Venice because he cannot drive his Mondeo there. The car only features in the last few seconds of the ad.

The trend is set to continue, forecasts Page. This sector of the car market may be about vehicles used primarily for work, 'but that doesn't mean there has to be an unnecessary focus on work'.

Whether life outside work extends to being ravished by a beautiful woman in a restaurant, as in the Peugeot film, 406 man can at least dream as he negotiates the traffic between appointments.

Source: Financial Times, 1 February 1996

15.2 It would seem that TV advertising by car manufacturers is aimed at the individual buyer, although, by far the largest purchaser of cars in UK is the fleet market. What benefits can there possibly be therefore, in continuing to advertise on TV?

15.3 Using any of the response hierarchy models as a framework for your analysis, which stage(s) do you think this particular series of advertisements is aimed at?

15.4 Is this an example of a push or pull strategy? Justify your response.

15C

Beauty and the advertising beast

Virginia Matthews looks at the crackdown on outrageous claims

Next month the Advertising Standards Authority will publish the results of a spot check survey into the claims being made in hundreds of health, beauty and slimming ads this summer.

The survey reflects mounting concern at the self-regulatory advertising watchdog that consumers' fears over anything from cellulite to impotence are being exploited by companies which promise the impossible.

The authority's move follows the granting of a High Court injunction against a series of advertisements for a hair restorer product which claimed that baldness sufferers could reverse their condition.

The 'cure' amounted to 'standing on your shoulders for a short period each day', according to John Bridgeman, director-general of the Office of Fair Trading.

In his submission to the High Court, Bridgeman referred to the ads – placed by Quest Hair Research on behalf of its product Restore – as 'a particularly blatant and persistent attempt to mislead consumers and frustrate the efforts of the ASA'. Another hair product to fall foul of the OFT was a depilatory cream which it was claimed could prevent, permanently, the growth of unwanted body hair. Although challenged to produce evidence to substantiate its claim, the company was unable to do so.

When threatened with court action by the OFT, distributor Anthony Green & Co, and its advertising agency Lavery Rowe, gave legally binding undertakings not to repeat the ads. The OFT yesterday won a High Court ban on advertisements for Citra-Slim, a slimming product also promoted by Green.

While the more outrageous 'miracle' claims for health and beauty products have, according to the ASA, begun to diminish, regular abuses of the codes of advertising practice continue to give 'cause for concern'.

The ASA's first detailed survey of so-called 'code compliance' by beauty advertisers took place last year. Of the 470 health and beauty ads examined, 23 per cent were either 'unacceptable' or 'borderline', according to the authority.

One, for Solgar Vitamins, with its 'advanced antioxidant formula', appeared to claim that using the product could alleviate dietary problems associated with the depletion of the ozone layer.

Complaints against a series of ads for Wellbeing Royal Jelly, which claimed the product could relieve 'cold symptoms, depression, nervousness, indigestion and aching joints', were also upheld.

Among the worst offenders, says the ASA, were slimming ads – 72 out of the 174 examined (41 per cent) flouted the codes by such tactics as presenting specially designed 'tight-fitting garments' as a permanent route to slimness – and anti-ageing products.

The perennial search for eternal youth continues to be exploited by manufacturers, says the authority, with some marketers even claiming to 'regenerate skin tissue or enhance cellular repair'.

While the ultimate sanction against a miscreant advertiser is a court injunction, or even a prison sentence, the ASA has also devised, in conjunction with the Newspaper Publishers Association, representing national newspapers, what it calls the 'ad alert system'.

Advertisers who have been the subject of three 'ad alerts' – where their claims are so outrageous that the media has been warned not to accept them – must have all their ads pre-vetted for a year before they can get anything published.

'Large health and beauty companies don't tend to give us great problems,' says an ASA spokesman. 'Some of these fly-by-night operators have given the entire industry a bad name.'

Source: Financial Times, 11 July 1996

15.5 In your work groups instigate a discussion with two teams taking opposite sides.

Team 1: believes that advertising need not be controlled because nobody forces the customer to buy. In any case, isn't it the customer's responsibility to make themselves aware of what they are buying? Even if it only makes the customer feel better, and it keeps people in work, haven't we all benefited?

Team 2: is adamant that customers need protection from unscrupulous advertisers who will take advantage of them given half a chance. There are a lot of people who believe in the 'lose two stones in a month', or 'get rich quick' schemes and they are being preyed upon.

Note: You will need to select somebody to act as Chair, Moderator or Referee!

15D

Party strategists may have the devil to pay

Labour's counter to the 'immoral' Conservative poster attack on Blair has risks of its own, reports John Kampfner

For all the denunciations of churchmen and high-minded politicians, there was not much contrition to be found at Conservative central office yesterday. Rather the reverse. Tory strategists appeared to be basking in the publicity produced by their latest advertisement, which shows Mr Tony Blair, the Labour leader, as the devil incarnate.

'There will be a lot more yet,' said a senior party official. 'It takes time for the message to seep through the consciousness of the voter, but I think we're getting there.'

The aim behind the 'New Labour. New Danger' campaign, using a range of shock poster images, is simple: to sow doubt in the minds of voters who might be considering voting Labour. With little chance of achieving a net gain in their total support, the Tories have one priority – to make the undecided have second thoughts about dumping them at the general election.

Labour's chief strategist, Mr Peter Mandelson – a consummate campaigner – argues that the Tory tactics are not only immoral but also counter-productive. 'Not only is the message unconvincing, but the medium is off-putting,' he said. 'People associate the Tories with sleaze, and they simply don't believe or trust them.'

Labour has responded with a risky counter-charge, through the slogan 'Same old Tories. Same old lies'.

By repeating some of the accusations made by government ministers, Labour is drawing attention to them. Yet its strategists maintain they have no choice. Experience in the US and other elections shows that any allegation has to be countered quickly. If ignored and left to fester, it does more to undermine confidence in the party under the spotlight.

The main parties claim their respective approach is working. There is probably an element of wishful thinking on both sides. Recent opinion polls have provided inconclusive evidence, both about the extent of the Tory climb back from the implausibly large gap of 30–40 points, and the success of its negative message.

Asked whether the posters made them better disposed to the Conservatives, most voters said they did not. Tories argue that they may not like it, but the voters who matter will eventually pay attention.

The next phase begins in September, in the run-up to the party conferences. The Tories already have several advertising ideas.

Some will attempt to put across a positive message about the government, others will focus more specifically on the 'dangerous' aspects of Labour policy.

It has become perceived wisdom to argue – with up to nine months still to go – that this election campaign will be the dirtiest yet. They said that last time, and the time before, and the time before that. There was not much subtlety in the Tories' 'double whammy' boxing advertisement in 1992, or its 'tax bombshell' or its famous 'Labour isn't working' which helped to bring Mrs Margaret Thatcher to power in 1979.

Many Tories feel uncomfortable with the idea of invoking satan, especially against a man who is a practising Christian. Only a few have gone public with their doubts; approval from others can be measured by the passion with which they defend the strategy. As for Mr John Major, the prime minister, he enjoys a political scrap, and there is no sign that he disapproves.

Ultimately, the morality of the strategy will not be judged in a vacuum. It seems inconceivable that voters will both disapprove of the Tories' sledgehammer approach and vote for them. Labour will claim the moral high ground. Mr Blair will be advised that there is political capital to be gained by staying in the pulpit.

Source: Financial Times, 14 August 1996

15E

Tories revel in success of controversial advert

By George Parker, Political Correspondent

The Conservative party yesterday celebrated the 'good value' of a controversial advertisement portraying a demon-like Mr Tony Blair, after a former Tory media chief kept the row alive by criticising the image.

Mr Hugh Colver, who quit as director of communications six months ago, said the advertisement – featuring the Labour leader and a pair of burning red eyes – represented the kind of 'negative campaigning' which partly led to his resignation.

His comments were quickly seized upon by Mr Peter Mandelson, Labour's campaigns chief, who said: 'The Tories are in a hole and should stop digging, by saying now they will not repeat the advertisement or anything like it.'

But the renewed controversy over the advertisement delighted some officials in Conservative Central Office, who believe it has offered the party some of the best free political publicity in recent years.

In spite of the week-long furore over the image, Tory sources pointed out yesterday that the advertisement, devised by M&C Saatchi, had featured in only three Sunday newspapers and was unlikely to be repeated elsewhere. 'This really is very good value advertising for us,' a Tory official said.

The party can look forward to yet more media attention if the Advertising Standards Authority decides to censure the party for breaching its code of practice, which covers protection of privacy of individuals.

The on-going row over the Tory demonisation of Mr Blair masked the gentler criticism of the Labour leader expressed by his deputy, Mr John Prescott, in an interview in yesterday's Independent.

Mr Prescott admitted some Labour MPs had voted for people they 'couldn't stomach' to sit in the shadow cabinet in the interests of party unity – thought to be a clear reference to Ms Harriet Harman, who angered colleagues by sending her son to a grammar school.

He also warned that Labour's election appeal had to be built on 'ideas, principles and substance', not image and said the party was 'uneasy' about the pace of change under Mr Blair's leadership.

In another barb, apparently partly aimed at Mr Gordon Brown, shadow chancellor, he said some policies 'seem to appear rather quickly'. Earlier this year Mr Brown surprised colleagues by announcing he was considering abolishing child benefit for 16–18 year-olds to help fund training schemes.

Source: Financial Times, 17 August 1996

15.6 In terms of the VisCAP model of presenter characteristics and communication objectives, assess the likely success of this poster campaign.

15.7 On the continuum between personal and impersonal methods of communication, where would you place the political parties' poster campaigns?

15.8 Poster campaigns are relatively poor at conveying complexity. Assuming that the politics of the UK is indeed a complex subject, why do you think all parties continue to use this medium?

15.9 The Conservatives seem highly pleased with their 'demon eyes' campaign and believe that it has offered the party some of the best free political publicity in recent years. It is often said, that there is no such thing as bad publicity, just publicity. How effective do you think all this is in persuading people to register a vote? Justify your response with supporting arguments.

15.10 As a media adviser to the Conservative party, what other methods of media communication would you recommend to Dr Mawhinney?

Public fed on a diet of eggverts

'Alternative' media are turning up in the strangest places, reports Diane Summers

Go to buy a London Underground ticket and there is a strong chance that, from now on, you will be handed a leaflet offering money-off vouchers for hamburgers or theatre tickets together with your tube ticket.

The scheme, just launched, is the latest in a steady stream of new ideas designed, it seems, to exploit every opportunity to promote a commercial message.

Recent months have seen the advent of, for example, 'eggverts' – advertising messages on eggs – videos on buses and ads on racehorses.

Aspen Specialist Media, the company which has formed a joint venture with London Underground for the ticket office leaflets, cornered the Post Office market recently with advertising-based TV programmes which are being shown to captive queues.

According to Marco Rimini, planning director with CIA, the independent media buying company, the developments are part of a wider trend away from rigid demarcations between areas where commercialisation is or is not acceptable. The surge in sponsorship of TV programmes and sporting events and trophies is another indication of the trend.

Transport-related 'alternative' media seem particularly popular. Liveried taxis, decked out in a company's colours and advertising slogans, are now a common sight. United Airlines, the US international carrier, has had the largest liveried taxi campaign to date, with 170 cabs on the road.

The airline's advertising agency, Leo Burnett, devised the slogan 'United Airlines, the best of both worlds' and decked out the front half of cabs as yellow New York taxis and the back half as regular London black cabs. Passengers also receive airline schedules and copies of in-flight magazines. The Financial Times has had a similar campaign with pink taxis and free copies of the newspaper.

Taxi Media, the company operating the advertising, charges £5,600 a year per taxi, plus a respraying charge of about £2,000. The panels inside taxis cost upwards of £4 each a month.

Advertising on buses might be mainstream, but last year The Economist magazine went one step further by putting a poster on the outside roof of the number 133 bus, which follows a City route, reading 'Hello to all our readers in high office'. Advertising agency Abbot Mead Vickers BBDO, which thought up the idea, said one of its art directors looked out of his eighth-floor office and noticed 'that the red bus tops were Economist posters waiting to happen'.

Freight Media also specialises in vehicle ads. It provides mobile poster lorries, special display vehicles and seat-back advertising on tourist buses.

Back on the Underground, escalator wall advertising is commonplace – less obvious but now available is advertising on the steps themselves. Not a centimetre is unexploited, with some travel tickets showing an advertising message on their fip side.

In the supermarket, there are ads on the floor, while Birmingham-based Swan Marketing offers 'trolley media' bringing, says the blurb to potential advertisers, 'your message, consumer and brand in perfect harmony at the point of purchase'. The advertising panels on the trolleys now reach nearly half of all households in Britain, the company claims.

At the golf course, advertising is sold on ball washers at the first tee and beer ads can be glimpsed inside the hole.

Eggverts have been used by Sky TV to launch a subscription drive, and BT to advertise reduced call rates. The ads are printed on the eggs using a high-pressure jet blowing tiny dots of food colouring on the shell of each one as it passes on a line.

According to Rimini, it is this kind of technological development, as much as a desire to do something different in a world where the existence of advertising has become commonplace, that is driving the 'alternative media' industry.

Alternative media can be closely targeted: it is possible to buy an advertisement on the visa form visitors to Australia are required to fill out, or place stylish postcards in London's most fashionable bars. The latter service, provided by a company called London Cardguide, might be the most cost-effective medium if, for example, an upmarket clothes retailer 'just wanted to talk to those 3,000 people in London who could afford their clothes,' says Rimini.

But, in most cases, the function of alternative media is to back up a mainstream advertising campaign. Space on the supermarket floor, eggshell or tube ticket is limited, so the advertiser's name needs to be well known already.

There is also the danger, Rimini points out, of looking cheap and tacky: 'Check that your brand is not being devalued. One of the arguments in favour of using television advertising is that people think if you're on TV, you must, by definition, be a big player. The reverse is also true. The danger with some of these things is that people will say you can't be very serious if that's the kind of advertising you do.'

Source: Financial Times, 12 January 1995

15.11 **In your work groups, think up as many ideas as you can to identify locations where promotional messages could be carried.**

15.12 **Would such advertising be a push or a pull strategy?**

15.13 **What types of products could best be advertised in this way?**

15.14 **From your lists in 15.11 and 15.13 above, select one combination and create a promotional message, with or without illustrations.**

16

Advertising

Advertising is perhaps the most powerful weapon in the promotional mix, and because of that, the most expensive. It is important, therefore, that the objectives of every advertising campaign are carefully thought through and evaluated before heavy expenditures are committed. Television advertising, in terms of time on screen for amount of currency spent, is by far the hungriest medium. The spiralling costs demanded by TV networks, is forcing manufacturers of heavily promoted branded goods to examine other, more cost effective ways of maintaining their advertising presence.

Working on the assumption that perhaps only 50 per cent of advertising reaches the target audience, and an even smaller percentage actually responds to the message then it can be seen that there is plenty of opportunity for money to vanish into thin air. The oft-repeated quote of 'I know that only fifty per cent of our advertising is working, the trouble is, I don't know which fifty per cent', rings very true, especially for those sectors which rely heavily on advertising to maintain a presence in the market.

Advertising, however, is not just the preserve of the large conglomerates, vehicle manufacturers and FMCG firms, although they do certainly dominate. Advertising can be used very successfully by other organisations, such as a local council for example, as a way of providing information on new developments or communicating views on a particular issue. Political parties have also realised the power of advertising and recent years have seen both the two main UK parties, Conservative and Labour, fight their battles through the roadside hoarding.

Competitive or comparative advertising, is a relatively new activity in the UK. In order to fully exploit its potential, the instigator has to make sure that all the facts are correct, otherwise litigation soon follows.

In order to successfully complete the tasks in this chapter you will need to be familiar with:

- formulating the advertising message;
- creative appeals;
- advertising campaign planning;
- TV advertising;
- competitive/comparative advertising.

Tobacco's pole position at risk

An anti-smoking campaign aims to invade one of the sector's last media bastions, says John Griffiths

If exploratory talks under way between a design engineer and potential corporate sponsors prove fruitful, the legislation- and lawsuit-harried tobacco industry may find itself at bay on its last global marketing platform: the race tracks of Formula One.

Hugo Spowers, whose Surrey-based Prowess engineering concern includes a Formula Three team and a classic cars restoration business, predicts that within the next two seasons grand prix cars will be circling the track funded by non-tobacco multi-nationals. The subtle but unambiguous message will exhort the young not to smoke.

Spowers, himself a racing driver and founder member of the notorious Dangerous Sports Club, says that 'several' potential sponsors are interested in advertising the campaign against children taking up smoking to the vast global television audiences – up to 800m per race – of Formula One. The campaign is already being waged on the circuits by Spowers's 'Extinguisher' Formula Three team.

Under-16s are estimated by Gordon McVie, scientific director of the Cancer Research Campaign, to spend £160m a year on cigarettes in the UK alone. Anne Charlton, a Manchester University academic specialising in the relationship between children and smoking, says most try their first cigarette between the ages of 9 and 11 and that 9 to 10 per cent of 11-15-year-olds now smoke.

Spowers, who has received support from a number of political and other public figures, ranging from former health secretary Edwina Currie to entrepreneur Richard Branson, insists that the Extinguisher project will be trying only to dissuade children from taking up the habit – it will not attack the freedom to smoke, passive smoking or even tobacco promotion.

Nevertheless, it is inevitably controversial for the world's most expensive branch of motor sport, where more than half the cars on the grid are funded by tobacco concerns collectively spending an estimated £90m to £100m annually.

Lord Alexander Hesketh, former grand prix team owner and now president of the British Racing Drivers' Club, has already accused Spowers of seeking to undermine motor sport.

Privately, grand prix teams admit that they can foresee other sectors readily taking over the tobacco advertising slots.

The campaign is being pursued at a particularly sensitive time. Not only is US President Bill Clinton's administration proposing sweeping regulations to curb smoking by teenagers, but the industry has been shaken by the decision by Liggett, whose best-known brand is Chesterfield, to seek financial settlement with two of many anti-smoking litigants with suits against the industry. No US tobacco company has paid compensation in an anti-smoking suit before and the decision is seen as a potentially devastating precedent.

A Stop Before You Start campaign launched at a House of Commons press conference recently saw such disparate figures as Currie, shadow education minister David Blunkett, Baroness Denton and former racing driver Sterling Moss all line up behind Spowers.

He is well-known in motor racing and has a deserved reputation for flamboyant eccentricity. It was Spowers who conceived a St Moritz downhill ski race for grand pianos, inflatable elephants and a rowing eight, and who broke neck, back and pelvis in pioneering the bungee jump from Bristol's Clifton bridge.

The seriousness with which he is pursuing the Extinguisher project threatens to put grand prix on the spot. The tobacco companies can hardly oppose the venture publicly as they are formally pledged to dissuading youngsters from taking their first puff. But there is no doubting their private displeasure at the prospect of such an intruder in one of the few sporting arenas left where they can promote their products relatively freely.

Grand prix teams such as Williams (whose major sponsor is Rothmans), Benetton (main backer Japan's Mild Seven brand) and McLaren (RJ Reynolds's Marlboro) are maintaining a discreet silence, except to indicate that they will take the Extinguisher project seriously only when Spowers can produce clearly identified sponsors matched to a competitive team.

So far, Spowers is refusing to name potential backers. But he is understood to have reached outline deals on partial sponsorship for the project with a

Japanese cosmetics group, which has begun assembling a consortium of complementary, non-tobacco Japanese companies to fund the projected £15m needed for each season.

The Extinguisher project's original goal was to develop the Formula Three activities into a grand prix team; but this has been discarded in favour of creating and matching sponsorship funds with an existing grand prix team.

Spowers is relaxed at the prospect of the tobacco industry threatening to withdraw its sponsorship if Extinguisher were allowed access. 'They will never leave grand prix until they are kicked out,' he says.

The teams acknowledge that rapid withdrawal of tobacco sponsorship from grand prix would be financially painful. Most are resigned to anti-tobacco laws and advertising bans eventually squeezing tobacco out of grand prix. They envisage tobacco sponsorship being replaced by advertising from other sectors – such as soft drinks or household goods – which may have been previously deterred by the strong associations with tobacco. 'They [the tobacco industry] spend millions on this absurd message that smoking is glamorous and at last we have a voice of reason in the sport,' says Branson.

Source: Financial Times, 22 August 1996

When smoke gets in your eyes

Marlboro retreats in US billboards dispute, writes Richard Tomkins

Cigarette advertising on television has been outlawed in most developed countries for years; but oddly, the ban has not prevented cigarette advertisements on viewers' television screens.

This is because manufacturers have often succeeded in getting around the ban by placing advertisements at sporting events in such a way that cameras are sure to pick them up.

In the US, opponents of this controversial practice seemed to triumph last week when Philip Morris, maker of Marlboro, the world's best-selling cigarette, agreed to move its billboards out of the view of television cameras at sports arenas after being threatened with a suit by the Justice Department.

The department alleged that Philip Morris had circumvented a 24-year-old US ban on television cigarette advertising by putting billboards next to the playing area or scoreboard at more than 30 sports arenas.

Philip Morris denied the charge, saying the ads were aimed solely at people who attended the games and that any television coverage was incidental.

However, it agreed to move all the offending advertisements out of the normal view of the television cameras 'to eliminate debate over placement'.

The agreement means US viewers can in future expect to catch only rare and fleeting glimpses of cigarette advertisements in televised baseball, basketball, football or hockey games. But it does not mean an end to cigarette promotion on television because it does not affect other televised sports – notably motor racing. In the case of the sports arenas, Justice Department investigators found the price paid for the space bought by Philip Morris had been set on the basis of how clearly it could be seen by the cameras.

At New York's Madison Square Garden, for example, Philip Morris was assured its courtside Marlboro advertisement would be 'clearly visible on all NY Knicks cablecasts/telecasts emanating from Madison Square Garden as well as on sport news programmes' and the display would receive about three or four minutes of television time per game.

Other cases may be much less clear-cut. In motor sport it might be difficult to prove a cigarette maker's sponsorship deal with a racing team was aimed at flouting a ban, however much that was suspected.

The Justice Department refuses as a matter of policy to say whether it is planning to widen its investigations, but Philip Morris seems confident it will not. 'Sponsorship is viewed as different by both parties,' Philip Morris said. 'It hasn't been at issue and we do not believe that it will be at issue in the future.'

Source: Financial Times, 15 June 1995

16.1 With the acknowledgement that smoking is extremely bad for your health, and given the enormous world-wide advertising exposure which grand prix events receive, why do you think that motor racing advertising continues to be dominated by tobacco companies?

16.2 When deciding to sponsor a Formula One racing team, what advertising messages do you think the sponsor is trying to achieve?

16.3 Given your answer to 16.2 above, assess whether any of them can be categorised within the two broad dimensions of creative appeal.

16C

Beef up your marketing by renting a cow

By Richard Wolffe, Midlands Correspondent

Last week they were just another tragedy of the BSE crisis, part of an unsold herd grazing beside the M42 motorway near Birmingham.

But yesterday these Friesians quit the troubled beef market for the go-go world of the adman. Wearing the latest in promotional clothing, they took to the fields on behalf of two clients to broadcast their slogans to passing motorists.

Ben and Jerry's, the US ice cream manufacturer is the herd's biggest account to date with 12 cows. A further eight won a week's booking from MarketingNet, a small Midlands marketing company.

The idea behind the bovine billboards came from a conversation in a pub between the farmer Mr Harry Goode and two executives from Axiom, a small public relations company in Leamington Spa.

Mr Goode said he was facing losses of more than £7,400 as the value of his older cattle had plummeted after the health scare. Because he preferred natural feed instead of intensive farming, Mr Goode said his 239-strong herd was growing too slowly to secure a profitable price in the post-BSE market.

The solution came in a flash. The motorway beside Mr Goode's farm, at Hockley Heath, carries thousands of motorists to and from Birmingham each day.

By charging advertisers up to £300 per cow for one week the beleaguered farmer could recoup some of his losses.

Mr Goode said: 'The interest we have had is unbelievable. It is an amazing gimmick, but it is also a serious matter because it will bring the whole issue to the attention of the public. If I can get some financial reward, that will help even more.'

Now the farmer is looking for other retail food producer clients. There is even a suggestion of recruiting a network of motorway cows for national campaigns. Mr Peter McGarry, senior executive at Axiom said: 'It was suggested half jokingly, but we soon realised it was a fantastic idea.

The inquiries are flooding in. As far as we are concerned it is the first time this has been done in the UK.'

Animal rights concerns have been allayed with specially designed coats of PVC and cloth, which fit the cows closely but avoid overheating.

But the pressing question for advertisers may be a little harder to answer – will the cows face the right way for people to see them?

'They will turn around for the cars,' said Mr Goode. 'They always do when they are feeding.'

Source: Financial Times, 28 May 1996

16.4 Why do you think that Ben & Jerry's saw Mr Goode's cows as a perfectly feasible advertising medium? What benefits do you think they could expect?

16.5 In terms of ratings, how could Mr Goode demonstrate the advertising value of his Friesian herd?

16.6 As an account handler with an advertising agency, you are wondering whether this wacky scheme is worth it. There are clearly some disadvantages in renting a herd of cows as an advertising hoarding and you have been asked to identify these and assess whether the benefits outweigh the drawbacks.

16D

All in the best possible taste

Virginia Matthews looks at a drive to promote
British food as wholesome and delicious

The beleaguered food industry is poised to mount a £20m-plus marketing and advertising campaign to reassure consumers that British food is safe and wholesome.

The campaign, which is already out to tender with two London advertising agencies, is being spearheaded by a small group of unnamed food manufacturers which are calling themselves the Campaign for Confidence in British Food, or CCBF.

A number of slogans for the publicity drive – including 'Eat The Best. The Best of British' and 'Delicious and Safe – That's British' – are among the contenders.

The aims of the group received backing this week from the Meat and Livestock Commission, whose marketing manager, Chris Lamb, would like to see 'a range of activities to back up the advertising', and the Council for Responsible Nutrition, whose director, Maurice Hanssen, says such a campaign is 'timely'.

J. Sainsbury, which already operates a 'buy British' policy, says it will 'look favourably' on such an initiative. Some 75 per cent of the food it sells is British and it has replaced £50m worth of imported goods with home-produced products in the past two years alone.

But the supermarket chain declines to say whether it has been officially approached for financial support.

The CCBF says that, while the campaign, scheduled to begin later in the summer, will 'avoid being overly-jingoistic', it will kick off by highlighting the strictness of UK food legislation – the new Food Safety Act in particular – and compare it with the apparent laxity of rules in other nations.

Phase two of the TV, press and poster drive is likely to involve setting aside a special week to highlight the diversity and superior quality of British food.

This may be modelled on the French 'Semaine de Gout' – 'Week of Taste' – sponsored last year by the French Ministry of Agriculture.

The CCBF says: 'Rather than bury our heads in the sand until the next food scare hits us, we believe it is vital that consumers are given a positive message about British food.

'The food industry is notoriously bad at showing a united front, but we hope that, given the current climate of suspicion and misinformation about our products, other firms will give us their support.'

While the CCBF membership is prepared to find as much as one-third of the necessary money, other companies will also be approached for cash.

Members of the CCBF want to remain anonymous at this stage for fear that their initiative may be undermined by politicians and, as one of them puts it, 'sacrificed on the altar of our EU membership'. They also fear the response of the industry's many critics, who might actively campaign against any hint of a flag-waving exercise. 'This campaign must not, like so many other initiatives on behalf of British industry, be strangled at birth,' says one CCBF member.

While there have been a number of 'buy British' initiatives by sectors of the food industry in the past – including fruit growers and speciality cheese producers – this would be the first generic campaign on behalf of the entire UK food industry in almost a decade.

The last, in the late 1980s, was run by Food From Britain, the promotional body for British food.

A cautious note was sounded this week by Unilever, which stressed that its sourcing policy was EC-wide, rather than purely British, meaning it could not commit itself to helping fund a purely British approach.

There are other potential problems. Leading food consultant Verner Wheelock says: 'It is no good advertising British food until the industry has totally cleaned itself up and, to be honest, there are still an awful lot of food firms that are cutting corners'.

The Meat and Livestock Commission's current Recipe for Love campaign is set to continue with its first TV advertisement specifically for beef.

The 30-second ad, which was postponed because of the BSE crisis, is in 'an advanced stage of preparation', according to the MLC, and will appear on TV screens either this month or next.

Source: Financial Times, 6 June 1996

16.7 **As a member of the team assigned to respond to the invitation to tender for this campaign, prepare a presentation to CCBF to cover:**

- **campaign responsibilities;**
- **target audience;**
- **campaign objectives;**
- **media selection;**
- **implementation and scheduling;**
- **evaluation.**

16E

Squeeze in TV hurts advertisers

As demand rises, companies say they are paying more for less, writes Diane Summers and Raymond Snoddy

Imagine what consumers would say if SmithKline Beecham raised its Lucozade drink prices and, at the same time, started selling bottles that were only two-thirds full.

Mr John Blakemore, advertising director for SmithKline Beecham's consumer brands, said that was exactly the trick the television companies had pulled on him with their advertising rates.

He will spend about £35m – almost all his advertising budget – on TV advertising this year, but each pound he spends with ITV and Channel 4 will buy him less airtime and fewer viewers during that time than he had last year.

He calculates that, for the first three months of this year, the average price of airtime, which is based both on demand and number of viewers, has risen by 11 per cent compared with the same period last year.

Mr Blakemore said he found it difficult to blame the TV companies for this 'media inflation', caused by increased demand for airtime in a fixed supply market. 'They're only doing their job, as I would,' he said.

As the recession has ended, more companies have wanted to advertise and there have been a number of new entrants to the market, including the National Lottery, the pools companies and, most recently, spirits manufacturers.

The Independent Television Commission, the regulating body, fixes supply by forbidding more than an average of seven minutes an hour advertising, with $7\frac{1}{2}$ minutes during peak times. Advertising on the new Channel 5 is unlikely to be available before late next year.

But Mr Blakemore is angry that as demand and prices have been rising, audiences have fallen. 'In effect, they're saying it's going to cost me more and they're going to give me less,' he said. He reeled off ITV viewing figures for May: down 15 per cent in the first week compared with the same week last year, down 10 per cent in the second week, 9 per cent in the third and 16 per cent in the last week.

Mr John Hooper, director-general of the Incorporated Society of British Advertisers, said: 'The number of eyeballs we're hitting for our money is down. I was sitting round the table the other day with some pretty heavy hitters from Unilever, Procter & Gamble, Mars, Guinness, Rover and SmithKline Beecham. They were unanimous in saying we've got to do something.

'Somebody has got to take notice of what we're saying. We are the customers and we are singularly unhappy.'

In particular, advertisers want to see:
● An extra 30 seconds an hour allowed for TV advertising. They believe this would take some of the steam out of the market by increasing supply. Advertisers say that the extra half minute would still mean the UK was well within European Union limits of nine minutes an hour.

The ITC, which last changed the rules in 1987, allowing an extra half-minute an hour during peak viewing, is unlikely to agree to a further increase and would usually act only if there were an obvious threat to ITV programme budgets.

The ITV companies are also opposed. Mr Barry Cox, director of the ITV Association, which links the ITV companies, said: 'We don't believe an increase in minutage is the answer. We will resist that. We don't want to take it out of the promotion time [for ITV programmes] or programme time either.'
● Increased spending on programmes and promotions to help revive figures. Mr Hooper said that the ITV companies made large savings by merging organisations and sales forces. 'There have been huge economies of scale, but is the money being put back into building the product? We're not totally convinced that it is.'

ITV is optimistic that it can reverse the ratings dip. Mr Nigel Walmsley, chief executive of Carlton UK, the biggest ITV company, said yesterday: 'Starting with the Rugby World Cup we have expectations of a strong ratings performance in the summer and autumn.'

ITV is, however, sufficiently concerned about the issue that a special meeting of the ITV council has been called for later this month to address the issue. The ITV managing directors will be asked to find several million pounds more to boost the autumn schedule in addition to this year's budgeted £550m for the national schedule, including Independent Television News.
● The prize of being allowed to advertise on BBC. Mr Hooper said that the BBC was increasingly moving outside its remit with aggressive scheduling aimed at ITV's weak spots. 'It really is unfair. The BBC is chasing ratings but is still not allowing us any airtime.'

The government has ruled out advertising on the BBC, at least until the end of the century, but Mr Hooper remains optimistic. 'We'll get it eventually, but let us at least have a reasonable amount of airtime available on ITV,' he said.

In the meantime, why do the 'heavy-hitters' agree to go on paying what they believe are inflated rates and why don't they get together to drive prices down?

Mr Blakemore at SmithKline Beecham said: 'A very, very good question. Unfortunately that is called a cartel and it's illegal.'

Source: Financial Times, 10 June 1995

16.8   If advertising on ITV and Channel 4 is supposed to be so expensive and somewhat inefficient, why do you think so many big names still persist in taking part?

16.9   The growth of cable and satellite TV stations has clearly expanded the market for TV advertising. Why is it then that major branded companies still feel it is important to be seen on ITV and Channel 4?

16.10   The ITV Association has decided that an increased allocation for product advertising is not acceptable because it cuts into programme promotion time. What do you think of this view, and do you think it is sustainable? Provide supporting arguments for your answer.

Light touch in battle for brands

A free speech issue, a clever marketing ploy or an unfair promotional device?
Diane Summers looks at EU plans to liberalise comparative advertising

Two chimps are locked up by scientists: one is given Coca-Cola to drink, while the other gets Pepsi. After six weeks, the Coke chimp can hammer pegs into holes and the scientists note his 'remarkable improvement in motor skills'.

The Pepsi chimp, meanwhile, has gone missing and is later discovered driving a Jeep full of young women along the beach into the sunset, to the accompaniment of rock music.

This Pepsi television advertisement – one of a series that seeks to differentiate the drink from the brand leader by giving it, in Pepsi's words, a 'hip and irreverent' image – was unveiled to a US audience of 130m viewers during a break in the Super Bowl football championship in January. The advertisement made it clear that Pepsi was being compared to Coke and both drink cans were displayed.

But when it came to showing the advertisement around the world, further versions had to be made, referring coyly to Coke as Brand X 'leading cola' or, even more elliptically, as Brand X 'leading soft drink'. Comparative advertising, which makes direct comparisons with a competitor's product, is a common and long-standing practice in the US, but is either restricted or banned in a number of other countries.

In Germany, for example, all comparisons are seen as unfair competition – the slogan 'Avis, we try harder' was not allowed because it was seen as implicating fellow car-rental business Hertz, even though the rival name was not mentioned.

Pepsi sees comparative advertising as a free speech issue, as well it might, since it is the number two brand. The convention is that the brand leader never stoops to the tactic. Alan Pottasch, a senior executive in charge of worldwide advertising for Pepsi-Cola International, says: 'As the world moves irrevocably towards free and open markets, we think it's high time that comparative advertising becomes an acceptable way to communicate the concept of choice to consumers everywhere. That's what we believe is at stake here.'

Coca-Cola's response – attempting to get the chimps advertisement and other Pepsi comparative commercials taken off the air in some countries – is, in effect, stoking the 'cola wars'. It has been sug-gested that the cola conflict appears manufactured and is in the interests of both brands – and that both Coke and Pepsi sales increase when their battle is being publicly fought.

Even if it is a marketing ploy, Pepsi is not alone in wanting comparative advertising laws liberalised. In the UK, the government is using a bill on trademarks, currently being considered by parliament, as an opportunity to clear the way for comparative advertising.

There is no absolute ban on the practice in the UK and there have been some famous examples, including Qualcast and Flymo lawnmowers. Duracell and Eveready batteries, St Ivel Gold and Flora spreads and, most recently, The Sun and Mirror newspapers. The latter has appeared mainly in the trade press, a sector which has produced some particularly strong comparative copy.

But, because of existing trademarks' legislation, an advertiser can run into trouble if a competitor's trademark – and names and packaging often form part of the trademark – appears in a comparative advertisement.

The proposed UK trademarks bill clearly specifies that the use of trademarks by others should be allowed 'for the purpose of identifying goods or services'.

However, not everyone is happy about such liberalisation. The Confederation of British Industry, the UK employers' organisation and representative of some of the largest brand leaders, opposes the development.

The CBI attempted to get the bill amended at an earlier stage of its passage so that trademark owners' permission would have to be granted, or, at the very least, owners would receive a warning that the trademark was to be used in comparative advertising.

Emily Marks, a CBI legal adviser, says trademark owners fear that brands in which they have invested could be damaged by competitors 'riding on their backs' to promote their own products. There could also be the danger of selective or subjective comparisons being made and by the time complaints are found to be justified, the damage to a brand would have been done.

Most of all, the CBI considers the trademarks bill provision ill-timed – a European Union directive on comparative advertising is in the offing.

'The European directive may overturn anything that's in the trademarks bill, so it'll all have to be gone into again,' says Marks.

European Commission plans for a directive have been around, in various forms, since 1978. A detailed set of draft rules, which would have allowed comparative advertisements – provided they were restricted to comparisons of objectively verifiable features of goods or services – was thrown out by member states as being overly-prescriptive.

A much simplified version is likely to emerge from the commission this year.

At present, eight EU countries allow comparative advertisements, with varying conditions, while four – Belgium, Germany, Italy and Luxembourg – either ban the practice or have restrictions making it virtually impossible.

If the EU directive does result in Europe-wide liberalisation, are there any lessons that can be learnt from the US experience, where comparative advertising has been used for the past 20 years?

Phil Dusenberry is chief executive in New York of BBDO, the advertising agency which has produced a number of advertisements for Pepsi, including the chimp one. It has also produced comparative campaigns for Visa and American Express, and Pizza Hut against its competitors. Dusenberry says the technique has many advantages but also numerous pitfalls. 'You have assiduously to avoid confusing the consumer. The casual television viewer will sometimes confuse your competitor with your product. That's like throwing money down the drain,' he says.

Dusenberry also believes that a light touch works best, particularly when the difference between brands is a matter of taste – as in Pepsi and Coke – rather than a clear-cut product advantage.

'If you come on too heavy-handed, you could look like a bully or a terrier nipping at the heels of the competition in a way that's off-putting and offensive. Usually the best kind of comparative advertising is done with a sense of humour, with a smile, rather than a sledgehammer,' he says.

Coca-Cola, meanwhile, fails to see the joke. A statement in response to questions about Pepsi's latest advertising reads: 'The Coca-Cola Company is not opposed to comparative advertising as long as the comparison is objectively chosen material, relevant, and scientifically measurable.' Somehow, one suspects Coca-Cola is unlikely to see the chimps experiment as scientifically valid.

Source: Financial Times, 31 March 1994

16.11   Outline the pitfalls in comparative advertising.

16.12   How can you avoid litigation in comparative advertising?

16.13   What is your view on comparative advertising? Does it really make consumers stop and think about the different brands or is it simply a case of one big brand taking a shot at another?

17

Sales Promotion

Sales Promotion is nearly always viewed as a tactical weapon in the promotional battlefield, and a battlefield it can be. Any initiative taken by a promoter by way of money-off vouchers, free trials, BIGIF, loyalty cards and volume discounts, is quickly matched by competitors. This is particularly evident in the FMCG sector where sales promotional tools and techniques reign and proliferate.

Smart operators have realised that it is now possible to get information in return for their 'give-aways' which is inevitably what a sales promotion becomes. This has provided the basis for database marketing, targeted mailings, slicker segmentation and more accurate customer profiling. It is less easy to cash in coupons or vouchers these days without the most basic requirement for a name and address to be added. Along with any till receipts which are required as proof of purchase, a more complete picture of purchasing habits is compiled.

The need for creative thinking to continually come up with new ideas for sales promotions, makes this an exacting and highly charged activity. It is no wonder that so many tend to mimic successful campaigns.

Only when the main objective of the sales promotion itself has been agreed can the appropriate tools be selected. Rewarding the customer can best be done through money based methods, whereas, the need to shift stock or encourage product trial is better executed though product based techniques.

One of the key advantages of the many sales promotional tools available to the marketer is that they all should be relatively easy to evaluate. The operator should know how many vouchers have been exchanged, how much additional product has been moved, how many competition entries have been received and how much more data is held in house for future use. This makes evaluation of the campaign's value and candidacy for a repeat run in the future more objective. It may also explain why sales promotion is a heavily used tool in the FMCG sector, but one which can also play a role in business to business marketing too.

In order to successfully complete the tasks in this chapter you will need to be familiar with:

- customer loyalty schemes;
- manufacturer-consumer sales promotion objectives and techniques;
- sales promotion evaluation;
- joint promotions;
- 11 P's of loyalty marketing;
- guidelines for good sales promotion practice;
- European sales promotion regulations.

17A

Train miles scheme launched

By Charles Batchelor

A voucher scheme designed to give supermarket customers free train journeys has been launched by Great Eastern, one of the newly created train operating companies.

Customers at 30 Tesco stores in Essex and London can from today exchange their till receipts for Train Mile vouchers, which can be used to buy cheap day returns or London Travelcards for local journeys, and trips to Paris and Brussels by Eurostar.

This is the first time a train operating company has offered a promotion of this kind but other operators have introduced schemes to persuade travellers to use the railways. The idea is based on the air miles offered by the airlines.

Great Eastern runs services from London Liverpool Street to Southend, Chelmsford, Colchester, Clacton, Harwich and Ipswich, carrying more than 80,000 people a day.

The company is dependent on peak-hour commuting to and from London and the Train Mile scheme is intended to boost leisure travel on off-peak trains.

Mrs Penny Austin, commercial manager of Great Eastern, said: 'This will encourage those who live and travel in our area to get added value from their shopping trips.'

For every £10 spent at Tesco before May 31 customers may claim a £1 Train Mile voucher. Journeys must be made before the end of the year. Purchases of petrol, medicines, lottery tickets and goods from the coffee shop or tobacco kiosk do not qualify.

Promotional campaigns by other train operating companies have included free children's travel from Gatwick Express and ScotRail's offer of travel for pensioners throughout Scotland for £5 return.

Source: Financial Times, 1 March 1995

The loyal route to gaining a computer

Many retailers now offer voucher schemes which ultimately benefit schools, reports John Authers

Retailers have recently discovered a new route to the parents of school-age children – through the schools.

Most of the UK's largest retailers now have loyalty schemes through which purchases are rewarded with vouchers redeemed by schools in return for equipment. Store chains involved include Tesco, Sainsbury, Asda and Dixons.

The model was Tesco's spectacularly successful annual Computers for Schools scheme, which starts its fifth year's campaign next month. Shoppers are awarded a voucher for every £25 of shopping they complete at Tesco. These can only be redeemed by schools, which receive computer equipment in return.

The scheme runs for 10 weeks a year. During the last four years, 12,000 schools have managed to collect enough vouchers to buy 21,000 computers, valued at about £22.4m.

Sainsbury launched its rival Schoolbags promotion last September. This has a 'green' twist – schools receive vouchers in return for plastic carrier bags, which Sainsbury's can recycle, with the aim of reducing its packaging costs. Carrier bags from other retailers are accepted under the scheme, as Sainsbury's is confident this will still help increase the total number of shoppers entering stores.

So far, vouchers have been distributed to 12,000 schools in return for 50m carrier bags – saving Sainsbury's 450,000 litres of oil that would otherwise have been needed to make new carrier bags. From this week, however, the scheme is being extended to cover normal shopping, as with the Tesco scheme, and vouchers will be available for every £10 of purchases.

The latest entrant, Asda, offers both computers and free Internet connections for schools in return for £25 vouchers. Vouchers are also available in return for taking carrier bags to be recycled. There are extra discounts if computers are bought directly through Asda, and there is an extra tie-in with the Daily Mirror newspaper, which also publishes vouchers. The company says it has 'taken a good idea and made it better'.

Qualifying for the computers involves big volumes of shopping – last year, a pocketbook palm top computer under the Tesco scheme needed 1,200 vouchers, or £30,000 worth of shopping. Under the Sainsbury's scheme, which expands beyond computers, a globe will cost 650 vouchers, while the most expensive multimedia personal computer available under the scheme is 22,000 vouchers – equivalent to £220,000 worth of shopping, or 22,000 carrier bags.

With hurdles this high, amassing vouchers becomes a collective exercise, co-ordinated by schools anxious to gain specific pieces of computer kit. Parents are more likely to listen to an appeal for vouchers from their head teacher or parent-teacher association, amplified by their own children.

The schemes quickly justify themselves. Already, head teachers interested in the Asda scheme are to be found in local papers encouraging local shoppers to send any spare vouchers to them – a phenomenon already widespread with Tesco vouchers.

The state of British education helps the initiative. Government reforms have encouraged governors and parent-teacher associations to take a much more active role. Computers have taken a much higher profile in education, thanks partly to the welter of publicity for the 'educational super-highway'.

Retailing tie-ups have also become a significant element in the battle between computer suppliers to establish a hold in the school marketplace.

Tesco's scheme buys computers only from Acorn, the traditional leader in the market. The company might easily have been overhauled without the extra influx of demand created by the Tesco scheme. Instead, it is extending the concept with the Acorn Advantage scheme, which allows vouchers to be collected from a range of retailers, to count towards a large catalogue of educational supplies.

Asda is linked to Compaq and Sainsbury's to IBM, both big computer manufacturers which have so far made comparatively little impact in UK schools. Both are likely to be helped by their involvement in the scheme.

Source: Financial Times, 29 February 1996

Retailers set to 'market learning like soap powder'

By John Authers

Retailers could give away vouchers for adult education and training in the same way airlines issue Air Miles, under a new scheme to be launched today.

The plan, part of the Royal Society of Arts' Campaign for Learning, already has the backing of organisations, including British Airways, J. Sainsbury, British Petroleum, British Telecommunications, and the Post Office. It is part of a package to 'market learning like soap powder'.

The vouchers – which would accumulate in a 'learning account' – would be transferable and could be redeemed for education and training courses in the way that Air Miles pay for air travel.

Rover Group, the motor company which already has one of the most ambitious learning account schemes for its own staff, is also considering offering free learning accounts as an extra incentive when selling cars.

Several training and enterprise councils already offer learning accounts for employees in particular need of training, and Labour has pledged to spend £150m on creating a national scheme for those most in need. There is also interest in the idea from the government, with 1994's white paper on competitiveness suggesting widespread use of 'learning credits' for adults.

The new proposals are the most ambitious attempt to use the prospect of cheap or free education for adults as a marketing tool. Schemes which allow shoppers to save towards discounted computer equipment for schools are already run by most big retailers, including Tesco, J. Sainsbury and Asda.

Sir Christopher Ball, the chairman of the campaign, said there was strong demand for extra learning. He cited a Mori survey carried out for the campaign which showed 71 per cent of adults thought extra education would improve the quality of their lives. He said: 'It's the motivation to do something about it that they were lacking. They cited not enough time, other responsibilities and sheer apathy as the reasons for their lack of action.'

Promising to market learning courses 'like soap powder', Sir Christopher said: 'Our mission is to persuade people that they should care about their personal learning in the same way that we are all gradually learning to care about the environment and our own health.'

The campaign will set up a telephone hotline for any other companies interested in offering vouchers towards learning accounts.

Source: Financial Times, 24 April 1996

These three articles appear to be reporting on similar schemes, yet there is a fundamental difference in the purpose of each of them.

17.1 Assess the benefits to the retailer in promoting:
- **the voucher system to schools;**
- **the learning voucher system to adults;**
- **the free train journeys to Tesco shoppers in Essex.**

17.2 What difficulties can you foresee in these schemes? Note those already stated in the article as well as those which result from your discussions.

17.3 Customers now seem to expect a reward simply for spending their money. Some would say, that if retailers are able to support such schemes, then they are either charging too much for their produce or making too much profit, or both. What do you think?

Ford to use virtual reality as sales tool

By John Griffiths

Ford is using virtual reality as a sales tool for a new vehicle for the first time.

If the project, undertaken jointly with International Business Machines, proves successful it may become a standard fixture at many of Ford's dealerships.

The immediate use of the technology is to help launch Ford's Galaxy, a multi-purpose vehicle developed jointly with Volkswagen and which is due to go on sale in the UK in the next few weeks.

A potential customer sits in a purpose-built pod, intended to represent the front passenger seat, wears a lightweight headset which generates the virtual reality scene and operates a hand control for a number of functions.

Using specially created software, the potential customer is taken on a four-minute virtual reality drive, through virtual countryside by a virtual chauffeur sitting alongside.

Before driving away the passenger is encouraged to watch as the seating and interior trim of the Galaxy change shape and colour, metamorphosing through the entire range of options available.

On the 'journey' the potential customer can operate all the equipment in the vehicle – for example, opening and closing the windows and sunroof and sampling the sound system. The pod and its hardware have been developed by IBM and the Virtuality Group, with Ford helping to create the software. For three months starting in July several of the units are to be taken on tour around county shows to assess consumer reaction.

If the response is strongly positive, it is expected that Ford will start exploring ways in which the system can be exploited by its dealers, both in the UK and in continental Europe.

Neither Ford nor IBM yesterday would put a precise figure on the likely cost of each unit, but IBM said 'it would certainly be affordable in terms of the amounts dealers typically spend on marketing and information technology'.

Ford sees the system as having much greater potential than a vehicle demonstrator.

Mr Steve Parker, Ford of Europe marketing communications manager, said: 'In future virtual reality technology could also be used by purchasers to select the precise vehicle specification they want from their dealer.

'Information about personal preferences could then be sent electronically to the Ford manufacturing plants enabling just-in-time delivery of customers' specific requirements.'

Source: Financial Times, 3 June 1995

17.4 Identify the benefits of Ford's new sales approach compared with the traditional vehicle demonstration. Which would you prefer?

17.5 How do you think this new activity could be evaluated?

17.6 What benefits do you think there will be for IBM if the idea really takes off?

After the dust has settled

Roland Adburgham and Diane Summers look at the impact of Hoover's ill-fated free-flights promotion

For well over half a century Hoover has been the generic term for a vacuum cleaner. However, after more than 18 months of being linked constantly to the phrase 'free-flights fiasco', the name may now be as readily associated in some minds with a disastrous sales promotion.

Last week Maytag, Hoover's US parent company, disclosed that the ill-fated promotion had cost the company more than £48m – more than double the sum originally feared when Maytag took stock of the damage early last year.

The promotion which caused all the trouble closes this week. In reality, Hoover will feel the reverberations of its free-flights offer for some time to come. There are also signs that consumer attitudes have hardened towards 'free offers' in general, with companies more cautious in their approach to sales promotions of every kind.

The problem for Hoover started in autumn 1992 when it promised customers who spent at least £100 on a Hoover product two free air tickets to continental Europe or the US. From the customers' point of view, it seemed the bargain of the decade. Demand was such that Hoover, which employs 3,500 people in the UK, had to step up production of vacuum cleaners which were just over the £100 threshold.

It rapidly became clear that Hoover had grotesquely underestimated the take-up of the offer. Thousands of customers were infuriated by delays in obtaining flights. Maytag intervened. Three senior executives lost their jobs and a taskforce, at its peak employing 250 people, was set up.

Peter le Conte, chairman of the Institute of Sales Promotion (ISP), says that Hoover could have done 'a lot more a lot earlier' when it became clear the promotion was going awry.

'Perhaps instead of wriggling, it would have been better to have come clean and try and do something else,' he says. Le Conte suggests, for example, that the company might have been able to fulfil its obligations on flights over a period of years.

The offer itself was flawed, from the first, he adds: 'In my book it doesn't stack up to be able to buy a product for £100–£200 and fly to America

for significantly more than the cost of the product you purchased.'

The sheer scale of the take-up of the promotion has been breathtaking: Hoover says 220,000 people have now flown or are booked on flights up to June. The taskforce is now winding down.

'By the end of this month, or by the end of June, Hoover will have fulfilled its commitments and obligations,' says Hoover spokeswoman, Caroline Knight.

Not so, claims a group of dissatisfied consumers which has organised itself as the Hoover Holiday Pressure Group. Last week three leaders of the group flew to Maytag's headquarters in Iowa accompanied by boxes containing what the group said were 7,000 letters of complaint, and on Tuesday the group's representatives spoke at the company's annual general meeting.

The group has yet to decide whether it will pursue legal action in the High Court in London. Hoover has already faced about 70 cases in small claims courts, all of which it has defended, and about one in five of which it has lost.

The Advertising Standards Authority (ASA), the advertising watchdog, is currently investigating seven consumer complaints and the ISP has also asked the ASA to examine whether the promotions industry's voluntary code of practice has been breached.

The code sets out, in general terms, promoters' responsibilities not to disappoint consumers and to make realistic calculations of the likely response to a promotion. However, according to Keith Richards, a barrister at the Consumers' Association, the code lacks teeth. The association, which is still dealing with complaints from dissatisfied Hoover customers, would like to see the ASA, or a similar body, having the power to fine companies which breach the code.

'I'm sure consumers are now shaken and will not be so readily willing to be taken in by sales promotions,' says Richards.

Le Conte agrees that the Hoover case has 'caused people to be more cynical, which is extremely unfortunate'. But he says the ISP has seen a big upturn in companies seeking legal and copy advice before they go ahead with promotions. 'Everybody is super-aware that promotions that go wrong can seriously damage your health,' he says.

Hoover denies that any long-term damage has been done either to sales or to the company's image. Says Knight: 'Customers are able to differentiate between a quality product and, regrettably, a flawed promotion. Our sales figures indicate that the brand has not suffered and we have maintained market share.'

There does not appear to be any evidence that Hoover sales have been damaged. Scottish Power, one of Scotland's largest electrical retailers, says there was a temporary dip in Hoover sales after the offer, which was promoted particularly hard in its territory and provoked a great deal of adverse publicity.

It may be, though, that this dip was caused by a glut of second-hand vacuum cleaners on the market, as people disposed of machines purchased only to fulfill the conditions of the promotion. Whatever the reason, sales soon recovered, says the retailer.

Hoover even had enough confidence last year to offer a new travel promotion and could do so again in the future. Says Knight: 'Travel remains a very key motivator in sales promotions.'

Although the company must be assuming the worst is over, it looks likely that the consequences of the offer will drag on for months, if not years. In the longer term it can only hope the 'free-flights fiasco' will be a relatively short-lived association and that Hoover will mean vacuum cleaners for at least another 50 years.

Source: Financial Times, 28 April 1994

17.7 **What alternative sales promotion techniques could Hoover have used?**

17.8 **Why do you think the 'free flights' scheme went so horribly wrong and what could Hoover have done to prevent this?**

17.9 **What other promotional tools could now be used to repair the damage done to Hoover? Draw up a plan of activities to cover the next two years.**

17F

The faithful shopper

Diane Summers examines Tesco's scheme to attract and retain customers

When Tesco broke ranks last week with the other big grocery retailers in the UK by introducing a national 'loyalty card', it cited two motives.

It wanted to 'say thank you to customers' and recreate, into the bargain, the kind of relationship that existed between consumers and local shops half a century ago.

The scheme works by awarding points for sums spent over a minimum amount each time the shopper visits a Tesco store. The points are added up each quarter and money-off vouchers, to be used against future grocery bills, are sent to the shopper's home. As the scheme was launched there was speculation that other food retailers would inevitably find themselves sucked into competing loyalty schemes.

But missing from the debate has been any wide-scale evidence of what shoppers think of these schemes. A study by the London-based Henley Centre, to be published shortly, is one of the first attempts to examine consumer attitudes to the concepts of 'loyalty' and 'relationship marketing'.

The language used by Tesco to introduce its Clubcard is unlikely to have struck many chords with shoppers, for the idea of loyalty means little to consumers, and relationships are reserved for people and not for companies, found Henley. Indeed suspicion of the very idea that a company might consider it had a 'relationship' was expressed in focus groups.

Qualitative research also revealed that consumers are very canny about evaluating schemes designed to encourage them to try new products or services.

It remains to be seen whether the estimated 1 per cent saved on shopping bills under Tesco's Clubcard will provide a sufficient incentive to switch to the store or continue to stick with it.

As can be seen from the chart, quantitative research among 1,000 adults also indicates that those participating in some recent loyalty schemes have changed their overall attitude to the companies comparatively little. Combining these results with other data, Henley suggests schemes may produce only marginal improvements in attitudes to companies, with participants expressing just 2–5 per cent more satisfaction than the average consumer.

The report questions whether this represents a good return for what may be a high level of investment: in Tesco's case, the company said start-up costs are likely to be about £5m.

Overall, the study concludes that most current loyalty schemes may have some effect on repurchase rates but will fail to sustain changes in consumer behaviour unless quality, price and service measure up and, at an emotional level, there is trust in the company. Trust emerged as one of the most important factors in true consumer loyalty and was decisive in whether an individual would recommend a product or service to others.

These conclusions are similar to those reached by Coopers & Lybrand in 1993 in its study for the Coca-Cola Retailing Research Group of customer loyalty in grocery retailing.

Customer loyalty schemes are 'not a durable substitute for a competitively deficient retail strategy', it stated. If a retailer's core strategy is weak then a loyalty scheme may suppress the symptoms but is unlikely to provide the cure.

The most successful schemes, it concluded, are an integral part of retail strategy: 'The key risk of a 'bolted-on' scheme is that it encourages tactical rather than genuinely loyal shopping.'

The same point has been made by Tim Denison and Simon Knox, researchers from the Cranfield School of Management, who have identified the following uncomfortable paradox: 'promiscuous' shoppers are those most likely to be interested in loyalty schemes, shifting their allegiance from one retailer to another to take advantage of the latest offer.

But the real test for Tesco, and other companies getting involved in similar schemes, is in exploiting the sizeable database they will be able to assemble of customers' names, addresses and shopping habits – an aspect of the Clubcard's operation most shoppers will be unaware of.

Food retailers have done little to date to understand their customers and focus on those who provide them with most profit. Says Marcus Evans, managing director of advertising agency Ogilvy & Mather's newly formed worldwide Loyalty Centre: 'There are people who are popping in for bread and milk, and others who are going in to spend £150. At the moment they are all treated equally.'

Tesco will be able to target its own-brand baked beans, for example, to customers who are known to purchase branded beans; it will be able to find out more about why one family buys its wines and spirits at the supermarket, but another does not; and it could also (although it says it chooses not to) sell information to a manufacturer about purchasers of rivals' products.

The power of such databases can be illustrated by the experience of Felix petfood in the Netherlands, says Evans. In a scheme that his agency helped develop, the names of 100,000 cats have been collected: the cats get their own junk mail, with details of offers and information on new developments.

When Felix, known mainly for its dry packet catfood, introduced a new wet canned product, club members were mailed and offered trial vouchers. Rather than a gradual build up of sales, says Evans, 'the product was moving off the shelves from day one'. Now Felix has introduced a variation on the usual 'member-get-member' scheme, where databases are expanded by existing members giving names of other who may be interested. A 'cat-get-cat' scheme is resulting in cats recommending their friends for membership of the Felix club.

As Henley points out, the ultimate accolade of the loyal shopper is the personal recommendation, rather than the mechanical collection of points on a card.

Source: Financial Times, 16 February 1995

17.10 **Using any one of the numerous supermarket loyalty cards now on offer, visit the store and test their performance against the 11P's of loyalty marketing. You may need to interview the store manager or a spokesperson in order to fully complete this task.**

17.11 Using the information gleaned from its database, what other sales promotion technique could the operators of loyalty cards use?

17.12 Do you think that loyalty cards really do produce loyal customers or do they simply reward customers who would have made the purchase anyway? Are they offered for the benefit of the customer or the operator? Justify your response.

17.13 If loyalty cards were classed as a 'Collector Device' which European countries would it not be possible to operate such a scheme? What alternative sales promotion tools would be available to a supermarket operating in the Benelux countries for example?

17G

We're all going on a plumber holiday

Overseas jaunts are among gifts being used by boiler makers
to boost trade, reports Peter Marsh

Las Vegas, Sardinia and Monte Carlo are the last places you would expect to encounter several plane loads of British plumbers.

But in recent months all three have been on the itinerary of plumbers and heating engineers on holidays paid for by the makers of central heating boilers. They are symptomatic of promotions and discounts in the boiler industry, which some say are getting out of hand, reducing price transparency and eroding profits.

Mr Steve Barker, purchasing director at Graham, a large builders' merchant, says that 'the size of the jolly' was often crucial in helping a plumber choose between different makes of boilers, all of which might be similar in technical performance or price.

The five biggest manufacturers, which account for about four-fifths of UK boiler sales of about £400m a year, are Potterton Myson, part of Blue Circle; Hepworth; Ideal, the boiler division of building materials group Caradon; Baxi; and Worcester, owned by Robert Bosch of Germany.

Between them they fund incentive schemes aimed at plumbers – ranging from free overseas jaunts to supplies of software or telephones – thought to cost about £3m a year. On top of this a complicated system of discounts can lead to a single boiler having dozens of different prices, depending on who is buying it. This can mean the product being sold for as much as 40 per cent less than the list (wholesale) price.

'In this industry there are rebates left, right and centre,' says Mr Alistair Clark, marketing manager at Ideal. 'If anyone can tell me the true price of a boiler, I'll eat my hat.'

Similar schemes are seen in virtually all parts of the building industry – and in other sectors such as pharmaceuticals or insurance where sales staff have to target a set group of customers in a tough competitive environment.

In the boiler industry the high level of incentives to stimulate custom has been encouraged by the sluggishness of the sector.

Sales have been virtually flat for six years, a result of the recession followed by only a subdued rise in consumer spending and the housing market. About 800,000 boilers are expected to be sold this year – at an average wholesale price of about £450 – with four-fifths of them replacements for worn-out systems and the rest going into new houses.

Another factor is the complexity of the supply chain for boilers. Most consumers have little interest in the technical merit of the products.

Instead, boilers are bought mainly by the UK's 40,000 or so firms of plumbers and heating engineers – from big gas installers such as British Gas to one-man businesses. They buy the products not from the boiler makers directly but from builders' merchants.

Since merchants have considerable freedom to set prices, efforts by the boiler makers to boost sales through price strategies alone have a limited effect –

so most of their marketing efforts are built around promotional schemes aimed at plumbers.

The leader in this field is Hepworth, which every year organises a free trip for plumbers who buy above a target number of boilers – perhaps 80 over nine months.

Last April the company took 800 plumbers to Las Vegas for a week. Next year the trip is to Paradise Island in the Caribbean. Other venues on the annual Hepworth jaunt have included Spain, Singapore and Hong Kong.

Mr Brian Powell, managing director of Hepworth's home products division, says the trips encourage customer loyalty and add 'excitement to a boring industry'. He takes personal charge of the visits and insists they are hard work. 'Looking after 800 plumbers on the pop in Las Vegas is a 22-hour-a-day job,' he says.

Hepworth does not disclose the cost of its scheme but this is thought to be about £1m a year – roughly a third of the estimated cost to the boiler makers of the industry's incentive schemes, some of which are organised by builders' merchants although largely paid for by the manufacturers through wholesale discounts.

Wolseley, a big firm of builders' merchants, recently took plumbers to Sardinia and Monte Carlo. Graham rewards plumbers who have met purchasing targets with a range of goodies from free telephones to Marks and Spencer vouchers.

Potterton eschews free holidays on the grounds that this seems too naked an inducement. Instead, it provides free software to help leading plumber customers run their business computers. Ideal has an incentive scheme based around inviting top customers to special training sessions on boiler installation.

While virtually everyone in the industry enters into the spirit of the promotional schemes, many wish there was a way of reining them back. 'We've almost got to the stage where there are too many [incentive schemes] for the health of the industry,' says Mr Andrew Hutton, managing director of Wolseley's builders' merchants division.

Even some of the plumbers do not seem to appreciate the deals. 'We would prefer to negotiate better net terms [on price] rather than be included in a lot of special offers,' says Mrs Edna Buswell, equipment buyer at Wintle Heating in Northampton.

Mr Jack Robinson, who runs the four-man Jack Robinson Heating and Plumbing in High Wycombe, Buckinghamshire, has happy memories of a golf trip to France and two days in Amsterdam which were part of industry promotions. But he adds: 'They [free trips] are not the reason I specify particular types of product.'

Mr Graham Allwood, purchasing director at Robert Prettie, a Nottingham plumbing firm, says the schemes are so deeply entrenched they have a life of their own. 'I don't think the industry will ever stop them.'

Source: Financial Times, 1 August 1995

17.14   How acceptable do you think this practice is, bearing in mind that all incentive schemes have to be paid for by someone?

17.15   Identify the people who benefit and the people who suffer as a result of such a scheme.

17.16   As a newly established manufacturer of technologically superior boilers you find the incentive schemes an increasing barrier to entry. You are tired of answering the 'what's in it for us' question from plumbers. The rewards seem to have got out of hand as manufacturers continually try to out-incentivise each other. Even if you had the funds to compete in this way (which you don't), you are determined not to join in. What can you do to break the vicious circle?

18

Personal Selling and Sales Management

Personal selling, traditionally used in organisational markets where the amount of time elapsed from initial enquiry to specification of product and delivery can take years, is becoming more common in consumer markets. However, there is quite a difference between the genuine concern for a customer's satisfaction which you might receive in a tailor's shop when buying an expensive hand-made suit and the pre-programmed, rhetorical, 'are you alright there?' questions emanating from a bored shop assistant in a high street fashion store.

Sales management and the act of selling particularly is not a job to be taken on lightly. It is hard work, can be demoralising and, depending on the product, rejection levels can be high. It is for this reason that many organisations, especially those in the FMCG sector, put their new graduates into the selling role. If they come through their 'apprenticeship' relatively unscathed, they can take on anything the company cares to throw at them, and to a large extent this is true. It is a question of earning your spurs, and the respect of all the others who have gone before you.

There will always be the born sales executive – the one who can't wait to meet each day's challenges and they are the diamonds of an organisation. Let's face it, without sales revenue, what else would the rest of us have to spend? If the sales team look after the top line, then there should be no problems on the bottom line. There are many 'quick routes to selling success' put out by consultants and gurus, but the only real way to learn how to sell is to do it. There are guidelines and procedures which help to provide a framework for the overall task but, in sales and customer relations, more than any other area in marketing, there is nothing to beat experience and a willingness to accept and learn from mistakes.

In order to successfully complete the tasks in this chapter you will need to be familiar with:

- training/motivation/compensation plans;
- telesales;
- handling objections;
- closing the sale;
- managing relationships;
- monitoring competitors;
- order takers/order makers;
- performance evaluation.

A picture of change

Anthony Thorncroft on new sales policies at Christie's and Sotheby's

For years Sotheby's and Christie's, the twin peaks of the international art market, were more or less indistinguishable. Smooth specialists sold treasures for comparable prices.

The old canard that Sotheby's was run by businessmen pretending to be gentlemen while Christie's were gentlemen pretending to be businessmen has lost its relevance. The aristocratic Mr Henry Wyndham took over as chairman of Sotheby's in London last year, while Christie's is led by a former backroom boy, Mr Christopher Davidge.

Clear water has now opened up between the two auction houses. Christie's has adopted a much more aggressive marketing policy which led to a 13 per cent rise in sales last year to £820m. Sotheby's saw its turnover dip slightly in sterling terms, to £868m.

A sign of Christie's new policy came in January when it took out full-page advertisements in the New York Times to promote its auction of the contents of the apartment of Rudolf Nureyev, the dancer who died in 1993. The auction brought in $8m, double the estimate, with every lot sold.

Having convivial experts in antiques is no longer enough. The company now plans a concerted sales campaign for every important collection. Marketing costs rose 40 per cent last year. In the Far East, which Christie's sees as the great untapped source of demand, it has brought in an IBM executive to head operations in Tokyo, opened an office in Shanghai, and will soon set up shop in Seoul.

However, Christie's has taken its quest for business one step further. To fend off competition from Sotheby's, it offered guarantees to sellers on three occasions last year. If the works of art failed to reach the guaranteed sum in the saleroom, the owners would get their cash and Christie's would be left with the objects.

This could prove a perilous policy if the market falls after a price is guaranteed. Last year, the company was left with a Cézanne after it only attracted an unsuccessful bid of $2.6m, half its assumed value – although it was quietly sold later. A Monet from another collection also went well below expectation.

In spite of these close shaves, Christie's is again offering guarantees on two collections. One is three paintings belonging to Pamela Harriman, the US ambassador in Paris, valued at $20m and including a Picasso that should make $10m. The other is the collection of Ralph Colin, a New York lawyer, which contains a Modigliani also valued at up to $10m.

Last week Christie's went a step further. Its 10 per cent commission charge for sellers was axed, and replaced with a sliding scale of costs. Goods which sell for more than £60,000 will attract a 9 per cent commission, falling to just 2 per cent for properties worth more than £3m.

The change will affect less than 20 per cent of the antiques handled by Christie's in terms of volume but cover 80 per cent of the goods in terms of turnover. It is a bold attempt to counter the power of the big vendors who have taken advantage of the fierce competition between Christie's and Sotheby's to bargain their charges to almost nothing.

After the collapse of the art market in 1990, the turnover of both companies dropped almost 60 per cent in one season. Both were so desperate to attract goods that they were prepared to undercut each other on commission. They could afford to cut their rates to sellers only by increasing their charges to buyers, and in 1993 these were raised to 15 per cent on lots selling for up to £30,000.

But there is a limit to how much buyers are prepared to pay on top of the hammer price. And loading the charges on the buyer also raises questions about whether this is fair when the auction houses are acting for the seller.

'We don't intend to negotiate the vendor's premium in future,' Mr Davidge says. 'We want to rely on the strength of Christie's, its level of expertise, to attract goods.'

Mr Davidge expects the new scale of charges to add up to £15m to Christie's profits in the 1995–96 season, virtually doubling them. Much depends on whether important sellers accept the line that they will gain from higher prices in the auction room what they lose in higher charges.

Much more, however, depends on the response of Sotheby's which is continuing to negotiate commission over the most valuable items. When Christie's first introduced a buyer's premium in 1975 Sotheby's followed suit within days. Mrs Dede Brooks, president of Sotheby's, reckons she has a month to decide whether to maintain the policy, follow Christie's initiative or adopt a different approach.

So far, Sotheby's has attempted to rebuild its profits, which – like Christie's – increased only marginally last year by keeping tight controls on its costs. Mrs Brooks says: 'Our operating expenses are $20m down on Christie's. Spending money is not necessarily the best way to sell works of art. When I see the market is starting to gear up then we will spend more on marketing.'

The next few months could see such an upturn. In addition to the Harriman and Colin collections, the best group of Impressionists for five years is due to be sold. Collected by the late Donald and Jean Stralem, of the Lehman banking family, it includes an early Picasso expected to fetch more than $10m. The whole collection should make well in excess of $40m and Sotheby's is selling it without a guarantee: it believes the quality of the pictures will secure the best possible prices.

And yesterday, Christie's announced it was offering the most important Van Gogh to appear on the market since it sold the same artist's portrait of Dr Gachet for $82.5m in 1990, still the record for any work of art at auction. In today's more subdued conditions a Van Gogh portrait has an estimate of $7m to $9m.

If these auctions go well, more valuable lots may come on to the market, with sellers tempted to accept the new, non-negotiable terms of Christie's. If they do so, Sotheby's cannot be far behind.

Source: *Financial Times*, 19 March 1995

18.1 Outline the changes which have taken place recently in both Christie's and Sotheby's.

18.2 How appropriate do you think this type of selling is to the art market?

18.3 Whatever your response to 18.2 above, what alternative(s) could you recommend? Bear in mind the unique relationship between seller, intermediary and purchaser in this sector.

18.4 How risky do you think the 'guarantees' scheme run by Christie's will be? Justify your response with supporting comments and make comparisons with a more familiar product which you know well.

Wrong number

'Junk mail' has spread to the phone. Diane Summers reports
on moves to keep telesales under control

Supper is on the table and the phone rings. The caller asks for the previous occupant of the house who died two years ago.

He then proceeds to claim it is you he wants after all, for he is convinced you will be fascinated to learn that a 'consultant' will be visiting your area next week to advise on replacement windows – or perhaps it is stone cladding, new kitchen units, or one of a host of other goods or services in which you have not the slightest interest.

If you live in some parts of the US, you may even find your meal interrupted by a randomly dialling computer and the sales spiel is the recorded message. This practice has such a potential for jamming lines and other misuse that it is outlawed in many countries, including the UK, and in some US states.

The potential of the telesales call to annoy – in particular 'cold' canvassing – is out of all proportion to the actual number of calls received by consumers. In the UK, for example, it is thought the average person receives no more than one call a month. Figures are hard to come by, but the tally could well be considerably higher in the US, where phone usage overall is about **four** times greater.

Once it was junk mail that was the focus of opprobrium; now it is more likely to be the phone that attracts the flak. Robert Leiderman, chairman of the UK's newly formed Telephone Preference Service (TPS), which aims to weed out consumers who do not want to be called, highlights the power of the phone. 'If it rings, it's answered. When was the last time you leapt out of the bath to open a piece of mail?' he asks.

Recognition of this power, its potential for abuse and the shadow this casts on the direct marketing industry led to the launch last week of the UK's self-regulating TPS.

At a federal level in the US, there has been a tightening of rules under a new Telephone Consumer Protection Act. Within the European Union, Germany takes the toughest stance by outlawing most cold calling. Meanwhile, at a pan-European Union level, at least three separate directives that touch on the subject are in the pipeline.

The UK's Direct Marketing Association-led TPS is very similar to a scheme that has been in place in the Netherlands for about six years. The UK body has the support of Oftel, the telephone regulator, charity fundraisers and the Glass and Glazing Federation, among others.

The scheme works, from the consumer point of view, as follows: domestic phone subscribers can phone BT (0800 398893) or Mercury (0500 398893) and ask for further information and a form to register the fact that they no longer wish to be cold-called by any company.

The information takes about three months to circulate, at which point most calls should cease. The consumer cannot be selective and will continue to receive calls from companies which do not sign up for the voluntary scheme. Excluded from the TPS scheme are: sales calls to business numbers, faxes, market research calls, and calls from companies with which the subscriber has some contact.

Businesses choosing to participate will foot the cost of the scheme by paying an annual licence fee of between £75 and £2,500, depending on size, plus extra for the lists or computer tapes containing the names and numbers of subscribers who have opted not to be canvassed. In return companies will get better-targeted prospects.

Such self-regulatory preference services could develop in other EU countries, and in order to deal with cross-border telesales, lists of consumers who have chosen to opt out could eventually be exchanged between countries.

Indeed, one draft EU directive – the Integrated Services Digital Network directive – contains a requirement that member states have a preference service which includes telephone market research on top of the items already covered by the UK scheme.

Proposed EU legislation – the other relevant draft directives are the Data Protection directive and the Distance Selling directive – are not expected to find their way on to statute books in member states for, perhaps, three years. A European Commission green paper on commercial communications, meanwhile, is expected shortly.

EU experts are bound to keep an eye on developments in the US, where telephone marketers are getting to grips with laws which now require them to restrict the hours of calling to between 8am and 9pm and which tighten up the use of automated dialling.

For example, phone lines must be released by automated systems no more than five seconds after a subscriber has hung up. There had been horror stories, according to the Consumers' Union in the US, of people unable to dial emergency services because their phone lines were jammed by pre-recorded messages.

According to Greg Daugherty, an editor on CU's magazine, Consumer Reports, the telephone sales call issue continues to be a huge irritant in the US. 'In my own household, it's a rare evening that the phone doesn't ring with someone trying to sell something. People come home from work and have so few hours of personal life to begin with. To have someone calling you on the phone and trying to sell you something is all the more aggravating.'

Connie Heatley, a senior vice-president of the Direct Marketing Association in the US, points out that the US has its own preference service, which has drawn less than 1m consumers on to its books, indicating that many people, like her, can find the cold call a valuable source of information.

'I only became involved with Mothers Against Drunk Driving because I received a phone call. Another person, who may be an avid skier, may be willing to receive a phone call about a new ski magazine,' she says.

For those who do not like their supper to get cold, Consumer Reports has a handy tip: don't sit down to eat until after 9pm.

Source: Financial Times, 2 February 1995

18.5 As a sales tool used for generating leads, telesales is very effective. Discuss.

18.6 When handling objections to a sales pitch, and presuming that the recipient does not put the phone down on you, how could you deflect their displeasure?

18.7 Your customer is teetering on the edge of making a decision. What alternatives are available to you to close the sale?

18C

Customer complaints venture pays off

By Neil Buckley

It may be the ultimate form of contracting out: let someone else handle your customers – and their complaints.

Customer service management, or handling customer contacts on behalf of other clients, is a sizeable business in the US, and is starting to catch on in the UK.

Non-business customers of Cellnet, the mobile phone company, for example, are connected to Cellnet's network, but their accounts, payments, inquiries and complaints are handled by a company previously known as Club 24, but which is today renaming itself Ventura – a subsidiary of the Next retail group.

The advantage of the arrangement for Cellnet is lower costs and the opportunity to use Ventura's skills in credit scoring, analysing customer behaviour and controlling 'churn' – or customers defecting to a rival service.

Mr Howard Ford, Cellnet's managing director, said he considers Ventura to be 'part of Cellnet'.

Ventura, which claims to be the UK's biggest customer service management company, began in 1968 as a credit card company operating the store card for Hepworths, the clothing retailer later absorbed into Next.

After falling into a £20.8m loss in 1992, it pulled out of large-scale retail credit funding and moved into customer service management, utilising account handling skills it had developed as a credit card operator. Today's name change recognises the break with the past.

Since 1992 Ventura's staff has quadrupled to more than 1,200, handling 9m telephone calls a year. Last year it made a £12.1m profit. Other large clients include the Co-operative Bank, and Time Retail Finance, the store card operator for retailers Comet, B&Q and Woolworths.

Some of the biggest US customer service management companies have similar origins. SPS started as the credit management arm of Sears Roebuck, the department store group, and handles millions of customer accounts for a dozen large companies. First Data Resources, another US company which also operates in the UK, was spun off by American Express in 1992.

Mr Mark Astbury, sales and marketing director, said Ventura offered clients call handling – typically contracting to handle more than 90 per cent of customer calls within 15 seconds – as well as mailing services and financial management. More important, it stores and analyses customer data, enabling it to spot trends and target customers at risk of 'churning'.

This concept of managing the 'whole customer life-cycle' is strongly related to development of customer loyalty schemes by retailers, such as Tesco's Clubcard.

'Businesses everywhere are starting to believe price is less of a differentiator, but customer service is an important differentiator,' said Mr Astbury. 'That means you have to understand the customer.'

Source: Financial Times, 9 October 1995

18.8 **Outline the benefits and pitfalls of contracting out customer service management in terms of managing relationships and monitoring competitors.**

18.9 **Would it be possible to turn these order takers into order makers? Justify your response.**

18.10 **Let's assume that your answer to 18.9 above, was 'Yes' (and it need not be), would it be possible to formulate a compensation plan for such a contracted out service? What would you recommend?**

18D

Closer to the customers

Deutsche Bank's huge branch network in Germany is undergoing one of the most fundamental transformations since the bank was broken into regions after the second world war. The slowly-growing competition for customers among German banks has forced it to rethink how services are delivered.

Deutsche recognised the need to give customers at its 1,500 branches a more personal and effective service – and thus have a better chance of keeping them – in 1990. It started pushing authority down to local branch managers, and away from its head and regional offices four years ago.

Not satisfied with the results, it is now trying to inject urgency into the process and involve staff more closely, with the introduction of Projekt Kundennähe (getting close to the customers). It involves visits to branches by board members, and training for staff.

Mr Michael Endres, a member of the managing board, says it will boost the confidence of the 55,000 domestic employees. 'This has to reinvigorate our activities in Germany. There is also the question of motivation. The blows we have received this year have had some repercussions on our people.'

Deutsche is keen to enhance links with the customer and strengthen a service mentality for which Germany is not exactly famed.

The bank also plans to develop advisory skills. It wants staff to give financial advice to customers, and persuade them to buy a wider range of products. 'You have to find a way of opening up the bank more fully for the client,' says Mr Hilmar Kopper, the chairman.

This is in line with efforts by banks in other European countries to sell more products such as residential mortgage loans and life insurance to customers. German customers have traditionally been as conservative as banks, but they are beginning to shop around for better deals.

'Three or four years ago, banks found it hard to compete with one another because customers not price-sensitive, but there has been an attitudinal change,' says Mr Chris Williams, analyst at the broker Fox-Pitt Kelton. Banks now offer more products such as money market investment funds.

They are also starting to charge companies for products and services that used to be included in lending margins before they were eroded. 'Banks are beginning to re-think, and they will attach price tags to individual services,' says Mr Hans-Peter Ferslev, head of Deutsche's strategy unit.

Deutsche has tried to remove administrative responsibilities from middle managers, to give them more time to focus on lending and giving advice. Paper processing is being taken out of branches and done in regional centres, while personnel issues are being handled from head office.

The aim is not simply to increase income, but to reduce the number of poor lending decisions. Mr Endres says the sharp rise in bad debt provisions on lending to small- and medium-sized companies last year was partly because managers had not devoted enough time to their customers.

'We saw in recent years, especially in our business with smaller and medium-sized companies, that we didn't take enough care of our clients,' says Mr Endres. He estimates that productivity (measured in profit per employee) has risen by about 30 per cent since reforms started in 1990.

To reinforce the idea of personal responsibility, Deutsche has introduced performance-related pay at the level of branch director, and wants to extend it throughout the bank. 'Everybody can be drawn at his nose if something goes wrong. He cannot say that it is someone else's fault,' says Mr Endres.

Deutsche has become a harsher place to work in other ways. Staff numbers fell by 2,800 in the domestic bank last year, with many middle managers taking early retirement. The impact of the changes in west Germany was partly cushioned by Deutsche's expansion into branch banking in the east.

Mr Endres says that a change in attitudes is the most vital aspect of reforms. 'It is not just a matter of drawing lines and boxes on a chart, it is important that everyone knows that his role has changed,' he says.

As competition grows in German banking, this will become increasingly apparent.

Source: Financial Times, 7 November 1994

18.11   In the eight-stage personal selling process, at which stage is Deutsche Bank's personal selling initiative expected to be most effective?

18.12   Which elements of the external environment have forced Deutsche Bank to change its approach to customers in this way?

18.13   What type of training, motivation and compensation plans do you think will now be necessary if this initiative is to be successful?

18.14   What methods of performance evaluation would you recommend?

19

Direct Marketing

It is within this section where the most disliked activity in Marketing usually occurs. Junk mail addressed to 'Mr Chestnut Avenue', unsolicited telephone calls trying to sell us anything from a fitted kitchen to life insurance and the ubiquitous 'You have just won ...' letter sometimes haunt our lives. Now that the technology has improved and databases are kept much more current, the early difficulties of direct mail have all but disappeared, even if the invasive image hasn't.

Direct marketing techniques have been around for a very long time in the form of coupons, samples and catalogues. Membership schemes have been used by various book and music clubs for several years, Readers Digest perhaps being the most well-known in the UK.

The growth in direct marketing has arisen largely because of considerable changes in consumer life styles, i.e. there isn't enough time to shop in the high street for every item one might need. There is also an increased confidence in buying through mail order, as legislation has sought to protect customers from shoddy goods and service.

The Internet, as an electronic intermediary, has also capitalised on the direct marketing boom. However, this increased access to goods and services appears to be much more acceptable, perhaps because it is customer driven. After all, if you download something which you subsequently find to be of no interest, the onus is on you to refine your searching skills rather than blame the vendor for being there in the first place.

There is no doubt that direct marketing techniques are here to stay and will play an increasingly more important role in defining segments and providing customised services. Many more of us expect customer help lines, freephone telephone ordering systems, and some familiarity with our purchasing record when we contact regular suppliers. The trick is to get it right so that true personalisation can take place without 'the computer' becoming so powerful, such that even the smallest deviation from a pre-determined list of responses isn't possible.

In order to successfully complete the tasks in this chapter you will need to be familiar with:

- techniques of direct marketing;
- mailing list;
- database;
- mail order;
- telemarketing;
- Internet.

Line cuts advice service

By Motoko Rich

Direct Line, the telephone-based insurer, is abandoning giving advice on life assurance products as it merges its life assurance and financial services activities.

The insurer, owned by the Royal Bank of Scotland, is withdrawing from giving advice only 18 months after it began testing the service.

The move could be seen as a set-back for Mr Peter Wood, founder of Direct Line, who had hoped the group could continue to expand in all areas of retail financial services, selling an increasing range over the telephone.

One analyst said: 'It is very difficult to give complex advice over the telephone. People are just not prepared to sit on the telephone for an hour and a half going through the nitty-gritty details of their financial situation.'

The group will now only offer life assurance products which directly complement those of its financial services business, which include mortgages, personal loans, savings products and personal equity plans. The life products being offered will be mortgage protection, fixed-term cover and disability cover.

Mr Jim Spowart, managing director of the newly merged Direct Line Financial Services, said: 'Direct Line is about offering the products that customers want and we keep our approach simple and straightforward. During the test period of the advice line customers identified mortgage protection and fixed-term life products as what they wanted.'

However, another analyst said: 'I am surprised they have given up so quickly. With their emphasis on direct selling I thought they would have given it a chance for longer.'

Mr Spowart said the group would rationalise its products, removing 'whole life' policies – those which provide cover in the event of death or disability over the course of the insured person's entire life, rather than a fixed period of a mortgage – from its portfolio.

The head office functions of the life assurance business will be moved from Croydon to Glasgow in Scotland. About 39 positions will be made redundant, but Mr Spowart said he hoped many of these staff would be re-deployed.

The financial services businesses continue to incur start-up losses, but the company said its mortgages and personal loans businesses were exceeding expectations.

Direct Line, which is the UK's largest motor insurer, has fallen on hard times recently as fierce competition on the general insurance side of the business and severe weather losses cut pre-tax profits from £45m to just £5m in the six months to March 31.

Source: Financial Times, 29 August 1996

19.1 Either individually or in a work group, make contact with Direct Line with a view to taking out a life insurance policy. Make notes of your conversation with them and prepare a presentation for the group which reports on:
- the way in which your enquiry was handled;
- the type of questions you were asked;
- your view of the suitability of the questions asked;
- any advice offered and your view of that advice.

19.2 In view of the above, draw up a list of information which you think Direct Line now has on its database about you. Outline how the company could use this in a direct marketing campaign.

Littlewoods set to expand direct mail order business

By Christopher Brown-Humes

Littlewoods, the family-owned retailing and football pools group, is strengthening its direct mail order business with the nationwide launch of its Index Extra catalogue after two years of trials.

Mr Bryan Mayoh, managing director of Littlewoods Home Shopping, said the strategy, to be supported by a £16m advertising campaign this autumn, would broaden and expand the group's home shopping business.

Littlewoods is the second largest participant in the UK agency mail order market with a 25 per cent share. But agency business is in gradual decline and Littlewoods, like its competitors, wants to build its direct business where annual growth exceeds 10 per cent. The latest sign of interest in the sector came last week when Burton, the clothing retailer, disclosed plans to buy the Innovations direct mail order group.

Mr Mayoh said Littlewoods hoped Index Extra sales would top £100m this year, three times last year's level. The aim is to recruit 400,000 new customers this autumn and winter.

'Index Extra will provide the growth for our mail order activities over the next few years,' he stated.

Mr Mayoh said Index Extra would work in conjunction with Littlewoods' high street chain of catalogue shops. Mail order customers will be able to order, pay for, and collect merchandise at the 129 Index stores, where they will also be able to see a sample of Index Extra goods.

'The combination of Index and Index Extra means none of our competitors will be able to match our breadth of range and sharpness of price,' said Mr Mayoh.

Littlewoods said last month it planned to invest £35m to expand Index in an attempt to rival Argos, the dominant company in the sector. It aims to add 40 to 70 additional stores over the next four years.

Source: Financial Times, 24 July 1996

19.3 Littlewoods already has a presence in nearly every high street, his competing with Argos through its Index operation, and runs a well established agency mail order business. What benefits do you think they will gain by introducing Index Extra?

19.4 Littlewoods now wants to increase its non-store activities and is looking for more imaginative ideas than simply adding 'Extra' to an existing operation. In your work group, identify the various options, rank them and with supporting arguments make recommendations.

19.5 In light of your recommendations in 19.4 above, what associated promotional activities do you think will be necessary in order to present the right image to the customer?

Heated debate on cold calling

Possible effects of proposed EU curbs on selling by phone are outlined by Diane Summers

The past week has seen a flurry of behind-the-scenes activity by many European companies which rely on the telephone to sell their goods and services. From financial services companies, to publishers, double-glazing companies and their trade associations, there is widespread anxiety about precisely what a European Union-wide ban on 'cold calling' could mean for businesses.

The anxiety has been sparked by the actions of a committee of Euro MPs, which last week voted in favour of a series of amendments to proposals to regulate 'distance selling' – sales contracts which do not involve face-to-face contact between the company doing the selling and the consumer.

The committee was discussing the proposals, commonly known as the draft distance selling directive, before a full session of the European Parliament which is due to vote on the measures during December. The amendment giving companies most cause for concern specifies that 'prior consent' should be obtained from consumers before they are contacted by phone. In another amendment, financial services companies, previously excluded, were brought within the scope of the proposals.

Fedim, the Europe-wide direct marketing association, forecast last week that this 'prior consent' measure could mean the loss of at least 10 per cent of the 1.5m-plus telephone marketing jobs in the EU.

In the UK, where selling by phone is particularly developed, the Direct Marketing Association asserted that 'selling over the telephone, whether to a 'cold' prospect or even to an existing customer, would become virtually impossible'.

Also, several areas of confusion appear to be causing many companies extra, unnecessary worry. Lionel Stanbrook, director of political and legislative issues at the UK's Advertising Association, warns: 'There are some over-zealous consultants looking for business.'

The first clarification needed is whether the measures cover only those calls made to consumers in their homes. A senior European Commission official emphasised this week: 'The point is to prevent consumers being disturbed at home at seven o'clock during dinner.'

The next area of confusion concerns which kinds of calls to consumers would be covered by the directive, and which would fall outside its remit. While the measures are commonly known as the draft distance *selling* directive, earlier this year it was agreed by the Council of Ministers that the title of the proposals should be changed to the distance *contracts* draft directive.

The difference between selling, as opposed to concluding a contract, is vital. Selling could mean any call that attempted to interest a consumer in a product or service; a distance contract, meanwhile, would clearly have to involve an actual sale.

It now seems likely that the intention of the draft directive is to cover only transactions which involve no face-to-face contact. A home improvements company would still be allowed, without prior consent, to ring consumers to gauge interest and make an appointment for a rep to visit. But if, for example, the normal procedure would be for a consumer to be phoned about a product or service and then sent a contract through the post or have a payment taken by credit card over the phone, prior consent for the first call would be required.

Then there is the question of what 'prior consent' actually boils down to, and here there are national differences in demands from MEPs. For example, in Germany, telemarketing is severely restricted and German MEPs want to ensure that German consumers have to give prior consent in writing before they are phoned. They want to see cross-border sales into Germany abide by the same rules.

Meanwhile, Phillip Whitehead, a British MEP and spokesman for the Socialist group on the committee which last week amended the draft directive, says he will be proposing that companies merely identify themselves and the purpose of the call at the start of the conversation. 'Consumers need to know a sales pitch is coming up,' he says.

According to the commission, prior consent may be gained in a number of ways. 'The basic idea is for the consumer to have the initiative,' says the senior official. So prior consent could be taken as given if the consumer had filled in a magazine or newspaper coupon requesting more information. If an existing customer had signed a contract which contained a clause specifying the company might make contact about other products, that would be deemed prior consent.

This area, like many other aspects of the draft directive, is still open to negotiation. Indeed, the entire set of proposals could still fall if, under the labyrinthine procedures of the EU, the parliament votes next month for the amendments and is not able to reach a compromise with the Council of Ministers, which has opposed them.

In the view of Alastair Tempest, Fedim director general, the draft directive – bar the prior consent amendment – contains many useful measures which will aid cross-border trade. To lose it entirely would be a step backwards.

'We've worked hard to get a directive that's useful. The amount of cross-border distance selling at the moment is pathetic when you consider we're living in a single European market – it's probably somewhere between 3 and 6 per cent of turnover. We should be able to sell kippers from Aberdeen to Athens without any problem, but that just isn't happening,' he says.

Source: Financial Times, 30 November 1995

19.6 Which aspects of telemarketing are the proposed EU curbs trying to control?

19.7 Which aspects of telemarketing would appear to be unaffected?

19.8 Outline the main operational and regulatory issues which firms who use telemarketing have to be aware of. Assess the usefulness of telemarketing for an international organisation.

19D

Online shopping plan claims better security

By Alan Cane

Uunet Pipex claimed yesterday that its new system for 'secure shopping' on the Internet not only met widespread concerns about security but was more secure than buying by phone or in a shop with a credit or debit card.

The company, the UK subsidiary of MFS, the US telecoms operator bought earlier this week by WorldCom of the US and one of the largest European Internet service providers, believes its system is in advance of US developments.

The British system is backed by National Westminster Bank, which will act as the clearing house for online debits and credit card transactions. Uunet Pipex said the system, called 'The Bureau', will enable customers to buy goods from electronic 'shops' on the Internet in safety and with security. Merchants trading on the Internet will be able to take advantage of an established payments mechanism without the cost of building their own.

Shopping over the Internet has been possible for some time but its popularity has been held back by concerns over security. Potential customers are reluctant to trust the Net with their credit card information. Nevertheless, online electronic commerce is believed to be worth $300m (£193m) annually at present and rising.

Among the organisations seeking to develop secure shopping and payments systems are card companies Visa, Mastercard and American Express and software developers Microsoft, Netscape Communications and Verifone.

Internet merchants sign up with Uunet Pipex and pay 5 per cent of the purchase value per transaction. The system is activated when a customer presses the 'buy' key and enters his or her credit information. It is then stored securely by Uunet who instructs NatWest to pay the merchant for the purchase. When the deal is complete electronic confirmations are generated for customer and merchant.

Mr Richard Nuttall, Uunet Pipex director of electronic commerce, said: 'Until now, security concerns have deterred buyers and sellers from doing business over the Net. We have created a comparatively low cost system that is more secure than buying goods on an ordinary credit or debit card.' Four merchants have already signed up to use the system.

Responsibility for establishing an electronic shop on the Net remains with the merchant. Many believe the quality of the images of goods for sale is a more effective deterrent to Internet commerce than fears over payment security.

The principle advantage of 'The Bureau' over competitive systems seems to be the ease and low cost of adoption. Mr Susen Sarkar of the London technology consultancy, Ovum, said: 'The launch of The Bureau will remove anxieties for both merchants and consumers.'

Other UK groups, notably Barclays Bank, already offer Internet shopping services and British Telecommunications is testing a large-scale online shopping service.

Source: Financial Times, 29 August 1996

19.9 Internet service providers, think that payment security is a major barrier to the growth of its shopping and payments system. How real do you think this fear is? Identify other issues which might inhibit Internet shopping.

19.10 For some, shopping is an important and enjoyable social activity. Do you think that this segment would be able to adapt to Internet shopping and what would be needed to attract them?

19.11 Among your friends, colleagues and associates, initiate a discussion about the Internet and try to establish how many have:

- experience of accessing the Internet;
- regular access to the Internet;
- seen anything they would like to buy on the Internet;
- bought anything through the Internet.

Report on your findings and also draw up a summary of their views on the topic.

19E

Downloading on the farm pays off

The small number of farmers using the Internet have reaped the benefits, writes Alison Maitland

Mr Nigel Joice, an arable farmer near Fakenham, Norfolk, was surfing the Internet one night and discovered that US wheat futures had tumbled. He sold about 250 tonnes of wheat 'before the market fell out of bed in the UK' and saved himself between £500 and £600.

'What affects us is global events: if it's raining in America, or there are floods in China – this means more grain imports. Some information is not as detailed as we need. But it keeps us in touch,' he says.

The number of UK farmers using the Internet is still tiny. A year ago there were as few as 10, but now there are a few hundred, according to Mrs Marie Skinner.

She and Ms Diane Wright run an Internet course for farmers in a tastefully converted piggery at the Skinners' High Ash Farm, at Caistor St Edmund, near

Norwich. More than 200 farmers have attended the course and agricultural companies – including Rhone Poulenc and Norsk Hydro – have sent delegates, as has the National Farmers' Union.

Mrs Skinner – who farms 200 hectares of cereals and sugar beet with husband Chris – started the courses just over a year ago because she wanted to learn more about the Internet.

'I think 99.9 per cent of what you could use is not relevant to business needs and most of it is quite boring,' she adds. But she believes the remaining 0.1 per cent can give isolated farmers, often living in inaccessible rural areas, an unprecedented commercial advantage and lobbying power in their dealings with multinational agricultural supply companies.

Top attractions are satellite weather pictures updated every half hour, Chicago grain futures prices, available with a 10-minute time lag, e-mail and a wealth of information about pests and diseases from non-commercial sources such as the US Department of Agriculture or the UK's Institute of Arable Crops Research.

It helps that many farmers already have computers for their records. The NFU estimates that 40 per cent have office computers and 25 per cent more are considering buying one.

As the number of farm users grows, so more UK-based agricultural supply companies are taking sites on the World Wide Web. In January, says Mrs Skinner, there was only one UK agricultural group site worth visiting – an East Anglian fertiliser supplier. The sector was dominated by US companies. 'Now we look at pretty much nothing outside the UK.'

According to the European Network, a Web site funded by the European Commission, Britain already has far more agricultural sites than any other EU country.

Farmers' use of the Internet is likely to be given a boost by a service to be launched in October by the National Farmers' Union, the Country Landowners' Association and Adas, the farm consultancy. Their £1m Rural Business Network brings together a wide range of information and services of use to farm and countryside users.

It will give the farming organisations the chance to consult thousands of members instantly by e-mail.

Mr Joice thinks farmers would welcome up-to-the-minute Internet information direct from the European Commission in Brussels on policy issues such as changes in set-aside rates or support payments.

For livestock producers caught up in the bovine spongiform encephalopathy crisis, the Internet has provided desperately needed knowledge.

When Alison and Laurie Ritchie began using the net in April, they found research on the disease was predominantly American. Since then, many UK universities have put their findings on the Web.

'We've learned a lot more about BSE, from the medical and veterinary point of view, from the Internet than we ever did from the ministry [of agriculture],' says Mrs Ritchie. 'It could be half the trouble that the information wasn't readily available in the past.'

Source: Financial Times, 24 August 1996

19.12 **Identify the advantages and disadvantages for farmers connecting to the Internet.**

19.13 **Segmenting the customer base into its two main sectors, i.e. livestock and arable, how could farmers use the system proactively?**

19.14 **You are the marketing assistant in an old-fashioned firm which supplies all types of agricultural and horticultural goods from lettuce seeds to milking machines and combine harvesters. What arguments would you put forward to connect your firm to the Internet?**

20

Public Relations and Sponsorship

It is easy to mistake public relations for press relations. Public relations entails all relationships with the outside world through promotional events, moulding of the corporate image, internal and external publications such as the annual report and house journals through to the sometimes very elaborate Annual General Meeting. Press relations is an activity which makes sure that the print media gets to know all that the firm wishes them to. It is often the role of public relations though to handle the damage limitation exercise which occurs when the press gets hold of a story the firm would rather it didn't have.

PR can be a very exciting area to work in, but it does have its problems. First, it has always been difficult to measure the effect of good PR, whereas bad PR is quickly quantified via a fall in share price or company resignations. Second, it is an activity that most companies know they have to have but would really rather avoid the cost. Hence the PR department is frequently not recognised for the good work which it does.

Sponsorship has been embraced by many organisations as a method of widening the exposure of either the corporate or brand name. Sport is a common vehicle for sponsorship because of the inherent benefits in subsequent TV programmes, but it all has to be paid for. There is also a danger in that a large sum spent on sponsorship cannot then be spent elsewhere, therefore, other media forms suffer. Sponsorship of the arts is perhaps seen as a more altruistic activity and per event, a lot more affordable. The exposure a brand name would get from being connected with the Stately Homes Music Festival, would be considerably less than that achieved via sponsorship of a televised Pro-Am Golf Tournament. This is of course, reflected in the price paid. Sponsorship is perhaps one of those areas where the phrase 'You only get what you pay for', rings very true.

> **In order to successfully complete the tasks in this chapter you will need to be familiar with:**
>
> - techniques in PR;
> - evaluating PR and sponsorship;
> - types of sponsorship;
> - role of sponsorship;
> - corporate hospitality.

Coca-Cola's return of serve

Is corporate sponsorship of sporting events worth the money?
Patrick Harverson reports

When the 'Summer of Sport' draws to a close next month, the image that will linger longest in our memories may not be that of a gold-medal winning athlete or a championship-winning team, but the bright red logo of Coca-Cola.

The soft drinks giant has been everywhere in sport this year – including the Euro 96 championship, the Tour de France and the Olympics. Exactly how much it spends on sport is not published, but Sergio Zyman, its chief marketing officer, reveals that in an average year about 20 per cent of the company's $1.5bn (£960m) annual consumer marketing budget, or roughly $300m, is used to 'support' sports.

However, 1996 is not a typical year, and Coca-Cola's spending on sports events this year is likely to be well over $300m. It has spent $40m alone on buying the rights to be an Olympic sponsor, and it plans to spend another £62m on television commercials during NBC's coverage of the Games in the US. It has also built a 12-acre 'Olympic City' for visitors in downtown Atlanta.

With corporate involvement in sport growing rapidly every year, it is worth asking if Coca-Cola and other sponsors get a good return on their huge investment in sports. Is sports sponsorship value for money?

Andy Smith, broadcast director at Zenith, the London media buying group, says sponsors can measure the impact of their involvement with sport by tracking the screen time and column inches their brand logos enjoy in the media.

He points to Tetley beer, which backs the England cricket team. 'Looking at the coverage of the Tetley logo on television and in press photographs, you can see it easily covers the cost of the sponsorship,' says Smith.

For non-consumer companies, measuring the impact of sports sponsorship is harder. Mava Heffler, head of global sponsorships at Mastercard, says one of the key objectives behind the company's backing of Euro 96 was to reinforce Mastercard's brand image in the UK, particularly among Access card holders who might have been unaware that their card was part of the Mastercard stable.

The anecdotal evidence so far suggests that this objective was achieved, says Heffler. 'When we started our programme in the UK nine to 12 months ago, we asked Access cardholders if they had a Mastercard. Most said they didn't. Now when we ask the question, people show us their Access card straightaway.'

However, companies have to invest a lot of money to get the best out of their deals. Smith says of event sponsorship: 'You have to be there at the events to put hats on people and make sure the camera angles are right. There is a lot more to being an event sponsor than a broadcast sponsor – you have to spend a lot more to achieve a lot more.'

The official sponsors of Euro 96, for example, paid £3.5m for the rights to the tournament, but some spent as much as 10 times that on advertising their association with the event. The Olympics are even costlier, and advertisers are expected to spend an estimated $5bn worldwide on Olympic-related marketing.

While sport is becoming increasingly popular with corporate sponsors – 'sport is highly televised, highly interactive and has very large fan bases', explains Heffler – the crucial factor is sport's ability to transcend national boundaries. It can help companies overcome cultural, language and political barriers.

Bridgestone-Firestone, the Japanese tyre company, has used its sponsorship of Indy car racing in the US to build brand recognition in Italy through a television programme it produces for Italian broadcasters.

The company pays $60,000 for the Italian rights to Indy racing, and spends about another $190,000 making five 25-minute programmes on the main Indy races. It gives the programmes to an Italian broadcaster in return for advertising slots worth more than $400,000.

However, sponsoring sports events is not a risk-free proposition. IBM's embarrassment this week at the failure of its Olympic computer systems to provide accurate data is an example of what can go wrong. The company spent $40m acquiring the sponsorship rights and as much again on setting up the technology for the Games in Atlanta, but all the spending and preparation could be wasted if press coverage of the computer problems ultimately overshadows IBM's contribution to the Olympics.

Ultimately, sports sponsorship has become popular because it allows large corporations to identify closely with customers or prospective customers in a way that traditional advertising and marketing cannot possibly achieve.

Thus, the thrust of Coca-Cola's sports campaign this year has focused not on the events, or the teams, but on the ordinary fans. As Zyman puts it: 'Sport allows us to say to consumers: "We like what you like".'

Source: Financial Times, 25 July 1996

20.1 Coca-Cola has clearly identified all aspects of sport as being appropriate for sponsorship. What alternatives are available to the Coca-Cola management when looking for sponsorship opportunities? How would you rank them in order of importance to the company?

20.2 What criteria should a manager use when evaluating sponsorship opportunities?

20B

'Fun' at the Olympics

The Games helped Swiss watchmaker Swatch to change its image in the US, says Andrew Baxter

'I'm supporting Angola, isn't that where those nice sweaters come from?' With 197 countries competing, one could forgive the occasional geographic slip among spectators at last month's Olympic Games in Atlanta.

But if on occasion some of the 1,200 guests brought in from around the globe by Swatch Timing had lost their geographic bearings, the Swiss producer of 'fun' plastic watches had a clear idea of why it was in Atlanta.

Swatch was official timekeeper at the Games, which meant it paid for some $30m (£19.2m) worth of timekeeping and scoring equipment and services. By the end of this year it estimates a further $40m will have been paid to the Atlanta Committee for the Olympic Games and to national Olympics committees from sales of special Olympic Swatch watches.

Teams of technicians from Swatch sister companies within SMH, the big Swiss watchmaking group, spent a year in Atlanta setting up the timekeeping equipment.

Hundreds of companies were in Atlanta simply to sell, but Swatch had a different agenda. The company was keen to dispel the image of a Swatch product as something that is worn for a while and then thrown away.

In the fiercely competitive US market, Swatch has never been as successful as it has been in Europe. 'People had a tendency to identify plastic and colour as cheap and lacking in quality – and it's not true,' says Nicolas Hayek Jnr, Swatch's vice-president for international marketing. Hayek's father is SMH's chairman and chief executive.

'In Europe there is an understanding of the credibility and quality of the product that isn't there yet in the US, perhaps,' says Barbara Khouri, president of Swatch US and head of the company's Olympics project. So the Games gave Swatch an opportunity to broaden the awareness in the US of the product's quality by linking the Swatch name with the sophisticated timing and scoring equipment at the Games.

The linkage was echoed subtly at the Swatch Pavilion, a temporary exhibition hall set up in Centennial Park, close to many of the main events and to the site of the pipe bomb blast at the end of the first week.

Surrounded by display cases of Swatch watches past and present, a mock-up finishing line had been rigged up to allow children and adults to experience the Swiss group's latest photo-finish technology.

So was it all worth it? Market research in the first week of the Games showed that Swatch's role as official timekeeper had registered with US consumers, says Khouri, enhancing the product's credibility.

Swatch was the only company whose name could be displayed inside the venues, albeit discretely on the equipment. This produced the kind of publicity that money simply cannot buy: the widely used pictures of the double-gold hero Michael Johnson posing by a Swatch timing board showing his world record 19.32 secs time in the 200m.

Hayek says US Swatch sales are up 60 per cent so far this year, compared with 1995. The Olympics have played their part in that, and have had a very immediate impact on sales, he says, but new stores and products were also responsible, and in the longer term it looks as if these will have a more sustained effect on building sales.

As both Hayek and Khouri point out, it is easier and more appropriate to link a mass-market, broadly distributed product such as Swatch with a global event such as the Olympics than it would have been with the more serious brands such as Omega, which are sold only in jewellers. In promotional terms, says Khouri: 'There's a lot more you can do with Swatch, you can have a little fun with it.'

Even with this advantage, though, Swatch can claim with some justification to have had a successful Olympics, given the potential pitfalls of being associated with such events. Nothing went wrong with the timing and scoring technology, which would have been damaging to the broader marketing aims.

That helped Swatch avoid being linked with the embarrassing initial glitches in the results service supplied to the world media by IBM, even though the two companies had been co-operating closely for months.

The Swiss company also benefited from some of the changes introduced in the run-up to the Games by Khouri – who had joined Swatch only three months before they began. Apart from trying to integrate more closely the many activities involved in the project, Khouri increased the number of PR and other special events.

Sales of Swatch watches at the Games were secondary to the broader marketing aims, but one of Khouri's changes was to expand the retail outlet at the pavilion, where sales reached 6,000 watches a day. Three days were lost with the closure of Centennial Park after the bomb, but even so the cost of the pavilion was covered entirely by the watch sales from it, says Hayek.

And the corporate hospitality? That was not very expensive for Swatch either, claims Hayek, because it was financed through increased sales. Most of the guests were on incentive programmes and had won the trip through winning sales drives, window displays and other competitions.

Source: Financial Times, 15 August 1996

20.3 **Identify the role that Public Relations played in improving the image of Swatch in the US and state the known benefits achieved.**

20.4 **What other PR techniques could Swatch have used to complement its activities at the 1996 Olympic Games?**

20.5 **Increased sales was a clear measure of the PR campaign's success. What other measures could Swatch have employed to further assess its effectiveness?**

20.6 **Is the Swatch campaign an example of Marketing PR or Corporate PR? Justify your decision.**

Beware the PR stuntman

By Helen Jones

Covering a newsagent's shop in orange fur, laser-projecting a supermodel in her underwear on to the side of Battersea power station and smuggling a 40ft flag of footballer Eric Cantona into Manchester United's games are just some of the publicity stunts that companies are pulling to increase awareness of their brands.

Tango, Playtex Wonderbra and Nike, the beneficiaries of these ideas, have been the most conspicuous so far, but PR stunts are playing an increasingly important role in marketing strategies for a range of companies.

Tango's advertising agency, HHCL & Partners, has even set up a division called Environment Marketing to create PR 'happenings'.

Environment Marketing was responsible for decking out the newsagent in fur. During Prime Minister John Major's leadership battle with John Redwood it used characters from Tango's advertising campaign to hover around live news broadcasts drinking the product and waving at the cameras. Emma Jenks of Environment Marketing says: 'Because it was all live news coverage we were able to direct the actors to get in shot using a mobile phone. Tango drinkers recognised the characters and the fact that the news had been "Tangoed".'

As well as communicating directly with existing consumers PR stunts increase brand awareness in highly competitive markets. Mike Perry, managing director of Nike's advertising agency Simons Palmer Denton Clemmow & Johnson, says: 'Because the media is increasingly fragmented it is less and less easy to hit people via traditional TV or press advertisement. You have to stand out.'

Perry and his team created a flag from Nike's Eric Cantona Nike poster which was unfurled during an important match between Manchester United and Barcelona. An estimated TV audience of 80m watched as the flag was passed around the ground.

The biggest advantage of PR stunts is that they save money. Perry says: 'The Nike flag cost £5,000 to make but for that sum we were seen by 80m people. The cost of that sort of advertising airtime would have been huge.'

Alasdair Ritchie, chief executive of Playtex Wonderbra's advertising agency TBWA, agrees that it is a cheap way of getting your brand into the public eye. 'Wonderbra cost £20,000 to laser project on to Battersea power station. A 30-second TV commercial costs £60,000 but we got much more than £60,000 worth of media coverage.'

Perry says: 'The media was never really very interested before but now advertising and brands are sexy and the media is much more prepared to accept stories about them. Perhaps it says something about the trivialisation of news.'

Sony is spending £20m on the launch of its computer game, Playstation, this month and is rumoured to be running an anarchic advertisement backed by the release of a novelty record into the charts. And next week HHCL & Partners intends to run a TV teaser campaign for Martini which will ask viewers to audition for a part in its next commercial. Jenks says the company expects significant tabloid interest.

However, Ritchie says agencies have to keep developing really new ideas to excite jaded tabloid journalists and an increasingly media-literate public. 'You can't just laser project an advertisement on to a building, because we have already done it,' he says.

He believes that perhaps the best publicity stunt was one of the first: 'In the 1980s the glue brand Araldite stuck a chair to a poster site on London's Cromwell Road. It said a lot about the brand and got worldwide coverage.'

But, he says: 'There was also a man who tried to sell advertising space on his cows which grazed alongside the Euston to Birmingham rail track. It was a great idea on paper but it never took off.'

Source: Financial Times, 14 September 1995

20.7 How valuable do you think PR stunts are in terms of brand awareness and incentive to buy?

20.8 Why do you think that PR agencies have started to adopt this type of activity?

20.9 It is becoming increasingly difficult to generate new ideas. Pick a product and draw up a list of PR stunts which could be used to promote the product.

Hitching a ride on the corporate gravy train

Diane Summers considers where to draw the line on freebies

When does an expenses-paid trip, a day at the races or a night at the opera stop being part of normal public or corporate life and start to look like sleaze?

Even the most junior manager is likely to have been faced at some time with a freebie dilemma.

The gift of a calender from a supplier will probably not cause a second thought, but what about a case of wine? A nice lunch to keep in touch with a client is one thing, but does a free golfing trip to somewhere warm add up to an improper inducement, or just a longer opportunity to cement relations?

Journalists are faced with an abundance of freeloading opportunities. The 'Private Eye test', which is the standard in operation at the Financial Times, can be adapted for use elsewhere when it comes to deciding whether a gift, meal or trip is acceptable or sleazy. To apply the test, visualise whether a mention of the arrangement in Private Eye would cause embarrassment.

Lobbyists and public relations specialists also have reason to consider these matters more than most. Mr Mike Beard, president of the Institute of Public Relations and head of PR at Taylor Woodrow, the construction company, has developed a couple of useful tests of his own.

The first is the 'means test'. He draws the line at entertainment 'way beyond the level the person would normally be able to afford for themselves'. This level will vary with the individual. A steak in a wine bar at lunchtime is not beyond the means of most journalists but, said Mr Beard, 'if you want to talk to the chairman of a major company on a piece of business, you may have to meet him in more expensive surroundings'.

The second is the 'wow test'. When you open an envelope containing an invitation you either groan or you say 'that's nice', said Mr Beard. But if you find yourself saying 'wow', then it is time to consider.

It also pays to do an audit from time to time, to check that entertaining is reciprocal, he said. 'The rule in my department is that we're quite happy to be bought lunch by our suppliers but we sometimes buy them lunch back. You must not have a relationship which is too oppressive.'

In Mr Beard's view a night at the opera, with a ticket for an accompanying partner, is particularly useful when overseas visitors need to be entertained in the evenings – although Mr Beard is more likely to be spotted at a rock concert. 'I can't stand opera, to be honest. A rock concert is low-cost and it's a bit different.' Taylor Woodrow also arranges weekend outings to theme parks for contacts. 'We have a little barbecue and it's a chance to talk to them – the cost is incredibly modest. We're buying a bit of their private time to talk to them about the company,' said Mr Beard.

But in the experience of Mr David Willis, who runs a corporate hospitality business, there is little point trying to encroach on people's private time. Hospitality should aim to be in the hours the boss is paying for.

Mr Willis said: 'Sunday is absolutely out. The hardworking executive is locked away with his family, mowing the lawn and polishing the Daimler. Saturday is possible if it's a really monster event, like the cup final, or the rugby international. But people view both offering and accepting hospitality as part of work.'

Even though such events are seen as part of work, very little work is actually talked about, said Mr Willis, a director of the National Sporting Club. 'It's almost infra dig to do any selling at a hospitality event. The idea is to get Ron and Brenda out for a jolly good day, pour a lot of champagne down them and give them a few tips for the Derby winners. They then feel good about you, and the next time you or your sales rep calls you'll be received in front of the competition.'

The cost of corporate hospitality at top sporting events can approach Ritz-bill proportions these days. Mr Willis said that it cost upwards of £1,500 a head to entertain at the last Wimbledon men's finals, but 'people pay if they've got major international customers coming into London for deals that are worth millions.'

The British may frown on cultures where baksheesh and special favours to family members are an expected part of business life. But it would seem that British standards are, in turn, frowned on by the Japanese and Americans.

According to Mr Willis the Japanese are notably absent from the hospitality scene. While they will visit clubs in their own time they are shocked by the notion of taking a working day off to go to a sporting event.

In his experience 'Americans would think it barmy to spend thousands of pounds at Wimbledon. An MD of a big American company might entertain a senior partner at the ball game, but they'd buy each other a hot dog and sit in the public seats. How near you are to the Royal Enclosure, and all those other layers of importance, is very British.'

Mr Willis said a few companies, such as the supermarket chain J. Sainsbury, actively discouraged employees from receiving such hospitality. But in his view 'most Brits don't have a problem on the morality or ethics side of all this'.

For those who do, the 'Private Eye', 'means' and 'wow' tests remain reasonable starting points.

Source: Financial Times, 24 October 1994

20.10 You work for the Marketing Director of an electrical components manufacturer and have been given the job of organising next year's traditional corporate hospitality event. Previous years have seen rather extravagant events at the Cheltenham races, the Five Nations Rugby Tournament, Cowes Sailing Regatta and the British Open Golf Tournament, to which senior managers, customers and suppliers are usually invited. Being a male dominated industry, these events are rarely attended by female managers and spouses of male managers have never been invited on the assumption that they wouldn't want to go anyway. Having always been regarded as a 'boys day out' it has become an opportunity for food and drink to be consumed in great quantities.

You are uneasy at continuing with this 'great' tradition and think that as the industry becomes more competitive, with shop-floor redundancies commonplace and global players eating into your market, this current practice is not only outdated but could actually be damaging the firm's reputation.

(i) Draw up a list of advantages and disadvantages for continuing with the current practice and assess whether it is still necessary to reward managers, customers and suppliers in this way.

(ii) Assuming that the firm still wishes to put on some sort of event, make alternative proposals, with supporting arguments for the Marketing Director's consideration.

Fire brigade's 999 sponsorship call

By Diane Summers, Marketing Correspondent

Businesses trying to find new ways to advertise their company names through sponsoring worthwhile causes are being offered a unique opportunity by Greater Manchester Fire Service.

The Manchester brigade is believed to be the first to put its fire engines up for sponsorship by companies, as a way of raising funds for safety campaigns.

However, full-scale advertising on engines will not be allowed. Mr John Weaver, the brigade's assistant divisional officer, said advertising would be limited to a simple safety message, plus the company's name and logo.

'We are not talking about having the machines painted in a company's livery or with garish adverts on the side,' he said. 'It will need some discussion, and it would have to be something appropriate in view of some of the harrowing incidents we attend.'

The fire service said cuts of £2m in its £78m annual budget meant sponsorship was the only way of extending community education campaigns. It is looking at a number of ways of getting companies involved and is holding a sponsorship day at Manchester United Football Club next month.

Mr Weaver said that a company making products for children might, for example, want to sponsor a schools campaign. 'We are also looking at an annual award for members of the public who have acted bravely or commendably and that could well be sponsored,' he said.

He added: 'We have to be realistic. The budget cuts have concentrated our minds on how we can expand our campaigns that have been successful in reducing death and injuries.'

While Greater Manchester Fire Service, the busiest outside London, may be the first to think of sponsorship for its fire engines, other parts of the public services have been benefitting for some time from sponsorship funds.

Volkswagen has sponsored the uniforms worn by lollipop patrols at school crossing points for more than four years. The company said the jacket logos helped reinforce associations between the VW name and safety issues.

Source: Financial Times, 20 March 1996

20.11   Do you agree with the proposal for allowing sponsorship on fire engines? Justify your response.

20.12   How far do you think sponsorship should go in its infiltration of public services? A Volkswagen logo on a school crossing control warden's uniform might be acceptable but what about ambulances carrying the Dettol or Elastoplast logos?

20.13   What sort of sponsorship link would you find completely distasteful?

20.14   The article mentions sponsorship of school campaigns. In recent years, teachers and schools have been bombarded with very high quality, comprehensive, free teaching material, produced by organisations such as McDonalds. All of this material inevitably carries the McDonalds logo and often, money-off coupons for its products. Cuts in education funding make these very attractive propositions for over-worked teachers, but there have been complaints that targeting school children is unethical.

(i)   How do you view this type of PR and should it be encouraged?

(ii) How genuine do you think this type of activity is? Is it philanthropic or manipulative?

(iii) Do the teachers have a valid argument or are they simply being naive in thinking they can get something for nothing?

(iv) How acceptable would you find it to have your brother, sister or child taught arithmetic on the basis of the cost of ingredients in a Big Mac?

21

Strategic Marketing

The very word 'strategy' suggests the long-term view, and this may well involve significant changes throughout the organisation, not just marketing. Indeed, for anything to be considered a long-term strategy, it has to involve something more substantial than a seasonal price cut or a quick burst of advertising and promotional activity to sell the product.

It is a fascinating area of marketing in which to be involved, there are so many variables to consider and, of course, there is a need to look into the future – the unknown. At best we can produce informed forecasts on what is likely to happen when we implement a strategic change, at worst we can just wait and see what happens. Although strategic marketing portrays the image of a high-risk, intellectual activity, really it isn't. I would even go so far as to suggest that a sales executive dealing with customers, has to make many more instant decisions based on imperfect information than most strategic marketers who have the benefit of many analytical tools and techniques to help in the process.

The problem of paralysis by analysis is quite possible and firms which have relied too heavily on the analytical process while allowing no place for the 'gut feeling' or 'hunch' have come to rue such an approach. Having said that, the tools and techniques covered in this chapter, are in frequent use and provide a framework within which to discuss ideas and recognise limitations. Please remember though, that few of these models are meant to be applied in a rigid diagnostic fashion. Just because a product appears as a 'dog' it does not necessarily mean that it should automatically be divested. Many well-known products such as Scott's Porrige Oats, Fairy Soap Powder and the very desirable Morgan car, all have low relative market share in low growth markets, but still generate satisfactory cash flow for their firm. So tread warily. Use the models and tools of analysis to illuminate and suggest sensible options rather than simply direct. Always ask yourself 'does this make sense?'.

In order to successfully complete the tasks in this chapter you will need to be familiar with:

- influences on marketing strategy;
- Ansoff matrix;
- BCG matrix (Boston Box);
- Shell Directional Policy matrix;
- defensive strategies;
- integrative growth strategies;
- competitive position and posture;
- generic strategies.

21A

Railtrack prescribes doctors and shops to revive stations

By Chris Brown-Humes

Railtrack will today open the first doctor's surgery at a mainline UK station, marking the first stage of ambitious plans to expand retail, leisure and other services at many big rail terminals.

The company, which owns the rail network infrastructure, hopes facilities such as health clubs, bowling alleys, multi-screen cinemas, virtual reality centres, libraries, business centres and crèches – as well as doctors' and dental surgeries – will eventually be offered. The aim is to attract passengers and people living and working near stations, even if they do not travel by train.

The private doctor's surgery at London's Victoria station will be run by Medicentre, part of Sinclair Montrose Healthcare, the personnel group recently floated on the Alternative Investment Market. The walk-in service will operate six days a week, with normal GP functions, screenings and vaccinations. The cost would be £32 per consultation.

Ms Carol Davies, Medicentre operations manager, said the aim was to expand the service first to other mainline London stations, including Waterloo and Liverpool Street, and eventually to airports and shopping malls. The scheme is based on a US concept.

Railtrack operates 14 mainline stations, including eight in London, and leases 2,500 stations around the country. It believes many of them are significantly under-exploited and points out that up to 200,000 passengers a day pass through its biggest stations.

The company said yesterday that the monolithic structure of British Rail, which owned the network before privatisation this year, had prevented the potential of the stations being released.

A model for the future is Liverpool Street station in London. Following a big development programme in the early 1990s, it boasts a range of shops, restaurants, a health club, pub and travel centre. It is already busier at lunchtimes than during rush-hours, said Railtrack, but there is potential to develop it further.

Railtrack said much space would be freed at Liverpool Street, Euston and King's Cross stations by the relocation of Royal Mail services to Willesden, north London. This could enable Railtrack to provide car-parking, which many see as essential to the development of a successful retail and leisure complex.

In many cases, Railtrack would provide concessions to retailers, just as BAA, the airports owner, has done successfully at leading UK airports.

'Instead of being places people pass through, we want stations to be places people go to,' Railtrack said.

Mr Richard Hyman, the chairman of retail consultants Verdict, said: 'There is massive potential to develop rail stations because they have two major prerequisites of a good retail location – space and a high customer traffic flow.'

Source: *Financial Times*, 19 August 1996

21.1 Draw up an analysis of influences on marketing strategy which will impact on Railtrack.

21.2 In terms of Ansoff's matrix, what type of growth strategy would you call this?

21.3 Do you think this idea will work? Justify your response with supporting arguments.

21B

Nestlé's portfolio of possibilities

Many peripheral businesses could be worth more to other owners, writes Roderick Oram

Like the attic of a thrifty Swiss burgher, Nestlé's huge product portfolio is crammed with possessions. But the generation moving into leadership are showing no signs of wanting to shed more peripheral businesses.

Admittedly, Nestlé sold its wine business last year for an undisclosed sum. But what British vinegar, German pork and Italian crispbread have to do with Nestlé's core products of coffee, confectionery, mineral water, milk, ice cream and pet foods is a mystery to many analysts and investors.

Just five products account for 35 per cent of Nestlé's European sales, 10 for 50 per cent and 18 for 75 per cent, according to an analysis by Goldman Sachs. Thereafter, the portfolio tails off through more than 20 other products making up the final 25 per cent.

Most of the lesser items, forming the longest tail of any leading food producer, have little to recommend them. Typically they achieve only minuscule market shares, geographic spread or profit in the greater group context.

Money is not a problem: free cash flow (after dividends and renewal of fixed assets) will be SFr1.3bn ($1.07bn) this year, estimates Mr James Amoroso, of Crédit Suisse in Zurich.

But managerial focus is, particularly for a multinational that still gives country managers autonomy. Moreover, lacklustre businesses only blunt Nestlé's efforts to hit demanding group targets such as 4 per cent a year volume growth and a return on capital better than 15 per cent.

Nestlé argues that products deserve to stay if they contribute reasonable profit with minimal managerial effort. But the size of the underperforming rump is hard to estimate. It could total as much as 10 per cent of Nestlé's portfolio, some analysts guess.

'We do not recognise that figure,' Mr Helmut Maucher, Nestlé chairman who hands over as chief executive to Mr Peter Brabeck next June, said in a recent interview. 'We always distinguish between where we are investing and do not have an adequate return yet, and where there is no hope.' The second category accounts for about 5 per cent of sales, some SFr3bn, he said.

Processed meat is the only large category which Nestlé identifies as one it would consider selling. It contributed operating profits of SFr55m on sales of SFr1bn in 1995, Mr Amoroso estimates. If these meats, with an operating profit margin of 5.5 per cent, had not been in the portfolio, group margin would have risen from 9.7 per cent to 9.8 per cent last year.

About 80 per cent of the meat business is in Herta, a German-based business. Nestlé likes part of the business, such as its higher margin products and chilled distribution chain, but would consider offers for the upstream primary processing and simpler processed meats, such as sausages and salami.

Nestlé has signalled its willingness to sell its meats, but the only offer to date is for Vismara, an Italian producer of ham and other meats, Mr Maucher said.

The most likely buyer of the meat businesses is Sara Lee, of the US. It has targeted European processed meats as a strategic imperative and has been acquiring companies. Neither company would comment.

Deeper in the Nestlé portfolio is a trove of small businesses that could be worth more to other owners. In the UK, for example, it owns Gales honey, Sun Pat peanut butter and Sarsons vinegar: strong niche brands, but in areas where Nestlé has no apparent interest.

In other areas, synergy may be a valid reason for keeping something. Buitoni dried pasta, for example, has a small and unprofitable share of the Italian market. But Nestlé bought Buitoni and built up a range of high-margin sauces to accompany the pasta.

Selling assets is only one tool for shaping portfolios. More important are acquisitions and canny management. Over the past 15 years under Mr Maucher, Nestlé has made large acquisitions, such as Perrier of France as part of a SFr3bn diversification into mineral water, and of Rowntree in the UK to double its confectionery business and to take it into impulse-purchase snack chocolates.

On management, Nestlé has poured resources into developing chilled foods almost from scratch. Buying Chambourcy in France in the 1980s gave it a big yoghurt brand and chilled distribution. But yoghurt became increasingly a commodity business, so Nestlé shifted into higher value chilled deserts and bio-tech enhanced yoghurt, while moving products from the Chambourcy to Nestlé brand.

Nestlé is prepared to invest for decades to reach critical mass. Its patient stalking of L'Oréal in cosmetics and San Pellegrino in water is typical. Ice cream and pet foods, however, are the top two products in its portfolio which it has targeted for rapid development. Particularly in Europe, they lack powerful market shares and lag behind the leaders – Unilever in ice cream and Mars in petfoods.

Only in Italy and France does Nestlé have reasonable petfood market positions with 23 per cent and 15 per cent, respectively, making it second to Mars. A new pan-European management team for petfoods, however, is wringing more from the business. Petfood sales rose 14 per cent to SFr413m in the first half of this year.

Acquisitions will play a part in building petfoods in Europe to complement the number one position it has in the US. Nestlé said it has twice had inconclusive talks with a company it declined to identify, and could well talk to it again.

Competitors believe the target is Royal Canin in France, owned by Paribas, which has an 8 per cent market share and may be worth about FFr800m ($158m). Acquiring it would make Nestlé a credible second to Mars.

Such in-fill acquisitions fit the strategy of Mr Maucher and Mr Brabeck to achieve Nestlé's overall growth one-third by acquisition and two-thirds by organic growth. They pose no financial strain, one London analyst says, but might make the company more aware of the benefits of shedding peripheral businesses.

Source: Financial Times, 8 August 1996

21.4   Using the information in this article and that obtained from any additional research you carry out, draw up an analysis and assessment of Nestlé's business activities.

21.5   With such a broad portfolio of interests, what difficulties do you think Peter Brabeck will face as new Chairman?

21.6   How would you assess Nestlé's attitude to change and risk? What evidence can you give to support your response?

Sony's defence of the living room

The Japanese giant has had to redefine its strategy to compete in the digital age, explains Michiyo Nakamoto

Sony, the Japanese electronics giant, has always exuded an air of self-confidence. With a name that is the best-recognised brand in the US, a proven knack for setting the trend in consumer electronics, a history marked by its achievements in paving new paths for the industry, the inventor of the Walkman and the compact disc, it has had good reason to feel sure of itself.

But as Sony's management looks to the challenges that lie ahead, it will need to muster all the collective self-confidence it can to attain the goal the company has set for itself. In a year in which it celebrated its 50th anniversary, Sony has outlined its ambition to become 'the leading maker of consumer electronics in the digital age,' as Nobuyuki Idei, Sony's president, puts it.

Idei, who has been at the helm for just a year and a half, is the first to admit the enormous challenges this presents. The ongoing spread of digital technology 'will affect our way of making things in very fundamental ways', he says.

Sony's growth from a small company selling transistor radios in war-ravaged Japan to a $4bn (£2.5bn) global business has been the history of the development of consumer electronics using analogue technology. 'But after 50 years, the industry which depended on analogue technology is coming to an end,' Idei points out.

In the past several years, digital technology has spread through the consumer market in the form of compact discs and MiniDiscs – products which Sony pioneered. But two impending developments, in particular, make it certain that the impact of digital technology on the consumer market will usher in more fundamental changes in future.

For one thing, the shift to digital broadcasting in the European Union, the US and Japan means that the boxes that receive entertainment in the home – TV and radios – will have to become digital. PCs and networks, or information technology, will encroach further into Sony's core business of providing home entertainment, ensuring that digital technology dominates the living room.

This will happen in a big way when the Internet moves from narrow-band to broad-band networks, through cable and satellite, allowing more visual information to speed down the information highway. 'The Internet will quickly become more like TV,' Idei notes.

These changes, which Idei sees happening rapidly, represent the convergence of information technology and consumer electronics – particularly the audio-visual products which have been at the core of Sony's business.

In the face of what has been a rapid march towards that convergence, Idei recognised that Sony would need to change in order to defend its position in the living room.

He saw a need for a 'regeneration' of the company that would enable Sony to be the one to offer the new digital TV services, the games and other home entertainment on the PC and through networks.

'Sony wants to be the company that brings the PC into the home,' says Kunitake Ando, president of Sony's information technology company. But to do so it will have to change from an analogue to a digital company.

One of the first steps Idei took towards that objective was to redefine a strategy for Sony in the digital age. He coined the phrase 'digital dream kids' to send a message to employees that the company would have to shift the focus of its products from analogue to digital technology.

But making digital consumer products will not be enough to achieve that goal, Idei believes. The company needs to expand into information technology, that is to make and sell PCs which have an undeniably important role in shaping the new age of digital entertainment and participate in online networks.

That decision by Idei led to the establishment of a new IT company within Sony's 10-company structure in Japan and a strengthening of its IT research and development. Earlier this year Sony unveiled the Vaio, an upper-end PC made by Intel, the US semiconductor manufacturer, which will go on the market in the US under the Sony brand this month.

The move into PCs is a gamble for Sony. The company is already deeply involved in the computer business through the peripherals and components it makes, such as monitors, floppy disc drives, CD drives and semiconductors.

However, as far as PCs are concerned, its record has been unimpressive. Sony failed to make inroads into the PC market with an early home-use PC which was developed in the early 1980s under Idei. It has since brought out a palm-top PC, which was dropped after a year, and a workstation, which has a limited market.

Competition in the PC market is already fierce and, consequently, profits are difficult to come by. Critics have questioned what Sony can offer PC users – a market it has little familiarity with. 'Sony, unfortunately does not have strength in PCs,' concedes Kenji Tamiya, senior managing director in charge of communications. 'All the expertise it has in the audio visual world, it is beginning to build up in the PC world.'

'The rules of the game are different,' adds Ando. 'In the audio-visual world, Sony has been a holder of the technology format. But in the IT world not only is Sony a latecomer, and therefore unlikely to be a standard-setter for some time, if ever, it also faces a market in which it is very difficult to differentiate your products from those of your competitors.'

At the same time, the digitalisation of Sony cannot be accomplished without some fundamental changes to the corporate culture as well. For one thing, since software will become increasingly important Sony has had to nurture a new kind of engineer who can understand both hardware and software, such as operating software, says Minoru Morio, executive deputy president responsible for technology.

An engineer who designs a video recorder, for example, must also understand the semiconductors that will determine what the video will be able to do and how it will do it. Trying to educate hardware engineers on software 'is equivalent to realising a cultural revolution', says Tamiya.

Breaking with age-old habits which have no place in the digital age has also been an important issue, Idei admits. 'Past experiences led to unwritten rules about what Sony will or will not do,' he says. 'For example, since Sony made magneto-optical discs, it was taken for granted that it would not make hard discs which compete. But we have to remove such restrictions.'

At the same time, Sony, which has fought its fair share of bitter standards wars and has a reputation for going it alone, acknowledges that it needs to co-operate with others to overcome its weaknesses and to embrace the open culture of the Internet. 'My message is that Sony will be open and wants alliances,' Idei emphasises.

Furthermore, these changes to the way Sony operates have made it necessary to re-think the corporate identity. 'Sony used to make things that were different from those made by everyone else. That is what made a product, a Sony,' says Idei. 'We ourselves may have come to think that being Sony meant doing something different.

'But I think this is wrong. I think it is possible to make the same things as everyone else and still make something that is uniquely Sony. For users, what makes something a Sony is that it is good. It is a perception of reliability, good design, sophistication and something slightly unique. In the age of the network, we have to continue to redefine what makes something a Sony,' he notes.

Whether or not Idei's message to become 'digital dream kids' takes hold at Sony will have a crucial bearing in achieving its goal. But perhaps the biggest risk Sony faces in its gamble may be the impact that its new PC business could have on its image.

That image, one of the company's greatest assets, will be more fully exploited in the IT market where products it now sells under other companies' brands will increasingly be sold under the Sony name.

The problem is that Sony is not used to dealing with the kind of customer queries and demands that are a part of life in the computer world. 'In the audio-visual market, users expect to be able to use a product as soon as they bring it home. But there is a 15 per cent return ratio in the US PC market. This is unthinkable in the audio visual world,' says Ando.

Against such obstacles, Sony nevertheless still feels it needs to be in computers because knowledge of computers and what people want from them will be crucial to maintain its status as the leading provider of home entertainment in the digital age.

'Vaio is an entrance fee,' Idei says categorically. Because 'if you are not making computers, since change is happening so rapidly, you can't keep up', he explains. 'I don't aim to take market share in PCs, but to use the PC as a step to go on to the next step.'

Sony's management is also driven by the conviction that their company can be the one to bring the PC into the living room. 'Existing PCs do not offer any of the features of a home-use product,' says Ando, who admits that he himself finds it difficult to use Windows, the operating system launched by Microsoft which was supposed to make PCs easy to use.

Not only are PCs difficult to use, the quality of the sound and graphics they offer are far below the standards expected from a TV or CD-player.

With its experience in mass-producing consumer products which people find easy to use, its expertise in designing and packaging those products attractively, its knowledge of what consumers want, its global distribution network and, above all, the power of its brand, Sony executives are confident that the company is well-placed to lead the convergence of information technology and consumer electronics by making IT 'more fun', as Idei says. 'Sony knows the living-room culture,' Morio emphasises.

Having defined a future direction for Sony and instigated a cultural revolution within Sony, Idei is preparing to further the company along that route through a number of alliances which he sees as crucial in determining its success in achieving its goal. 'The next three years, I think, will be a very exciting time,' he says.

Source: Financial Times, 26 August 1996

21.7 Where would you place Sony's proposed entry into the PC market on a Shell Directional Policy matrix? Specify exactly what you mean when you use the descriptors: weak, average and strong for the 'competitive capability' axis, and unattractive, average and attractive for the 'prospects for sector profitability' axis.

21.8 Given your answer to 21.7 above, would you advise Sony to invest in this area? Why?

21.9 In terms of the Ansoff matrix, how would you classify this move?

21.10 What are the implications of your answer to 21.9 above, in terms of marketing mix activities and risk?

21.11 How successful do you think Sony will be in this venture? Justify your answer.

21D

Macfarlane plans to buy smaller packaging rivals

By Simon Kuper

Macfarlane Group (Clansman) is planning to acquire some of its smaller rivals in the packaging industry including one with sales of £20m.

Lord Macfarlane of Bearsden, chairman of the Glasgow-based group, said yesterday it would also spend up to £6m opening packaging plants. 'We are investing money in every one of our companies,' he said.

He was presenting annual results showing a 30 per cent rise in pre-tax profits to £21.2m. Sales rose 36 per cent to £158.6m, thanks largely to increases in raw materials prices, which were passed on.

Organic growth came 'almost entirely' from Macfarlane's packaging division, where pre-tax profits rose 40 per cent to £14.5m. Profits from the plastic moulding division grew 13 per cent to $6.54m, held back by the flat whisky industry.

The final dividend is 2.5p for a total up nearly 25 per cent to 3.9p (3.13p), payable from earnings of 12.03p (9.19p).

Sales and profits in 1996 were 'ahead of the same period last year', said Lord Macfarlane. Aged 70, the chairman said he had no plans to leave the company he founded.

'Nobody will know better than me when the time comes,' he said.

● Comment

Macfarlane almost never disappoints the market and is likely to please it again this year. Analysts forecast pre-tax profits of £24m and earnings per share of 13.6p, making a forward p/e of 17. That is high: most small packaging business tend to have a p/e of about 12.5 – but Macfarlane easily deserves its premium.

The company is wary of throwing money around. When it does make capital investments and acquisitions, as it plans to now, these almost always enhance earnings. And the £24m forecast could well be bettered – the company creates some unnecessary uncertainty among analysts because it is less communicative than most. As long as the economy does not collapse and leave Macfarlane with empty new plants, the shares look well worth having.

Source: Financial Times, 29 March 1996

21E

Appetite for acquisition beats competitors on their own ground

James Whittington reviews the strategy that keeps British Polythene Industries ahead of the game

Mr Cameron McLatchie, chairman of British Polythene Industries, balks at the suggestion that his expansionist methods might be described as ruthless. He prefers to be thought of as the architect of a well thought out rationalisation of the polythene industry.

Over the past 10 years, while many of his UK competitors have been losing market share or going bust, he has built the company into Europe's largest polythene film producer.

As the fragmented industry comes under further strain from the increasing costs of raw materials and competition from east Asia, BPI is again adapting to change.

Typical of BPI's strategy is the opening of a polythene bag factory in China later this year. Hounded by east Asian competitors who have been making inroads into the UK market for lightweight bags used at supermarket counters, it has taken the view: 'If you can't beat 'em, join 'em.'

Eighteen months ago BPI became the first European investor to enter China's polythene market when it signed a £5.5m joint venture agreement with China's High Point Corporation, a state-owned conglomerate, to build a factory in the southern Guangdong province.

The factory is being equipped by BPI and manned by Chinese labour. It will begin manufacturing an initial 15m lightweight plastic bags a week in April, about 10m of which will be exported to UK supermarket chains.

The joint venture company, called Xinhui Alida Polythene, is 60 per cent owned by BPI and 40 per cent by High Point Corporation. Mr McLatchie says the agreement will enable BPI not only to compete with other east Asian manufacturers in the UK, but also to tap the huge market in China and other countries in the region.

Since 1988, when it was Scott & Robertson, BPI has developed an extraordinary appetite for acquisition. It has spent more than £120m on the purchase of more than 30 companies. Mr McLatchie says the two main acquisitions were British Visqueen, from ICI, in February 1988 and Alida Holdings in July 1989.

'After that it was just a game of Pac-man,' he says. 'We swallowed up every smaller company we could find and integrated them into our operations.'

By following a strategy of buying out competition wherever possible, BPI sales grew nearly fivefold in 10 years to more than £250m in 1994. It now dominates the UK polythene market by controlling nearly a third of volume turnover with its 270,000 tonnes a year.

Mr McLatchie argues that the key is rationalisation. 'When we buy a business we focus on what they do best. Either they'll develop a profitable specialism or we'll close them down and shift their equipment elsewhere. This is the only way to get economies of scale.' As a result, BPI is UK market leader in a range of niche products such as wide agricultural film, recycled carrier bags and heavy sacks for fertilizers.

The latest casualty of rationalisation is the Alida Polysack plant at Telford, in Shropshire, which manufactures 27m lightweight carrier bags a week for the supermarket chains. After losing an order from one supermarket which accounted for 25 per cent of the plant's £10m–£11m turnover, the group this week announced that it would be closed in May with the loss of 150 jobs.

Half of Telford's output, and its plant and machinery, will be taken up by the Chinese plant at Xinhui; the rest will be integrated into other UK facilities.

Mr McLatchie maintains that closure was unavoidable in the light of massive rises in raw material prices and pressure from the supermarkets to reduce selling prices. According to BPI, the price of high density polyethylene, the basic polymer used in plastic bags, has risen from £400 to £720 per tonne since August.

Its customers, including Safeway, Tesco and Marks and Spencer, say they are constantly assessing their suppliers of plastic bags, to find the most competitive prices. Although the retailers would give no details about the sourcing of the plastic bags, one industry analyst estimates that east Asia has about 25 per cent of the market and rising.

BPI's growth has been matched by a strong showing in its share price, from a low of 134p in 1988 after the Visqueen acquisition to 528p in July 1993. Yesterday it closed 3p up at 487p.

By comparison, Sidlaw Group, a competitor in the packaging business, last week saw its share price plummet by nearly 25 per cent after issuing a profit warning as a result of raw material price increases.

Analysts are bullish about BPI. Profit forecasts for 1994 range from £17m to £18.5m, growing to £21m in 1995, against £15.39m in 1993. 'BPI has become a dominant player in a fragmented market,' says one. 'Its ability to look ahead of the others makes it a stock well worth having.'

Source: Financial Times, 8 February 1995

21.12 What type of defensive strategy do you think Macfarlane and BPI is engaging in by acquiring rival firms? What type of integration is being proposed?

21.13 What are the benefits of such a strategy?

21.14 Obtain a copy of BPI's latest Annual Report along with any other secondary information you can find. Form a view on whether BPI's acquisitive strategy has continued to be successful.

21.15 As a customer of Macfarlane's packaging division, what benefits and drawbacks do you think you could expect if their plans are successful?

21F

Gains via R&D, market share and cost-cuts

Three leading European manufacturers employ very different strategies against their international competitors

ROCHE by Tony Jackson

The Swiss pharmaceutical giant Roche is an example of European industry at its most effective. Last year, the steady rise in its share price made it the most highly valued drug company in the world, overhauling Merck of the US.

Roche's success is based on the performance of European workers at home and European managers abroad. Swiss-based researchers have discovered a wealth of commercially valuable drugs. Roche has also proved shrewd in acquiring assets overseas, notably Californian biotechnology company Genentech.

The achievement owes much to the immense and, no doubt, excessive profitability of the international drug industry, which governments around the world are now seeking to control. The results for Roche have been extraordinary.

Its spending on R&D has been heavy even by the standards of its industry: in 1992, for instance, its pharmaceuticals research bill came to SFr1.6bn ($1.1bn), or 24 per cent of its pharmaceutical turnover.

It was also able to plank down $2bn in 1990 for 60 per cent of Genentech, a company which had only $500m in sales and very little profit. Despite all that, Roche has cash and securities currently estimated at SFr20bn ($13.5bn).

In the field of conventional drugs, it is worth recalling that Roche's success represents a fairly recent comeback. It had a previous glory phase in the 1960s, based largely on the tranquilliser Valium.

As Valium went off patent, Roche spent heavily on the search for replacement drugs. For a while, it seemed the money was being wasted. The real strength of the resulting research pipeline has become apparent only recently.

Roche has also built a formidable position in hospital drugs, claiming to sell more drugs to US hospitals than any other company in the world.

At the same time, the purchase of Genentech was a particularly bold strategic move, since biotechnology is a field in which the US has a clear lead over Europe. Roche has thus hedged its bets against a possible shortfall in European technology.

MICHELIN by John Ridding

Michelin of France, the world's biggest tyre maker, made it the hard way. In 1960 it was 10th biggest, by 1970 it was number six and by the end of the 1980s it was number one. Michelin's approach had a Japanese ring: aggressive international expansion and concentration on market share.

Greenfield investments, followed by the acquisition of Uniroyal Goodrich in 1990, have resulted in a 20 per cent share of the world market and a clear lead over Goodyear of the US and Bridgestone of Japan. At the same time, Michelin has invested heavily in quality and in R&D, being the first company to develop and market the radial tyre.

Michelin's rise has been far from smooth. The Uniroyal acquisition was completed as the US market collapsed. Last year, the European market did likewise. For several years, the group suffered large losses. But most industry observers believe the worst is over.

Michelin's ability to pursue its aggressive and sometimes risky strategy partly reflects its ownership. As a family-controlled group in the continental European mould, it can afford to be less concerned with quarterly earnings and more with dominance in markets and technologies. The benefits are evident in the initially costly but ultimately lucrative development of radial tyres and in the strengths of geographical diversity.

But now a different message is emanating from Michelin's headquarters at Clermont-Ferrand. With its market position established and little remaining scope for growth through acquisitions or new capacity, the company is shifting emphasis towards increased efficiency and higher margins.

This is to be achieved partly through new, higher value-added products, such as the green tyre, which reduces fuel consumption.

The company has also embarked on job cuts which have seen staff numbers fall from 140,000 at the end of 1991 to 125,000. Further reductions are expected from the introduction of its C3m automated and flexible production process.

PHILIPS by Tony Jackson

Philips, the Dutch electronics group, is a classic case of a once-great European company caught between the Japanese hammer and the American anvil. On the one hand, its battles with Japan in consumer electronics have led to huge losses. On the other, it has been obliged to abandon high-tech areas in computers and semiconductors.

Philips's basic problem can be illustrated by comparison with one of its chief competitors, the Japanese electronics company Matsushita. A decade ago, Matsushita's sales in dollar terms were smaller than Philips's. They are now twice as large. The growth of the Japanese company in the 1980s owed much to the strength of its domestic market, from which Philips was largely excluded by a combination of protectionism and the peculiarities of the Japanese retail system.

But the Japanese advantage, whether fair or foul, was a fact of life. Philips' determination to tackle the competition head-on has been impressive, but also smacks of arrogance and inflexibility. Despite the company's recent enormous losses, the struggle continues. In the field of consumer audio, Philips is confronting Sony's mini-compact disc with its new digital compact cassette. It has also just opened a factory in Holland to make flat screen panels, a vitally important technology in which even the Americans have conceded Japan a virtual monopoly.

Philips could be past the worst. Its cost-cutting and rationalisation in the past couple of years have been on a scale to suggest that even the notorious Philips bureaucracy has become genuinely alarmed. And the Japanese electronics industry is facing problems which may prove structural rather than cyclical.

Certainly, the investment community is inclined to optimism. In the past year, Philips's shares have outperformed the Dutch market by two thirds.

However, the company has seen false dawns before. For the pessimists, it may be more relevant to reflect that the shares have halved relative to the Dutch market in the past decade.

Source: Financial Times, 25 February 1994

21.16 Draw up an analysis on the activities of each of these three firms. (Additional desk research may be necessary.)

21.17 Identify the strategies which are associated with each firm in the article and determine whether they are still in place today.

21.18 Assess the competitive position and posture which each firm might be taking in relation to its key competitors.

21G

Volvo takes the wraps off expansion strategy

The group has ambitious plans, writes Kevin Done

Volvo is taking the wraps off its strategy for expanding its automotive operations independently, more than a year after the spectacular collapse of its planned merger with Renault, the French majority state-owned carmaker.

The moves outlined yesterday are the first steps towards expanding its successful truck operations in Europe, while providing a broader base for its car division with the development of new products outside the narrow confines of its established car business.

Volvo acted quickly last year to set the priorities for its new corporate strategy. This is centred on the plan to concentrate resources on its car and commercial vehicle operations (it will retain its aero and marine engine activities), with the divestment of most of its non-core activities.

By late 1994 it had regained control over its strategic auto operations by dissolving its alliance with Renault and removing the cross-shareholdings binding the two groups' car and commercial vehicle operations. It also began the disposal of unwanted activities with the aim of strengthening its balance sheet.

The expansion of its automotive operations will not be achieved cheaply, but Volvo's finances are improving rapidly, fuelled both by the disposal programme and, more important, by the turnround of the automotive operations.

Net debt had been driven down from SKr14.5bn ($1.9bn) at the end of 1993 to SKr700m at the beginning of October last year. The group's equity-to-assets ratio had risen to 30 per cent from 21 per cent. Mr Sören Gyll, chief executive, aims for a ratio of 50 per cent.

Profits are rising fast as Volvo benefits from the tough cost-cutting programmes it was forced to implement during the recession, as well as from an upturn in its main markets and a favourable response to new car and truck products launched in the last two years.

Volvo Truck had record sales year last year, with volumes climbing by 33.5 per cent to 68,500. Operating profit in the first nine months rose to SKr2.697bn from SKr183m in the corresponding period a year earlier. Volvo Car increased sales volume in 1994 by 15.9 per cent to 361,500, with operating profits in the first nine months rebounding to SKr1.95bn from SKr10m.

The truck operations are embarking on a far-reaching expansion in Europe and Asia, with the first move aimed at expanding production capacity outside North America to 60,000 trucks a year with an investment of SKr1.7bn.

Some 42,000 trucks were produced outside North America last year. About 27,000 trucks a year are produced in the US.

The planned expansion will take place in Europe with heavy investment in the production of cabs and components – engines, gearboxes and axles – in Sweden, and the expansion of assembly capacity in four countries, Belgium (up by 4,000 to 26,000), the UK (up by 1,000 to 5,500), Poland (up by 500 to 1,500) and in Sweden (up by 2,000 to 17,000).

Also under consideration are ambitious plans for the development of a new range of trucks to allow Volvo to enter the European light truck market, as well as for the establishment of a joint venture in China with the aim of adding a production centre in Asia to its three regional truck manufacturing operations in Europe and North and South America. It has also launched a feasibility study into establishing production in India.

Asia is Volvo's 'number one priority' in the geographic expansion of its truck operations, says Mr Karl-Erling Trogen, chief executive of Volvo Truck.

Volvo is among the world leaders in the truck sector, but in the car industry it is one of the smallest producers in the mainstream industry.

Mr Per-Erik Mohlin, president of Volvo Car, has made clear that it will need a number of partnerships to replace the alliance with Renault.

The joint venture with TWR, the UK automotive engineering group controlled by Mr Tom Walkinshaw, is a first step.

It will develop small volume niche products, initially a cabriolet and a coupe, from Volvo's main 850 large car chassis platform.

Volvo is strong in the 'family market', says Mr Mohlin, but it must develop a strategy for broadening the customer base to gain more 'pre-family' and 'post-family' buyers.

'We know it is possible to develop more cars from a single platform. The trick is to utilise common components but to differentiate the products,' he says.

To achieve this flexibility Volvo has chosen to join forces with Mr Walkinshaw, the entrepreneurial and technical talent behind JaguarSport (a previous Jaguar/TWR joint venture) and the Benetton grand prix team.

Volvo Car already has in place one other big alliance, namely its joint venture in the Netherlands with Mitsubishi Motors, which will provide Volvo with a replacement for its current 400 medium car range starting in 1996.

Source: Financial Times, 19 January 1995

21.19 In your work group, discuss each of Porter's Generic Strategies in relation to Volvo.

21.20 Which generic strategy do you think Volvo is now following?

21.21 Why do you think Volvo selected this one as the most appropriate? How well do you think this fits with the firm's strengths?

22

Marketing Planning, Management and Control

Marketing planning done well, is the foundation for a firm's effort and eventual success. It involves a great deal of analysis and an assessment of both the macro- and micro-environment. A particular problem which can occur when first embarking on marketing planning, is the elapsed time between the initial enthusiastic effort and a tangible result of that effort. Any plan, and particularly a marketing plan, does not provide a quick-fix solution.

Planning takes place at all levels in the organisation. The Board of Directors should be looking at strategic direction and long-term issues. Capital investment needs, resource allocation, risk analysis, company structure and sometimes an assessment of Government activity over the next ten years are typical concerns.

Medium-term plans typically cover the period between one to three years and will concentrate on competitiveness, product development and market position. Senior functional managers are usually expected to be concerned with this type of planning.

Short-term planning takes place at the operational level and may involve issues such as stock levels, market performance and an assessment of current competitor activity. A decision to try and capture more market share in the existing market has an impact on how the marketing department design their pricing and promotional strategies. Similarly, the objective of increased market share which is supported by heavy promotional effort and sometimes price cuts, has an immediate impact on other areas, such as purchasing, manufacturing, warehousing, transportation, recruitment and credit control. A sales strategy pursued in isolation from the rest of the organisation is almost certainly doomed to failure.

Planning is essential for all organisations, but it is wrong to automatically assume that it always exists in a formal way. Owner/managers of small- to medium-sized enterprises, may well boast that they have never produced anything more detailed than the initial business plan required by the bank to support the firm's launch, but just because it isn't written down doesn't mean it isn't there. Owner/managers often have an intimate knowledge of their product, their customers, their suppliers and the market and all the decisions are theirs alone to take. This is acceptable, and in some instances it would be positively harmful to stifle creativity by demanding that their activities are reflected in a formal planning process, but, in the larger, more publicly accountable organisation, the need for everybody to be pulling in the same direction is vital. It is here that the formal planning procedure is most valuable not only in ensuring a coherent approach from all areas of the organisation, but also in providing the platform for any course of any action taken.

In order to successfully complete the tasks in this chapter you will need to be familiar with:

- SWOT analysis;
- marketing objectives;
- marketing strategies;
- mission statements;
- control and evaluation;
- market/sales potential;
- sales forecasting;
- sales analysis;
- organisational structure.

22A

Telecoms operators stripped of duopoly

By Alan Cane

The government yesterday stripped the last vestiges of monopoly power from British Telecommunications and Mercury Communications, the duopoly of UK-owned telecoms operators which controlled the domestic telephone business between 1984 and 1991.

It announced the end of restrictions which prevent competing operators from owning and operating their own circuits for international calls. At present, a rival operator must either lease international circuits from BT or Mercury – or pay an agreed rate for each call carried.

The end of the international duopoly will mean sharp falls in the cost of international calls.

Rivals to BT and Mercury will have the right to construct and use their own infrastructure including sub-sea cables and satellites, and to conclude their own contracts with operators abroad.

The decision, announced in the Commons by Mr Ian Taylor, the science and technology minister, will maintain the UK's reputation as Europe's most liberal telecoms regime ahead of Europe-wide liberalisation on January 1, 1998.

It also raises the prospects of an adverse balance of payments in telecoms – if foreign operators continued to charge UK-based carriers high rates for calls abroad while taking advantage of their own infrastructure to deliver calls cheaply in the UK.

Mr Taylor said yesterday, however, that the decision would mean big gains for the UK. In addition to the inward investment expected from firms relocating to the UK because of its telecoms environment, he expected the country to become the European hub for global telecoms traffic.

He said steps would be taken to ensure fair play. 'In particular, we will wish to give the director-general of telecommunications powers to prevent one-way bypass or discriminatory practices between affiliate companies,' he said.

'In parallel, we will be continuing to press for improved access for UK operators both within the EU through strict application of the new Community liberalisation rules and in other countries through the World Trade Organisation,' he added.

Mr Don Cruickshank, the director-general of Oftel, the telecoms regulator, welcomed the liberalisation of international facilities and said Oftel would start discussions immediately with BT, Mercury and prospective licensees to determine how facilities might be shared and access to international gateways obtained.

Ruling may cut phone cost for network services

The cost of services sold over the domestic telephone network could fall after the publication yesterday of new proposals by Mr Don Cruickshank, the telecoms industry regulator, designed to encourage competition, Alan Cane writes.

The proposals will make it possible for British Telecommunications, the UK's dominant operator, to charge independent service providers (ISPs), companies which sell services over networks to the public, rates that are lower than its conventional retail prices.

In exchange for the new freedom, however, Mr Cruickshank is insisting that BT agrees to a new licence condition giving him broad powers to outlaw anti-competitive behaviour.

BT and Mr Cruickshank have been at odds over the new licence condition for the past six months.

Last week he announced controls on BT's prices until 2001 which seemed broadly deregulatory; their implementation, however, was again dependent on acceptance of the licence conditions.

ISPs typically provide data services over the public telephone network. Current regulations require BT to charge these companies retail prices for carrying its traffic.

Under the new proposals, the regulator would have no power to determine the prices which are offered to ISPs by BT. A definition of ISPs is to be drawn up, however, to identify companies entitled to ISP prices.

Mr Cruickshank also proposes to redefine which of BT's businesses are basic network services and which are enhanced services.

The mix is being powerfully affected by technological change as networks increasingly use digital technology which does not distinguish between voice and data traffic.

ISPs must be able to buy network services from BT on the same terms as BT's enhanced service business if they are to compete effectively.

BT and Mercury said yesterday that they supported the government's decision. Mercury said its turnover and profits had doubled since the introduction of full domestic competition in 1991.

Among the companies expected to make immediate application for international licences are AT&T, the largest US operator, Energis, the telecoms arm of the National Grid, and MFS, a US operator targeting the business market in the UK.

Mr Merrill Tutton, AT&T's UK president said: 'AT&T welcomes the opportunity to obtain an international facilities licence and looks forward to utilising these new freedoms.'

MFS said it would be seeking permission from both US and UK regulators to build out a new sub-sea fibre optic cable between the US and the UK.

Source: Financial Times, 7 June 1996

22.1 Carry out a SWOT analysis for British Telecom.

22.2 In the face of new entrants into their previously closed market, what do you think BT's marketing objectives should be over the next three years?

22.3 Weinburg (1996) identified the trade-offs which take place when setting objectives. Identify the trade-offs you made when completing your answer to 22.2 above.

22.4 What strategy, or mix of strategies, can be employed to achieve the objectives you propose?

The man who would sell coals to Newcastle

Derby's chief executive takes the 'lean' route to achieving global success, reports Peter Marsh

The village of East Preston on England's south coast is not normally associated with multinational manufacturing companies. Yet from a room in his house close to the West Sussex seaside Mr Alan Finden-Crofts runs a £300m annual turnover business making bicycles around the world.

Mr Finden-Crofts was chief executive of Dunlop Slazenger, part of the BTR group, before setting up Derby International in 1987.

He eschews a head office and works half his time from home, with the rest of his week spent in his company's sales, production and distribution operations in Germany, China and Canada.

Derby, of which Mr Finden-Crofts owns just under a quarter, has emerged as one of the UK's most noted industrial success stories. In 1987 it took over the Raleigh bicycle-making operations of Tube Investments (now TI) – which in the previous five years had lost £35m.

Since then the company has been restored to profit and turnover has roughly doubled on the back of a number of global acquisitions. The company is now thought to be worth about £150m. Its non-executive chairman is Mr Ed Gottesman, a New York lawyer who owns about 5 per cent and controls investment trusts accounting for more than 50 per cent of the Derby stake.

Mr Gottesman and Mr Finden-Crofts have already used the Derby approach in setting up another company in which they are the main shareholders – Exeter International, which owns the Royal Worcester and Spode china companies and has annual sales of about £60m. Mr Gottesman said the idea of combining a 'lean' management style and privately owned status could serve as a model for the takeover of other companies, and that he and other Derby shareholders were considering a range of further acquisitions.

A large part of Derby is its operations in the Far East, particularly in China where the company is pursuing a 'twin track' strategy. At the same time as trying to fend off heavy global competition from Chinese bicycle makers, Derby has a series of big supply contracts with Chinese component makers and is trying to set up innovative licensing deals with independent bicycle makers in the country.

Raleigh China has been set up to broaden and deepen Derby's existing licensing operations in China under which the company collects royalties on sales of about 2m bikes a year produced by two Chinese companies, Zhejiang Phillips Bicycle and Anyang Bicycle Industry. These deals involve only minimal transfer of technology and few design ideas.

On the supply side, Derby has a 40-strong trading company, based in two offices in Taipei, Taiwan, and Shenzen, China, which handles the purchasing each year of about £120m worth of bicycle components from several hundred companies in east Asia, – mainly in China, Taiwan, and Japan.

This is part of the company's policy of scouring the world for low-cost components. Roughly two thirds of the factory price of the bicycles Derby makes around the world is accounted for by bought-in components.

Derby's total bicycle production under its own control adds up to about 2.5m bikes a year. Existing licensing deals including the Chinese agreements and similar deals in India, Scandinavia and South America, provide royalties of several hundred thousand pounds a year, covering the manufacture of 3m bikes a year.

According to Mr Finden-Crofts, Derby has prospered by becoming 'more focused' on control of component supplies, researching sales trends and production discipline.

Since 1987 Derby has spent £55m in investments at its factories – of which the main one is in Nottingham, home of Raleigh bicycle making for more than 100 years, and where employment is down to about 1,500 compared with more than 8,000 in the early 1980s. Nottingham accounts for just under half of Derby's total staff, with most of the others working in its two plants in Germany, and factories in the US, Canada, South Africa and Holland.

Mr Finden-Crofts keeps in touch with his company's operating units through a near-continuous tour of Derby's plants and sales offices. Every quarter he also presides over a meeting of Derby's 10-strong executive board, which brings together the top executives from the subsidiaries.

Derby has three main committees – covering product design, manufacturing systems and component purchasing – which involve another 40 or so managers and assemble twice a year. 'Companies waste a lot of time and money calling in their people to some grand head office – I'd rather spend my time going out to the subsidiaries to see what's going on,' said Mr Finden-Croft.

Much of the chief executive's time is spent ensuring that Derby's finances are under control. This particu-

larly applies to borrowings which tend to rise early in the calendar year when cash flow is under pressure prior to the surge in deliveries before Christmas.

Roughly 15 per cent of Derby's 3,600 staff are on temporary contracts to cope with the peaks and troughs in demand. Derby is also geared up for swift switches in strategy. For example, its base in Seattle was until recently little more than a trading operation, importing 220,000 bikes a year from China and Taiwan for sales in the US. However, after the quality of the imports turned out too low, the company recently started assembly operations.

Source: Financial Times, 4 December 1995

22.5 Propose a mission statement for the bicycle division of Derby International.

22.6 To what extent does your answer to 22.5 above, encompass the four characteristics identified by Day (1992) as evidence of a well thought out mission statement?

22.7 What type of management control does Alan Finden-Crofts utilise?

22.8 How appropriate do you think this is for this type of business and what alternatives would be available to him?

22C

Milking the niche trend

Dairy companies are now freer to promote products in more innovative ways, writes Deborah Hargreaves

Consumers shopping for a pint of milk have, until recently, been faced with few decisions about what to buy: semi-skimmed or full fat, bottle or carton. But shoppers could soon face an array of different quality specifications including milk claiming to be from local farms, as producers try to differentiate their supplies in a commodity business.

Tomorrow sees the launch of the first nationwide cow-to-consumer quality assurance scheme, by Northern Foods. The Northern Milk Partnership, which supplies roughly half of Northern Foods' 2bn litres of fresh milk direct from farmers, will provide certain quality guarantees on aspects of hygiene and animal welfare. It will reassure consumers that its milk comes from happy cows and can be traced back to the individual farms that supplied it.

The move highlights a trend in food retailing towards greater accountability on the part of suppliers, higher standards imposed by supermarkets and the drive for more expensive, niche products.

Richard Smith, chairman of the Northern Milk Partnership and a dairy farmer, says he is not necessarily looking to create new sales with his assurances: 'It is a question of whether we can capture and keep our market. Everyone will have to go this way eventually – I want to be at the forefront and don't want to be forced by the supermarkets to do it.'

Milk producers are anxious to secure their market share following the rapid demise in doorstep sales in recent years and aggressive price competition between supermarkets. Deregulation in the dairy industry a year ago when the government's statutory purchasing body was scrapped has given companies the opportunity to be more innovative.

The success of farmhouse cheeses, such as Dairy Crest's Davidstow brand where milk supplies come from Cornish farms, have given dairy producers a chance to move into higher value products. It also fills a consumer demand for tasty local produce which looks as if it comes from a farm rather than a factory. 'People are keen to know where their food comes from, they are interested in regional variations and quality of the produce,' says John Houlistan, chief executive of Dairy Crest.

Supermarkets have also launched ranges of free-range meat or established high welfare standards for farm suppliers of meat.

Continental food producers have traditionally been more sophisticated about marketing regional produce and food with quality guarantees. Farmhouse cheeses dominate the French market. Philippe Vasseur, French minister of agriculture, recently commented that promoting and developing regional produce which is marketed under various quality symbols, was 'one of the linchpins of my policy'.

In the UK Marks and Spencer launched the first small-scale quality scheme in May with its 'Milk from Specially Selected Farms' in stores in the south. 'We are always looking to provide products with an edge and this is one way to differentiate,' says the company.

The milk, which is marketed in distinctive cartons and has a special quality guarantee, is supplied by Unigate from around 100 farms with which the company has long-standing arrangements. M&S says that so far it has had an encouraging response from consumers.

Until a year ago, all the nation's milk was collected and sold by the Milk Marketing Board. Now, many dairy companies buy direct from farmers and even Milk Marque, the voluntary farmers' co-opera-tive which succeeded the board, offers milk from specific regions.

Milk producers must be able to trace supplies in order to comply with strict health requirements in the event that milk becomes contaminated. Smith says that providing the consumer with guarantees about milk quality is only publicising suppliers' best practice.

There is also a growing trend for manufacturers, such as cheesemakers, and supermarkets to be able to market milk as coming from a specific region. Northern Foods will sell its quality-guaranteed milk under labels such as Derbyshire or Yorkshire milk.

Milk Marque says that since August the co-operative has been offering supply contracts tailored more closely to customers' needs, such as Stilton. 'We can supply milk from a specific county although we don't sell much milk on that basis,' says Andrew Dare, chief executive of Milk Marque.

Although some shoppers are willing to pay a premium for farmhouse cheeses and other branded products, milk sales are so competitive that retailers do not plan to charge more for the additional quality guarantees.

Other commentators say that offering specific quality assurances on certain supplies of milk could be self-defeating. 'It could become a two-edged sword because guaranteeing the quality of some supplies could cast a doubt in people's minds about the rest,' says Michael Landymore, food analyst at London brokers Henderson and Crosthwaite.

But Neil Davidson, director of milk activities at Northern Foods, says consumers will not be very aware of the quality guarantees unless there is some sort of problem in the market with contaminated milk. Then the ability to trace milk directly to the farm gate and provide reassurances about quality will come into their own.

Source: Financial Times, 16 November 1995

22.9   The Northern Milk Partnership has asked you to help them assess the market potential for their 'quality' product idea. How would you explain to them the difference between market potential and sales potential?

22.10   Assuming that they go ahead with their proposal, what choice of sales forecasting methods would you recommend? Outline the benefits and drawbacks of each method.

22.11   What type of promotional activities would you recommend to help this product idea reach its potential?

One step ahead of the pack

Peter Marsh reports on what three industry leaders are doing to remain at the top amid increasing competition

You are a world champion sprinter and you want to stay at the top for the foreseeable future. But the rivals snapping at your heels are employing ever more skillful techniques to narrow the gap: how do you stay ahead?

This is the sort of question faced by a handful of companies, global leaders in their fields, as they try to remain number one at a time of increasing international competition, changing technologies and spiralling demands for better service and more enhanced products from consumers and industrial customers.

Three such companies, in disparate areas but facing related dilemmas, are Otis, part of the US's United Technologies group and the world's biggest elevator business; the privately-owned Danish Lego group, the largest worldwide maker of construction toys; and John Crane, part of Britain's TI engineering company and the global leader in supplying complex mechanical seals used in pumps and similar products with a vast range of applications.

All three companies are mindful of how a range of other businesses in the past – which include IBM in computers, Perkin-Elmer in chip fabrication equipment and the British company Plessey in machine tool controls – built up a commanding lead over rivals in their field only to see it whittled away by events apparently beyond their control.

'A lot of world leaders are realising they've got to re-position themselves, not because they're in crisis but because of wider changes,' says Donald Marchand, professor of information management and strategy at the International Institute for Management Development (IMD) in Lausanne, Switzerland. Marchand is involved in advising about 30 such companies, including Otis, on what their responses should be.

A common thread is that Otis, Lego and John Crane are each in fairly mature industries, with few signs of large spurts in demand for their products in their main markets in Europe and the US.

Each in the past year has instituted a range of programmes aimed at speeding up their responses to market pressures, in particular trying to capitalise on increased demand from regions with fast-growing economies such as East Asia.

A common theme is their determination to capitalise on advances in information technology, either through the ability to bring out new products or add to their efforts to provide a better service. Additionally, each of the three is trying, in differently ways, to hone the 'think global, act local' maxim of many big companies with international businesses.

The specific challenges facing the three companies, however, are different. Otis, headquartered in Connecticut, but with its $5bn (£3.2bn) of annual revenues split between some 220 operating companies around the world each with a fair degree of autonomy, is experiencing flagging demand for its main products of lifts and escalators in the developed world, a by-product of the general slowdown in construction in the main developed countries.

It is therefore switching its resources to concentrate more on the 'service' end of its business – supplying spares and updating existing equipment – as well as putting more effort into marketing and sales in regions undergoing construction booms such as southern China and the Philippines.

Lego, maker of the ubiquitous plastic bricks and miniature figures, with sales thought to be about $1.2bn, needs to respond to the rapid inroads into its markets recently by makers of electronic toys. Traditionally highly centralised at its headquarters in Billund, central Denmark, Lego is trying to push more responsibility for decisions to local managers – a process which it believes will heighten responsiveness to market trends.

Chicago-based John Crane, with annual sales of about $800m, has a style of operating some way between Otis and Lego – less centralised than Lego but more so than Otis.

With its heavily customised product range – its mechanical seals sell in approximately 750,000 different variations and fetch anything between $1 and $1m – Crane's challenge is to try to engineer a new way of developing product 'families', through the use of common design elements cutting the development cycle but at the same time providing leeway for engineers to adapt basic products to specific customer needs.

At the helm of Otis is Jean-Pierre van Rooy, an ebullient multilingual Belgian who believes in the company developing a strongly international character while reflecting local characteristics and following the views of customers.

He is particularly optimistic about sales prospects in East Asia. 'By 2010 China will be the biggest country [by sales] in the Otis world and in the first 50 years of next century we will have a Chinese president,' he says. At present, China accounts for only a small part, about a fifth, of Otis's total Asian revenues, now about $1.5bn a year. North and South America account for some $1bn a year of business, and Europe virtually all the remaining slice of some $2.5bn annually.

Otis's approach to doing business must vary depending on the market characteristics of these different regions, van Rooy says. In the fast-growing economies of East Asia, the split of Otis's revenues is roughly 70:30 between new equipment and spares and service, reflecting the large number of buildings being erected. In Europe and North America, the split is the reverse.

The greater importance of service-linked revenues has meant Otis has to develop a new 'service culture', according to van Rooy in which managers have to get closer to customers to react to their demands. They must also look out for opportunities to fit new hardware to existing lifts and escalators that will enhance performance.

These ideas are enshrined in what the company calls its Service-2000 blueprint. This was formally launched last autumn. Following this up is a programme being worked out for Otis by IMD in which 120 senior managers from the company's European division (which also takes in Africa and the Middle East) are being trained in new ways to respond to customers.

In development terms, Otis is also putting greater accent on new computer techniques – such as remote monitoring of elevators for faults using a combination of radio waves and electronics sensing – by which it reckons its products in the next century can be differentiated from competitors.

In the European division, the ideas about getting close to customers are being rammed home through two-day training packages which some 15,000 Otis employees (out of a total of 26,000 in the division) are going through in the next year or so and which draw on lessons from the IMD programme.

While van Rooy first sketched out the main elements of his Service-2000 blueprint during a vacation on the French Riviera in 1994, the ideas behind the new management programme at Lego came to Kjeld Kirk Kristiansen during a long illness in 1993 and 1994, from which he is said to have made a full recovery. Kristiansen, a quietly spoken, intensely private Dane is president of the company and grandson of its founder.

'In the 1980s and early 1990s, we had in a way been too successful,' he says. 'We were being driven too much by the past, and not concerned enough with the future. I realised we had to become less structured in what we do and react more quickly to external events.'

Kristiansen's plans are contained in a project he calls Compass – signifying a clear direction. Under this the company's top 300 managers – half of whom are outside Denmark – cut down on formal meetings and spend more time 'coaching their employees and getting them to develop their skills rather than trying to control them'.

A central element is that managers in key countries such as Japan, the US, Germany and Britain, are given much more autonomy over decisions related to mix of products (such as the different Lego kits featuring figures like Pirates or Black Knights) which they will push towards retailers, and also over questions such as the type of packaging which they think will do best in specific markets.

Lego is also honing its product development plans, as a result of which about a third of its 300 or so product types are changed every year, to speed up the development cycle. It is bringing in to these conversations much earlier than in the past marketing people from different parts of the world. Up until a year or so ago, most decisions over new products were taken almost exclusively by headquarters staff in Billund.

The company, via product development groups in Denmark, the US and Japan, is also planning to use the Lego brand in a new series of interactive computer systems (one of which it is developing in collaboration with Mindscape, the Californian software developer owned by Pearson, publisher of the Financial Times), in an effort to hit back at companies such as Sony, Nintendo and Microsoft which have through their own products been eating into Lego's revenues.

By contrast with Kristiansen, John Potter, the chief executive at John Crane, is a no-nonsense British manager keen on cementing links between marketing people and engineers. He carries around with him a file marked 'Philosophy' which sets out ways to bring this about, for example through interdisciplinary product development committees.

At John Crane, interest in information technology has culminated in a grandiose scheme to link the company's sales centres in 50 countries via satellite, so that customer requests (for specific assemblies of parts) can be met more readily from the company's two main factories, in Chicago, and in Slough, UK. According to Potter, such communications links are vital if John Crane is to make progress in meeting demands from customers for replacement parts – which account for two thirds of its business – as quickly as possible.

Another big effort has been to establish a world-wide system of product development to get ideas more quickly into the market. A 'new product' committee of 10 senior people from around the world, drawn from divisions of the company covering sales, engineering, finance and marketing, meets under Potter's supervision every three months to review new ideas for new 'families' of seals – which use, for instance, a new material or radically different design.

The good ideas get pushed immediately into a crash development programme – stewarded by a 'product champion' who is appointed for that particular scheme. As a result, Potter reckons new ideas are getting pushed to the marketplace in less than two years, compared with roughly seven years at the beginning of the decade.

While John Crane's culture is rooted firmly in the engineering tradition, before setting up its new development system the company talked in detail to companies in non-engineering fields including 3M, Procter & Gamble and Coca-Cola about how they managed the product development process. Flexibility of mind will be increasingly important according to Potter. 'The product champions are a case in point. We have six of them at present and their numbers will grow. They will be people able to shift focus fairly quickly, reporting to the marketing side of the company but being able to pick up influences from a lot of different directions.'

Source: Financial Times, 13 May 1996

22.12 Distil the information from this article into one comparative table and assess the different ways in which the three organisations operate.

22.13 Identify the dominant philosophy regarding organisational structure in place at each of the three companies.

22.14 Assess how the new initiatives in each of the three companies will help them maintain their position in the market.

22.15 Do you have any ideas or advice for these organisations which might better equip them for the future?

22E

The Co-op celebrates a century on the land

Geoff Tansey looks at the diverse operations of, probably, Britain's biggest farming group

Mike Calvert is certainly Britain's largest dairy farmer – and probably runs the country's largest farming operation. As general manager of CWS Agriculture – which is celebrating its centenary this year – he is responsible for an operation that milks some 4,000 cows a day and produces 32m litres of milk a year.

Today sees the official opening of a £2.2m, 500 cow unit at Frisby on CWS's Stoughton estate. The cows are managed as two 250-head herds in a high-tech facility that is divided into two halves. One stockman is responsible for each herd, out of a five-man team.

Standing in the glass-fronted office where computers will record data on each cow, the stockpens on either side and twin milking parlours are visible. The cows are milked three times a day and each milking takes about 3 hours from start to finish. A computer-controlled sweeper continuously clears the muck behind each pen and an underground conveyor-belt system takes it to a 'weeping wall' enclosure, which can hold a year's worth of solid waste. Slats in the wall allow the liquid to drain off into large storage tanks before it is used on the land.

This is the biggest of 15 dairy units on six estates and two under joint venture agreements run by CWS Agriculture. It owns over 28,000 acres and farms over 50,000 acres (20,000ha) through a number of farm management contracts. The operation has come a long way since it began with the purchase of the 714-acre Roden estate near Shrewsbury on June 6, 1896 for £30,000. In 1995, a turnover of £28m yielded a profit of £5.6m, up from £4.7m in 1994. The target this year is £6m.

CWS Agriculture is an operating group within CWS (the Co-operative Wholesale Society), which runs fairly autonomously according to Mr Calvert. Dairying accounts for no more than a sixth of the business, which has 30 different farming enterprises – each is run as a profit centre and managed separately. There is a deliberately diverse range of enterprises – from soft fruit to arable and from dairying to bees. The farms stretch from North East Scotland to the southern half of England and include the management of the Castle Howard Estate in Yorkshire.

Although it is part of CWS, it does not have to sell to either the wholesale or retail co-ops, nor do they have to buy from CWS Agriculture. Even so, about 60 per cent of its milk goes to Associated Co-operative Creameries at Uttoxeter and most of its peas and sprout production ends up in Co-op branded frozen packs. The cereals are sold across the board and fresh vegetables are sold both to Co-op retailers and through growers co-operatives.

'Our business is big enough, diverse enough, that no one part can bring it down,' says Mr Calvert. 'I reckon it's easier for me to run this business than for the average family farmer to run his farm.'

With about 260 full-time employees, he has a wide range of skills to draw on and people with whom he can talk through problems – something he's been glad of during the 'mad cow disease' crisis. There is also a management training system and career structure for the staff. Size has also given them the flexibility and opportunity to experiment – and on a fairly grand scale not on small-scale trial plots.

'We approach it as a farmer, experiments must be able to handle big kit. If you have 10-acre fields you need the technology for that,' says Mr Calvert. The company has been operating a 260-acre organic farm within the Stoughton estate as a completely separate entity since 1989. It is divided into a traditional, mixed farming part and a stockless arable system. The full results from the rotation are due after another year.

'Organic farming is extremely remote from farm systems today but no doubt some of the systems used are effective in suppressing diseases and pests,' says the enthusiastic trials manager Alastair Leake. He wanted to try something between a full organic system and high-input intensive systems. This led to a 'Focus on Farming Practice Project' co-sponsored by fertiliser manufacturer Hydro Agri and Profarma, an agro-chemical distributor, that started in 1993.

Today the results can be seen across a lush valley, lined with hedgerows, and a series of seven fields covering a total of 150 acres, each split in half, one half farmed with a lower-input system, the other intensively. There is a seven-year rotation – two years grass, winter wheat, beans, winter wheat, set-aside and winter wheat. Only the darker green colour in one half of the winter wheat field gives any indication of the difference. The slightly lighter half has lower inputs – using only 27 grammes per hectare of a pesticide compared with 600g the other half, for example. Although the trials are incomplete, the key point of results so far, says Mr Leake, is that although reduced inputs do affect yields 'profitability has been maintained'.

Source: *Financial Times*, 12 June 1996

22.16 What type of organisation structure do you think is in place at CWS Agriculture?

22.17 If you were to suggest a more marketing led approach at CWS Agriculture, what type of structure would you recommend?

22.18 Mike Calvert is concerned that he does not have a sufficiently rigorous approach to sales analysis. Advise him on how he might achieve better control in this respect.

23

Services Marketing

The marketing of services is not so different to the marketing of products, but there are some subtle differences between them. It is still important to design a good product offering, systematically segment markets, target them appropriately and design attractive promotional campaigns but there are five additional characteristics of service markets which make the marketer's job somewhat more complex.

The most prominent issue is one of lack of ownership. The recipient of a service rarely gets to own the service, rather they are party to an agreement, written or verbal which might be:

- a rental agreement for property or vehicles;
- a hire charge for capital equipment;
- an annual subscription for a health club or;
- an agreed fee for professional services.

There can also be an element of intangibility with the provision of services. Often it is difficult to quantify the entire package. For example, you might belong to a health club in order to gain access to their well appointed gym, sauna and swimming pool, but there is an intangible element which makes you feel better for having just been there.

The issues of perishability and inseparability are particularly obvious in the case of sporting events. If you missed the 1996 Wimbledon Tennis Final, nobody on earth can re-create it for you in exactly the same way it happened the first time round. Of course, you can always buy the video, but videos rarely capture the full atmosphere of a live event. That's why a Centre Court seat on Finals Day will cost several hundred £'s, and the video, around £12. You have to be there to get the full benefit.

Similarly, a half-empty Boeing 747 about to take off for New York will always be half-empty once the doors are closed. There will never be another opportunity to sell the seats on that particular flight and those empty seats become losses.

The close involvement of the consumer with the service provision leads to a situation of heterogeneity, i.e. it is different for each and every customer involved. The individual personalities of both consumer and service provider has the potential to produce millions of possible conflict situations. Franchise operators are particularly aware of this and the better ones strive for service consistency through procedures manuals, unannounced site visits, mystery shoppers, personnel training and restricted service offerings. This can help to avoid any failures in service quality, either through identifying gaps, managing expectations or anticipating perceived outcomes.

In order to successfully complete the tasks in this chapter you will need to be familiar with:

- service quality, expectations, perceptions and gaps;
- SERVQUAL;
- 7P's;
- service training;
- service productivity.

23A

Service, but not with a smile

Is there a 'customer respect deficit' in the US? Diane Summers reports on findings which suggest that standards are slipping

Every term Leonard Berry, professor of marketing at Texas A&M University in the US, sits down to read what he describes as a deeply depressing pile of documents.

They are the diaries his students have kept for three weeks, detailing every single 'service encounter' they have had, including trips on the bus, visits to the library, and shopping expeditions. The students describe the service they have experienced and detail in their diaries how it made them feel.

The resulting diaries have convinced Berry that there is a 'customer respect deficit' in the US today. Consumers are treated constantly to rude, impersonal and unhelpful non-service, he recently told a US retailing and banking conference organised by computer group ICL. His own Top 10 of the worst types of service behaviour are shown on the right.

A survey conducted recently for Bozell Worldwide, the advertising agency, and US News and World Report, the magazine, appears to back Berry's findings. The poll of more than 1,000 adults found 89 per cent of Americans considered incivility a serious problem, and 78 per cent thought there had been a decline in manners over the past 10 years. Almost none of those questioned considered they might be to blame themselves – 99 per cent said their own behaviour was impeccable.

All this is in the US, where service standards are generally considered to be among the highest in

---

TOP 10 ways to annoy customers

1 **True lies**. Blatant dishonesty or unfairness, such as the selling of unneeded services or deliberately quoting unrealistically low estimates.

2 **Red alert**. Assuming customers are stupid or dishonest and treating them harshly or disrespectfully. Treat customers like visitors in your home, says Berry.

3 **Broken promises**. Not showing up as promised; careless, mistake-prone service.

4 **I just work here**. Powerless employees who lack the authority, or the desire, to solve basic customer problems.

5 **The big wait**. Waiting in a long queue because checkouts or counters are closed.

6 **Automatic pilot**. Impersonal, emotionless, no eye contact, going through the motions, non-service.

7 **The silence treatment**. Employees who don't bother to communicate with customers who are anxious to hear how a service problem will be resolved.

8 **Don't ask**. Employees unwilling to make any extra effort to help customers, or who seem put out by requests for assistance.

9 **Lights on, but no one home**. Clueless employees who do not know (ie will not take the time to learn) the answers to customers' common questions.

10 **Misplaced priorities**. Employees who chat to each other or conduct personal business while the customer waits.

the world. If there is perceived to be a customer respect deficit in the US, is the deficit even greater in the UK?

FT writer Lucy Kellaway tried the Berry diary test, below. Her conclusion is that 'service is patchy but, on the whole, not as bad as it is cracked up to be'. And often where service is dire, it may be less to do with staff attitude and more related to lack of money or people.

The British undoubtedly start with lower expectations, although these are rapidly rising, believes Patricia Manning, Laura Ashley's group director of marketing. She is an American who has lived in the UK for the past 18 years and makes frequent trips back to the US. 'The British consumer is getting more demanding. The more people travel, the less they will tolerate,' she says.

Overall, the US is still streets ahead, she says: 'I see the difference every time I'm back in the States, whether for business or holidays.' Particularly for the first few days back in the UK, she is extra aware of 'the sales associate who doesn't make eye contact, or pushes your change across the counter to you'.

One area where service *is* much better in the UK than the US is on the domestic front, according to Manning. Workmen visiting the home in the US are far more brisk and commercial in their attitude, she says: 'I can never remember wanting to offer a cup of tea to a plumber in the States.'

Source: Financial Times, 11 July 1996

Dear UK Diary

Wednesday lunchtime. Pub by the Thames. I ask woman assembling sandwiches for ham with mustard. 'You'll have to put the mustard in yourself,' she snaps. Changes her mind and dumps a tablespoon of mustard on to the ham.

5pm. St Paul's Underground Station. Elderly Evening Standard vendor. 'Thank you, darling,' she says as she accepts my 30p. She apologises for being unable to fold the free poster of the England football team into the paper and explains that her knuckles are swollen.

7pm. Wembley Stadium. Hand ticket to man who grabs it, tears it in half, and checks hologram for authenticity. Impersonal, emotionless, no eye contact. But then how much eye contact can you give to 80,000 people?

Thursday 9.15am. Highbury and Islington Underground Station. Ticket machine closed. Long queue. No visible signs that anyone is trying to fix it.

Friday 9.30am. Call Islington Council to find out why it has taken more than three months to process my application for planning permission. The man handling it does not answer his phone. Later track him down. He is friendly but vague, and says it has been cleared for approval. Then changes his mind, and says there might be a conservation problem.

10.30am. Waitrose supermarket. No queue at the till. 'Would you like a packer,' asks the woman politely. She rings a bell and another woman packs my shopping neatly and tickles my baby's toes.

3.20pm. Return to car to find a man attaching a wheel clamp. He greets me like an old friend and promises to wait by the car while I find a phone and pay by credit card. Am so relieved not to have to wait for four hours to be unclamped that I don't mind so much about the £58.

Saturday. Local village shop, Norfolk. Wait 12 minutes to be served while shopkeeper chats aimlessly to customer in front about the weather, the garden, local bird life, the football. Am beside myself with frustration by the time I buy a loaf of bread.

Sunday afternoon. Telephone British Rail to discover train times. Try five times at two-minute intervals. On sixth attempt get ringing tone, and after a minute and a half the phone is answered and information supplied. The whole process took 15 minutes.

Monday 12.15pm. Phone First Direct. Phone answered promptly. 'How can I help you, Miss Kellaway?,' says the man. Supplies me with my bank balance. Manner is friendly and professional.

3pm. Phone the doctor. Am told that the soonest available appointment is in two-and-a-half weeks' time.

Lucy Kellaway
Additional research by Hannah Williams

23.1 As suggested in the article, keep a diary over the next three weeks of every single service encounter you experience. Describe the service, identify good and bad points and state how it made you feel at the time.

23.2 In your work groups, compare notes and using Professor Berry's 'Top ten ways to annoy customers' list as a basis, prepare a presentation to show how many times each of these poor types of behaviour occurred. Any others which merit attention can be added to the list.

23.3 In your presentation identify what might have been the cause of such poor service and suggest ways in which it might be rectified.

23B

At a clogged crossroads

London is feeling the crush of record numbers of tourists, says Antony Thorncroft

It was not quite what the London Tourist Board wanted to hear. London's West End area was 'repellent'; it was 'filthy'. If you avoided treading on a sleeping vagrant you were likely to slip on beer dregs or worse.

The disenchanted observer speaking his mind recently was Trevor Nunn, one of the UK's leading theatre directors. He was no more flattering about the dramatic output of the theatres that spread out from the city's focal point, Piccadilly Circus, describing it as 'pusillanimous' and 'superficial'.

For the tourist board this was a particular blow to the heart. It cannot promote London for its weather or its charm. Instead it promotes its culture, especially its historic monuments and museums, and its theatres. One in three of the record 11.9m tickets sold in the West End last year went to a foreign visitor, and another third to UK tourists.

Fortunately the board can afford to brush off Trevor Nunn's attack. Last year a record 23.6m visitors came to London, more than 13m of them from overseas. This was an appreciable increase over the 20.1m in 1994. This year is looking even busier, with more than 28m tourists anticipated, pumping £6bn into the capital's economy.

The London Tourist Board wants more, but there are already signs that the pressure of tourists, at least at certain times of the year and in certain locations, is causing strain and stress. Trevor Nunn's outburst was just an expression of the feeling that London is becoming clogged.

Mr Neil MacGregor, the director of the National Gallery, whose Trafalgar Square building is hemmed in by tourists spilling over its narrow exterior pavement, speaks for many. 'It is not the number of tourists. By tiny adaptations we can cope with more visitors. It is the lack of a transport policy for London; a public space policy for London, that causes the problems.'

London is notorious for being a world capital without a mayor. The absence of a powerful figure to represent, and oversee, the whole city creates a feeling of malaise, of irresponsibility. London faces a crossroads: some modest changes would make life more enjoyable for the current number of visitors and enable more to be happily absorbed.

Modest changes are under way. The National Gallery processes 4.6m visitors a year by opening later on Wednesday evenings and earlier on Sundays. But this hardly improves its immediate environment. It is supporting with enthusiasm plans from Westminster Council, backed by English Heritage, for a pedestrianised area between the gallery and Trafalgar Square. There are also ambitions to pedestrianise Parliament Square, which fronts the Houses of Parliament and Westminster Abbey.

But pedestrianised areas can create their own problems. One of the insoluble ironies of tourism is that improving the environment attracts more visitors. Nearby Leicester Square has been smartened up in recent years, with the result that it has become a *paseo* for London. The crowds attract street entertainers and traders, who attract more crowds, who attract petty criminals. An area can go from happy throng to claustrophobic mess quite quickly.

If London suddenly seems overcrowded it is a tribute to its recent ability to push up visitor numbers. It is particularly appealing to younger tourists. There has been a pronounced loosening of controls by the authorities: more bars and clubs have late-night drinking licences. Warm summers have created a café society.

London has become a haven for the gay community. For the first time since the 1960s London is hip. This has turned Soho at the weekends into one big party – with the consequence of unsightly rubbish strewn across the district by Sunday mornings.

Leicester Square and Soho can just about cope. Further north in Camden the strains are showing. Camden Town has become the greatest magnet in London for the young, attracting 10m visitors a year who cram into a short half-mile stretch of street from Camden station to Camden Lock to buy cheap clothes and ethnic curiosities.

Camden, which has just appointed its first tourism director, has realised it is breeding a monster. The hope is that the traders will go slightly up-market, attracting fewer but freer-spending tourists.

Like other London boroughs it does not want to frighten away tourists. It wants to spread them around the year, and direct them to more sedate sites, such as Kenwood House and the Sir John Soane Museum. London is rich in overlooked treasures – the Wallace Collection, Kensington Palace, Ham House, the Courtauld Institute – but tourists, with their cramped schedules, have an annoying habit of hunting in packs.

The problem of inadequate facilities to cope with increased numbers is particularly acute at the Tower of London, the capital's main heritage site, with 2.5m visitors a year and rising. 'Squalid' and 'sewer-like' are not Trevor Nunn's description of the environs of the Tower but those of its governor.

However, a £50m development project involving the Tower, local Tower Hamlets council, and private developers, is in train, which aims to smarten the landscape, improve access and fill the moat with water. Its achievement – like the plans for Trafalgar Square and Parliament Square; like the British Museum's scheme to improve the flow of its 6m visitors with the creation of a new Great Court; like the Tate Gallery's development of London's first museum of 20th century art on a revitalised Bankside, south of the Thames – depends on lottery funding.

London may lack the political will to improve its facilities and environment but, thanks to the lottery, it has the cash.

There is, however, one London tourist attraction which is quite happy with crowds. Madame Tussauds is the main paying tourist attraction in London, with 2.7m visitors in 1995, 70 per cent of them from overseas.

They actually like to queue; anything less than an hour's wait cheats them of a battle honour to impress friends back home.

Source: Financial Times, 19 August 1996

23.4 Carry out a services marketing mix analysis, using the 7P's framework.

23.5 Using your answer to 23.4 above as a basis, how could you improve the experience for a UK resident visiting London?

23.6 How could you improve the experience for an overseas visitor to London and would this differ from your response to 23.5 above? Why?

Ploughing a new furrow

A computer-guided vehicle is set to revolutionise farming, reports Alison Maitland

The wheel has turned full circle. A century after western farmers began exchanging hand tools for machines, the idea that plants need individual attention is making a comeback. This time, however, a computer-guided vehicle will be doing the work.

Scientists at Silsoe Research Institute in Bedfordshire this week unveiled the experimental machine which they hope will revolutionise farming in the 21st century.

It moves at a walking pace through the crop, analysing live images of the ground ahead of it from a video camera mounted at the front. These infra-red images differentiate between plants, weeds and soil. The machine's spray nozzles can then target liquid feed at the plants and not the soil, or herbicide at the weeds and not the plants.

'This is a world first,' says Brian Legg, Silsoe director. 'Never before have we been able to identify and treat individual plants automatically from live images.'

The three-year, £400,000 research project was driven by pressure for farming methods that are both efficient and environmentally friendly, using fewer chemicals. Development of the machine fits well with the trend towards 'integrated crop management', which combines crop rotation and biological controls with minimal use of chemicals.

Legg says the new system could lead to 90 per cent reductions in pesticide use. 'This would mean high-quality "consumer friendly" produce, significantly less impact on the environment and big savings for farmers.' Eventually it may even be possible to spray aphid-eating insects through the nozzles on to individual plants instead of insecticides.

Current technology allows farmers to treat fields in patches of, for example, 2 sqm. The new machine takes this down to the level of the individual plant with the aid of a computer which analyses 10 images per second. The infra-red images enhance the contrast between plants, weeds and soil, which show up as white, grey and black respectively. These data are fused with readings from a compass and measurements of the vehicle's speed and wheel rotations to ensure accuracy. The computer then issues instructions to spray the right dose at the right moment.

The vehicle is programmed to turn round at the end of the field – when it can detect no more crops – and progress along the next row. In theory it should also be able to work at night.

Nick Tillett, project co-ordinator, says the machine could be ready for commercial use in five to six years. Silsoe is talking to the Ministry of Agriculture about funding for the most promising short-term use of the technology – guiding tractor-mounted hoes. Concern about excessive use of weedkillers on crops such as sugar beet has led to a return to mechanical hoes, but these can damage the crop as they move rigidly through the field. The new 'plant-scale' technology would be able to identify rows and provide better steering. Silsoe's research has attracted interest from growers, food processors and machinery manufacturers. Eventually the vehicle could work with any crop, possibly even rice in paddy fields, although the camera might find it difficult to distinguish the rice plants on the reflective surface of water.

Although development costs are high, the machine is likely to be relatively cheap once it is commercialised. This is not, however, the answer to a gardener's prayer.

'It is suitable for straight rows, precisely planted, and most gardens aren't like that,' says Legg.

Source: Financial Times, 7 June 1996

23.7 Your brother is Managing Director of a large agricultural machinery contracting firm and he decides to invest in one of these computer-guided vehicles. As with all his other farm equipment, he will be hiring it out to farmers, but this time, with a skilled operator, thus making it a service rather than simple equipment hire. As the money for the vehicle purchase will have to be raised via a bank loan, your brother needs to prepare a convincing presentation on how he will manage the service. He has been reading about Services Marketing and has heard of the 7P's, the need for staff training and the generic differences between services and physical goods, but he is getting confused.

Knowing your interest in marketing he has asked you for help. Prepare either a presentation or a report which sets out:

- How existing and prospective customers can be targeted.
- The reasons why this service is considerably different to straight forward equipment hire and highlights the additional elements present in the marketing mix.
- The quality expectations which customers might have of the service.
- The steps you propose to take to measure the quality of the service.

Seeing Orange

Orange Communications, the soon-to-be floated mobile phone operator, believes 90 per cent of the UK population is now within calling distance of its national network.

Which is why 6,500 posters throughout the country this week are drawing attention to hamlets such as Pott Shrigley and Snodland where the Orange service is now available, as well as better known towns like Bootle.

Last year Orange spent £30m on advertising, twice as much as any of its cellular rivals. Its latest campaign alone will cost £4m, only a million pounds or so less than Vodafone, the largest mobile operator, spent in the whole of 1995. The Orange posters are tacit warnings to its rivals that they must devote more time and money to advertising and promotion.

The reasons are diverse, but pricing is key. Orange had about a 30 per cent advantage in price in digital services last year with an innovative series of pricing packages and 'per second' billing.

This, coupled with its advertising, helped it to a 25 per cent share of the UK digital market in less than two years. Now both Vodafone and Cellnet, the second largest UK operator, have cut their prices; marketing rather than price – on paper at any rate – is likely to determine success in the future.

The mobile phone market is changing dramatically. Customers are becoming more sophisticated. In the past operators have left much of the marketing to dealers and service providers whose principal selling point has been low handset prices. The absence of a boom last Christmas, however, indicated that mobile phones are no longer an impulse buy and customers now have a keener eye for value.

The business market, the most lucrative area, is saturated and operators will have to market increasingly to brand-sensitive but inherently less profitable residential customers. Vodafone and Cellnet, with more than 4m customers between them, have to move customers from the older analogue networks to modern digital systems which are expected to dominate the industry by the turn of the century.

The four operators are mounting distinctly different campaigns. Vodafone, the oldest of the four, spent only about £5m on advertising last year; this year the total will be closer to £20m as it unveils a campaign due to be launched in April.

It has been seen as the premier choice for business users, but this has left it with a slightly stuffy image among residential customers. The aim is now to re-establish the name as a generic term for mobile phones: 'Vodafone does not have a bad image, but it has been dormant,' says a spokesman.

Last year it announced new tariffs and 'per second' billing. 'The playing field is much more level,' the spokesman adds; 'Now the game is marketing.'

Cellnet, in which British Telecommunications has majority stake, spent £15m on advertising last year and 'will not spend less this year' according to Paul Leonard, head of marketing support. Two weeks ago, it cut charges for its digital services by about 30 per cent and introduced per second charging in an aggressive move which signalled open price warfare. Its soon-to-be-launched ad campaign will emphasise simplicity and value for money.

Mercury One-2-One, the UK's first PCS (mass market mobile telephone) operator has the task repositioning itself after finding itself caught with a parcel of wrong strategies. It emphasised local coverage – at first within the London M25 motorway ring – and found customers wanted to use their phones nationally. It neglected the business market in favour of residential customers who took advantage of its offer of free off-peak calls to saturate the airwaves.

Paul Donovan, sales and marketing director, says it will now emphasise its commitment to building out the network – 37 per cent coverage at present and 65 per cent by the end of the year – and try to broaden its appeal to business.

Last year it spent £7.5m on advertising; this year the figure will double. The key message will be One-2-One's low running costs – the 'true cost of ownership' – for both business and residential users.

The fact remains, however, that Orange's iconoclastic approach has left its rivals with much to do. Despite television adverts featuring bicycle-riding Asians which many believed too esoteric, its image is innovative and futuristic.

It has successfully conveyed the concept of a lifestyle of which a mobile phone is an essential component, according to Lisa Gernon, marketing director. 'We did not want people to be disappointed by what they got when they started using the phone,' she says, adding that Orange ads work 'at an emotional level. They are visually interesting and they involve you'.

Source: Financial Times, 15 February 1996

23.8 Visit any high street outlet specialising in mobile communications as a prospective customer and assess them on the ten main criteria outlined in SERVQUAL.

23.9 Do you think that such outlets are selling mobile phone products or communication services? Justify your response.

23.10 What improvements would you need to see before being sufficiently convinced to buy from this outlet? If you think that no improvements are necessary and that the outlet already has an excellent performance, say why you feel this way.

24

Marketing and the Smaller Business

For the smaller business, more than any other, it is absolutely critical that the marketing effort is productive. Poor product quality, late deliveries, inappropriate pricing or an ill-advised promotional campaign, are almost certain to kill off a fledgling enterprise. The firm just cannot recover from the wasted expenditure, the bad publicity, or the knock to its fragile reputation. Indeed, the main cause for so many small business failures can often be laid at the door of poor decision making by an often inexperienced management team. As with the product life cycle referred to in Chapter 8, recognition of the business's position in its life cycle helps to illustrate what is needed to achieve continued growth, if indeed that is the firm's objective.

The specialised nature of the smaller business, usually means that the firm has either a very small share of a large market, or is operating in a clearly defined niche. Cash flow problems are almost certain to arise very quickly, whatever the situation, and it is here that an understanding bank is worth its weight in gold. By competing on price, the firm's profit margins inevitably will be slim, but if competing with a highly differentiated product or service, albeit with better margins, then at best, revenues are going to be erratic. Having said that, it is still more likely that you will become a millionaire through entrepreneurial activity than by buying a lottery ticket. Many of the newly wealthy individuals have become so through starting, developing and then selling their own business. Some of course, such as Anita Roddick and Richard Branson are still heavily involved with their ventures.

Franchising has offered a relatively safe way for a business to grow rapidly, and as you might expect, there are good and bad franchisors, just as there are good and bad franchisees. An idea which hasn't been thoroughly market tested is not going to cost you as much to buy as say a McDonald's, Burger King, Body Shop or Dynarod franchise and this reflects the risk you are taking.

In order to successfully complete the tasks in this chapter you will need to be familiar with:

- business launch and development model;
- influences on the growth of small firms;
- influences on the start-up decision;
- franchising.

Patent problem for dancing K9

An orthopaedic opportunity is going begging, says Richard Gourlay

Michael Reid is a serious shed-maker. His company has built new stands for Aston Villa's football ground and aircraft hangars for China, and re-equipped parts of the old Subic Bay naval base in the Philippines.

He also has a sideline – a small one – making three or four orthopaedic scooters a week that are sold by word of mouth to hospitals and trauma clinics through out the UK.

The diversification was by accident more than design. Ten years ago Reid fell down the hatch of his boat and injured his foot so badly that he faced the prospect of keeping his leg in the air for eight weeks.

Had he tried to move around on conventional crutches, a build-up of body fluids could have led to persistent swelling that would have slowed the healing or, worse, led to a recurrence of gangrene.

He lay back and designed what he now calls the K9 orthopaedic scooter, named after Dr Who's mechanical dog. It resembles a stubby four~legged trolley on which the patient kneels.

The K9 scooter needs new backers

He offered one of his mechanics a pint to knock together a prototype and to smuggle it past nurses, wrapped in brown paper. He tried it, had its use approved by his doctor and says he was back at work in five days.

'My surgeon not only approved, but asked me for some for the hospital,' Reid says.

Not only does K9 remove the effect of gravity on the foot, avoiding the damaging build-up of fluids, but it also leaves the hands free for ordinary activities and allows the upper leg muscles to continue working so they do not atrophy.

The Royal Orthopaedic Hospital in Birmingham even discovered that the scooter demanded 25 per cent less energy expenditure from patients than they would require on conventional crutches.

K9 is of equal use for a variety of lower-leg injuries. James MacLean, a consultant orthopaedic surgeon at the Royal Perth Infirmary, has used it both for patients and when he ruptured his Achilles tendon playing squash. 'I was back at work in two weeks and giving injections standing up,' says MacLean, who claims to have performed Scottish dancing on K9. 'The alternative is elbow or axillary crutches which are tiring and occupy both limbs.'

Reid patented his scooter and his company, John Reid of Christchurch, Dorset, which has annual sales of £12m from its shed business, has been making and selling the device at a rate of about three a week. He has even tried some modest advertising in medical magazines.

But now he must deal with the kind of problem many inventors face – justifying the cost of maintaining the patents when they lack the time or do not want to commit the resources to marketing the product in a manner that would justify the expense.

Under pressure from the board, which is not keen on him spending the £8,000 needed to maintain the patents in Europe, Japan and the US, Reid is now contemplating finding a new home for K9.

'It's not a commercial proposition for us,' he says. 'What I need is someone to take over the marketing. I just want K9 to make enough profit to keep going so it can be useful to people.'

Source: Financial Times, 2 July 1996

24.1 At which stage of the business launch and development model would you place the K9?

24.2 What would be the marketing implications of your answer to 24.1 above?

24.3 You are intrigued with the K9 idea and have offered your services to market the product. When you meet Mr Reid next week, what questions would you ask and what would be your key concerns? Divide these into concerns about the product and concerns about the organisation.

24.4 You accept the job as Marketing Manager for the K9 and you are due to meet the Board next month. Like you, they know little about orthopaedic supplies. In preparation for the meeting, research the market and draw up an outline marketing plan.

Cutting its cloth for new markets

Kieran Cooke on how a Donegal tweed manufacturer has responded to the demands of fashion

Walk into the Donegal town premises of Magee, Ireland's premier tweed manufacturer, and there are echoes of another, more gentrified, era. A tweed jacket, thick enough for walking through a hedge, hangs in a display case. Rolls of tweed from cottage industry producers in remote parts of County Donegal are piled on the floor.

But behind the traditional exterior at Magee is a different world. Philip Carder runs Magee's weaving plant. He stands among rolls of cloth ready for export. 'Cloth manufactured here might be destined for a suit to be sold in one of the top US outlets,' he explains.

'The trousers could be made in China, the jacket in Portugal and the waistcoat in Morocco or Hungary. We might be a small company in an obscure part of Europe but nonetheless the global market place is very real to us.

'Our orders come in and out via computer. We are contemplating a site on the Internet. Clothing is one of the world's oldest industries but we have to marry it to the most modern manufacturing and marketing methods. If we don't adapt, we won't survive.'

Magee is privately-owned and has been run by the locally based Temple family since the start of the century. The firm has been producing its distinctive, speckled Donegal tweeds for more than 120 years.

Yet tweed is now only a small part of its business, accounting for about 5 per cent of total sales in Ireland and the UK. Magee uses a wide range of other fabrics. 'We realised that we could not survive on tweed alone,' says Lynn Temple, chairman at Magee.

'The hallmark of our products used to be hardiness – making a suit that lasted a lifetime. People are not so interested in durability any more. Now there is a very different marketing approach. The most important thing is satisfying the whims of fashion. We sell on design more than cloth. Even a small company like ours has to be on its toes all the time, trying to anticipate next season's styles,' Temple adds.

Magee has a weaving division and a clothing factory, based at two plants, one in Donegal in the Irish Republic, the other at Ballymena in Northern Ireland, employing 600 in total. Clothing sales were £15m last year. The weaving plant had a turnover of £3m.

While other small textile manufacturers have been swallowed up by the big chains or disappeared in the face of low-cost competition from overseas, Magee has successfully kept its niche near the top end of the market. 'We are not in the volume business,' says Temple. 'Our aim is to sell highly designed, high-quality natural fabrics and offer customers variety. We are not producing row upon row of identical suits.'

Each day Magee produces about 400 suits in various cloths, colours and designs. It markets a wide range of styles – from morning coats sold to stores such as Moss Brothers, to pinstriped suits and clothes with a more rugged, country look.

Organising such a varied output is a logistical nightmare but it has paid dividends. Magee now exports 15 per cent of its clothing outside Ireland and the UK. Two years ago the company started making women's jackets and skirts: women's wear now accounts for 40 per cent of export sales.

One successful marketing ploy has been a 'stocks special' scheme, through which a customer can walk into a Magee stockist in Düsseldorf or Derby, select a cloth and be guaranteed delivery within four weeks. Orders are sent back to Donegal where suits, jackets and skirts made and dispatched.

'We want to bring customer waiting time down to only 15 days,' says Temple. 'That mean streamlining our production still further. The land is poor in Donegal and over the years people have been forced to develop various crafts. Our workforce is highly skilled and dedicated.

'Despite that, we have to keep investing in new equipment. We are about to put in a new £250,000 computer system for processing orders. For a small company like ours that represents a big investment.'

Many of the smaller, more upmarket suit and jacket retailers in the UK and elsewhere in Europe have traditionally relied on German cloth suppliers. Magee sees a change.

'The cost of labour in German factories is so high that now they are outsourcing increasing amounts of their cloth from eastern Europe,' says Temple.

'Quality is suffering as a result. People also want a bit more flair and colour in their clothes and have become tired of the rather predictable German look.'

Keeping up with the latest design trends is crucial. Magee's designers attend the big fairs and monitor changing tastes. 'We put a lot of resources into working with the Italian market.

'Italy is still the final arbiter in much of the clothing industry. If you can sell to the Italians you can sell to anyone.'

Source: Financial Times, 16 July 1996

24.5 At which stage of the business launch and development model would you place Magee?

24.6 Identify the organisational and marketing elements which you think have influenced the growth of this firm.

24.7 What difficulties might you expect Magee to experience if it continues to grow?

24C

Intoxicated by success down at the local

Entrepreneurs like Michael Cannon have transformed the face of the British public house, writes Roderick Oram

The small convoy of vans bearing the logo 'Magic Pub Company on Tour' poured into Bradford-on-Avon in Somerset early one morning last year and pulled up at the King's Arms, a pub that had been closed for seven years. A gang of workmen piled in, shooed out the nesting pigeons and began refurbishing the premises. By 7pm, it had reopened as the Sprat and Carrot.

Michael Cannon, 55, has 'cannonised' more than 700 British pubs over the past 22 years, making him almost £100m in the process. Some £70m of that came this week as his share of the £197.5m paid for the two-year-old Magic Pub Company by Greene King, the regional brewer.

'He is a genius at visualising how to turn round pubs,' says a City analyst, who as a young brewery employee extended trade credit to Cannon in his first venture, a £20,000 half-share in a Bristol pub. 'Others call in teams of architects and designers but he turns up with Sally (his wife) and a team of his own tradesmen.'

Entrepreneurs such as Mr Cannon have been transforming the face of the British pub. Once the local offered little more than a pint of beer and a packet of crisps, but today's pubs provide a cornucopia of exotic food and drink, amenities from children's playrooms to no-smoking bars and special events.

Mr Cannon has become something of a 'serial entrepreneur' in the business. His penultimate venture was at Devenish, the west country pubs group which he sold to Greenalls Group for £214m in 1993. He created the Magic Pub Company in 1994, renovating three or four pubs a week in the first year. 'His foot was absolutely flat to the boards,' says a colleague. He invested £31m in his 277 pubs, almost all acquired from Scottish & Newcastle for £100m.

Three others have been similarly successful: David Franks, managing director of Regent Inns, the listed company worth £200m; Tim Martin, chairman of J.D. Wetherspoon, valued by the stock market at £400m; and Peter Dickson, managing director of Yates Brothers Wine Lodges, worth £160m at its current share price.

The big breakthrough for Messrs Cannon and Franks came in 1989 when the government ordered national brewers to shed large chunks of their pub estates to increase retail competition. The brewers sold off what they regarded as their least promising premises – pubs that with investment and good management have proved highly profitable.

'The right bloke with the right idea can turn round any backstreet pub,' says one pub chain creator.

Messrs Martin and Dickson took a different approach: they built their chains by converting disused high street and town centre premises such as banks, post offices and building societies. They overturned the conventional brewers' wisdom that it was very difficult to get licences for new places.

There is plenty of scope for further growth, with more than 5,000 pubs that could come on the market. Some are ex-brewery pubs owned by institu-tions such as Nomura, the Japanese investment bank. Pubmaster, part of the Brent Walker empire, has 1,700 pubs which could be sold to reduce the group's debt. And Bass, the brewer that owns 4,300 pubs, may have to sell many to avoid a reference to the Monopolies and Mergers Commission if it goes ahead with its long-rumoured takeover of fellow brewer Carlsberg-Tetley.

For Mr Martin of Wetherspoon, there are three challenges. The first is to find prime sites for new pubs. The second is to manage and motivate a large workforce in a business where customer service is vital – '1,000 little components make a Wetherspoon pub like the 1,000 that go into a BMW'. Finally, he wants to further improve Wetherspoon standards of value and service – 'we're where British supermarkets were 35 years ago. We've everything to play for'.

Ten years ago, muzak and frozen food were two essential ingredients in Cannon pubs, recalls Philip Snook, a Cannon associate for 11 years and managing director of the Magic Pub Company. Now it is hi-fi sound systems and fresh pasta.

'I say to our people, "Go see what Marks and Spencer are selling because that's what we'll be selling in a year's time",' says Mr Snook.

With the sale of the Magic Pub Company, Mr Cannon's competitors are speculating whether he will re-enter the market. His first retirement after the sale of Devenish lasted a year. He cancelled a world cruise and set up Project Sinatra to buy the pubs that formed the Magic Pub Company.

But if he resists the temptation and retires to his west country shooting estate, the landlord of his local pub had better watch out. Mr Cannon will never be short of a few ideas for doing it up.

Source: Financial Times, 23 June 1996

24.8 Apply Cooper's model of influences on the entrepreneur's start-up decision to Michael Cannon.

24.9 How far does this go towards explaining the motivation for this venture?

24.10 Why do you think that Michael Cannon sold the Magic Pub company to Greene King, and why do you think Greene King wanted to buy it?

24.11 What else could Michael Cannon have done with his chain of pubs?

The ebb and flow that hampers Midlands

DTI says small companies suffer low productivity, investment and innovation, writes Peter Marsh

Janice Reynolds admits her company has problems. The family-owned Bracebridge Engineering, based in Birmingham, has survived a difficult 15 years for manufacturing, but has fallen behind on the latest production and management techniques.

'We recognise we're not as advanced as we should be,' says Ms Reynolds – who is joint managing director at Bracebridge with her sister, Debbie Parker. Both are among the family shareholders in the 86-year-old company, whose annual sales of £1m come from making metal parts mainly for bathroom equipment and central heating.

Ms Reynolds is not alone in her musings. According to a report this week from the Department of Trade and Industry's west Midlands office, the region's small manufacturers suffer from low levels of productivity, investment and innovation.

The industrial heartland of the west Midlands contains an estimated 20,000 to 30,000 small companies in manufacturing, many of them privately owned and key suppliers to the big names of UK engineering, particularly large car producers.

'A lot of these companies ebb and flow with the economic cycle but never achieve much more,' says Mr Jeremy Woolridge, chairman of the west Midlands branch of the Confederation of British Industry and also chairman of B.E. Wedge, a Willenhall-based galvanising company.

'The problems of these smaller companies are holding back the prospects for the bigger businesses,' says Mr Chris Voss, an expert on UK industrial competitiveness at the London Business School. Among the specific difficulties are believed to be lack of resources by the companies to invest in training and new management skills, as well as lack of awareness about what the rest of the world is doing in their industries.

Mr Larry Freeman, of the Birmingham Training and Enterprise Council, a private sector body which is trying to improve the position of industry in the west Midlands, says: 'One of the difficulties is psy-chological. A lot of the companies have been here for generations, and don't want to change.'

In the case of Bracebridge, Ms Reynolds is open about what she regards as the failings of her company – whose customers include the Caradon building products business and Armitage Shanks, maker of bathroom hardware.

She accepts that Bracebridge, which has a staff of 25, has been too inward looking. But the company is now trying to investigate new techniques in areas such as production methods and staff motivation.

More optimistic is Mr David Cooke, the joint managing director of Walsall-based Cooke Brothers, which specialises in making hinges for industries such as furniture, vehicles and construction. Mr Cooke's brother Philip is the other managing director.

The family-owned company has annual sales of £4m, and although profits have been hit in the past year, Mr Cooke reckons it is making progress on a wider front. Over the past four years it has stepped up training for its 80 workers and invested 'several tens of thousands' of pounds in modern computer-aided design systems to improve products for customers such as Jaguar and the JCB excavator company.

Mr Cooke says his company is open to new ideas but says some of his customers 'want higher quality but often they don't want to pay for it' in higher component prices.

Mr Roger Varley, managing director of family-owned Birmingham Stopper, which makes metal parts mainly for the car and office-equipment industries, says that one of his difficulties is recruiting high-calibre staff.

In the past three years Birmingham Stopper has nearly doubled its annual sales, to £5m, and increased employees from 85 to 120. Over this period, it has invested £1m in new machinery, including the latest laser systems for punching holes in metal sheets. This has helped the company to improve quality levels three-fold over the past three years, as measured by the number of defective parts.

Mr Varley refutes suggestions that, as a family-owned business his company has become complacent. 'We're willing to change at a fair old pace to keep up,' he says.

His message is that many Midlands manufacturers have moved on a lot in the past decade, even though they realise the gap between them and some of their international rivals is still wide.

Source: Financial Times, 11 July 1996

24.12 At which stage of the business launch and development model would you place the businesses discussed in this article?

24.13 What marketing and organisational implications should this have on their future plans?

24.14 What could these organisations do to obtain and develop new product/ business ideas?

24E

Competitors learn the hard way

The UK leader in educational software is teaching its rivals a few lessons, writes Paul Taylor

Just outside Macclesfield in Cheshire, a small, family-owned company is proving that you do not have to be a colossus like Microsoft to create innovative software for the home and educational markets.

Europress was founded in 1965 by Derek Meakin, a former journalist, free-newspaper pioneer and computing magazine publisher. It now ranks as the UK's leading producer of educational software with a market share of more than 55 per cent.

Buoyed by a rapidly expanding portfolio of educational, lifestyle and multimedia software titles, turnover has risen six-fold in the last three years and is now expected to double each year.

In the early 1980s growth was fuelled by the home personal computer boom and Meakin's passion for technology. 'I am a *Tomorrow's World* freak,' says the 70-year-old entrepreneur. 'I just love anything to do with inventions, developments and futuristic stuff.'

His first computer magazine focused on the Apple II. The second – called The Micro User – was devoted to the BBC Micro developed by Acorn Computer and reached a circulation of about 90,000. The Micro User included computer program listings so that readers could program their own machines.

'I think that many of the top developers in computer software, the ones who are doing the major games at the moment, cut their teeth on The Micro User and BBC Basic, and we did a very powerful educational job in showing them how it was done. It was very satisfying,' says Meakin.

The computer magazine and an associated exhibitions business proved highly successful, but Meakin decided it was time to move on. The exhibition business was sold to Blenheim Exhibitions and then in October 1994, IDG, the US publisher, bought the computer magazine operations which then accounted for more than 90 per cent of turnover. For the last two years the Europress management, now led by Derek Meakin's 41-year-old son Michael, who is managing director, have been able to concentrate on growing the software portfolio.

Europress launched its first software package – a suite of productivity programs which it still sells, called Mini Office – in the early 1980s. Since then Mini Office has sold more than 500,000 copies.

In the first 18 months after disposing of the magazine operations Europress launched about 15 new titles. Meakin says the company had three main targets: 'Firstly, to maintain and reinforce our position as the number one educational software supplier in the UK; number two was to repel the American invaders and number three was to make a determined move to export British educational software all round the world.'

As part of this process Europress has redesigned its software packaging to present a distinctive, uniform identity on the shop shelves. Sensing an imminent invasion from the US, the company has been securing its market position. 'We were determined they would not overtake what we can do,' says Meakin. Part of this strategy has been to keep its own software prices low. Most of its products, which now break down into five ranges – education, lifestyle, multimedia, bookshelf and productivity – sell for between £19.99 and £29.99.

Its pre-eminence in the UK market has been based largely on the popularity of the Fun School range which is now a fifth-generation product with sales of more than 1m copies and is used extensively in the home as well as having strong appeal to teachers and educational establishments.

'We have made learning a fun experience, kids are playing games but they are learning and they are learning some very difficult subjects through the medium of games,' says Meakin.

The Lifestyle range also covers a wide spectrum, from packages which help the user design a garden or home to a driving test tuition program. However, the group's innovation is perhaps best seen in its game creation package Klik & Play which is available in 16 languages and distributed in more than 35 countries.

The package, initially developed by two French programmers, François Lionet and Yves Larnoureu, costs a fraction of many similar multimedia creation tools and has won widespread praise from games developers and the computing press for its speed and flexibility. Users can create multilevel games using the Storyboard editor, animate their games and add music.

Europress has used the software to create educational titles. The Bookshelf series of interactive CD-Rom-based children's classic stories includes *Alice in Wonderland* (which uses Sir John Tenniel's original steel engravings, coloured and animated), *Treasure Island*, *Journey to the Centre of the Earth*, *Peter Pan* and most recently Mark Twain's *Tom Sawyer*.

The skills used to produce Klik & Play have also been applied to the world of multimedia with Klik & Create which allows users to create a range of multimedia programs. Earlier this year Europress signed a worldwide distribution agreement for Klik & Create with Corel, the Ottawa-based software house.

Reflecting the growth of the business, the Europress team of programmers has expanded from just four, 18 months ago, to more than 50 today in addition to about 10 external developers. The creativity of its programmers is backed by professional teams of producers, artists, storyboard editors, animators, writers and musicians, in the UK and France.

But, as Meakin notes: 'However good your products are, unless you have an efficient sales and marketing team you won't get anywhere.' The challenge for Europress is to build on its success in the UK market.

'There is a lot of innovation, capability and creativity in Britain,' says Michael Meakin. He is now focusing on expanding the group's sales overseas by building an innovative franchise network – thought to be the first time a software publisher has used this route to market.

Source: Financial Times, 16 July 1996

24.15 **Assess the influence that Derek Meakin might have had on his son Michael and his success at Europress.**

24.16 **Identify the advantages and problems that Michael Meakin might have if he pursues the franchise network idea.**

24.17 **What would you recommend he does in order to ensure that the franchise network has as a good chance of success?**

25

International Marketing

The move into international markets for a firm which has traditionally only operated in its home country, is not one to be taken lightly. It is hard enough for a firm to succeed within the domestic market where the surroundings are familiar, and easy to see how simple it can be to get it wrong where there is so much more to learn and many more factors to take into account.

There are many reasons for firms wishing to operate internationally, the most common being to:

- spread risk through broader activity;
- enter new markets;
- escape small or saturated domestic markets;
- seek or achieve economies of scale;
- engage in international production;
- respond to competitor moves;
- strengthen the firm's overall competitive position.

The entry method for international markets also differs and can range from simple exporting from a domestic base to full-scale investment in the host country to provide production facilities, sometimes on a green field site. Exporting offers the least risky option and is often a firm's first move into an international market. However, the traditional route of an incremental level of activity from exporting, to the transfer of expertise to full-scale investment is now too slow an option. Firms which are serious about an international presence, are much more likely to bypass the early stages and prefer to make a full commitment to their internationalism by commissioning new facilities or becoming involved in contractual arrangements such as joint ventures and strategic alliances.

As you might imagine, each of these also come with varying degrees of risk and certainly the willingness of a firm to embrace the differing business objectives, culture and management styles of its partners is a crucial factor in determining success. Joint ventures can be a very successful way of achieving an international presence, but they are prone to failure. More often than not, this is due to a lack of awareness of the needs of all the partners or inappropriate behaviour which offends. For UK firms wanting to do business in Japan, France or Germany, for example, the most basic courtesy would be to at least learn the language, but few organisations can even manage this. Prospective joint venture partners also need to exhibit a willingness to recognise that cultural practices, social customs and norms in another country are by no means inferior to their own – just different, and that stereotypes are simply that – generalisations. In fact, your host may well be viewing you with exactly the same preconceived notions, so it is your responsibility to dispel those just as quickly as you can.

As trading blocs become less powerful, previously restricted markets open up to western trade, domestic markets get more saturated and currency exchange becomes quicker and easier to perform, then it is a fair assumption that more firms will find it worthwhile to spread their wings outside national boundaries.

In order to successfully complete the tasks in this chapter you will need to be familiar with:

- types of investment;
- joint ventures;
- market entry options;
- market selection factors;
- product adaptation/standardisation.

25A

Rolls-Royce in China joint venture

By Tony Walker

Rolls-Royce and Aviation Industries of China (Avic) yesterday announced the formation of a joint aero-engine company to manufacture components for Rolls-Royce jet engines as a step towards building complete units. Investment in the new company would total $30m.

Rolls-Royce officials say the venture would receive a significant boost if China goes ahead with plans to build 100-seater aircraft in partnership with overseas companies, including British Aerospace as part of a European consortium.

China has said a decision is close on the 100-seater project. The European consortium, in which Aérospatiale of France is expected to play a prominent role, is the leading contender in competition with Boeing.

The venture between Rolls-Royce and the Xian Aero Engine Company will make several items, including turbine blades for various Rolls-Royce engines such as the BR715, which is being proposed for the new 100-seater aircraft.

The joint venture agreement was announced by Mr Zhu Yuli, president of Avic, and Mr Gordon Gurr, president of Rolls-Royce China, in the presence of Mr Michael Heseltine, Britain's deputy prime minister, who is on a week-long selling mission to China.

Mr Gurr said Rolls-Royce had a 'vision that one day Avic and Rolls-Royce will design and build a complete new engine together'. He said the new venture, which begins operations in 1998, would gradually extend its activities to include a wide range of aero engine parts.

'We have a plan that by the year 2000 China will be responsible for complete modules,' said Mr Gurr. 'Once this capability is in place, Rolls-Royce will help the Chinese facilities to build and test complete engines.'

Rolls-Royce has a long relationship with the Xian Aero Engine Corporation, located in Shaanxi province, south-west of Beijing. XAE has been manufacturing components for Rolls-Royce engines since the mid-1970s.

Mr Heseltine's mission to sell 'UK Plc' to China comes in the shadow of a trade row between Beijing and Washington over intellectual property rights. About 270 UK businessmen, including representatives of leading companies, are accompanying Mr Heseltine to Beijing and Shanghai.

British officials in Beijing said they did not expect present difficulties in Sino-US relations to affect the Heseltine mission, although one noted there were areas such as aerospace where UK companies were engaged in intense competition with the US.

Mr Heseltine's main focus will be on pushing UK interests in aerospace, the power sector and telecommunications. GEC-Alsthom is hoping Mr Heseltine's visit will boost its prospects in bidding for a power sector project in Zhejiang province, south of Shanghai.

■ Thyssen Aufzüge, a subsidiary of Germany's Thyssen steel group, yesterday announced a $25m joint venture with Qinghe Group Corporation to manufacture elevators for the fast growing Chinese elevator market, writes Tony Walker.

The venture, located in Shandong province, south-east of Beijing, will be called Shandong Thyssen Elevator. Thyssen Aufzüge will be a 51 per cent shareholder. This will be the German company's second venture in China. Thyssen aims to capture 10 per cent of the Chinese lift market by 2000 against competition from local producers and Otis, Schindler and Mitsubishi.

Source: Financial Times, 21 May 1996

25.1 **What type of investment is Rolls-Royce making in China?**

25.2 **What other methods of market entry to China could Rolls-Royce have used?**

25.3 **What are the benefits to both Rolls-Royce and AVIC in this venture?**

25.4 **Advise Rolls-Royce on the key factors that they will need to get right in order to make sure the venture succeeds.**

25B

War declared on chintz

Virginia Matthews sees IKEA launch a campaign against the William Morris tradition

Ikea, the Swedish home furnishings giant, declares war this weekend on what it sees as England's moribund tradition of English decor.

Backed by a £4m-plus TV and press advertising campaign through the advertising agency St Luke's, Sweden's best-known export since Abba will call on home-owners to 'chuck out that chintz' in favour of bolder and more modern designs.

The 70-second commercials – which mock the pastels, pelmets and flowery prints that dominate English sitting rooms from Scunthorpe to St James's – mark a new and aggressive phase of global expansion by the 53-year-old company from Smaland in southern Sweden.

Thurrock, the giant shopping centre in Essex, will become home to the UK's seventh IKEA store in November, with two further openings planned each year between now and 2001.

The company's international ambitions, which have already seen the establishment of 126 outlets in 25 countries including the US, Hungary and Poland, are also to receive a boost with plans to move into China, and possibly Russia, in the coming years.

While the privately owned IKEA – which began life as a mail-order company selling everything from Christmas tree baubles to ballpoint pens – refuses to divulge any detailed financial information, its strategy of low-cost products sold in out-of-town sites has helped build a company worth more than £3.5bn, say industry analysts.

IKEA's founder, 70-year-old Ingvar Kamprad, believes that a stock-market flotation would distract the company from its core aim of providing 'a better everyday life for the majority of people' via budget-priced, high-quality furniture in a flat pack.

Although the UK furniture sector continues to be dominated by giant chains such as MFI, which has an 8 per cent share of an estimated £6bn market, IKEA's 4 per cent slice of the business is augmented by sales of smaller items from kettles to duvets and lights to picnic rugs.

While more than 6,000 people a day already flock to the group's flagship Brent Park site in north London – where rigid design allows shoppers to go only one way around the store – the company will not be content until it has converted English flounce into modern minimalism, says Hilary Pepler, IKEA's communications manager.

'Our research shows that two-thirds of consumers like the flowery, somewhat overblown style that is associated with William Morris and, more recently, Laura Ashley,' she says.

'But that leaves not only the one-third of people who prefer sleeker, cleaner lines to frills, but also many thousands more who would love to try something other than "Victorian parlour" or "country cottage" but who simply need a shove in the right direction.'

While IKEA's sometimes stark approach to interior design has always appealed more to the young-on-a-budget than to their grandparents, the store has in recent years begun to stock rather more luxurious items such as £900-plus leather sofas in an effort to broaden its clientele.

Ikea is prepared to make small concessions to local tastes in each of its markets – after years of selling generous Swedish-sized beds in Britain, for example, it has reverted to stocking our more modest singles, doubles and kings. However, more than 95 per cent of the goods sold in the store in Warrington are identical to those on offer in Warsaw.

The philosophy of sameness does not end with the Pixbo armchairs and Nejde yarn rugs or the Kronvik dining tables set with Klunk glassware.

In defiance of the American hamburger or British fish and chips, Ikea aficionados across the world consume the same traditional Swedish fare of meatballs and herrings, no matter whether they are seated in an Ikea restaurant in Pittsburgh or in Brent Park.

However, in spite of the apparent move for Swedish domination – be it in cuisine or in curtain fabric – IKEA rejects any suggestion that it is as culturally imperialistic as Walt Disney: 'We're not saying that people should strip their sitting rooms of roses and pastels and start all over again,' says Pepler. 'We simply hope that by gently mocking the English style in our advertising, we may encourage people to be a little more adventurous.'

These are brave words: IKEA's mission to rid the world of fitted carpets and magnolia in favour of wooden floors and magenta faces an uphill task in Britain.

'Second only to the Belgians,' says Pepler, 'the British probably have the most entrenched views about home styling in the world.'

While the new ads – which will be reinforced this autumn with the distribution of 6.8m copies of IKEA's 1997 catalogue – could never be accused of being racy, the same cannot be said of the marketing strategy in the US.

Earlier this year IKEA drew protests after a TV commercial featuring a bi-racial couple discussing how best to time the conception of a baby.

In the finest Benetton tradition, the ad, which followed other story lines about divorce and homosexuality, attracted an avalanche of publicity for the company and its goods.

In Britain, says Hilary Pepler, the more immediate task is to tackle the tyranny of William Morris.

Source: Financial Times, 29 August 1996

25.5 What type of investment has IKEA made in the UK?

25.6 How does this differ from the type of investment between Rolls-Royce and AVIC in the previous article?

25.7 Given that IKEA has a view that the 'British have the most entrenched views about home styling in the world', why do you think IKEA still decided to invest in the UK?

25.8 How much product adaptation does IKEA use in its marketing strategy for different countries and how important do you think this decision is to the firm's success?

Headlamp deal puts pressure on small suppliers

By Peter Marsh

Two of Europe's four biggest makers of car head-lamps have agreed to cross-supply their products to each others' UK distributors in a move designed to squeeze out small suppliers.

The move by Hella of Germany and Valeo of France is likely to shake up the highly competitive UK business of selling replacements for headlamps, a business estimated to be worth £150m a year at the retail level.

The agreement comes as Europe's big four makers of headlamps attempt to increase their combined share of the market – which is characterised by highly intricate distribution chains where small independent suppliers have a large presence.

The big lighting manufacturers, which also include Magneti Marelli of Italy and Germany's Bosch, are thought to account for no more than about a quarter of the UK market for replacement headlamps.

Lucas, the UK engineering company which no longer makes car headlamps but imports them from Taiwan, is estimated to have the biggest share in the business, with about 10 per cent.

The Hella/Valeo agreement applies only to the UK aftermarket and does not affect the original equipment business of selling headlamps for new cars.

It is the first agreement of this sort between Valeo and Hella, which are continuing their existing distribution operations in other parts of Europe.

Under the deal, each company will supply its own lamps to the other's distributors – which in turn make them available to shops, independent garages and repair outlets which are part of the car manufacturers' franchise networks.

Hella said the deal meant that both sets of distributors would have access to 'the largest single lighting range' from original equipment manufacturers.

At present, distributors that are part of the separate Hella and Valeo selling networks are unlikely to handle each others' products.

Hella concentrates on making lights for German-made cars while Valeo has a corresponding bias towards lamps for French cars.

Both companies hope that the move will bolster their relatively small presence in the UK headlamp after-market. This business has been strongly affected by efforts by small suppliers to gain market share though selling cut-price lamps.

In turn, all the big four lighting companies – which dominate the European business for making lights for new cars – are trying to persuade consumers that their products are of higher quality and so worth buying even at higher prices.

Of the big four lighting makers, only Hella and Magneti Marelli have UK factories. Hella is spending an estimated £10m, doubling its UK supply capacity from its factory in Banbury, Oxfordshire.

Source: Financial Times, 2 February 1996

25.9 Identify the area of business where the Hella/Valeo agreement will take effect.

25.10 How robust do you think this agreement is and do you think it will be successful?

25.11 What other options were available to Hella and Valeo if they wanted to gain entry into this sector within the UK?

25.12 Given your answer to 25.11 above, and assuming that the two firms had considered these, why do you think they chose the route they did?

Third world looks to first world cast-offs

Developing countries are eagerly snapping up used factory machinery and plant, writes Andrew Taylor

There are more than 5,000 miles between the tired urban landscape of Romford in east London and a greenfield development site at Baoding, south of Beijing.

This journey has just been completed by the former Romford Brewery, once renowned for its John Bull beer, which has been dismantled and shipped to China in 130 containers.

It is being reassembled by new owners San Miguel, the Philippines based brewer in partnership with Bada, a local company from Hebei Province.

The volume of secondhand factory equipment and plant being exported from industrialised countries to emerging nations is rising rapidly, says Ove Arup, UK consulting engineers assisting the move from Romford to Baoding.

Developing countries and industries cannot afford to pay new prices for all the new equipment they need, says Arup. Secondhand equipment is cheaper and has the added advantage of a proven track record.

Mature industries in developed nations need to invest in more efficient modern plant to meet rising environmental standards and to combat increased competition from low wage economies. They now have a ready market for their old equipment, even if they are assisting potential competitors.

Just before the end of last year, Kuwait Raffinazione e Chimica, the Italian subsidiary of Kuwait Petroleum, announced it had sold an oil refinery in Naples to Petro Energy Products Company India (Pepco).

The cost of dismantling 10,500 tonnes of refinery equipment and moving it to Pondicherry in Tamil Nadu is estimated to be between $400m and $500m.

This represents a savings of up to 70 per cent compared with the cost of $1.2bn–$1.5bn to build a new refinery according to Henry Butcher, international plant and property consultants which handled the sale.

The refinery which attracted strong interest from eastern European and south east Asian countries, is planned operational within two to four years.

Mr Peter Harriman, Henry Butcher partner, says: 'Over the past 10 years the pace of industrialisation

in many developing countries has quickened. In particular China, the Indian sub-continent and other countries in southeast Asia and South America have acquired a great deal of equipment from Europe and North America.'

The company has been instructed by BHP Minerals of Canada to find a buyer for the assets of one of the world's largest copper mines on Vancouver Island which is closing. It is also nearing the end of a four-year programme to sell plants and equipment used in the construction of the Channel tunnel.

Buyers have come from all over the world, according to Mr Harriman.

The cost of shipping the former Romford brewery to China is estimated to be about £50m, about a fifth cheaper than designing and building a completely new plant.

Mr John Dunwell, vice president of San Miguel, says that Carlsberg Tetley closed the Romford works because of overcapacity in the UK brewing industry.

China by comparison is one of the world's fastest-growing beer markets and is the third largest producer behind the US and Germany.

Ove Arup also has advised the construction of a new combined heat and power station for the Baoding brewery which will produce San Miguel pale pilsen, one of the best selling foreign brands in China.

The last of the brewery equipment arrived at the beginning of December accompanied by 300 police and officials and celebrated with fire crackers, having travelled overland in a five kilometre long convoy from the Chinese port of Tianjin. The plant is expected to produce the first beer by the end of March.

Arup says that chemical production and vehicle manufacturing are the most popular industries for relocating plant but demand is spreading to other industries.

Kimberley Trading, a small London based export company specialising in selling new and secondhand machinery and spares to Kenya, is currently looking at the possible purchase of equipment from a British disposable nappy factory which it would send, lock stock and barrel, to Nairobi.

It says: 'Deals like this are increasing. It provides export earnings and further useful life to equipment which would otherwise be sold for scrap or remain idle.'

Last year the company arranged the sale of 50 weaving looms from an old French abbey. The looms which were up to 30 years old are now working in a Nairobi factory.

Source: Financial Times, 16 January 1996

25.13 Why do you think that developing countries are so attractive to the firms mentioned in the article?

25.14 Identify the benefits that developing countries receive from international activity such as this by industrialised countries.

25.15 'Selling worn-out equipment at a profit to developing countries is immoral. These firms are just getting rid of their scrap to unsuspecting buyers – it is nothing more than a con job.' Discuss.

25E

Brewers thirsty for Romania

International groups are seeking to establish dominant position, reports Kevin Done

International brewing groups' thirst for expansion in east Europe is leading them to stake out a growing presence in Romania, a market still regarded as too risky by many other industries.

Interbrew of Belgium, Germany's Brau und Brunnen, and South African Breweries have taken the lead, but investment bankers in Bucharest are confident that more deals are imminent.

Carlsberg of Denmark and Efes, Turkey's leading brewer, are also joining the race, but have chosen to develop new breweries on greenfield sites rather than to acquire existing outdated capacity.

The brewers are attracting increasing financial support.

The European Bank for Reconstruction and Development is to sign a deal shortly to provide a $43m loan for the Carlsberg project. Significantly, the EBRD also expects to syndicate up to $24m of the loan to a commercial bank in western Europe, and it is keen to back more brewery ventures.

Carlsberg is taking a 20 per cent stake in the venture, with the Danish state Investment Fund for Central and Eastern Europe taking a further 10 per cent. The driving force behind the project is a group of Israeli interests led by Central Bottling Company, Carlsberg's partner in Israel, which will hold close to 60 per cent.

About $55m is to be invested in a brewery on the outskirts of Bucharest with capacity of 500,000 hecto-litres a year. Construction is to begin by the end of the year, with production, mainly under the Tuborg brand, due to start in about two years.

The most ambitious brewery project in Romania is being planned by Efes, a subsidiary of Turkey's Anadolu group.

It has leased land at Ploiesti, an industrial city north of Bucharest, and is planning to invest more than $60m in the first phase to create capacity for 750,000 to 800,000 hectolitres a year.

Mr Ilker Keremoglu, chief executive of Efes beverages group, said building permission had been granted recently, and construction was scheduled to begin by the end of the year with production starting two years later.

Efes had also drawn up plans, he said, to spend a further $60m–$80m in a second stage to expand production to as much as 3m hectolitres.

This would create one of the biggest breweries in the region, which could also become an export centre for other markets in central and eastern Europe.

Before the arrival of the big international groups, the Romanian brewery industry was highly fragmented, with about 40 small, regional producers. Development of national brands was hampered by poor product quality and inadequate distribution.

That picture is changing rapidly, however, as the international brewers engage in an intensifying contest to establish a dominant position in the Romanian market. The push into Romania also forms part of a wider strategy for expanding throughout central Europe.

In Romania, an early move to local production has been encouraged by prohibitively high import tariffs on both beer and raw materials, although brewers still face serious seasonal problems in gaining sufficient local supplies of barley and malt.

The pioneers in Romania are Interbrew, the family-owned Belgian group and producer of Stella Artois, which includes Labatt of Canada; Brau und Brunnen, the leading German brewery group; and South African Breweries.

Interbrew entered central Europe in late 1991, in Hungary, and has since made acquisitions in Croatia and Bulgaria. In Romania, it holds majority stakes in two breweries: in Blaj, central Romania, and in Baia Mare in the north.

Both are being expanded to give Interbrew overall capacity of close to 1m hectolitres a year, two nationwide brands – Bergenbier and Hopfenkönig – and a market share of about 10 per cent, although it has already set a target of 20 per cent.

The foreign brewers are rapidly expanding, helped by the introduction of modern technology, greatly improved product quality and investment in national marketing, sales and distribution.

'The big problem earlier was the variable product quality,' says Mr Gérard Fauchey, Interbrew external affairs director. 'The maximum shelf life was only about 7 days, because they did not pasteurise the product. The small, local brewers could not distribute nationally because of the short shelf life.'

The Romanian beer market is estimated at between 9m and 10m hectolitres a year, with a per capita consumption of 45 litres a year, compared with 140 litres in Germany, 39 litres in France and 103 litres in the UK.

Competition is growing rapidly. Brau und Brunnen is currently the largest foreign brewer in Romania. In the past year it has acquired a 75 per cent stake in the Pitber brewery in Pitesti, about 110km west of Bucharest. Its first significant move was the acquisition of a stake in the Ursus brewery in Cluj-Napoca, north-west Romania, in 1992, where it now has a stake of more than 60 per cent. It is developing Ursus as its national brand.

The Pitesti brewery is being modernised, with plant and equipment from the group's closed Elbschloss production site in Hamburg being transported to Romania for re-assembly in Pitesti.

The most recent arrival is South African Breweries, which is adding Romania to operations in Hungary and Poland. Earlier this year it purchased a 70 per cent stake in the Vulturul brewery in Buzau, north-east of Bucharest, which has capacity of 500,000 hectolitres.

It is investing about $18m during the next five years, with $10m to be spent on the modernisation of the brewing facilities, as well as packaging, distribution and marketing.

Creditanstalt, the Austrian bank which is advising the Romanian State Ownership Fund on the sale of controlling stakes in several companies, including breweries, believes there are still attractive investment opportunities in the sector.

There will be a restructuring of the brewing sector 'and those breweries which either have no critical mass, poor quality beer products or no cost advantage will be driven out of the market', it says.

Source: Financial Times, 20 August 1996

25.16 **From the information in this article draw up an analysis of the activity of the different firms involved, which will cover at least:**

- **collaboration arrangements;**
- **market entry route;**
- **capital committed;**
- **forecasted production capacity;**
- **aims and objectives.**

Include any other elements which might be relevant to provide a fuller picture.

25.17 Compare the current market situation to that which existed prior to the involvement of the large international brewers.

25.18 Given your answers to 25.16 and 25.17 above, what other marketing activity do you think the international brewing firms will have to engage in to generate sufficient profits to cover their activities in Romania?